What God Has Joined . . .

What
GOD HAS JOINED...
The Sacramentality of Marriage

Rev. Peter J. Elliott

Official of the
Pontifical Council for the Family

ALBA · HOUSE   NEW · YORK

SOCIETY OF ST. PAUL, 2187 VICTORY BLVD., STATEN ISLAND, NEW YORK 10314

Library of Congress Cataloging-in-Publication Data

Elliott, Peter J.
    What God has joined — : the sacramentality of marriage / by
  Peter J. Elliott.
        p.   cm.
    Includes bibliographical references.
    ISBN 0-8189-0568-9
    1. Marriage — Religious aspects — Catholic Church. 2. Catholic
  Church — Doctrines. I. Title.
  BX2250.E45   1990   89-18533
  234'.165 — dc20   CIP

Nihil Obstat:
Reverend James T. O'Connor,S.T.D.
Censor Librorum

Imprimi Potest:
Reverend Pietro Rossano
Rector Universitatis Lateranensis
Romae, die 20 Iunio 1989

Imprimatur:
Reverend Patrick Sheridan
Vicar General
Archdiocese of New York
November 15, 1989

The Nihil Obstat and Imprimatur are
official declarations that a book or pamphlet is free
of doctrinal or moral error. No implication is contained therein
that those who have granted the Nihil Obstat and
Imprimatur agree with the contents,
opinions, or statements expressed.

Details of Australian edition

National Library of Australia
Card Number and ISBN 0 949080 53 5

Published by
ST. PAUL PUBLICATIONS — Society of St. Paul,
60-70 Broughton Road, Homebush, NSW, 2140

Printing Information:

Current Printing - first digit 1 2 3 4 5 6 7 8 9 10 11 12

Year of Current Printing - first year shown
1990   1991   1992   1993   1994   1995   1996   1997

St. Paul Publications and **Alba House** are activities of the Priests and
Brothers of the Society of St. Paul who proclaim the Gospel through the
media of social communication.

Matri Boni Consilii

Abbreviations

A.A.S. - *Acta Apostolicae Sedis.*

C.C. - Pius XI, *Casti Connubii.*

C.F.M.F. - *Cuéstiones Fundamenteles sobre Matrimonio y Familia*, Il Simposio Internacional de Teología de la Universidad de Navarra.

C.I.C. - *Codex Iuris Canonici* (1983).

DS - Denzinger, H., Schonmetzer, A., *Enchiridion Symbolorum, Definitionum et Declarationum de Rebus Fidei et Morum.*

F.C. - John Paul II, *Familiaris Consortio.*

G.S. - Vatican II, *Gaudium et Spes.*

H.V. - Paul VI, *Humanae Vitae.*

I.T.C. - International Theological Commission (1978), *Propositions on the Doctrine of Christian Marriage.*

In IV. - Saint Thomas Aquinas, *In IV. Sententiarum.*

L.G. - Vatican II, *Lumen Gentium.*

P.G. - Migne, J.P., *Patrologia Graeca.*

P.L. - Migne, J.P., *Patrologia Latina.*

S. - Saint Thomas Aquinas, *Supplementum.*

S.C.G. - Saint Thomas Aquinas, *Summa Contra Gentiles.*

S.T. - Saint Thomas Aquinas, *Summa Theologiae.*

V.II. - Flannery, Austin, *Vatican Council II, The Conciliar and Post Conciliar Documents.*

Foreword

I am sure that many readers will share my own reaction to the publication of this substantial work — at last a book is available which is devoted entirely to the *sacrament* of Marriage. But why has there been such a lack of emphasis on the sacrament in modern writing in English on Christian Marriage?

All the time we have had before our eyes the most obvious truth that Marriage is a sacrament. Did we perhaps tend to avoid looking closely at the sacrament because it is too much of a challenge to us? The "great mystery" of Christ's nuptial union with his Church is awesome, but it becomes a personal challenge to faith once couples know that this deathless love is meant to be lived out in their Marriage. It is easier to reduce the central truth of the sacrament to something holy tacked onto Marriage — "and Marriage is also a sacrament. . . ." Therefore there is a great need today for a study which sets forth "sacramentality" in both its specific and wider meanings, which explains the scope and methods of this work.

Father Elliott has integrated systematic theology with history and a study of the living reality of Christian Marriage. The scriptural foundations are set out by way of biblical theology rather than textual analysis. The reader is brought into contact with the wisdom of the great minds of the Church: the Fathers, especially St. Augustine, and theologians such as St. Thomas Aquinas, St. Robert Bellarmine and Matthias Scheeben, each contributing to the developing teaching of the Magisterium on holy matrimony. Fresh insights into Marriage emerge in the light of the personalism of Pope John Paul II. For these reasons, I hope that this work will become a standard text for priests and seminarians and a useful resource for Marriage and family apostolates. Such a study should be an inspiration for couples who are searching for a deeper understanding of their sacrament of life and love.

WHAT GOD HAS JOINED . . .

 This timely book also raises pastoral questions. How many Marriage preparation programs and enrichment courses center around the *sacrament*? How far have we allowed the social sciences to displace the central reality? Is the sacrament set out well in our catechesis of the young? Does our spirituality of Marriage spring forth from the supernatural heart of Marriage?

 There is a sensitive spirituality of married life within the theology of this book, derived in part from the author's pastoral experience with families and his current work within the Roman Curia. Therefore, *What God Has Joined. . . ., The Sacramentality of Marriage* may well be described as a call to grace, that is, an invitation to rediscover the grace of Marriage and to believe in the power of this precious gift of God.

Edouard Cardinal Gagnon, P.S.S.
President,
The Pontifical Council for the Family,
Vatican City State

Acknowledgments

I wish to thank His Eminence, Edouard Cardinal Gagnon, P.S.S. who supervised my research and the Most Rev. Thomas Francis Little, the Archbishop of Melbourne, for the opportunity to complete this project. The work was made possible through the assistance of professors at the John Paul II Institute for Studies on Marriage and the Family, Rome, in particular Msgr. Carlo Caffarra, the President of the Institute, and Msgr. Inos Biffi, Fr. Bonifacio Honings, O.C.D., Fr. Tadeusz Styczen and Fr. Louis Ligier, S.J. I also thank Fr. Kilian Dwyer, O.P., Msgr. Diarmuid Martin and Msgr. Anthony La Femina.

Having chosen to make a wide but detailed study of the sacrament, a series of methods was necessary: biblical and patristic theology, historical theology, a phenomenology of the sacrament within a Thomist structure. The Catechesis on Marriage of Pope John Paul II was a constant source of inspiration and insight. Soon after completing *What God Has Joined. . . ., The Sacramentality of Marriage*, I was pleased to find that much of my methodology had been suggested already by Fr. Thomas Norris of Maynooth, although my approach was more "Pauline" than "Johannine".[1] Discussion with Bishop Eugenio Corecco of Lugano also endorsed my thesis that marriage is a sacrament which *constitutes* the Church, thus opening a new perspective in ecclesiology.[2]

The publication of this work fulfills the final requirement for the Doctorate in Sacred Theology, John Paul II Institute for Studies on Marriage and the Family, the Lateran University, Rome. Therefore, I am particularly grateful to the fathers and brothers of Alba House for making it possible to offer this book to the People of God, especially to those who live the sacrament of Marriage day by day.

I also place on record the advice and encouragement of three leaders of the Church who died soon after my work was completed: the Most Rev. Kevin McNamara, the Archbishop of Dublin; the Most Rev.

Guilford Young, the Archbishop of Hobart, Tasmania; and the Most
Rev. John A. Kelly, Auxiliary Bishop of Melbourne, whom I served as
secretary before commencing work in Rome. However, there is a
"presence" in this work which is beyond the gratitude of words and that
is the witness of the Christian married life of my late father and of my
beloved mother.

P.J.E.

Contents

A Great Sacrament

Porque en todo semejante	*Exactly, in all things like they are,*
El a ellos se haría	*He would cause Himself to be.*
Y se vendría con ellos,	*He would traffic in their dealings*
Y con ellos moraría.	*And in their daily life agree.*
Y que Dios sería hombre,	*And so the God would be the Man*
Y que el hombre Dios sería,	*And the Man be the God: and then*
Y trataría con ellos.	*He would roam amongst them freely*
Comería y bebería.	*And eat and drink with other men.*
Y que con ellos continuo	*He will stay with us forever.*
El mismo se quedaría,	*As a Comrade He will stay,*
Hasta que se consumase	*Till the present dispensation*
Este siglo que corría.	*is consumed and fades away.*

Saint John of the Cross, *Romance IV*

The Catholic Church solemnly teaches that Marriage is one of the seven sacraments of the New Law, instituted by Jesus Christ.[1]   This teaching of the Council of Trent has been consistently echoed by the Popes and more recently embodied in the teachings of the Second Vatican Council.[2]   Yet, so often the sacramentality of Marriage has been neglected as a focus for theological research and reflection. Study of the sacramentality of Marriage has been overshadowed by the work of specialists in the fields of Canon Law and pastoral theology. However necessary and important such practical work may be, in our times especially there is a great need for a deeper understanding of the sacramental mystery of Marriage. We need a thorough theological investigation of the divine activity at work in this unique and specific union of man and woman.

This work is devoted to just such an investigation. It treats of Marriage as it is understood by the Church, viz. as a monogamous union between a man and a woman which is permanent, indissoluble and exclusive, a life partnership only established by the free and mutual consent of two baptized persons who are not impeded from entering such a union.[3]   Baptism is the criterion for the essential distinction between sacramental and non-sacramental Marriage. This fundamental sacrament must have been received by both partners before they can make the contractual consent which is a sacrament.[4]   Incorporated in the redeeming work of Jesus Christ by baptismal regeneration, justification and sanctification, "man and woman are definitively placed within the new and eternal covenant, in the spousal covenant of Christ with the Church."[5]

Therefore, before proceeding to a specific analysis of its distinctive sacramentality, it is important first to place Marriage within the whole context of the Catholic sacramental economy or system. As a sacrament, Marriage does not exist in a vacuum. Although its sacramentality will be found to bear rich qualities which are distinctive, it relates to all the sacraments in various ways, both as a sign and as an effective means of Grace.

A SACRAMENT AMONG SACRAMENTS

Any initial reflection on Marriage as a sacrament should return at once to that which is basic to all seven sacraments: that they are God's effective remedies for sin, that they raise us into Christ's work of sanctification in this life, with the ultimate end of our salvation in eternity. The salvific meaning and purpose of Marriage is the reason why some carefully chosen verses from the mystical poetry of Saint

John of the Cross (1542-1591) have been included at the beginning of each chapter of this work.[6]

In his poetry, Saint John of the Cross expressed his mystical experiences. At the same time, he set forth a theology of our salvation, the Incarnation and Redemption as Christ uniting himself to each of us. Often expressed in outpourings of intensely romantic joy, he used Marriage to describe the ineffable mystery of divine union. Would it not therefore be presumptuous or even irreverent to reverse his mystical symbolism, reapplying this delicate and central theme in his poetry to Marriage itself?

If Marriage, as a sacrament among sacraments, is ultimately salvific, if spouses minister Grace to one another through this union on earth for their salvation, then we can apply the poetic logic of the great mystic to Marriage. Saint John of the Cross set forth the spousal archetype, the beloved Son, sent from his Father to seek his spouse, the Church, bonded to her in the Incarnation, his love consummated on the Cross, a love in turn relived by the members of his Mystical Body — "one flesh," his flesh, one body, his body, one with the Bridegroom.[7] But this is the "great mystery" of Ephesians 5:32. Saint Paul's words in this passage are central to this work because they are central to the way the Church understands the sacrament of Marriage.[8]

Marriage is one specific incarnational way in which the saving work of Christ enters people's lives. In the bond of this sacrament, the spouses minister Grace to one another in daily life. As spouses, they will be judged ultimately on their fidelity to the sacramental covenant. As spouses, they will enter, God willing, into the eternal saving union with God which will replace the union of the earthly sacrament which signified and even foreshadowed it.

Marriage, a sacrament among sacraments, is one response to God's call. As the Second Vatican Council teaches, we are all called to holiness.[9] But this universal vocation, and each specific vocation, including Marriage, is ultimately a call to divine union. In their union as "one flesh," spouses anticipate the blessed union in heaven, described by another John with mystic insight, as the nuptials of the triumphant Lamb of God (cf. Revelation 19, 21 and 22).

Vocation is involved in each of the seven sacramental invitations of God. The poetry of Saint John of the Cross helps us to see the ultimate salvific purpose of the vocation of Marriage. Furthermore, by applying his poetry to Marriage, we affirm the sacred value of that higher state to which this saint was called, a consecrated life of virginity for the sake of the Kingdom. But we affirm this higher state as a different kind of espousal. With John Paul II, we do not separate consecrated virginity from Marriage and family; rather we keep Marriage and virginity or celibacy together, each enriching and supporting the other: . . . two ways of expressing and living the one mystery of the covenant of God with his people.[10]   Whether called to Marriage or to celibacy in the Church, each embodied "acting person," in and through bodily life, is redeemed, transformed, sanctified by incarnational means, the tangible bodily acts of the sacraments. We are to be saved finally in an incarnational way, by bodily resurrection. The complete "nuptial meaning of the body" for all of us is fulfilled in the eternal bliss of perfect union with God.[11]

MEMORIAL, ACTUATION, PROPHECY

In proposing the poetry of Saint John of the Cross as a way into the "great mystery," I have implicitly suggested the three dimensions which Marriage shares with the other sacraments: 1. an *anamnesis* or memorial of past events; 2. a saving reality in the present, and; 3. a pledge of glory yet to come.[12]   Thus Marriage recalls and re-lives the acts of God, our Creator and Redeemer. It is an effectual means of Grace to husband and wife. It leads them towards an eternal future which is signified in its celebration and lived vocation. Pope John Paul II described these three dimensions of Marriage as "a memorial, actuation and prophecy."[13]

With the pastoral consequences of a deeper understanding of Marriage as a sacrament in view, the emphasis of this work falls on *actuation*, what God does in and through the husband and wife in the sacrament. To develop the actuation of Marriage, four major components of Marriage favored by theology or law are used: *signification* in chapters one and two on the "great mystery," and in chapter three on the history of sacramentality in Marriage; *consent* in chapter four; the *bond* in chapter five; and the *covenant* in chapter six. Specific problems related to the sacramentality of Marriage are covered in chapter seven and some conclusions concerning the sacrament and the family are offered in chapter eight.

However, if the emphasis falls on actuation, it is impossible to dissociate the memorial and prophetic dimensions from it. What happens in the sacrament is determined by the incarnational archetype: Christ's espousal of his Church, the "great mystery" (chapter one). The ultimate purpose of the sacrament is the salvation of married Christians. They are called to give prophetic witness to this ultimate purpose in the way they live the sacrament (chapter eight).

Memorial, actuation and prophecy also come together in Marriage as a covenant (chapter six). Interpreted as doctrine rather than law, the covenant brings together and synthesizes the other three components. As God's own mode of spousal consent and contract, the covenant includes: 1. the sacred *signification* (*signum matrimonii*) or source and meaning of matrimony as a sign; 2. the *consent*, as the effectual human "sign" or contractual "form" of the sacrament, vowed and lived by husband and wife; 3. the *bond* as the permanent abiding matrimonial reality and sign (*res et sacramentum*).

Having introduced some technical terms at this introductory stage, let us review the meaning of these and other useful terms which relate to the three-fold distinction of "memorial, actuation and prophecy."

When presenting the sacrament of Baptism in his *Summa Theologiae*, our perennial teacher, Saint Thomas, made distinctions which apply in varying ways to all the sacraments. In each sacrament there is: the *sacramentum tantum*, the visible sign only (for example, the action of water and word in Baptism); the *res et sacramentum*, the abiding reality brought about by that sign (for example, the permanent character in Baptism, Confirmation and Orders); the *res tantum*, the Grace bestowed through God's action and the human response of faith (for example, inward justification in Baptism).[14]   These three distinctions may be perceived in Marriage and they may be integrated with the three dimensions of "memorial, actuation and prophecy."

Marriage is a "memorial" in the profound sense of the Greek *anamnesis* found in the eucharistic narratives (1 Corinthians 11:24 and Luke 22:19). "Memorial" is a sacred re-presentation, a "re-play." It "re-calls" and makes present Christ's espousal of his Church in the

Incarnation and his self-immolation for his beloved spouse on the Cross. As a man and woman "reenact" this "memorial," the phenomena we see are the signs and acts of a man and woman coming together and entering into a covenant based on mutual consent in which they pledge to one another unity of body and life. Their consent, visibly entered into and lived out, is the *sacramentum tantum*.

As "actuation," Marriage consent and consummation establishes the abiding reality, the indissoluble bond, "that which God has joined together." In his *Scriptum* on the *Sentences* of Peter Lombard, the young Saint Thomas showed that this bond is analogous to the character permanently imparted in Baptism, Confirmation and Orders.[15] Thus he developed the teaching of Saint Augustine who compared the indissolubility of Marriage to the character sacraments.[16] Therefore, like the characters, the bond of Marriage is the abiding *res et sacramentum*.

As "prophecy," Marriage may be seen in two ways, because "prophecy" means both God's word concerning our present condition and God's word concerning our future. Through the sacrament, husband and wife minister Grace to one another, day by day. In this lived sacrament, we behold a twofold "prophecy": one having to do with our present condition, the dignity and meaning of the human person; and the second having to do with our future, the eternal destiny which God has prepared for those who love him. This prophetic witness of husband and wife is the most fruitful ecclesial and evangelical form of the *res tantum*, the life of Grace in the family.

Therefore, with "memorial, actuation and prophecy," this work maintains Saint Thomas' distinctions. From the "great mystery" of Ephesians 5:32 in chapters one and two, our study moves to the historical quest for the true *sacramentum tantum* in chapter three and human consent as this *sacramentum tantum* in chapter four. The *res et sacramentum*, the Marriage bond, is covered in chapter five. The *res tantum* is implicit in chapter six where the response in faith to the Marriage covenant (derived from God's covenant) is treated, and explicit in chapter eight where conclusions regarding the life of husband and wife in the family are set forth. Again we see that these distinctions are not neatly separated parts of the sacrament. Rather, they depend closely on one another. They "order" the holy mystery without exhausting its powers and meanings. For example, the simple sign of consent not only establishes the bond, but also runs through married life, the continuous Grace of a daily consent to give, to share, to love.

This example indicates another distinction, also not made by way of separation. Marriage "*in fieri*" is "Marriage becoming." It is the act of consent. Marriage "*in facto esse*" is Marriage in its actual existence, the state of two people who are married.[17]   It is the "lived sacrament," which is inseparable from consent and consummation. Therefore, the "sacramentality" of Marriage, in the dimensions already mentioned, must include the community of life and love, as well as the important moments of sacramental consent.

However, just as there are human problems in the way marital consent is given, so there are problems in the way the sacrament is lived. The former area will be considered in the context of faith and the sacramental consent.[18]   The latter problem is the concern of pastoral theology and practice but it may concern a sacramental theologian in one important way.

The saints may well receive the sacraments perfectly, in ways which are completely fruitful (*fructuose*) in terms of their effects in Christian life. Most of us receive the sacraments imperfectly, as pilgrims called to holiness, yet as sinners. This is obviously true of the sacrament of Marriage, as it is lived, in the failure of so many spouses to respond to the Grace of the sacrament. Even the best marriages are subject to tensions, trials and moments when God's ways are rejected.

Failure to "live up to" the sacrament is usually a failure to discern the sacrament, a precise parallel with St. Paul's warnings concerning failure to discern the reality of the Eucharist (1 Corinthians 11:27-32). How often Christian spouses have lost sight of their own marriages as a "memorial, actuation and prophecy." This means that they have lost sight of Marriage as a sacrament.

In the light of this failure, one could easily be tempted to give into the pessimism which afflicts so many, even Catholic, discussions of Marriage. Admittedly, in the light of the nature of their work, canonists may tend to be pessimistic in their writing on Marriage, and pastoral theologians have to be realistic in an age when marital breakdown is so widespread among the faithful. But the sacramental theologian is called to present the ideal: Marriage as it is intended to be celebrated and lived by Jesus Christ, with his Grace accepted, welcomed and mediated in the lived sacrament. The "ideal" is the revealed *truth* of Marriage.

Therefore, no apology is made for proposing the sacred truth of sacramental Marriage in this work. By explaining and reclaiming that truth as attainable, this study rejects any attempts at a spurious "realism" that would, for example, separate the secular "reality" of Marriage from the sacramental "mystery."[19]   The human and the divine are *one* in this sacrament. Indeed, all the sacraments are specific extensions of the one Person of Christ, God and man, the Redeemer incarnate.

Sacramental Marriage is attainable. Pessimism concerning Marriage should challenge us not to separate the sacrament from some alleged secular "reality," but to proclaim Marriage as, above all, a sacrament. Proclaiming the sacramentality of Marriage calls people to remember what God has done, what He offers in married life, what He promises for those who are faithful, that is, a simple understanding of a "memorial, actuation and prophecy."

AMONG THE GREAT SACRAMENTS

The success of sacramental Marriage depends largely on people linking their consent and shared life to the other sacraments they have received or habitually receive. Saint Thomas gives us a key to the dependent status of Marriage when he groups Marriage in a special category with three other "great" sacraments: Baptism, Confirmation and the Eucharist. Each is "great" in its own way: Baptism because of its effects; Confirmation because of its minister, the bishop; the Eucharist because it contains the whole Christ; and Marriage because it signifies the union between Christ and his Church.[20]

Today, we would regard Baptism, Confirmation and the Eucharist as "great" because these are the sacraments of Christian Initiation. The Church links them to Marriage by recognizing that only a baptized man or woman can administer the sacrament of Marriage to his or her spouse, and by encouraging Confirmation before Marriage.[21]   Penance, as the renewal of the justifying Grace of Baptism, and the Eucharist are also strongly commended as preparation for the fruitful reception of Marriage as a sacrament.[22]   Ideally, when possible,

Marriage is celebrated within the action of the eucharistic sacrifice, the Nuptial Mass.

In her practice and law, the Church reflects the inner realities which bind these four holy mysteries together. Baptism makes Marriage possible and shares with Marriage the signification of a "memorial" of creation and Redemption. In Baptism, the water and blood of the Cross is conjoined with the waters of creation, overshadowed by the Spirit, waters of a new creation in the unsealed fountain of cleansing from sin. In Marriage, we see the "memorial" of Eden, yet more wondrously healed and restored by the Redeemer who comes to espouse his beloved Church by taking our flesh and dying for us, the themes which will be developed in chapters one and two of this work.

Baptism is the true pre-nuptial ablution of Christian spouses, cleansed in the water of the new creation and the Blood of the One who makes all creation new. "Husbands, love your wives, as Christ loved the church and gave himself up for her, that he might sanctify her, having cleansed her by the washing of water with the word. . . ." (Ephesians 5:25-26). The Greek term for "washing," *loutron*, is only found elsewhere in Paul in an explicit baptismal context: "the washing of regeneration and renewal in the Holy Spirit" (Titus 3:5).

Confirmation is also strongly encouraged before Marriage, and by popular custom or local discipline is required in some countries. The Spirit who hovered over the waters of creation, who was the life breath of our first parents, who came upon the apostles, this same Spirit should seal, sanctify and strengthen those who are to be consecrated in Marriage. In this way, they can claim the Grace of the Holy Spirit in their marriage, which was given to our first parents within the process of the first marriage before the Fall, according to Matthias Scheeben.[23]

The Eucharist is fittingly joined to Marriage, not only by the tradition of the Church, attested by Tertullian,[24] but also so that the first act of married life together may be the offering of that Sacrifice which they signify in their union. The first food that they share should be that Body and Blood "given up" in Christ's offering of spousal love for his Church. The Nuptial Mass and first Communion shared as husband and wife brings them into communion with the Sacrifice which they are called to live out each day as Christian spouses. This is meant to be the first of many Communions shared together, as spouses and as parents with children of the Church around them. Again the sacrament *"in fieri"* calls us beyond its moment of consent to the sacrament *"in facto esse,"* the lived sacrament.

Yet the link between Marriage and Baptism, Confirmation and the Eucharist is more profound than an association required or commended by Catholic practice and law. As a sacrament, Marriage reflects the three sacraments of Christian Initiation, and they in turn reflect Marriage in certain interesting ways. The catechumenate is not only the phase of a convert's instruction, but of his or her final choice. This is like the change from courtship to engagement before Marriage. The choice is for this specific person, for *this* good, such specificity being the ground for any understanding of consent, both as a rational act and as the basis of married love. In the catechumenate, the convert chooses a specific Person, Jesus Christ. In the "catechumenate" of marriage, engagement ideally combined with pre-Marriage catechesis, ought we not to show Christians that their choice of one another and for one another, is a choice of and for Jesus Christ, the third partner of their union?

Baptism and Confirmation embody their own kind of "marriage," a consent, a contract, a bond, within a personal covenant between God and the neophyte, raising that person into the divine life of Grace, into the Covenant offered by God. Permanence is established by the indelible seals, the character, the created Grace which is the *ex opere operato* basis for a response of fidelity to the New Covenant between Christ and his spouse, the new Christian. By these espousals, the Holy Spirit consecrates people, constituting them as the Body of Christ, the Church. Marriage, in turn, reflects Baptism and Confirmation as it is the covenant and consecration of the Church in its specific and typical unity, the family, the Church in miniature (*ecclesiola*).

The Eucharist is the consummation of these espousals, His Body for our bodies, our bodies for His Body, unconditional self-giving which is to be mutual, exclusive and fruitful. There is nothing shameful in the redeemed sexuality of Marriage. Rightly may it be linked to the union and communion of the Eucharist, but with reverent awe, for we find Saint Paul himself reminding us, with eucharistic nuances, that "the body is not meant for immorality but for the Lord, and the Lord for the body." These words lead into his use of the sexual union and the "one flesh" of Marriage as a warning against fornication (1 Corinthians

6:13-20). By their married union spouses become "one body," just as we become one in the communion, the *koinonia*, of the Eucharist: "Because there is one bread, we who are many are one body . . ." (1 Corinthians 10:17).[25]

The link between these two passages in 1 Corinthians is found explicitly in Ephesians 5:28-30: "Even so husbands should love their wives as their own bodies. He who loves his wife loves himself. For no man ever hates his own flesh, but nourishes and cherishes it, as Christ does the church, because we are members of his body." Marriage and the Eucharist come together in the mystery of the Church, already introduced by Saint Paul in the earlier verses concerning Christ's head-ship of the Church (vv. 23-24), his spousal love unto death for her (v. 25), her sanctification and perfection through his water and word (vv. 26-27).

In Ephesians we find a synthesis of the four "great" sacraments, as sacraments of the Church. The ecclesial meaning of Marriage will be evident later in the deeper *signification* of Marriage. At this point, we note what Marriage shares with the ecclesial sacraments of Christian Initiation.

The Church is not merely the context for Marriage. The Church is partly formed by sacramental Marriage. Some may object that only personal conversion through the sacraments of Christian Initiation forms the Church. But if this were the exclusive sacramental mode of forming the Church, we could regard the Church as a society without any natural social basis. Lacking social, structural or institutional bases in the created order, such a Church would be less incarnational in its human dimension. In such a Church, the regeneration of Baptism would be re-birth out of human society into a society of baptized persons. Something would be lacking, and is, indeed, evidently lacking in some ecclesial communities which require adult Baptism so that only adults are "members." That "something" is the basic natural unit of the human race, the family.

The Fathers of the Second Vatican Council provide us with a key to this ecclesial meaning of Marriage; the family and the Baptism of children in the family perpetuates the People of God in history.[26] Marriage sacramentalizes the family because Marriage makes the family, which is the domestic Church or the Church in miniature. But the Council Fathers also taught that the Church herself is a kind of sacrament: "Since the Church, in Christ, is in the nature of sacrament — a sign and instrument, that is, of communion with God and of unity among all men. . . ."[27]   Therefore, we may properly apply this sacramental quality to the domestic Church, the lesser included within the greater. Marriage thus constitutes the family as a kind of sacrament, in the Church and in the world. We see the domestic church as an effective "sign and instrument," vital and fruitful, whenever we find spouses faithfully ministering the sacrament of Marriage to one another, strengthened by the other "great" sacraments.[28]

Just as the family is the context for the sacraments of the New Law, imparted to the children of the Church, so the Family of Nazareth was the context for those rites of the Old Law which foreshadowed the sacraments. Guided by Our Lady and St. Joseph, Jesus Christ observed those rites, but he sanctified that home by his presence. Now he links all Christian families to Nazareth, through his work in the sacraments which extend his Incarnation. As the saint and mystic put it:

> "Exactly, in all things like they are,
> He would cause Himself to be.
> He would traffic in their dealings
> And in their daily life agree."[29]

A REVELATORY SACRAMENT

All the sacraments are known to us by Divine Revelation, that is, through the words and deeds of Jesus Christ, which come to us in Scripture and Tradition, through the Magisterium of his Church. Divine Revelation is public; it closed with the end of the age of the apostles. In its normative form it is propositional, the classical view which is assumed throughout this work.[30]

Nevertheless, the Church's understanding of Revelation develops. Indeed, the numbering of the seven sacraments and the recognition of the sacramentality of Marriage is a major instance of such development. A study of this development,[31]   along with the tests proposed by

Cardinal Newman[32]   for the genuine development of doctrine, will be covered in chapter three.

However, there is a revelatory quality *within* the revealed sacraments themselves. This secondary level of Revelation is only known by those who celebrate and receive sacraments. It depends completely on Divine Revelation, yet, in turn, it throws light back upon those great truths of the normal, primary level of Divine Revelation. We will find this evident in the light Marriage throws upon the "great mystery" of Christ espousing his Church. But there is a further revelation to be noted at this stage, namely, how Marriage reveals the human person, our fallen, yet redeemed, human nature.

The specific anthropology of Marriage centers around the reality, meaning and importance of gender in our creation and Redemption. Addressing the youth of the world, Pope John Paul II, prophetic interpreter of this matrimonial anthropology, said: "God *created human beings, male and female* thereby introducing into the history of the human race that special 'duality,' together with *complete equality*, in the matter of human dignity; and with *marvellous complementarity* in the matter of the division of the attributes, properties and tasks linked with the masculinity and femininity of the human being."[33]

A separate work would be required to develop fully the spousal anthropology of the papal teaching of 1979-1983. Others have already begun such a task.[34]   Yet within a sacramental theology of Marriage we will find the glory of man and woman, their "special 'duality', complete equality" and "marvelous complementarity," but disrupted by the Fall, and redeemed by the healing, elevating sacrament.

The wonder of gender is revealed in married love, when the sacrament is truly fruitful, when man and woman live in a bond which comes not from themselves, but from God. In their gender, two persons *themselves* are ministers, matter, form, gift and lived vocation of this unique sacrament. Gender is sacramentalized in Marriage, because gender was deemed necessary by God both in our creation — the Man and the Woman in Eden — and in our Redemption, the new Adam and the new Eve, Jesus and Mary.

If Marriage is the sacramentalization of gender, it reveals to us the human body in a sacramental way, for gender is inherent in the "special 'duality' " of the body of man and woman. I have already used the terms "the nuptial meaning of the body," which I understand ultimately in our bodily destiny of eternal union with God, as resurrected persons. Yet, for married people, "the nuptial meaning of the body" has an immediate meaning — the capacity for self-giving in the consummation of marriage and redeemed sexuality and the daily self-giving of two acting persons living as one. The "one flesh" or "one body" of sexual union is meant to be a supreme expression of the continual union of faithful love, embodied in the life of the family. This is the "language of the body," fruitful, faithful and free.[35]

The bodily union of husband and wife is meant to be fruitful. Indeed, the sacrament which unites their bodies is truly fruitful in its primary and supreme end, procreation. By way of gender, and only by this way, is the first divine command to man and woman realized: "Be fruitful and multiply and fill the earth and subdue it. . . ." (Genesis 1:28). The language of the body is likewise fruitful in the union of bodies as "one flesh." Sexual union is not only an expression of love, but a gift. Therefore, the Pope has properly identified a kind of "sacramentality" of the body in Marriage, the body revealed as an efficacious means of Grace.[36]

But this temple of the Spirit is still subject to the fallen tendency within each of us. The Pope deliberately, and in the face of criticism, devoted a major phase of his Marriage catechesis to the unfashionable problem of concupiscence.[37]   Because Grace is not irresistible, Marriage reveals a tension. Marriage is "meant to be" fruitful, faithful and free. But even a Christian Marriage can be reduced to a relationship in which procreation is thwarted, fidelity betrayed and people no longer feel free. The problem lies within us, the struggle of concupiscence, vividly depicted by Saint Paul in Romans 7:13-25 as division in the human person.[38]   In Marriage it can divide what is meant to be "one flesh," through lust, conflict, deception and exploitation. As in the Fall in Eden, gender is reduced to an instrument of division and conflict.

Yet, even at this negative level, in the very tension, the sacrament reveals the fundamental optimism of Catholic Christianity. If the sexuality of man and woman is a most vulnerable area, it can become an efficacious means of Grace. In their bodies, in masculinity and femininity, in the biological finality of gender as they transmit human life, man and woman can find a way to true communion of life and love. Such healing love is "as strong as death" (Song of Songs 8:6), even stronger, for it destroys that "death" in Marriage, the fruit of the Fall, its effects within us. Therefore, before the "resurrection" of Marriage, reconciling love is etched in the stark lines of suffering, so that the world may receive a revelation of the Cross in the lived sacrament, a love far beyond and above the pallid romanticism or eroticism of our age.

Such love also reveals its price. The Pope has proposed an asceticism in Marriage, the need for purity, self-control and self-denial.[39] The world cannot comprehend this love which requires sacrifice, but which draws its power, not from finite human resources, but from the infinite bounty of God's Grace. In its most fruitful form, the sacrament thus reveals the dignity of the human person, man and woman as being capable of being raised to the supernatural order, deemed worthy of such a gift, which nonetheless retains its divine gratuity. So the optimism of the Church remains intact, for Marriage reveals our fallen frailty and yet our dignity, more wondrously restored.

FROM SIGN TO ACTION

So far, the conventional definition of a sacrament — which may be variously expressed as "an effectual sign," "an outward sign which confers inward Grace," "a visible sign which causes Grace," "a sign which causes what it signifies" — has been used. But, as a sacrament, Marriage is a complex of closely related signs: consent, consummation, community of life. As with other sacraments, Marriage raises a question: Is "sign" an adequate basis or definition for the understanding and study of the sacraments? Some time ago, I raised doubts elsewhere as to the validity of talking of sacraments primarily as "signs," especially in the English language.[40] The reasons for questioning "sign" as a basis and working definition are linked to the way we think and live in Western secularized societies, together with a certain evident decay in post-conciliar sacramental theology — sacraments being reduced to signs *only*.

We live in an age which has demystified "sign," reducing it to a pragmatic meaning. A sign is a means of information (a street sign, for example), or it may convey meaning in human discourse (gestures,

facial expressions, and the like). The richer term "symbol" is unfortu-
nately linked to "sign," but is itself reduced in meaning: "symbol" as
opposed to "reality." There is a profound religious and cultural meaning for "symbol," and all sacraments are symbols in that sense, as a
complex of religious signs expressing a further reality. But even when
we add terms such as "religious" or "mystical" to signs and symbols, we
find it hard to conceive of signs or symbols which *cause* anything, with
the exception of legal instruments such as banknotes or contracts. The
loss of the Platonic view of reality has weakened the perception of sign
as cause, of sign as an expression of some transcendent reality at work in
our midst.[41]

Sacramental theology in recent years has suffered from assuming
secular understanding of the signs in sacraments, evident in the defective eucharistic theology of "trans-signification." Meaning, significance,
becomes more important than the reality signified. This may be linked
to a psychological understanding of sacramental "memorial" as a communal or personal memory, rather than as the re-presentation and
renewal of past events. Such tendencies may lead us in the direction of
the errors of Zwingli, whose non-biblical, simplistic psychological concept of sign and memorial was the source of his reduction of the
sacraments to memory-aids for believers.

The signification of Marriage is important. It requires close investigation. But it is a signification of actions, of God at work in human acts.
In this specific sacrament, we see, through faith and reason, that God is
at work through the Incarnation, in the Church, in the Marriage of two
members of the Church. Not only pastoral reasons — the difficulty with
"sign as cause" in catechesis — but also reasons emerging from the
complex of signs in each Marriage attract us to a sacramental theology
which emphasizes divine and human *actions* in concurrence in each
sacrament. Saint Thomas pointed out that, in Baptism, the sign is a
complex action: water, washing and word, not the water only as
sign.[42]   In Marriage we see the complex action of husband and wife
corresponding with a divine action. God bestows Grace in their consent,
consummation and life together. In turn, those human actions enable
the spouses to participate in the "great mystery," the action of Christ
espousing his Church.

While the signification of Marriage as essential and important is retained, a theology of sacraments primarily as *human actions where God acts*[43] is assumed throughout this work. Sacraments are only a concurrence between human and divine activity because, as revealed by Christ, God has decreed this to be so.

In proposing action as a theological basis for sacraments, we need to balance the various schools of thought on the problem of the causality involved in these sacred actions. The *ex opere operato* principle is affirmed strongly in action theology. This could favor the "perfective physical causality" view, that outward rites are real causes of Grace, with little emphasis on the signs involved. But these human actions have to correspond properly to what God wishes to confer in the sign. Therefore, willful defects or obstacles in the human action can impede the full effect of the divine action.

In the "dispositive physical causality" view favored in this study, God provides a reality in a sacrament, *res et sacramentum*, which disposes the recipient for the full benefit, *res tantum*, of that sacrament. The indelible character in Baptism and the indissoluble bond in Marriage are examples of the reality granted by God, disposing the baptized or the married person for the full benefits of these sacraments. The "dispositive physical causality" school of thought retains a proper place for "sign," as the way we know that God is at work, what he does and what he offers us in our actions in cooperation with him.[44]

A theology of sacraments as human actions where God acts responds to the dynamic ecclesiology of this century, especially the doctrine of the Mystical Body of Christ. Sacramental actions are essential to the worship, vitality and activity of that Body. Sacraments bring into operation "the sacred nature and organic structure of the priestly community."[45]   This approach also responds to the liturgical revival of the Second Vatican Council where the sacraments were described as Christ present and acting in the liturgy of the Church.[46]   Furthermore, it responds to the deeper appreciation of the whole "action of Christ" within the human actions of the Sacrifice of the Mass.

Marriage rightly finds its place in this ecclesial context as an act of worship, a dimension of the sacramentality also to be developed in this work.[47]   The principal worshippers in Marriage are the ministers, the husband and wife. Their action in the sacrament also strengthens this action theology of sacraments which places value on the intentional acts of acting persons, made one in the Acting Person, Jesus Christ our Lord. Thus the action theology of sacraments helps us to value the Christian anthropology of human dignity and responsibility which is revealed in Marriage.

Moreover, there are two principles of sound sacramentalism which are maintained by the emphasis on action rather than sign: (1) the principle of sacramental causality, and (2) the principle of sacramental transformation. These principles are not maintained by an over-emphasis on sign and signification which fails to bring out the effective causality of sacramental signs.

The principle of causality has been summed up in the terms *ex opere operato*, used by the Council of Trent to describe the inherent causality of all the sacraments.[48] The terms cannot be rendered literally into good English, for example as "by the work worked," but make sense if expanded to "by force of the action itself," where we note the clarity given once "action" is used.[49] The terms mean literally that "something is happening" when a sacrament is celebrated so long as there is no grave factor which would render the sacrament invalid. The terms take us beyond the indefinite theology of the pre-Tridentine "occasional causality" school of thought, that is, that sacraments provide occasions or conditions for divine Grace to become operative. Yet we would slide back into that kind of theology if signification were to dominate sacramental theology, especially if "memorial" were to be over-emphasized at the expense of what God does here and now.[50]

The principle of transformation depends on causality. Father Leeming gave us a key to this in his succinct comment, ". . .grace is not merely a psychological change, but an ontological change."[51] The sacraments are given by God to transform us, to raise us to the supernatural order, the divine life, to "divinize" us. The principle of our transformation is expressed most perfectly and finds its source in the objective reality, beyond and around us, in the ultimate transformation of bread and wine into the Body and Blood of Christ, eucharistic transubstantiation. In turn, the transformation inherent in the sacramental characters of Baptism, Confirmation and Orders tends towards that same eucharistic "summit," and flows from that eucharistic "source." The bond in Marriage, as a sacrament of the new creation, embodies this same principle of transformation.

What is at stake in sacramental realism is our whole doctrine of God. The God who is the Cause in the sacraments of his created order, the God who transforms us here and now, raising us to a real share of his life, this is the God who is truly transcendent in his Sovereignty, and truly immanent in the Incarnation. Sacramental realism depends on the true God who causes and continues to act in his material creation. He is neither a dispassionate distant deity nor the prisoner-god of Pantheist immanentism. He is the God of creation, the Incarnation and Redemption, as real historical events and acts.[52]   He is the God who acts in the human actions of a husband and wife, at once affirming and revealing in this gracious sacrament his binding creative power and his loving redemptive will.

JESUS CHRIST, SACRAMENT OR SOURCE?

God is at work in the actions and signs of the sacraments in his beloved Son, Jesus Christ. This raises a final problem as we relate Marriage to the other sacraments. His work for us in Marriage will be found to be a way in which human beings are elevated and introduced into the "great mystery" of his incarnate life among us and his saving death on the Cross. He is the immediate source of sacramental Marriage just as he is the Source of all the sacraments.

In recent years there has been an unnecessary complication and dangerous weakening of Christology by describing Christ as "the Sacrament."[53]   When Our Lord said, "He who has seen me has seen the Father" (John 14:9), he went beyond what we can affirm and see even in the Eucharist. He did not make himself to be only a sacrament of the Father. Rather, he affirmed: (a) his Person as the Incarnate Son, and (b) because of this, his being the second Person of the Holy Trinity.[54]

There is a union, the Hypostatic Union, of God and Man in Christ Jesus, which is absolute, total and objectively real. Therefore, we cannot say of Our Lord that he is some kind of "sacrament," an effectual sign of God, or even that he is a human acting where God acts. Such language implies and leads to an instrumental or functional Christology: Jesus is a designated man endowed with a divine mission and function. But this is not the teaching of the Church and if it sets up a false Christology, so it also undermines the sacraments which become sacraments of a sacrament.

The matter becomes more complicated if we add the licit extension of "sacrament" to the Church, even though we do this by way of analogy, derived from the seven sacraments themselves. Analogy may also permit careful extension of the term "sacrament" to husband and wife, as persons, especially if they respond to the Grace of Marriage. Analogy may likewise permit the term "sacrament" to be extended, with due caution, to the human body, particularly in a context such as Marriage. But even here we must be careful lest we divide the union of the person as a body-soul entity. Such a third extension of "sacrament" by analogy is preferable to misapplying the term to Our Lord, for the visible body is the way we know an acting person. It is through the body that the sacraments are celebrated, given and received. But our use of "sacrament" is by analogy in each of these instances, derived always from the seven sacraments.

Jesus Christ remains the source of these sacraments. In this passing life, they are the tangible means whereby he communicates himself to us and unites us to himself. But he abides with us in sacraments because he has already united himself to us in the Incarnation.

> "He will stay with us forever.
> As a Comrade He will stay,
> Till the present dispensation
> Is consumed and fades away."[55]

The poem suggests his real presence in the sacraments. In the Marriage covenant and community, this is the presence of a third Person, the unseen guest of the Cana of the Church. But this Guest is himself the loving Source of the bond between the spouses.

Newman expressed the truth that the Incarnation is extended sacramentally in us by Christ's indwelling presence: "Our Lord, by becoming man, has found a way whereby to sanctify that nature of which his own manhood is the pattern specimen. He inhabits us personally, and this inhabitation is effected by the channel of the sacraments. . . ." In this same synthesis of the doctrine of Saint

Athanasius, Newman developed this indwelling both as our salvation and our glory so that ". . . soul and body become, by the indwelling of the Word, so elevated above their natural state, so sacred that to profane them is a sacrilege. . . ."[56]

In Marriage, the Word Incarnate truly elevates soul and body above their natural state, when husband and wife come together as "one flesh." To profane that "one flesh" is indeed a sacrilege against the temple of the Spirit. To respond to all that Christ offers in Marriage is to find, together as "one flesh," both salvation and glory.

Newman also expressed more vividly, in a sermon, this real presence of Jesus Christ in his sacraments: "At times we seem to catch a glimpse of a form which we shall hereafter see face to face. We approach, and in spite of the darkness, our hands, or our head, or our brow, or our lips become, as it were, sensible of the contact of something more than earthly. We know not where we are, but we have been bathing in water, and a voice tells us that it is blood. Or we have a mark signed upon our foreheads, and it spake of Calvary. Or we recollect a hand laid upon our heads, and surely it had the print of nails in it and resembled his who, with a touch, gave sight to the blind and raised the dead. Or we have been eating and drinking: and it was not a dream, surely, that one fed us from his wounded side and renewed our nature by the heavenly meat he gave."[57]

This is the same Christ, present, at work, in the human actions of countless Christian Marriages. He is Jesus of Nazareth who rejoiced in the marriage feast of Cana, the historical Christ of the Gospels who is the risen Lord and Redeemer of our race. To him we must turn, to his "great mystery" of the espousal of his bride, the Church, if we are to understand better the "great sacrament" of Marriage.

What God Has Joined...

CHAPTER ONE

The "Great Mystery"

Una esposa que te ame,	*I wish to give You, My dear Son,*
Mi Hijo, darte quería,	*To cherish You, a lovely bride,*
Que por tu valor merezca	*And one who for Your worth will merit*
Tener nuestra compañía.	*To live forever by Our side.*
Y comer pan a una mesa,	*And she will eat bread at our table,*
Del mismo que yo comía:	*The selfsame bread on which I've fed:*
Porque conozca los bienes	*That she may know the worth and value*
Que en tal Hijo yo tenía.	*Of the Son whom I have bred,*
Y se congracie conmigo	*And there enjoy with Me forever*
De tu gracia y lozanía.	*The grace and glory that You shed.*

Saint John of the Cross, *Romance III, Of the Creation*

Speaking to the youth of the world, Pope John Paul II proclaimed the supernatural principles of the "great matter" of Marriage: "I want you to believe and to be convinced that this great matter has its *definitive dimension in God* who is love — in God who, in the absolute unity of his divinity, is also a communion of persons: Father, Son and Holy Spirit. I want you to believe and to be convinced that your human 'great mystery' has its *beginning in God who is the Creator*, is rooted in Christ the Redeemer who, as the spouse, 'gave himself,' and who *teaches* all husbands and wives how to *give themselves* in the full measure of each one's personal dignity. Christ teaches us all married love."[1]

The sacramentality of Marriage can only be understood in terms of the "great mystery" of Christ giving himself for his beloved spouse, the Church. In turn, the "great mystery" of the Incarnation and Redemption takes us back to creation, to God as Creator, and into the very Mystery of the Holy Trinity, three Persons, One in love, the ultimate source of all love and union. In the light of the Pope's compact summary of the supernatural principles of Marriage, we will approach the "great mystery" in three stages: (1) in terms of man and woman in Eden, created in the image of God, and the nature of their Marriage and its subsequent problems; (2) in terms of the Incarnation and Redemption, since Jesus Christ is the immediate Source of redeemed, sacramental, Marriage; (3) in terms of the ultimate Source of Marriage, God the Father, Son and Holy Spirit.

"MYSTERY"

Forth from the Father, Son and Holy Spirit comes the "great mystery" which Saint Paul described as "the mystery hidden for ages and generations (*or* from angels and men) but now made manifest to his saints . . . this mystery, which is Christ in you, the hope of glory" (Colossians 1:26-27). In his later epistle incorporating much of the content of Colossians, the Letter to the Ephesians, Saint Paul explained that God "has made know to us in all wisdom and insight the mystery of his will, according to his purpose which he set forth in Christ as a plan for the fulness of time, to unite all things in him, things in heaven and things on earth" (Ephesians 1:9-10). This is "the mystery" made known to St. Paul by revelation, "the mystery of Christ" revealed by the Holy Spirit, how Gentiles and Jews are "fellow heirs, members of the same body and partakers of the promise in Christ Jesus through the gospel" (Ephesians 3:3-6).

These verses, leading towards the "great mystery" of Marriage and Christ and his Church, show us different emphases, but the common theme: the Paschal Mystery of God Incarnate, crucified and risen, to whose Body the Church all the baptized are joined, the unity of "things in heaven and things on earth." Yet, in Ephesians 5:32, Marriage is identified with the "great mystery." In some real sense, Saint Paul sees

Marriage as a unity between heaven and earth, at once a Christological and ecclesial mystery.[2]

"Mystery" means, in this context, that which is hidden in the heart of God, but which proceeds forth in God's good time, to be revealed in the events of the history of our salvation. It retains a certain degree of the "secrecy" with which the English language invests the term, "mystery." It retains the sovereign freedom and autonomy of the "hidden God," yet it involves men and women who can know God's "purpose" and "plan" by both the apostolic teaching and by their sacramental incorporation into the supernatural life. It is of heaven, yet embodied in the events of earth; at once transcendent, as an impenetrable "mystery," and immanent, as God taking us to himself in our world. In Ephesians 5:32, the term remains "mystery," not "sacrament," contrary to the Vulgate text, *sacramentum hoc magnum est.*"

Nonetheless, the Vulgate's rendering of the Greek *mysterion* as *sacramentum* is fortuitous, not only for Marriage in this verse, but also for our deeper appreciation of the more accurate translation, "This is a great mystery." The term "mystery" has a double function, meaning both an efficacious sign (for God's "great mystery" is not merely revealed information but also God's work among us) and, at the same time, a great reality into which our lives are inserted, the mystery of the Incarnation and Redemption. Both meanings, efficacious sign and sublime reality, must be kept together. The latter corrects any naive attempt to impose our developed concept of "sacrament" in a limiting sense onto Ephesians 5; but the former meaning banishes any attempts to eliminate sacramental Marriage from Ephesians 4.[3]

The "great mystery" which we propose to examine in Scripture may be summed up as "the very reality of salvation in its entirety, the reality within which Christian marriage is located, from which it emerges and which it also brings to expression."[4] Using the scholastic sacramental categories, this "great mystery" in Marriage is both signified and, in a sense, "contained" in the sacrament. Developing this in terms of biblical and patristic tradition, this "great mystery" in Marriage is signified as it raises man and woman, by their human actions, into the divine work of our salvation. But we must return to "the beginning" if we are to enter into the "great mystery."

I. MARRIAGE IN CREATION

In Eden, the Creation Accounts

Jesus Christ our Lord took Marriage back to Eden, saying, "Have you not read that he who made them from the beginning made them male and female and said, 'For this reason a man shall leave his father and mother and be joined to his wife, and the two shall become one flesh'? So they are no longer two but one flesh. What therefore God has joined together let no man put asunder" (Matthew 19:4-6; Mark 10:6-9).

In "the beginning" in the Book of Genesis, we find two accounts of the creation of human beings which Jesus Christ brought together in his definitive teaching on Marriage: Genesis 1:26-28 and Genesis 2:7-9, 15-25.[5]

In the first account God says, "Let us make man in our image after our likeness. . . ." (Genesis 1:26). The "image" in Hebrew is *selem*, the term also used in the Old Testament for a graven image or idol, *e eikon* in the Septuagint. Man is thus distinct from God, not some reproduction of God or extension of God, but subject to him. Yet man is also a "likeness," *demuth*, an exact copy, model or correct blueprint of God.[6] Thus the text shows both man's distinctness and dependence on God and his likeness to the divine nature.

After affirming man's likeness to God in having dominion over all other creatures, the first account continues, "So God created man in his own image, in the image of God he created him; male and female he created them. And God blessed them, and God said to them, 'Be fruitful and multiply, and fill the earth and subdue it. . . .' " (Genesis 1:27-28). Creating man "in his own image," an ikon who is also a true "likeness," God at the same time creates gender, male and female. In some sense, gender is thus derived from the Creator who takes counsel with himself, "Let *us* make man . . .," as he creates.

Reading Genesis in the light of Christ, we should respect the tradition which recognizes some hint of a "plurality" within God in these texts. Man (*adam*), of the earth (*adamah*), is distinct from God, subject to God, yet the plurality of "male and female" in some sense is an ikon of

God in himself, for the "image" is also a correct, true "likeness." In the revelation of the Trinity, in Christ, Adam as a type of Christ may be seen as a true reflection of the Triune God, of the relating divine Person, in the "male and female" dimension of humanity. The Christological and Trinitarian meanings of Marriage are implicit in the Genesis text and it is in this light that these texts are to be read.

In the simpler first account we also find God's matrimonial "blessing." This is not to be understood in our Christian sense of a nuptial blessing. God's blessing in Jewish thought was his gift of fertility, a blessing of procreation. Within his covenant relationship this fruitfulness came from Israel's "knowledge" of the Law, not, as with pagans, from any orgiastic cults.[7]

The "blessing" makes "male and female" more perfectly a true likeness and image of their Creator, for it is in the gender partnership that the human person becomes God's co-creator — fruitful, multiplying, filling the earth, subduing it by creative skill, and having dominion over all other creatures. Therefore, already in the simpler first account, Marriage is found within the divine act of creation, as the specific human way of more truly being the divine "likeness" and "image." God's blessing assures both male and female of their status, for the terms of the blessing are at once a divine wish and mandate, to procreate and to control creation in a god-like way.

The second account of the creation of the human person (Genesis 2:7-9, 15-25) fills out the gender relationship in more specific and personal terms. The male is created first, from the earth, a "living being" with the life-breath of God animating him. The man is set in the garden to tend it, but he is alone, which is "not good" in God's sight. His creation, which *is* good, is somehow incomplete. The beasts are created to end Adam's loneliness. Man, the lord who reflects God, names the animals, but none of them is a "fit helper" for him in his loneliness. God puts the man into a deep sleep and from his side creates the woman and brings her to the man — the nuptial presentation of the bride.

The complementarity of gender is expressed in Adam's ecstatic cry: "This at last is bone of my bones and flesh of my flesh; she shall be called Woman (*ishshah*), because she was taken out of Man (*ish*)" (Genesis 2:23). Adam has lost his loneliness. His cry reveals what may be termed that capacity for personal relationship which is inscribed in each person, the capacity for love.[8]

Man is not "Adam," however, until man is *ish* and *ishshah*. Certainly the text shows the male as the material source of the female, and still exercising his lordship in naming the female, as he named the animals. This will be a factor in the problem of male "headship" in Marriage (cf. 1 Corinthians 11:2-16). But there is no complete "Adam" until the human person is gendered, as *ish* and *ishshah*, for only in losing his loneliness is man properly a "likeness" and "image" of the Creator. He is even incomplete in being the "living being" with God's own life-breath in him, even incomplete as gardener and lord of Eden. Only in being espoused is the human person complete as God's unique creation.[9]

The text continues with the words quoted by our Lord: "Therefore *(for this reason of created gender)* a man leaves his father and his mother and cleaves to his wife, and they become one flesh. And the man and his wife were both naked, and were not ashamed" (Genesis 2:24). The woman is now the "wife," although that was implicit already in *ishshah*, woman taken from the side of her man, *ishah*.[10] In their union, husband and wife are one: one flesh, one body. At this stage, their nakedness is innocence, innocent sexuality.[11] It is not the later, shameful, nakedness of lost innocence.

However, there is an important element in the text which leads to conclusions relating to Marriage in creation. When God creates the woman from the side of the man, he puts the man into a deep sleep, *tardemah*. In this divinely-induced sleep, Adam is completely passive, helpless. Whatever mystical meanings may be given to this deep sleep, the scriptural text reveals one important truth: God created the woman, not Adam. God did not require any co-operation from Adam in this creative act of "building" her, a procreative term. Thus, gender is part of the *one* act of God creating the human person. Gender is "given," bestowed gratuitously by the Creator, while Adam slumbered.[12]

Adam's equality with Eve in creation, his completeness and delight in her, in this second creation account, should be combined with truths revealed in the first account: the "likeness" and "image" of God in "male and female," and God's nuptial blessing. If gender is inherent in the creation of the human person, as God presents Eve to Adam in a nuptial union, then every time a man "leaves his father and mother and cleaves to his wife," we see a re-enactment of creation itself, of Eden. Every human spouse is another Adam or Eve. Even in its natural state, Marriage is thus a kind of "sacrament" of God's act of creation.

Therefore, the nuptial meaning of Genesis will be the basis for our understanding of the sacrament of Marriage. God is the Source of Marriage. In the primal nuptial union he expressed and communicated something of himself. His very act of creation was also a divine espousal — with us.

Marriage and the Fall

Marriage is found in the creation of the human person, but in Marriage the human person fell. We see this in the psychology of the account of the Fall of our first parents. God established a divine-human communion as he expressed himself in creating gendered persons. But this harmony was disrupted by the Fall, itself enacted in the human terms of the first matrimonial dispute. Adam's cry of recrimination echoes across time: "The *woman* whom you put here with me — *she* gave me the fruit of the tree and so I ate it" (Genesis 3:12). So the first effect of the Fall was guilt, lost innocence and the "knowing" of fear, shame and vulnerability in nakedness.[13]   But the "knowing" of the Fall, the fear and the shame, strikes first at the nuptial nature of the human person. Marriage is the target of the serpent, first as his tactic of seduction, playing upon the nuptial bond between man and woman to get them to fall, and then in disrupting that bond.

The mutual infidelity of Eve leading her husband to sin and of Adam blaming her for his own fall is played out in the specific matrimonial consequences of the Fall. To the "multiplied" pain of childbirth is added the woman's "desire" for her husband, a disordered desire, linked to submission to him, ". . . and he shall rule over you" (Genesis 3:16). Through the woman, the sexual dimension of concupiscence disrupts the primal Marriage. But the woman no longer enjoys the equality implicit in the state of being both flesh of Adam's flesh and "one flesh" in union with him. Indeed, it is in the light of this new abject submission to the man, that we can look back through the Fall to the ideal Marriage in Eden, when the man and the woman are different, but equal.

The Fall includes the fall of Marriage, just as the creation included the formation of the ideal Marriage. Henceforth, for the sons and daughters of Adam and the woman he now names Eve, "the mother of all the living," Marriage will be so reduced from what the Creator intended "from the beginning," as to require a radical healing and redemption of its own. In the Fall, the serpent Satan succeeded in attacking life itself, the creation itself at its highest point, in the assault on the bond between man and woman. Only a new Adam, himself a true spouse, will be able to provide a new kind of Marriage for a new kind of creation. The new Adam will come in God's own time, in the "great mystery" of an espousal of humankind more wondrous still than God's creative love in Eden.

Marriage, A Created Reality

In spite of the Fall, the natural union of Marriage was never totally corrupted or destroyed. Like human nature itself, and as a reality inserted in that created nature, Marriage before the coming of Jesus Christ was subject to the effects of Original Sin, but not immersed totally in those effects. The Catholic thus resists both a pessimism, which sees all non-sacramental Marriage as sinful or distorted, and an evolutionism, which sees monogamous Christian Marriage as only the best development so far from some primal swamp of primitive vice and polygamy.[14]

The best way to maintain such a balance is to give respectful regard to Marriage before Christ as a *created reality*, rather than a "secular reality." We inform ourselves in the light of Genesis and the Old Testament record of Marriage in Israel, that is, in the light of Revelation. We inform ourselves through a sound theology of the human person, neither as totally depraved nor as some evolving animal, but as the unique creation, fallen yet open to Grace and capable of Grace. We inform ourselves in the light of human sciences, such as comparative anthropology. From these founts, we conclude that Marriage as some "secular reality" is a later, modern distortion, the civil union of the secularized or secular state — and we dare not impose that regrettable reality onto ancient cultures or onto the customs of non-Christians.

Marriage is a created reality, that is, always bearing some reference to God or the numinous in the way people celebrate it, even if such celebration lacks the later ritual and ceremony of various Christian customs, for example, the presence of a priest. The domestic marriage customs of Israel and ancient Rome were religious rites nonetheless. Marriage in "primitive" tribes is not a secular contract. Even in its simplest forms, even when afflicted by polygamy, we do not find Marriage as an agreement made which specifically excludes any reference to God or to gods. The vulgar grandeur of the Soviet palaces of marriage is at least an unwitting admission that there is "something more" to the natural union than a relationship of sexual convenience or social convention.

Marriage from Eden retains God's blessing. It is potentially sacramental, because fallen man and woman are fit subjects for sacramental re-birth. But natural Marriage can only lay claim to what God offered man and woman in their creation, his blessing on the natural ends of their natural union. As a created reality it nevertheless may seek from God or even claim his protection, guidance and help when it embodies the binding force of a solemn oath (*sacramentum*) which all who believe in God or in gods relate to the transcendent order.[15] The dignity of such natural marriages may be further enhanced, and indeed in a way known to God alone, bear some kind of "sacramentality," when such unions are regarded with reverence as strictly monogamous and not open to infidelities. God's act in Eden is maintained in such unions, and reflected with respect by men and women who are surely bearers of un-covenanted Grace to one another, at least *ex opere operantis*.

If, from creation, Marriage ideally tends towards the sacramental order, as a created reality it is also subject in many situations to the lower instincts of fallen man. Polygamy is the major instance of such debasement of Marriage, for in no way can it reflect the created reality in Genesis. But, until Christ comes to make Marriage a sacrament, specifying monogamy as essential to Marriage, it is difficult to provide strong Natural Law arguments against polygamy. Saint Thomas provided the best arguments in his apologetic directed at Islam.[16] Yet one senses what is lacking in such arguments, where he limited himself to reason and the Old Testament. In arguing that matrimony should be indivisible, he added the Revelation of Christ to strengthen the natural arguments.[17] Even if only in terms of a further revelation, the natural union at its best was still in need of redemption. Yet God's created reality was destined to be raised to a higher dignity by such a redemption, as we find in the prophetic witness of Israel.

Israel: Towards the "Great Mystery"

Marriage in Israel, according to the Old Testament, presents us with a changing complex of laws, customs and social conventions. It shares both the dignity and the decadence of the fallen state of Marriage after Eden, the ambiguity which allows for the romantic fidelity of the Song of Songs, the dignity of the honored wife in Proverbs 31:10-31, the chaste love of Tobias and Sarah, and yet which uncritically records the polygamy of the patriarchs and kings. Its laws and conventions were included in the Law, especially under the sixth word of Yahweh: "You shall not commit adultery" (Exodus 20:14). It can be described in admirable terms.[18] On the other hand, if the status of women is clear in Israel, they are subjected to men in ways which reflect the abject state of Eve after the Fall.[19] The well-known provision for divorce in Deuteronomy 24:1-4 is further evidence of the loss of the primal ideal of the created reality of Marriage in Israel.

Therefore, taken in detail and as a whole, we cannot find any clear line of potential sacramentality in Marriage in Israel, except insofar as marital fidelity was required by the Law. As Jesus revealed in his teaching against Deuteronomy 24:1-4 (see Matthew 5:31; 19:7-9), Marriage in Israel was in need of reform. If our Lord told the Jews that Moses allowed divorce on the grounds of adultery, "for your hardness of heart . . .," then he implied that a new age was beginning when "hardness of heart" would give way to hearts of flesh, not of stone, hearts created anew by God (see Ezekiel 36:26-27). But such a new age would only come by way of a new Covenant.

The metaphor is direct and works simply. The Covenant is expressed as a Marriage. The basis may well be the recurring tale found in many cultures, of the poor girl rescued and raised to noble Marriage by the great king. But the poor girl abuses her status and the king punishes her, reducing her to her former state. His punishment was to correct her, for after it the king brought her back to her former glory.

Hosea was the first prophet to use the metaphor, apparently enacting it in his own life as a sign to the people, by marrying Gomer, the harlot (Hosea 1:2-3). This union is the basis for the message of Israel's adultery (2:2), her humiliation (2:10-13), and of Yahweh wooing her once more (2:14-23). In Ezekiel 16 the metaphor is expressed with greater vehemence and urgency. Jeremiah (3:20; 4:29-31; 14:17-18; 18:13-17; 30:14; 31:2-6) extends and vividly develops the Hosea metaphor which is also taken up in Lamentations 1 and 2, the sorrow and shame of the "Daughter of Sion." In Isaiah (49:18; 52:1, 2; 54:4-10 and 62:1-5) we find the metaphor repeated but with a sense of hope for Yahweh's bride.

The hope of fidelity to the Covenant was tested repeatedly by the events of history, captivities and conquests, the intrusion of foreign cults and (in the later years before Christ) of foreign cultures. The family of Israel as a nation was oppressed by all the pressures which came upon the family circle. In the time of Christ the moral options of covenantal faith were clear: fidelity to the Covenant-Law or rejection of it, where "idolatry is prostitution, infidelity is adultery, disobedience to the Law is abandonment of the spousal love of the Lord."[21] Yet God would never change. He remained faithful. His Covenant was his gift, not some agreement between equals, but he would honor it, if the gift were welcomed in faithful obedience.

With the coming of Christ we see that faithful obedience in Jesus and in Mary, his Mother. But we see a point of dramatic transition for Israel and the whole of the fallen creation. An old Covenant gives way to a new one, in new terms of faithful obedience. The old prophecies are fulfilled but in new terms, a true Messiah, a second Adam, a second Eve. In this context the coming of Christ, the metaphor of Yahweh seeking his bride, Israel, becomes an historical reality as one great metaphor of the prophets becomes the "great mystery." But the metaphor is reversed. The created reality of Marriage is raised to be an integral part of the new creation.

How can this be? We are about to reflect on the "great mystery," Christ espousing the New Israel, his Church. But the events of the

Incarnation and Redemption involve an objective reality. God unites us to himself in the God-Man, Jesus Christ, who immolates himself in love for us. The prophetic metaphor becomes a fact: God "marries" his beloved in a union more absolute than the finest Marriage. The created reality of Marriage no longer merely indicates what God is like. God reveals what Marriage can become, how he can be present *in* the created reality, transforming it into the sacrament of his "great mystery."

II. MARRIAGE TRANSFORMED IN CHRIST

The Incarnation

The divine nuptials began when "the Word became flesh and dwelt amongst us." We begin with the Incarnation in order to discern the nuptial theme in the New Testament, which forms the sacramentality of Marriage. It is a subtle theme, running through the Gospel of Saint John like a delicate thread, suddenly revealed in the Synoptic Gospels in short passages. It is filled out explicitly by Saint Paul and completed in the Book of Revelation. But we must begin with the Incarnation, because the espousal of the Church begins there, in Jesus Christ and in Mary his Mother.

Mary is the key figure in providing us with a nuptial interpretation of the Incarnation. She is the spouse of the Holy Spirit, in whose virginal womb the *union* between God and man is achieved in her Son. But, before we consider the hypostatic union of God and Man in Christ as the source of the sacrament, we must see Mary in her espousal to God as beginning the "great mystery" of her own Son's espousal with his beloved Church.

Mary is the "Daughter of Sion," a rich title which has much to contribute to contemporary Mariology.[22] In her, the prophetic metaphor of God wooing his fickle bride, Israel, becomes a perfected reality. By creating her immaculate, God finds in her the true spouse, the faithful one, who is the perfect "remnant" of Israel, giving obedient consent to his new Covenant by her consent to be the Mother of the Messiah (Luke 1:38). This Daughter of Sion also represents the ark, or holy of holies in the temple of Sion, herself the shrine overshadowed by "the power of the Most High" (Luke 1:35). In her virginal maternity, she is the glory of Israel, greeted as Queen Mother, "the mother of my Lord," by Elizabeth (Luke 1:43). God has looked upon her "low estate" and has exalted her in fulfillment of the spousal prophecies (Luke 1:48, 49, 52), to a glory beyond the hopes of Hosea, Jeremiah, Ezekiel and Isaiah.

Her glory as Daughter of Sion, in terms of the Incarnation, is evident in Revelation 12, the Queen who is Virgin and Mother, bringing forth the Messiah, at once a threefold overlay of symbols: Mary, the Old Israel perfected and the Church revealed. This apotheosis of the Daughter of Sion may be extended in the Sion figure of the New Jerusalem, mother of us all, whose nuptials are celebrated with the Lamb of God in the celestial visions of Revelation 21 and 22.

In Mary, Daughter of Sion, God has found the true spouse he sought and wooed. But these espousals take us back beyond the history of Israel, even to "the beginning," for Mary is also the second and true Eve. Her consent reverses the sin of Eve, in a recapitulation of history.[23] Yet as her consent made her Mother of the second and true Adam, it was in that instant a consent to nuptial union with God. Her obedience in faith is a spousal commitment to God, which we usually appropriate to the third Person of the Trinity, making her "spouse of the Holy Spirit." Yet that is appropriation, for she is equally spouse of the Father and spouse of the Word.

However, through Mary the second Eve, the second Adam enters the world as her Son, not as her husband. The disobedient spouses in Eden are replaced by the obedient Son and Mother. Yet Mary's role will not remain simply that of the Daughter of Sion who is the Mother of the God-Man. She will assume another, spousal, role representing the "great mystery" of her Son espousing his beloved Church. We will see this at Cana and on Calvary where she is "the woman," the second Eve who is mother of the re-born sons and daughters of God, Mary and the sign of the Church.

The Coptic rite of Marriage does not hesitate to identify the bride with Mary, hailing her as the elect member of the Church, the New Jerusalem. The angelic salutation becomes a bridal hymn. But the

Incarnation is only the beginning of the divine espousals. In that same Coptic rite, Ephesians 5:22-6:3 is read at the crowning of the spouses.[24]

Because Mary's spousal union will change into an ecclesial sign on Calvary, it is a preparatory symbol of divine nuptials in the Incarnation. The central reality is the Person of Jesus Christ, and the hypostatic union of the divine and human natures in him. Mary's mystical nuptials with God mediate the God-Man to us. His Person reveals and makes real God's true "marriage," his union of the human and the divine, his union with us, the unity of "things in heaven and things on earth" (Ephesians 1:10), the "great mystery."

The "great mystery" begins with the Incarnation. This is evident in an interesting theological approach to Marriage as an extension of the Incarnation in the thought of Saint Thomas. In his *Scriptum* on the *Sentences* he examined a problem not uncommon in his day, whether before a Marriage was consummated a spouse could enter religion. He argued that before consummation Marriage signifies the union of Christ with the soul by Grace, but after consummation it signifies the union of Christ with his Church, through the Incarnation, the assumption of human nature into the unity of the Person, which hypostatic union is altogether indissoluble.[25] Yet later, in his *Summa Contra Gentiles*, he was cautious about comparing Marriage to the Incarnation because Nestorius had used Marriage as an analogy in arguing for his Christological error, the union of two persons in "one flesh," as Jesus Christ.[26]

Thus we should see that the Incarnation of the divine Word relates directly to Marriage as the signification of indissolubility, the bond. It provides us with the nuptial ground for the "great mystery," the union between God and Man in Christ, in which we participate, to which we are raised in our Baptism into his Mystical Body. Even as he proposed the sacred Passion as the cause of all the sacraments, Saint Thomas nevertheless derived the visible, tangible sacraments from the sacred humanity of Christ, offered on the Cross.[27] The nuptial consent of Christ the Bridegroom, to die for us, was itself initiated by the divine decree whereby "the Word was made flesh," coming into this world to do the will of his Father. Within that supreme consent we also find the spousal consent of Mary immaculate, the consent of the espoused Church.

In these terms of God coming, in Christ, to unite himself to our nature and to seek his bride, we can make sense of Saint Thomas' interpretation of the citing of Genesis 2:24 in Ephesians 5:31: "For this reason a man shall leave his father and mother and be joined to his wife. . . ." Saint Thomas gave a mystical interpretation: Christ, the Son, "left" God his Father and the synagogue, his mother, to cleave forever to his wife, the Church, adding, ". . . I am with you always" (Matthew 28:20).[28]

The Incarnation united all humanity to Christ. As the Second Vatican Council taught: "He who is the 'image of the invisible God' (Colossians 1:15), is himself the perfect man who has restored in the children of Adam that likeness to God which had been disfigured ever since the first sin. Human nature, by the very fact that it was assumed, not absorbed, in him, has been raised in us also to a dignity beyond compare. For, by his Incarnation, he, the Son of God, has in a certain way united himself with each man."[29]

Yet, beyond this "certain way," the Incarnate Son has united himself in a specific way with us, in the specific redemptive form of the visible, fleshy, Church. Thus Saint Augustine taught: "The Spouse of Christ is the whole Church, whose principle and first fruit is the flesh of Christ: there the bride is joined to the bridegroom in bodily union."[30]   Thus, it is only by becoming flesh, by *already* uniting himself to us, that the Son of God can form and seek his bride of flesh, the living Church. By becoming flesh of our flesh, the Son of God enters our lives, penetrates our human actions, raising them to be his own saving actions in and through his spouse, the Church.

To summarize the incarnational basis of the "great mystery," we can say that: Through Mary, the spouse of God, "the communion between God and his people finds its definitive fulfillment in Jesus Christ, the Bridegroom who loves and gives himself as the Savior of humanity, uniting it to himself as his body." But this requires the Incarnation, so that his revelation of the original truth of Marriage "reaches its definitive fullness in the gift of love which the Word of God makes to humanity in assuming a human nature, and in the sacrifice which Jesus Christ makes of himself on the Cross for his bride, the Church."[31]

Saint Gregory the Great summed up the espousals of the Incarnation which will lead us into the "great mystery" and its sacrament, Marriage: God the Father prepared the nuptials for God the Son when he united the Son to human nature in the womb of the Virgin, when he wished him who was God before all ages to become man at a later age of the world. After rejecting the Nestorian error, that Christ is two persons, he continued, "Hence. . . we may say that the Father arranged the marriage of his kingly Son by joining to him the holy Church through the mystery of the Incarnation.[32]

Jesus Christ, the Bridegroom

The Bridegroom came into the world in the Person of Christ. In the union of the human and divine natures, his spouse the Church was being formed for him. Yet we must keep in mind that he is also the second and true Adam.[33] His coming is a new beginning, a new creation, and as such it will transform all human ways and institutions, including Marriage.

The Bridegroom who is the second Adam knows himself as a Person. Thus he is aware of himself as "the bridegroom." "Then the disciples of John came to him saying, 'Why do we and the Pharisees fast, but your disciples do not fast?' And Jesus said to them, 'Can the wedding guests mourn as long as the bridegroom is with them? The days will come when the bridegroom is taken away from them, and then they will fast' " (Matthew 9:14-15 and Mark 2:18-20, Luke 5:33-35). This self-identification with "the bridegroom" makes sense of the Marriage parables, the "king" who gives "a marriage feast for his son" (Matthew 22:1-14), and the wise and foolish virgins going "to meet the bridegroom" (Matthew 25:1-13).

The Bridegroom is an eschatological sign, one who "is taken away" but who will return, one who is awaited by the virgin attendants, one who celebrates his nuptial banquet to which his Father invites all. But the sign is an implicit claim to identity with Yahweh himself, seeking his bride, Israel, yet now inviting all to the nuptial feast, for the test of election is no longer membership in Israel but the "wedding garment" of personal faith and good deeds (Matthew 22:11-14).

This Bridegroom, as we have said, is also the second Adam, already entering into his mystical nuptials. This is the emphasis we find beyond the Synoptics in the Gospel of Saint John. If the divine nature of the Bridegroom is implicit in the Synoptics, Yahweh seeking his spouse in the chosen time, so we also find the human nature of the Bridegroom evident in the Fourth Gospel.

At Cana we know nothing of the bride and bridegroom whose nuptials were being celebrated. Jesus Christ, the guest, becomes the eschatological Bridegroom, providing the new wine of his Kingdom for the wedding feast, "the good wine" kept for the final moments (John 2:1-11). The compliments after the miraculous provision of wine are given to "the bridegroom," but already John the Baptist has borne witness to the true bridegroom: "This was he of whom I said, 'He who comes after me ranks before me, for he was before me' " (John 1:15). After Cana, John the Baptist reminds his own disciples that he is not the Christ, but one sent before him. And he adds, "He who has the bride is the bridegroom; the friend of the bridegroom who stands and listens for him, rejoices greatly at the bridegroom's voice; therefore this joy of mine is now full. He must increase, but I must decrease" (John 3:28-30).

At Cana, the Adamic symbol is evident in Mary, as Christ addresses her with the formal, yet blunt, term "woman" (gynai). She is "the woman," but "the woman" of a new creation, a new Eden, who calls the new and second Adam to a work of justice, not to sin. This work involves obedience, as Mary exhorts the servants, "Do whatever he tells you." At Cana, Mary becomes a Church-bride figure, already directing the economy of the household of God, as the nuptials are celebrated which point to eternity, "the good wine" kept for last.[34]   But this only can be seen by reading Cana in the light of the Cross where once again the second Eve will be addressed as "woman." There, on Calvary, the nuptials of the Bridegroom reach mystical perfection, and Mary's role is definitively changed into that of the Church-bride figure.

As the Bridegroom, Christ by his actions is already rendering Marriage sacramental. We may discern a similar institution of sacraments enacted in the Person of Christ, by deed and word, as he undergoes a baptism in the Jordan, as he has the Spirit poured out upon him, as he heals and absolves, as he links the cup of the Last Supper to "the cup" he must drink, his Passion, as he ordains and sends out his own friends. Likewise, he is the Bridegroom, whose spouse is not revealed in the Gospels, yet his espousal is the archetype for the sacrament of Marriage in his new creation.

The Bridegroom is not alone. He has a witness and bridal attendant, John the Baptist, and he has his "friends." This secondary theme is important, lest we isolate Christ in some mystical realm where he may both be Yahweh seeking his bride and a new Adam, but not related to the world of men and women. The friends of the Bridegroom are the beginning of his Church, invited guests destined to be the new Israel of his Kingdom.

John the Baptist is the Bridegroom's male attendant or "page" in a Jewish wedding. This *paranymphus* prepared and guided the ceremonies, led the bride and groom in procession to the husband's house and even prepared the bridal bath and helped the bride to adorn herself. He presented the bride to the bridegroom.[35] John the Baptist identified himself with this role, but as a servant of Christ, "the thong of whose sandal I am not worthy to untie" (John 1:27).[36] Yet this servant and friend, presenting the Bridegroom to his Church, as his "witness," would die for his beloved Bridegroom. Rightly is this witness, servant and friend of the Bridegroom hailed in the Syrian rite of Marriage.[37]

The apostles are the other friends of the Bridegroom, rejoicing in his presence in the Synoptic Gospels. In Saint John's Gospel they are servants who become friends of Jesus Christ at his supper table (John 14:14-15). But, by doing the Father's will, they can be admitted to the family of Christ, as "brother, and sister, and mother" (Matthew 12:49-50). This intimacy, from servants and friends to kin, will be revealed on Calvary. Another John, a friend of the Bridegroom, will become a son of Mary, son of the Church, and the witness to the supreme moments of the nuptials of the Bridegroom (cf. John 19:26-27). Yet all the friends of the Bridegroom are witnesses to his nuptials, for they have been with him "from the beginning" (John 15:27).

In the royal marriage procession of his ministry among them, the friends of the Bridegroom escort their beloved Master to his mystical nuptials, which even they cannot comprehend. His nuptial progress is towards Jerusalem, towards the marriage banquet of the Passover table, towards his ultimate self-giving on the Cross.

However, we cannot impose the exact pattern of Jewish marriage rites and customs onto the events of the "great mystery."[38]   Already that mystery has disclosed its complexity: its origins in Eden, God's nuptials in and through man and woman, the prophetic metaphor of Yahweh seeking Israel, its beginning in the Incarnation of the Son of God through Mary, and in his own awareness of himself as the Bridegroom. A divine mystery may not be forced into human patterns. It is mystery precisely because it evades total definition; but it remains open to ever greater human understanding. To gain some insight into the nuptials of the Bridegroom it will be helpful to proceed in terms of his three-fold office: as Prophet, Priest-Victim and King. Through that three-fold office, imparted to his Church, we may know his spouse, the nature of his espousals, and then examine Saint Paul's teaching in Ephesians.

The Bridegroom as Prophet

The self-awareness of Jesus Christ as the Bridegroom, is itself part of the proclamation of the Kingdom, thus included in his prophetic work. But the Bridegroom theme is subtle and mysterious. Jesus only explicitly applies the term to himself once, although we find this in all three Synoptic Gospels (Matthew 9:14-15, Mark 2:18-20 and Luke 5:33-35). His explicit prophetic role includes specific teaching on Marriage itself. In this authoritative teaching he reveals in word what he will reveal in deed, namely God's will for Marriage.

In word, he speaks as a new Moses, yet greater than Moses. He mediates a new Covenant. Within that Covenant, the covenant of Marriage is to be strictly monogamous and permanent unto death. In an expansion of his sermon on the mount, the radical change in Marriage is introduced: "But I say to you that every one who divorces his wife, except on the ground of unchastity, makes her an adulteress; and whoever marries a divorced woman commits adultery" (Matthew 5:31-32). "And I say to you . . ." reappears in the debate with the Pharisees on divorce (Matthew 19:3-9 and Mark 10:2-12). It is in this passage that we find the definitive revelation which raises Marriage to the level of a sacrament.

Jesus goes back beyond Moses to "the beginning." In the face of the
Pharisees' devious attempt to draw him out, he rejects both schools of
thought on the law of divorce. Neither Rabbi Shammai, allowing divorce only on the ground of adultery or immorality, nor Rabbi Hillel,
allowing a wider range of grounds, would bind Jesus.[39] He cuts
through their permissions and casuistry. He adds his own rabbinical
comment to Genesis 1:27 and 2:24. To the creation "from the beginning," male and female, "one flesh," he adds: "What therefore God has
joined together, let no man put asunder."

It is God who joins man and woman in Marriage, not man. It is God
who determines the permanent and monogamous nature of this union,
as in Eden. Implicit in this return to Eden is God's own blessing on
Marriage, to be developed in the Church — the theology of the grace of
the sacrament. Implicit in the authoritative way the teaching is given is
an unwritten "henceforth . . .": that Marriage is part of the new Covenant, the new Law, replacing the Mosaic divorce provision
(Deuteronomy 24:1-4), a new Law of "grace and truth" (John 1:17). As
John Paul II described this prophetic teaching of Christ our Lord, "He
reveals the original truth of marriage, the truth of the 'beginning,' and
freeing man from his hardness of heart, he makes man capable of
realizing this truth in its entirety."[40]

As prophet he not only calls mankind into the new Covenant; he
also points to the future. Again confronting the assumptions of his time,
he proclaims celibacy "for the sake of the kingdom of heaven." But this
higher form of nuptial union shares with Marriage a divine origin.
Celibacy for the kingdom is a gift of God: "He who is able to receive this,
let him receive it" (Matthew 19:12).

As prophet, he lives out this celibacy himself. He will have but one
mystical spouse, yet to be revealed, united to him in a union stronger
than death itself. Arguing with the Sadducees, who rejected the resurrection of the dead, he sets limits on the union of Marriage, which
cannot last beyond death: "For in the resurrection they neither marry
nor are given in marriage, but are like angels in heaven" (Matthew
22:30, and Mark 12:25, Luke 20:35-36). Yet he embodies in himself the
union of God and Man, source of the new nuptial union and beginning
of the "great mystery" of his espousal with his own bride. That union
cannot die, even when subject to death. That union is to be revealed in

the Paschal Mystery of Calvary and the empty tomb, a union revealed as deathless and perfect. Into that union of the divine and human natures, Christ will invite all who hear and welcome his prophetic revelation, all who wish to live, married or celibate, "for the sake of the kingdom of heaven."

This prophet lives out and fulfills that of which he speaks. In deed, not only in word, he reveals and realizes the "great mystery" of our redemptive union with him, in his spouse, the Church.

The Bridegroom as Priest-Victim

The nuptial procession of Christ Jesus led to Jerusalem, to Sion. In the Synoptics clearly (e.g., Matthew 16:21; 20:16-19), and implicitly in John (7:8; 12:55-57), we find his consent to die in this turning towards Sion. But as we are seeing the "great mystery" of his work of Redemption in *nuptial* terms, the work of the Bridegroom, so we see his nuptial consent as a consent to die, a love unto death itself.

When he enters Jerusalem, his spouse is evoked in prophetic words: "Tell the daughter of Sion, Behold, your king is coming to you, humble, and mounted on an ass, and on a colt, the foal of an ass" (Matthew 21:5, from Isaiah 62:11 and Zechariah 9:9). But his spouse is not Jerusalem, "killing the prophets and stoning those who are sent to you...." (Matthew 23:37). His spouse is symbolized by Jerusalem, but is yet to be revealed.

The Last Supper shows us the second phase of his consent to die. In word and deed he anticipates what will happen on the Cross. But even here the nuptial theme may be discerned. In Saint John's account, the Bridegroom washes the feet of his friends, a strange reversal of roles. The first among the apostles, Peter, objects, and Christ replies, "What I am doing you do not know now, but afterward you will understand. . . . If I do not wash you, you have no part of me." Peter then demands a total washing, hands and head as well, but Christ replies, "He who has bathed does not need to wash, except for his feet (*a phrase omitted in some texts*), but he is clean all over. . . ." (John 13:3-11). In the action of Christ and in his explanation, we find the baptismal washing, hence a sign of the washing of the spouse, which we will see is such an important element in the traditions of the "great mystery."

In Saint John's account we also find Christ's nuptial promise to his spouse: "Let not your hearts be troubled; believe in God, believe also in me. In my Father's house there are many rooms; if it were not so, would I have told you that I go to prepare a place for you?" Then follow the words which bear a nuptial meaning: "And when I go and prepare a place for you, I will come again and take you to myself. And you know the way where I am going" (John 14:1-4). The Bridegroom begins his ultimate nuptial progression, through death to resurrection, for the sake of his beloved spouse — addressed as "you," that is, the Church represented by the apostles, no longer servants, friends of Christ, yet to become more, for, "I will come again and take you to myself."

At the supper table, the eucharistic words of Jesus Christ may also be seen in their nuptial meaning. But these words anticipate the self-immolation of the Bridegroom, freely giving up his Body and Blood for his beloved spouse. In the Jerusalem tradition handed on by Saint Paul, our Lord says: "This is my body which is for you. . . . This cup is the new covenant in my blood" (1 Corinthians 11:24-25). In Luke, in the same tradition, the Body of Christ is "given for you" (Luke 22:19). The words reveal the spouse, again "you," the apostles as representing the new covenant people, the new Israel, the Church.

In Saint John's account, the spousal consent to die is found at the supper table, but in the "High Priestly Prayer." Reading this through the nuptial tradition we find his consent to die incorporated into two dimensions of love, specificity and union. Both of these intentions of the Bridegroom will inform the consent of the sacrament of Marriage, the love for *this specific person*, the true spouse, and the love which aspires to *union of body*, a union of "one flesh."

In that majestic prayer to his Father, Our Lord singles out those for whom he is offering himself specifically: "I am praying for them; I am not praying for the world but for those whom you have given me, for they are yours; all that is mine are yours, and yours are mine, and I am glorified in them" (John 17:9-10). Here is the spouse once more, presented to Christ by the Father, taken from the world, soon to be cleansed and so re-presented to the Son by his own act of love on the Cross, through which Christ can be glorified in his Body the Church.

Once again a collective pronoun identifies the spouse of Christ, "they," and he adds, "and for their sake I consecrate myself, that they also may be consecrated in truth" (John 17:19). This specificity, this sacred choice imparting the divine life to human beings, is wider than the apostles, for, "I do not pray for these only, but also for those who believe in me through their word" (John 17:20).

These last words introduce the second dimension of spousal love in Christ's priestly consent to die. A union, derived from God, a union reflecting the union in God, is what Christ establishes in his self-immolation for his bride: ". . . that they may all be one; even as you, Father, are in me, and I in you, that they also may be in us" (John 17:21). His sacrifice will impart glory to his bride, his own glory. "The glory which you have given me I have given to them . . .," but at once he returns to divine union as the purpose of this imparting of God's glory to the beloved and chosen bride, "that they may be one even as we are one, I in them and you in me, that they may become perfectly one" (John 17:22-23).

The world is to behold this union between the Bridegroom and his Church. The world is to be converted by the fidelity and love of this union, effected ". . . so that the world may know that you have sent me and have loved them even as you have loved me." At that point our nuptial interpretation of the "High Priestly Prayer" is at one with the ecumenical interpretation of these words as a prayer for unity. The Church as spouse of Christ should show the world the unity she receives by union with God in Christ.

We also find, in this last part of the prayer, a repetition of what we saw as the nuptial promise, Christ going to "prepare a place for you" and coming again to "take you to myself" (John 14:1-4). He desires that his spouse should be with him, with the Father, in the glory of the Father: "Father, I desire that they also, whom you have given me, may be with me where I am, to behold my glory which you have given me in your love for me before the foundation of the world" (John 17:24). The nuptial union of Christ and his Church has an eschatological goal, union in heaven, in "my Father's house," where a place has been prepared for the beloved spouse.

Through Gethsemane, through the trial and testing of his consent to die, through the halls of judgment and shame, the Bridegroom goes to his Cross. But what is the nuptial meaning of his self-immolation on Calvary? It may be seen in two ways: (1) Christ, Priest and Victim, dies out of love for the bride he has *already* espoused in the Incarnation, cleansing and perfecting her by his death; and (2) Christ, Priest and Victim, is espoused to his Church *in the act of self-immolation*, when the Church comes forth from his pierced side. We are at the heart of the "great mystery," and here both meanings may be held together, remembering that it is impossible to impose a literal human nuptial process (for example, the Jewish customs) onto events which are at the same time historical and supernatural realities. Ultimately, the deeper nuptial meanings of Calvary are accessible only to a true mystic.[41]

The first nuptial understanding of the Cross, Christ dying for his bride, may best be understood in terms of Mary, Daughter of Sion. On Calvary, as at Cana, Jesus Christ addresses her as "woman." This is to be seen in the context of his words to her, "Woman, behold your son!", and to John, "Behold your mother!" (John 19:26-27).

In the Incarnation, Mary is already espoused by God. She thus both fulfills the prophetic hope of Israel's espousal and she personifies the New Israel, the Church. Uniting herself, by her will, to her Son's death, she represents the death of the Old Israel according to the flesh expecting only a political Messiah, and the birth of the New Israel espoused to the true universal Messiah.[42]

First let us consider her role as the "woman," the Second Eve. She is the new Eve, a new creation, in the perfection of her Immaculate Conception. She is the faithful Eve, reversing the fallen Eve's disobedience in her consent and childbearing, her espousal with God in the Incarnation. Therefore, Mary stands at the Cross already redeemed by the anticipated merits of her Son, offering himself on the Cross.[43] She stands there already espoused in the Incarnation. Thus her own perfect participation in the Redemption and her spousal union with God make this Second Eve become the image and sign of the Church. Jesus, who is "the first-born among many brothers" (Romans 8:29), says, "Behold your mother!" And John becomes the son of the true Eve, Mother of the new humanity, sign of Mother Church. [44]

Her second role is that of Daughter of Sion, the espoused Virgin. She is both a sign of the faithful remnant, faithful to the Old Covenant, hence sought by the King who comes to Sion in his nuptial procession, and she is a sign of his New Covenant, espoused in a new fidelity of faith. Thus she becomes also an eschatological symbol of the Church of faith which replaces Sion, the community of the law. She personifies the New Jerusalem, "Mount Sion . . . the city of the living God, the heavenly Jerusalem" (Hebrews 12:22), "the Jerusalem above . . . our mother" (Galatians 4:26), whose offspring "keep the commandments of God and bear testimony to Jesus" (Revelation 12:17).

The Immaculate Conception is the new creation, providing God with a new spouse, a new beginning, as we see Mary both as the Second Eve and Daughter of Sion. The spousal and ecclesial meanings come together in the text of the Preface of the Immaculate Conception, nuanced with its nuptial reference from Ephesians 5:27. Mary was preserved free from Original Sin, "that in her, thanks to her aforementioned fulness of grace, you [God] might prepare a worthy mother for your Son, a sign of your favor to the Church at its beginning, the promise of its perfection as the Bride of Christ, radiant in beauty, without wrinkle or stain."[45]

Therefore, in her Immaculate Conception and in the Incarnation itself, Mary includes in herself the origin of the Church from creation and from Israel, the life of the Church espoused to God in the union of Grace, and the destiny of the Church, the celestial Sion, taken to himself by the Bridegroom in his eternal bridal chamber. Past, present and future meet in the "woman" on Calvary, in the dramatic change of her role from Mother of Jesus Christ to that of the mystical ecclesial spouse. The "woman" of Cana is once again the "woman" on Calvary, but now "the hour" of the Second Adam has come, and in dying he seals his espousal of the Second Eve, by the death which brought her into existence, immaculate and full of Grace.

We have passed into the second, deeper, nuptial meaning of the "great mystery." If Mary anticipates in herself the past, present and future of the Church, so she also represents the espousal of the Church made by Christ in the act of his self-immolation for his bride. She consents to his death, uniting her consent to his consent to die for us. Her role as co-redemptrix is best understood in ecclesial terms, in her personification of the whole co-redemptive community, the Church. In her spousal fidelity, she enters and, by Grace, participates in his

redemptive act, becoming part of that mystery in the consent of the
perfect harmony of her will with his Will.

Mary on Calvary is thus the perfect member of the Church, complete in her faith in God.[46] Her spousal union with God is a consent
even unto death, a sharing in the consent to immolate himself out of
love which is the consent of the heart of Christ. Both as the perfect
Christian espoused to God by the union of redemptive Grace, and as the
faithful Christian whose acts of consent are acts of faith, Mary provides
a model for the sacrament of Marriage, even at the central moments of
the "great mystery" signified in that sacrament. As we shall see, only
those united to the Redeemer in the objective order of Grace, in
Baptism, and only those who make an act of faith in matrimonial
consent, can minister the sacrament of holy Marriage.

At the heart of the "great mystery," we consider the greater consent, to which Mary united herself, the consent of the Bridegroom who
dies for us. He came to Sion in a nuptial procession with his friends, one
of whom stands with his Mother at his Cross. Now, as Priest and Victim,
having set his course at the supper table, his death becomes at once the
birth and espousal of his Church.

In his dying, out of love, the deep sleep of Adam is recapitulated.
As the Fathers of the Second Vatican Council taught of the work of our
Redeemer: "He achieved his task principally by the paschal mystery of
his blessed passion, resurrection from the dead, and glorious Ascension,
whereby 'dying, he destroyed our death, and rising, restored our life.'
For it was from the side of Christ as he slept the sleep of death upon the
cross that there came forth 'the wondrous sacrament of the whole
Church.' "[47]

If the Church is born from the side of Christ, so the Church is
espoused by Christ in his dying. The blood and water pouring forth
from his pierced heart, is the fountain of the sacraments, as the Preface
of the Sacred Heart proclaims: raised on the Cross, Christ offered
himself for us. "From his wounded side flowed blood and water, the
fountain of sacramental life in the Church. To his open heart the Savior
invites all men to draw water in joy from the springs of salvation."[48]

As the bride is born, so she is washed in the water and blood of her
nuptial ablutions. The blood and water is at once birth and re-birth. As
the Church is born, so all the Grace of the New Covenant is poured

forth from Jesus Christ, the Source. But as she is born, so she receives the Holy Spirit, the divine breath of a new creation, breathed forth by the Incarnate Logos on the Cross. Rightly Scheeben has drawn attention to an analogy and parallel between the Procession of the Holy Spirit and the creation of Eve from Adam's side; ". . . the Holy Spirit who proceeds from the Father and the Son," "*Spiritus de Spiritu*," and woman (*ishshah*) coming forth from man (*ish*).[49] The Procession of the Holy Spirit can also be compared to the birth and cleansing re-birth of the Church from the side of Christ. In Saint John's Gospel, for example, we read, ". . . and he bowed his head and *gave up* his spirit" (John 19:30). Saint Luke records the words of Jesus: "Father, into your hands I *commit* my spirit" (Luke 23:46). The Spirit "given up" and "committed" to the Father is the same Spirit of Pentecost, "poured out" upon the Church, yet already in the Church as bride, because the Church is "the body of Christ" whose creation was accomplished on the Cross: "It is finished!" As the Body of Christ (in the nuptial sense the "two are no longer two but one flesh"), the spouse participates in the Son's union with the Father and the Spirit. That union is at once her birth and cleansing in Grace. Once again our eyes are drawn to Mary.

As Body of Christ, the spouse born in the "great mystery" is the extension of the God-Man. Adam's cry is echoed, as it were, on the Cross: "This at last is bone of my bones and flesh of my flesh" (Genesis 2:23). In the paschal mystery, the Redemption is at once Christ's work *for* us and his extension of himself in his Mystical Body which is his beloved bride. The course set with his words at the supper table, "This is my body. . . . This is my blood," is accomplished in his sacrifice of love which extends himself into our race, into the new humanity nourished and joined to him by his immolated body and blood: "It is finished!" Thus Saint Paul in Ephesians can combine Adam's cry of delight in Genesis with the "great mystery" of the Bridegroom, redemptive and eucharistic: "Even so husbands should love their wives as their own bodies. He who loves his wife loves himself. For no man can ever hate his own flesh, but nourishes and cherishes it, as Christ does the Church, because we are members of his body" (Ephesians 5:28-30).

The birth and espousal of the Church on Calvary is not some isolated divine act beyond human participation. As Saint Paul added, ". . . *we* are members of his body." The proceeding-forth of his Mystical

Body, his spouse, is an inclusive birth and espousal, the potential incorporation of the bodies and souls of many millions of human beings. Of this objective, saving, union in Grace, we see Mary as the personification of the Church. But we also should see the beloved disciple, Saint John, as incorporation into the Church, the redeemed humanity embodied in the Church. Failure to appreciate John's role on Calvary may reduce the espousal of the Church to the level of a mystery religion symbol, a celestial event which does not involve us.

John, son of Mary, son of Mother Church, is no longer a servant, and more than a friend. Through his sonship in the order of Grace (cf. Romans 8:14-17), he is co-heir with Christ. He is among those "children of God who were born, not of blood nor of the will of the flesh nor of the will of man, but of God" (John 1:12-13). He is part of that collective "you" which we have seen as anticipating the communal nature of the bride of Christ, the Church. He stands with Mary, the first and perfect member of the Church and, by his incorporation into the espousal of the Church, she is his sister in Christ, just as she is his Mother.

In Christ's binding Mary and John together we see the loving provision of his last will and testament. But we also see these two virgins raised from the loneliness, brought to them both by his death. In the Church they have one another. Thus this moment in the "great mystery" is contained in human simplicity, held in an exquisite vessel — the family.[50]

Any understanding of the espousal of the Church by the crucified Lord would be incomplete without some reflection on the nature of the love of this Bridegroom for his spouse. Pope John Paul, as Cardinal Karol Wojtyla, perceived that the self-giving of Christ to his Church is the bestowal of "purification, sanctification, grace and all the joys of salvation. So the love of Christ-the-Bridegroom stems directly from the cross and the sacrifice. The Redeemer is the Bridegroom in virtue of being the Redeemer! He is able to bring his Gift (*the Eucharist*) to the Church precisely because he has already given himself in the sacrifice of his blood."[51]

Jesus Christ, "the Bridegroom in virtue of being the Redeemer," is espoused to his Church in redemptive love, in total self-immolation, freely laying down his life for his friends in the greatest form of love (cf. John 14:13). This redemptive love is the perfection of the "steadfast love" of Yahweh for his wayward, weak and sinful spouse, Israel. It is that unchanging love which accepts the sinner. In that acceptance, as bestowal of his very self, and in the radical experience of being accepted, the Church is born and espoused. Within the Church, each individual sinner is redeemed in that accepting love.

Contemplating such redemptive love, Saint Paul observed, "God shows his love for us in that while we were yet sinners Christ died for us" (Romans 8:8). The objective power of that Sacrifice is the Redemption, but the price is suffering. The Bridegroom offers himself in intense suffering far beyond the physical pains of his Passion, even to the depths of abandonment as Jesus-forsaken-for-us. The Bridegroom empties himself for his spouse, renouncing even the joy of union with his Father, for the sake of his spouse, for the sake of sinners.

The bride must also suffer in this nuptial union of redemptive love. As personification of the Church at Calvary, Mary is at the same time the Mother of Sorrows, the stricken Daughter of Sion, suffering in her union with the crucified Redeemer. As the incorporation of many others into the Church at Calvary, John shares in her sufferings, but without her innocence. His is the suffering of the penitent, accepted, sinner, who participates in the Cross by the new life of penitent conversion. Saint Paul expressed this ecclesial union with the suffering Redeemer, found in Mary and John in differing ways: "I have been crucified with Christ; it is no longer I who live, but Christ who lives in me; and the life I now live in the flesh I live by faith in the Son of God." And he adds, in awe, the accepting love of this Bridegroom, "who loved me and gave himself for me" (Galatians 2:20).

We may draw together the nuptial meaning of the "great mystery" of the Bridegroom who is Priest and Victim. He came to Jerusalem to die for his spouse. His intention was expressed at the supper table in his nuptial promise to come and take that spouse to himself. In his eucharistic words he proclaimed his self-immolation for his spouse. In his "High Priestly Prayer" he revealed the identity of his spouse as the Church in his consent to die for his chosen spouse (specificity) and in his seeking divine union with that spouse.

On Calvary, the espousal of the Bridegroom is seen in two ways: in Mary becoming a sign of Mother Church already espoused in the Incarnation, for whom he dies and, secondly, in his espousing his bride

the Church in dying for her. Mary includes the past, present and future
of the Church in herself. She thus represents the perfection of the
Church in union with the Bridegroom. In being espoused in the act of
Christ's dying, the Church is born, re-born in his "water and blood," and
united to the Bridegroom in his self-immolation. The Bridegroom
extends himself in the Church, his own cherished body.

On Calvary, the figure of Saint John reminds us that the espousal is
of the whole community, and of each redeemed sinner in the Church.
The Bridegroom's redemptive love for sinners is both his objective
bestowal of saving union and his acceptance of sinners. In receiving his
gift of self and in being accepted, the Church is born and espoused.
Each sinner is redeemed in that nuptial union, but at the price of the
suffering of the Bridegroom and his bride. These are the nuptial
meanings of the heart of the "great mystery" at the Cross.

Three of the sacraments deemed as "great" by Saint Thomas are
evident in the work of the Priest and Victim: Baptism, in the cleansing
water and blood; Confirmation in the breathing-forth of the Spirit; the
Eucharist in the sacrifice of Body and Blood. But the fourth "great"
sacrament, Marriage, is evident in the redemptive love of the
Bridegroom. He sought his spouse by taking our human nature. He
sacrificed himself as the second Adam to bring forth, cleanse and wed
his beloved spouse so that, "In this sacrifice there is entirely revealed
that plan which God has imprinted on the humanity of man and
woman since their creation; the marriage of baptized persons thus
becomes a real symbol of that new and eternal covenant sanctioned in
the blood of Christ."[52]

The "great mystery" of Christ espousing his Church, and how that
can be extended into Marriage, cannot be proposed only in terms of the
Cross. We must accompany the Bridegroom into the glory of his
Resurrection.

The Bridegroom as King

As Prophet, Jesus Christ the Bridegroom proclaimed a new dignity
for Marriage based on the created reality in Genesis. As Priest and
Victim, he entered a mystical nuptial union with his bride, the Church,

giving himself for her in redemptive, spousal, love. As King, he perfects and completes his nuptial union, through the glorious Resurrection of his own body.

We may find the nuptial meaning of the Resurrection in his Johannine title, "the Lamb of God," given to him by John the Baptist (John 1:36). John the Baptist also described him as the "bridegroom" (John 3:29). But there is nothing nuptial in the term "Lamb of God" within Saint John's Gospel. This term makes sense only in the context of John's account of the Passion, which reaches its high point "on the day of Preparation of the Passover," at "about the sixth hour" (John 19:14). The crucifixion coincides with the sacrifice of the Passover lambs. Jesus Christ is thus the Paschal Lamb, pierced, but without a bone of his body broken, in accord with the Law (cf. John 19:36-37 and Exodus 12:46, Numbers 9:12). He is the lamb "led to the slaughter," the Suffering Servant (Isaiah 53:7).

The nuptial meaning of the Lamb of God is revealed in the Book of Revelation. First the Lamb is presented in redemptive terms: "I saw a Lamb standing, as though it had been slain . . ." (Revelation 5:6), but the Lamb lives and is worthy to open the scroll and the seven seals, receiving with the Father, the praise and worship of the company of heaven (Revelation 5:8-14; 7:9-12). He is the shepherd king of those martyrs who washed their (Baptismal) robes in his blood (Revelation 7:13-17). He is surrounded by a perfect number of virginal men (Revelation 14:1-5). He is the risen Christ, "Lord of lords and King of kings," who conquers the beast (Revelation 17:14).

To this risen Lamb a spouse is given, after Satan and his agents have been hurled into hell. A great multitude sings the hymn of invitation to the nuptials of the risen Christ: "Hallelujah! For the Lord our God the Almighty reigns. Let us rejoice and exult and give him the glory, for the marriage of the Lamb has come, and his Bride has made herself ready. . . ." And at once her mystical ecclesial identity is revealed as the hymn continues: ". . . it was granted her to be clothed with fine linen, bright and pure," that fine linen which is "the righteous deeds of the saints" (Revelation 19:6-8). The messianic eschatological banquet is revealed as the marriage feast of the Lamb and his Bride: "Blessed are those who are invited to the marriage supper of the Lamb" (Revelation 20:9).

Finally, the Bride herself is revealed, amidst "a new heaven and a new earth." "And I saw the holy city, new Jerusalem, coming down out of heaven from God, prepared as a bride adorned for her husband." Again, there is an immediate ecclesial interpretation provided, the union of God and man in community: "Behold, the dwelling of God is with men. He will dwell with them, and they shall be his people, and God himself will be with them . . .," but this is the triumph of the Church, for, ". . . he will wipe away every tear from their eyes, and death shall be no more" (Revelation 21:1-4). Again, the Bride is revealed in the glory of the Parousia, as the angel says: "Come, I will show you the Bride, the wife of the Lamb," which is "the holy city Jerusalem coming down out of heaven from God." As before, there is an immediate ecclesial interpretation provided, for ". . . the wall of the city had twelve foundations, and on them the twelve names of the twelve apostles of the Lamb" (Revelation 21:9-14).

The "headship" of this glorified Lamb of God is evident in his spousal union with the New Jerusalem: "And the city has no need of sun or moon to shine upon it, for the glory of God is its light, and its lamp is the Lamb" (Revelation 21:23). The Book of Revelation closes with the voice of Bridegroom and Bride, calling believers to the baptismal gift of eternal life, inviting them to the marriage feast in eternity, with the Holy Spirit as the voice of the Bridegroom: "The Spirit and the Bride say, 'Come.' And let him who hears say, 'Come.' And let him who is thirsty come; let him who desires it take the water of life without price" (Revelation 22:17).

In the Book of Revelation we thus see, in glorious terms, the same nuptial union between Christ and his Church that we saw in his suffering redemptive love on Calvary. Yet there is an important theological meaning in the royal triumph of the Lamb. His espousal to his Church is only complete in his Resurrection. The spouse he sought in his union with us in his Incarnation was brought forth and cleansed in his self-immolation. Yet the "water and word" of Baptism, the redemptive water and blood, is only effective through his Resurrection into which the believers are plunged in Baptism (cf. Romans 6:1-11). His headship over the Church, his spouse, is only effective in his triumph over death. The nuptial headship of Christ in Ephesians 5:23 is explained in the Resurrection triumph of Christ the King in Ephesians 1:20-23, for the

Father "has put all things under his feet and has made him the head over all things for the church, which is his body, the fulness of him who fills all in all."[53]

The Resurrection may thus be seen as the complete nuptial union, the Glorified Body of Jesus Christ united to his Church, united to the bodies of those in baptismal and eucharistic union with him. The Resurrection is eternal; the union is forever. We have thus the key to both the Grace and the permanence of the sacrament of Marriage in the glorious nuptials of the risen Lord. By death and Resurrection he takes his spouse to himself, takes her to the place prepared in his Father's house, forever. Thus we may take the eternal glory of the Book of Revelation and propose this celestial Marriage as both God's plan for the union of Christians with himself and of the earthly union of Marriage. The redemptive love signified and contained in Marriage participates both in the Cross and Resurrection, a love stronger than death.

There is a further dimension to the nuptial meaning of the Resurrection. In the life of Grace, in Christ communicating himself to his spouse there is a causal relationship between the Resurrection and our salvation. Saint Thomas insisted on the Cross as the meritorious cause of our Redemption, hence the cause of the sacraments.[54] But when he examined the Resurrection, he argued that the efficient cause of our own bodily resurrection, i.e., our ultimate salvation, is both Cross and Resurrection.[55] He further argued that the exemplary cause of our forgiveness of sins is the Passion, but that the exemplary cause of our justification is the Resurrection. Through the risen Christ, we rise to a new life of Grace. He cited Romans 4:25: ". . . Jesus our Lord, who was put to death for our trespasses and raised for our justification."[56]

In this light, the Resurrection enters Marriage in terms both of justification and the resurrection of our own bodies. Only those raised to divine life by baptismal justification can minister sacramental Marriage to one another. They can truly signify the "great mystery," of Incarnation, Cross and Resurrection because they already participate in the redeeming union with the Divinity and Sacred Humanity of the Redeemer who is the risen Lord. He is present in and through them in their consent and bond of Marriage, as they are "one flesh" in body and in a community of life and love. His Resurrection rendered him accessible, across time and space, to baptized spouses in his Church. Moreover, the permanence of their union and their fidelity to justifying Grace each day is set before them by the risen, glorified, Bridegroom.

His deathless love was vindicated by the Father's acceptance of his death, in the Resurrection. His love is truly spousal, because he is the Bridegroom in virtue of being the Redeemer.[57] He offers baptized spouses a share in such deathless love, if they purpose to live the justification of their Baptism, as "one flesh." He calls them to die and rise with him each day in the joys and sorrows of their pilgrimage together. So, the risen Christ, present in his Holy Spirit, makes the lived sacrament of Marriage their chosen way of justification and sanctification. Already we anticipate the theological themes of the next chapter, which centers around the Church spouse of the Bridegroom, and human spouses in the Church.

Again using Saint Thomas as our starting point, I would see the Resurrection in the nuptial meaning of the human body. The risen Lamb imparted his eternal light to his bride, the New Jerusalem. The apocalyptic symbols reveal the perfection and the completion of the "great mystery," which is the final incorporation of those who are saved into the eternal life of God in heaven. This involves the resurrection of the body, of which both the Cross and Resurrection is the efficient cause.

God has created us for union, for union with himself. Our bodies signify that capacity for union. We were formed for union and communion with God and with one another. Sexuality, an element in the capacity for union and communion, was created "at the beginning" for the community of life and love which is Marriage. In the sacrament it is redeemed, raised from its degradation in the Fall, and rendered chaste and fruitful in a new way — such that the love of spouses is directed not only to one another, but to God. As "one flesh," they are called to bodily resurrection, for their salvation is worked out as spouses, as husband and wife. They are called by the Bridegroom, who revealed the nuptial meaning of his own body, his body and spouse the Church, and our bodies — in his physical Resurrection.

The slain Lamb of the Book of Revelation is the Bridegroom, bearing the wounds of his Passion, in the glorified body of our flesh, taken into the perfect Unity of the Trinity. The suffering of his nuptials on Calvary is imprinted in his wounds, proof of his love for his bride, the cost of that deathless love. The Bridegroom's friends rejoiced when he showed them those wounds, for in the Resurrection he already anticipates the fulfillment of his nuptial promise: "And when I go and prepare a place for you, I will come again and take you to myself, that where I am you may also be" (John 14:3). But that promise was followed immediately by his revelation of himself as "the way." "And you know the way where I am going;" "I am the way, and the truth, and the life. No one comes to the Father, but by me" (John 14:4, 6).

In his risen body, he is "the way," the Bridegroom who "goes," by way of his Cross, and who "returns," by way of his Resurrection. He returns to take his spouse, the Church, on the final nuptial journey, to our Father's house, rendering back to the Father that mystical spouse given to him by the Father. That spouse, descending from heaven as the glorious bride in the Book of Revelation, personifies all of us called to the true nuptial union, no longer servants or friends, but kin and heirs, no longer wayfarers, but those raised in their own bodies for that ultimate union, of which all earthly unions and communions are a sign and foretaste.

Again our eyes are drawn to one who personifies the ultimate espousal in a perfect way, Mary Immaculate, spouse and Mother of God. If Christ is King of kings through his Resurrection, she is revealed in the Book of Revelation as the Queen, "a woman clothed with the sun, with the moon under her feet, and on her head a crown of twelve stars" (Revelation 12:1). In a superimposed pattern of images we may recognize in her: the "woman" of Genesis, but a new Eve; the old Israel giving birth to the Messiah in the fulfillment of spousal prophecy; the new Israel, mother Church, whose union with the Bridegroom brings forth many "offspring . . . who keep the commandments of God and bear testimony to Jesus" (Revelation 12:17). As the Daughter of Sion, her triumph is seen in the female figure of the New Jerusalem, the bride adorned in the glory of the Lamb.

Here, the solemn teaching of the Magisterium is our sure guide. The bodily Assumption of Our Lady is her spousal glory, and that of the Church she personifies in the "great mystery." Rightly the Preface of the Assumption praises the Father in describing Mary as: ". . . the beginning and the pattern of the Church in its perfection, and a sign of hope and comfort for your people on their pilgrim way."[58] Derived from the nuptial meaning of the body of her risen Son, the nuptial meaning of Mary's body is seen in her re-birth by resurrection. Her share in his Resurrection, truly mirroring the "head of the body, the Church . . . the beginning, the first-born from the dead" (Colossians 1:18), is a share in his Resurrection "birth," in which the Church is re-born.[59] The Church coming forth from his pierced side is only complete in the Resurrection and, as we have noted, the baptismal water and blood is only effectual as Baptism into his dying and rising again. Yet all this is complete in Mary, past, present and future. In her Assumption and Queenship she is and represents the triumph of the bride of Christ.

Thus the Bridegroom imparts even his kingly office to the bride he espoused in the "great mystery" of his Incarnation and Redemption. How significant and gracious is the Byzantine Christian Marriage custom, the crowning of the bride and groom, visibly celebrating the glorious completion of the "great mystery," to which they are called in sacramental Marriage.[60]

III. GOD: THE SOURCE OF MARRIAGE

The Bridegroom and the Trinity

Before we examine how the "great mystery" enters the lives of married Christians in the next chapter, let us contemplate the eternal Source of the mystery and of Marriage: God, the Father, Son and Holy Spirit. From him, in our creation, human Marriage proceeded, a created reality inherent in the complementarity of gender. From him, in the work of our Redemption in Christ, came a new dignity for Marriage. From him came the healing of Marriage, restored to its simplicity and fidelity by the teaching of Christ the Prophet, united to divine life by the spousal work of Christ the Priest-Victim, perfected in its nuptial destiny in the risen glory of Christ the King.

At the Last Supper, we saw Jesus Christ reveal his spousal intentions as consent, choice and a will to union with his bride, the Church. He referred his own nuptial mission and work back to its Source, to the

Father who had sent him into the world to seek, to form and to be united with his spouse. He prayed for his spouse, revealed in the collective "them" as his Church. Yet the Source was also his own union with the Father.

He willed a union with that spouse, with us, his Church. He willed a union that would be a participation in his glory (cf. John 17:9-10, 22-23). But the union is derived from God, "one, even as we are one, I in them and you in me, that they may become perfectly one" (John 17:23). Yet he had already established the basis of their own unity, as a gift from God, reflecting divine Unity, based on union with himself: "I am the vine, you are the branches. He who abides in me and I in him, he it is that bears much fruit, for apart from me you can do nothing" (John 15:5). Thus, his prayer to the Father can be uttered for the intention "that they also may be in us," one with the Father and the Son.

On the Cross we saw not only the mystical birth of his spouse in the cleansing water and blood, but also the breathing-forth, or *Spiramen*, signifying the Holy Spirit, breathed into his spouse. As the Body of Christ, as the extension of the second Adam, the spouse thus participates in the Son's union with the Father and the Holy Spirit. Her nuptial union is derived from the divine union of Persons, the Trinity. Her birth and re-birth in redemptive love comes from the Triune Source of all love, he who is Love.

Before we see how this "great mystery" derived from the Trinity is signified in the Marriage of Christians, we should contemplate the greater, indeed the greatest mystery of love. Through their participation in the work of the Bridegroom, human spouses, in the sacrament, show forth in this world something of the love of the Father, Son and Holy Spirit.

The Love of the Trinity

It would be only too easy to move immediately to that analogy of the Trinity suggested by Marriage, the family. Such an analogy is not wholly satisfactory, not only because it depends on our understanding of "person," in human terms leading to tritheism, but also because it raises the problem of appropriation. To whom in a family do you assign the terms "Son" and "Holy Spirit"? But, if the family can only give us a faint or inaccurate analogy of God the Trinity, moving in the opposite direction, from God, we can see something of the Holy Trinity given to Marriage and the family. The more difficult theological problem is to perceive in stricter, less analogical terms, what relational love the Triune Creator and Redeemer can impart to Marriage, hence to the family.

First of all, considering God in himself, we see that the union which is Father, Son and Holy Spirit is "Trinity," not a "tri-Unity," as Saint Thomas has pointed out.[61] The Persons of the Trinity are distinguished as Father, Son and Holy Spirit, yet the Trinity is One God, the "One in Being," one *ousia*.

Yet if we confess perfect unity and union, we must also confess the dynamic communion as absolute as the union. This is that interpenetration of inter-relationship between the Persons, the *perichoresis* or *circumincessio*. In this dynamic communion we are given no better term than "love" to describe the union and communion of Father, Son and Holy Spirit. If we appropriate this being One-in-love to the Holy Spirit, we do not mean that the Spirit is the principle or cause of the love of the Father and Son towards one another.[62]   Each is equal in the union and communion of love, even as each is distinguished because each is pure act. The Father, for example, is the act of begetting.[63]   In the union and communion, each Person is a divine Relation, but God who is One is in no sense divided by each Relation, for whatever is in God is God.

However, we must balance such a view of God in himself with the "economic" understanding of the Trinity, that is, the Trinity as known by us through God's revelation of himself in our creation and Redemption. The perfect union of one divine *ousia* and the dynamic communion of the *perichoresis* could suggest an incommunicable or only inward, "self-contained," interpenetration in eternal love. But God, as we known him in revelation, is not an impassive monad. He is revealed, through Jesus Christ, in the "economic" sense, in our creation and Redemption as the God who is open to us.

The "openness" of God shows us how the Triune God imparts himself to us, and draws us to himself in creating us and in raising us to the supernatural life of Grace. The family titles revealed in Father and Son are not mere names. They reveal a God who can extend his family by adoption.[64]   But this Triune God has already imprinted his own image and likeness upon us, so that we can be raised to the adoption of Grace, and so that we can relate with one another. The union of Father, Son and Holy Spirit is inclusive, not exclusive. Our Lady and Saint John on Calvary were caught up into the "great mystery" of the Triune God raising men and women up into his "plan for the fullness of time," uniting all things in Christ, "things in heaven and things on earth" (Ephesians 1:10).

Both union and communion are offered to men and women alike in the Redemption. In faith and Baptism the offer is accepted, and men and women are raised up into the Trinitarian life, sharing as creatures in that union and communion. In his fashioning and re-fashioning of Marriage, the Triune God further offers the baptized a way of sharing as creatures in his own union and communion, through the created reality of gender, through sexuality and procreation, through the community of life and love which is found in the family.

The Trinity and Marriage

God, Father, Son and Holy Spirit imparts a specific share of his inner life of union and communion to those who enter sacramental Marriage. In the history of salvation, seen in the nuptial tradition, we may appropriate different "roles" to the divine Persons. We may see the Father presenting Eve to Adam, the Son espousing his bride, the Church, in the Incarnation and Redemption, the Holy Spirit raising Christian spouses to a share in that "great mystery" of a divine-human espousal in the sacrament of Marriage. But there are limits to appropriating "roles" to the Persons, One in union and communion. All the Persons are "at work" in imparting a share in the Triune union and communion to men and women in the nuptial vocation.

The Triune God also imparts something of his own divine freedom in Marriage. As a created reality in the objective created human order, Marriage ought to be formed in a truly human way. In the creative wisdom of God, there is meant to be choice, freely made and freely accepted, in each truly human nuptial union. Such choice is obviously an act of the freedom of will God has imparted to those made in his own image and likeness. Yet in redeeming the way the Fall impairs such freedom of choice, God also imparts something of the specificity of his own loving choice of us. Spouses, in the sacrament of Marriage, choose redemptive love, which we shall see is a true share in the love of the pierced Heart of the Bridegroom himself. Thus they participate in the free choice, or ineffable divine decree, which was God reaching forth to redeem us in love. Saint John of the Cross expressed this simply as the will of the Father that his Son have a bride:

> "I wish to give You, My dear Son,
> To cherish You, a lovely bride. . . ."[65]

In our human condition, we experience spousal choice as truly ethical, since it is derived from God, in our creation as moral beings in his image and likeness, beings able to know his law and follow his will for our own good and the good of others. In our Redemption, ourselves chosen and accepted, we find a higher ethical choice in sacramental Marriage. The love of the Trinity, open to redeem us, forms the consent for the good of the other and for the good of the self, a mutually redemptive self-giving in love.

The Divine Author

Looking back across the "great mystery," in its nuptial meanings, we see God involved in a union and communion with us, including all the elements we shall discern in sacramental Marriage: covenant, choice, consent, redemptive love, suffering, fruitfulness, fidelity, permanence, a community of life and love and a joyous and glorious finality. This helps us to understand more deeply what the Fathers of the Second Vatican Council meant when they taught: "For God himself is the author of Marriage and has endowed it with various benefits and with various ends in view."[66]

As "author" of Marriage, God is not some celestial architect who draws up a spousal blue-print for human Marriage. He is not some abstract agent, distinct and apart from this institution. He himself has espoused us in our creation, and more wondrously and lovingly, in our Redemption. He imparts a share of his Triune love, union and communion to those who enter the shared life of Marriage. He is involved intimately in Marriage. This is the profound, yet simple, basis of the sacrament.

CHAPTER TWO

Marriage "In Christ"

Cuando se gozaran juntos	*Then, to a deathless music sounding,*
En eterna melodía;	*Bride to Bridegroom will be pressed,*
Porque el era la cabeza	*Because He is the crown and headpiece*
De la esposa que tenía.	*Of the Bride that He possessed.*
A la cual todos los miembros	*To her beauty all the members*
De los justos juntaría:	*Of the just He will enlace.*
Que son cuerpo de la esposa,	*To form the body of the Bride*
A la cual el tomaría.	*When taken into His embrace.*

Saint John of the Cross, *Romance IV.*

From the Triune God, Source of all life and love, we move to the human person, his creation. More precisely, from Jesus Christ the Bridegroom, we move to his beloved spouse, the men and women who are the Church. This transition from the "great mystery" to human beings is the way to resolve the sacramental problem: how the "great mystery" is signified in the Marriage of Christians. Thus, we establish the foundation for the sacrament of Marriage, before examining the history of sacramentality and before entering the divine and human dynamics of consent, bond and covenant.

SAINT PAUL

To this point, I have assumed the central place of Saint Paul's theology of Marriage, without a specific study of that theology. It seemed best to trace the "great mystery" of Ephesians 5:32 in terms of Jesus Christ, hence relying on the Gospel traditions, before relating that mystery to men and women in Marriage. Saint Paul's theology is the way we understand Baptism as essential to sacramental Marriage, hence the radical difference between "natural" Marriage and sacramental Marriage.

Genesis affirms the sacred nature of a good "natural" Marriage as a "created" rather than a "secular reality." Every good "natural" Marriage may be described as "a religious symbol that points to God's faithfulness."[1]   But Saint Paul understands a difference between "natural" Marriage and the Marriage of Christians, even a difference between "natural" Marriage and the Marriage of a Christian to a cooperative pagan (see 1 Corinthians 7:12-16). For Saint Paul, Christian Marriage belongs to a higher order than the Marriage of pagans. It is more binding. It has its own purity and is more demanding in terms of mutual love between spouses. It establishes a correspondingly firm and noble family life.

However, the basis for the difference between this higher form of Marriage and pagan Marriage is not of the moral order only. That more demanding and refined moral order rests on an ontological basis, the divine re-creation of persons, the re-birth from paganism to Christianity, the dying and rising which is the radical transformation of Baptism.

Various passages may be adduced from the letters of Saint Paul to show his ontological theology of Baptism. Two are especially significant for our purposes, from Ephesians and the earlier letter which evidently influenced the shape and content of Ephesians, Colossians. Both letters have direct bearing on themes in Saint Paul's theology of Marriage.

In Colossians 3:9-10, Saint Paul seems to be playing on the baptismal stripping of candidates and their re-clothing after immersion or ablution. In the light of the "dying" of Baptism (Col 3:3), a change from the "old man" to the "new" is expressed as an accomplished reality, to which the baptized are meant to respond in a new way of life: ". . . seeing that you have put off the old nature (*ton palaion anthropon*, literally the 'old man') with its practices and have put on the new nature (*ton neon*, literally the 'new man')." In Ephesians 4:22-24, this is expressed more in terms of an exhortation to new moral life: "Put off your old nature . . . put on the new nature (*ton kainon anthropon*), created after the likeness of God in true righteousness and holiness." However, in Ephesians we note that Saint Paul uses the richer term for "new," *kainon*, implying a total change of reality, rather than the simpler term, *neon*, he used in 1 Corinthians.

The baptismal transformation also is expressed in terms of the radically new reality in Galatians and 2 Corinthians, again with the use of the stronger term for "new." Galatians 6:15, for example, reads: "For neither circumcision counts for anything, nor uncircumcision, but a new creation" (*kaine ktisis*, "*sed nova creatura*" in the Vulgate, "but a new creature"). The Greek text can read, as does the Vulgate, "For *in Christ Jesus* neither circumcision. . . ." In 2 Corinthians 5:17, this "in Christ" principle is explicit, without variants, and the "new creation" re-appears: "Therefore, if any one is in Christ, he is a new creation (*en Christo, kaine ktisis*, which may also mean 'a new creature') the old has passed away; behold, the new has come."

The principle of "in Christ," *en Christo*, repeatedly used by Saint Paul is most important in helping us to see the ontological change of Baptism. It has various shades of meaning, depending on the context. It may take the form "in the Lord," applied significantly to Marriage when Saint Paul (1 Cor 7:39) admonished widows who wished to take a second husband to marry "only in the Lord" (*monon en kyrio*). This may be a variation of "in Christ," referring to Christian life in the Church rather than the more mystical meanings of "in Christ," the baptismal or ecclesial union with Christ the Lord. But, "in the Lord" is derived from baptismal union "in Christ." By being a Christian, a widow can enter a Christian Marriage, and Saint Paul only permits a Christian Marriage to widows.

I. EPHESIANS: THE CONTEXT

The "in Christ" principle of Saint Paul pervades the letter to the Ephesians, the epistle where we find the "great mystery" — ". . . the mystery of his will, according to his purpose which he set forth in Christ as a plan for the fulness of time, to unite all things in him, things in heaven and things on earth" (1:9-10) — related to Christian Marriage. In Colossians (1:27), we find the *in Christ* principle identified with the "mystery" — ". . . this mystery, which is Christ in you, the hope of glory."

In the early chapters of Ephesians, Saint Paul repeatedly uses *in Christ*, or similar phrases, in various ways. The opening words, "Blessed be the God and Father of our Lord Jesus Christ, who has blessed us in Christ with every spiritual blessing" (1:3) are echoed in terms of redemption in Christ and the eschatological destiny of the baptized (1:11, 13). The baptized are a new creation, "created in Christ Jesus" (2:10), former Gentiles reconciled in the Church (2:13-18), members of the household of God, made into "a holy temple in the Lord" and "a dwelling place of God in the Spirit" (2:19-22). Saint Paul twice reminds these Ephesians that they were once pagans,[2] but "the mystery" is also the divine dispensation which unites Gentiles in the Church with former Jews, such as Paul himself (3:1-6).

The communal, ecclesial understanding of being "in Christ" is balanced by the personal, individual meaning of Baptism. Twice he refers to the "seal" of the Holy Spirit: ". . . you . . . were sealed with the promised Holy Spirit" (1:13), and ". . . the Holy Spirit of God, in whom you were sealed for the day of redemption" (4:30). The seal (*e sphragis*) has an eschatological meaning. It is the permanent sealing of those who are re-born "in Christ" in Baptism, bestowed in the laying-on-of-hands which completes Christian initiation. This consecration is a way we understand the indelible character of Baptism, Confirmation and Orders.[3]   Paul urges the Ephesians not to "grieve" the Spirit by their sins (4:30-32).

Those who are "in Christ" are also sons and daughters of God. The adoption or filiation theme is evident when he describes these converted Gentiles as "fellow heirs" (Ep 3:6. See also Gal 4:6, Rm 8:14-17). They enjoy the unity of one body, one Spirit (cf. Ep 4:3-4).[4]

The wider context of Saint Paul's letter to the Ephesians was not only to remind these converts of their baptismal dignity, but to encourage them and to exhort them strongly to resist the temptations of their pagan environment. They enjoy a two-fold dignity "in Christ," that is, as individuals each baptized and re-created "in Christ," living "in Christ," and as the whole Church, one body "in Christ." But Paul speaks to them beset with the temptations of their rich, worldly city, especially sexual immorality (5:3-13). His moral exhortations have a sacramental and ecclesial context, that challenge to moral fidelity which compels him to say, "I, therefore, a prisoner for the Lord, beg you to lead a life worthy of the calling to which you have been called" (4:1).

The central place of the sacrament of Baptism in "a life worthy of the calling" runs through all of Saint Paul's letters. It is because they are baptized, because they live, as individuals and as a community, "in Christ," that Paul can expect so much of the Ephesians. Thus, when he exhorts them in terms of Marriage, he proposes a kind of Marriage, in itself of more sublime significance than that they once knew as pagans. It is logical for us to call this "Marriage 'in Christ'."

II. MARRIAGE IN EPHESIANS

The passage in Ephesians devoted to Marriage should be seen as a whole, but within a wider exhortatory section, characteristically presented in the latter part of the epistle. Yet Marriage is presented in a deeper fashion than moral exhortation. In its central "great mystery" theology, Ephesians traces itself directly back to the teachings of Christ on Marriage as recorded in the Gospels.[5]   Paul was well aware of the Old Testament prophetic traditions which presented Yahweh as seeking his spouse, Israel. He would have been aware, in some form, of the tradition of Christ as the eschatological Bridegroom, as we saw in all four Gospels, no matter at what stage those Gospels existed at the time he wrote (late in his life) his letter to the Ephesians.[6]

The Marriage passage may be integrated into the continuous flow of moral exhortation: against sexual license, to awake from sleep, to make the most of time and walk carefully, avoiding drunkenness and turning rather to the praise of God (5:3-20). It need not necessarily begin with a new paragraph at verse 21 or 22.[7] But the nuptial message as such does begin with verse 21. Two stages in Paul's teaching on marriage seem to be suggested by the Apostle's thought and his use

of two points with both ecclesial and mystical meaning: the headship of
Christ over his Church and his espousing that Church in self-sacrificing
love.

1. Headship

21. Be subject to one another out of reverence for Christ.
22. Wives, be subject to your husbands, as to the Lord.
23. For the husband is the head of the wife as Christ is the
    head of the church, his body, and is himself its
    Savior.
24. As the church is subject to Christ, so let wives also be
    subject in everything to their husbands.

The concept of the headship of Christ over his Church and of a
husband over his wife is found elsewhere in Saint Paul's letters. Paul has
already mentioned Christ's headship over all creation "for the church
which is his body" in Ephesians 1:22-23. He has also referred indirectly
to this headship in terms of Christ being the "cornerstone of the
Church" (2:20), and more precisely, in more complex terms, as the
"head," into whom Christians are to grow and from whom the whole
body of the Church grows and is ordered (4:15-16). As we shall see,
these last verses are the key to the deeper meaning of Paul's combination of Christ's headship and the headship of a husband (5:21-24).
What makes the Ephesians passage important is that it is the only time
Paul brings both concepts together, using Christ's headship to justify a
distinctively Christian form of headship in Marriage. In Colossians, for
example, we find Christ as "the head of the body, the church" (1:18),
but later in the epistle a call to wives to "be subject" to their husbands
only because it is "fitting in the Lord" (3:18). The closest he comes to the
Ephesians combination of Christ's ecclesial headship and that of the
husband is 1 Corinthians 11:3, a hierarchy of headship: Christ "the
head of every man," the husband thus head of his wife, and God (the
Father) being the Head of Christ. Already we can see that "head" and
"headship" are more subtle than the English language suggests.

When the nuptial passage from Ephesians is read in full at a
celebration of Marriage today, it may provoke hostile reactions from

those concerned for the rights of women. Is Saint Paul requiring the subjection of a wife to her husband? Is this subjection part of the sacrament of Marriage, to be included in the "great mystery"? These questions can be resolved only when we understand headship with Saint Paul, in cosmic and ecclesial terms. Then the derived headship of the Christian husband, reflecting Christ the head of his Church, need not be exaggerated or dismissed by either reaction or surrender to feminist ideology.

Together with the "great mystery" of the Bridegroom's spousal love, Christ's headship of his Church is what makes Paul's matrimonial exhortation distinct and different from the exhortations which surround it in Ephesians: to the believers in general, to children, parents, slaves, masters. The mystical ecclesial nature of Marriage itself raises his matrimonial exhortation beyond a simple appeal to moral law or natural justice.[8]   But headship in the Church, hence in Marriage, does convey serious moral meaning, and is too important to be lightly explained away.[9]

Understanding headship revolves around the Greek term *e kephale*, "head." This may refer to the "head" of the human body, the "head" in terms of excellence, or even the whole human person. Yet it has a further meaning, related to origin or source, for example, the "head" of a fountain or spring of water. From Paul's use of this term in other letters and his probable choice of this word in this context, it would seem that he intended to convey the richer meaning.[10]   There is a priority of male before female in the Genesis account of the creation of gender, and this is expressed in 1 Corinthians 11:8-9: "For man was not made from woman, but woman from man. Neither was man created for woman, but woman for man." Paul notes this in 1 Timothy 2:13: "For Adam was formed first, then Eve. . . ." He sees hierarchy as implicit, in the mode of creation, in male priority.

The richer understanding of "head" is already present in the letter to the Ephesians. Speaking of the unity of the Church, in Christ, of various gifts and of the threat of heresy, Saint Paul called believers to unity with Christ the head of the Church: "Rather, speaking the truth in love, we are to grow up in every way into him who is the head, into Christ . . ." (4:15). Then he expounded the dynamism of this head of the Mystical Body, ". . . from whom the whole body, joined and knit together by every joint with which it is supplied, when each part is working properly, makes bodily growth and upbuilds itself in love" (4:15-16).

Coming immediately before the baptismal call to "put on the new nature," and the moral exhortations leading to our Marriage exhortation, we ought to see "head" and "headship" in the light of this dynamic vision of Christ, source of growth and unity in the Church. This also makes sense of the call to wives to "be subject to" their husbands. In Ephesians 5:21, "the subjection" to one another is to be mutual, among all Ephesian Christians. This may allow the less forceful translation of the verse that follows as, "Wives, give way to your husbands. . . ." But the "headship of Christ over his Church" remains in verses 23 and 24.

The "giving way" of a wife to her husband is in no sense servile or abject. It seems, rather, to be Paul's expression of the need for the wife to accept her role, as delineated by her gender, but in the same way that all members of the Church accept their differing, yet complementary, roles in the one body, "giving way" to one another (verse 21). Saint Paul elsewhere insists strongly on this ordered, but complementary and dynamic, hierarchy in the Body of Christ (see Ep 4:11-12 on charisms, Rm 12:3-8 on charisms in one body, and 1 Cor 12:4-31, his fullest expression of this ordered hierarchy). In Ephesians the emphasis is on unity, the underlying message of the whole epistle. In the matrimonial exhortation the headship of Christ in his Church is the key to unity between husband and wife, in the unique union of Marriage "in Christ."

Saint Paul's hierarchy in Marriage is less socially conventional than that apparent in Saint Peter's first epistle: "Likewise you husbands, live considerately with your wives, bestowing honor on the woman as the weaker sex, since you are joint heirs of the grace of life, in order that your prayers may not be hindered" (1 P 3:7). Yet "the weaker sex," in the social context may well be an expression of tenderness.[11]   Saint Paul likewise seems to present the role of a wife in terms of dependence, if we note the parallel dependency relationships he addresses in Ephesians 6:1-4, children and parents, and Ephesians 6:5-9, slaves and masters. Saint Thomas did not see headship as subjection, rather as of benefit to wives, "for their advantage and well being."[12]

In his comment after his ruling on head-covering at worship, Saint Paul seems to qualify headship: "Nevertheless, in the Lord, woman is not independent of man nor man of woman; for as woman was made from man, so man is now born of woman. And all things are from God" (1 Cor 11:11-12). For those "in Christ," the ecclesial principle "in the Lord" determines a new Christian anthropology. Married people are first and foremost "baptized into Christ." They have "put on Christ" and "There is neither Jew nor Greek, there is neither slave nor free, there is neither male nor female; for you are all one in Christ Jesus" (Gal 3:28-29). Paul's concern for unity rests on the equality of Baptism into Christ and his Church. In Marriage there is to be the mutual giving-way and shared will of "one flesh," informed by, yet building up, the unity of the Church.[13]

Headship and giving-way "in the Lord" may also be seen in terms of sexuality. Saint Paul counselled spouses to give one another mutual marital rights: "For the wife does not rule over her own body, but the husband does . . .," so maintaining the husband's priority, but he adds at once, ". . . likewise the husband does not rule over his own body, but the wife does" (1 Cor 7:4). In this same passage, on the question of mutual salvation, he addresses the wife first (1 Cor 7:16). In Ephesians, the greater part of his exhortation on faithful love is directed at husbands, who perhaps were more culpable at Ephesus than their wives in the area of fidelity.

In terms of the male as the "giver" of life and in the complementary roles in sexual psychobiology, sexuality suggests a resolution of headship, "in Christ," neither male exploitation nor female autonomy.[14] However, headship needs to be filled out by the self-giving love of the second stage, in Ephesians 5:25-33. In turn, this will need to be treated in terms of consent and the mystery of spousal love, which Von Hildebrand included in his fascinating observation, "The difference between man and woman is a metaphysical one."[15]

2. Love in the Mystery

25. Husbands, love your wives, as Christ loved the church and gave himself up for her, 26. that he might sanctify her, having cleansed her, by the washing of water with the word, 27. that he might present the church to himself in splendor,

without spot or wrinkle or any such thing, that she might be
holy and without blemish.   28. Even so husbands should
love their wives as their own bodies. He who loves his wife
loves himself.   29. For no man ever hates his own flesh, but
nourishes and cherishes it, as Christ does the church,
30. because we are members of his body.   31. 'For this
reason a man shall leave his father and mother and be joined
to his wife, and the two shall become one.'   32. This is a great
mystery, and I mean in reference to Christ and the church;
33. however, let each one of you love his wife as himself, and
let the wife see that she respects her husband.

The whole passage can only be understood if we take verse 32 and,
as it were, re-locate it at the beginning, making it qualify the spousal love
of the other verses and the preceding headship verses addressed to
wives. This is Saint Paul's intention, ". . . and I mean in reference to
Christ and the church." Since Erasmus and the Reformation era, those
who saw that *to mysterion* does not mean *sacramentum* as "sacrament,"
have taken a further, but unwarranted step, saying that "this is a great
mystery" is a passing reference to Christ and his Church, only taken by
analogy from Marriage and not referring to Christian Marriage as such.
Traditional Catholic exegetes have accepted the correct meaning of *to
mysterion*, showing how the "mystery" refers not simply to Christ and his
Church, but includes married Christians as well.[16]   Prat called the
anti-sacramental interpretation of "this is a great mystery" a "tiresome
tautology," for it is surely stating the obvious to limit "great" to the
mystical union between Christ and his Church in the context of
Ephesians.[17]

That the whole passage should be read in the light of the "great
mystery" may also be inferred from the Magisterium. Both the Council
of Florence and the Council of Trent referred to Ephesians 5:32, but
not to prove the sacramentality of Marriage. The Tridentine use of this
text is simply: "Saint Paul *suggests* this when he says: 'Husbands. . . .' "[18]
The Magisterium thus gives the mind of the Church, that the text refers
to Christian Marriage as a sacrament of the "great mystery." The only
respected source which seems to equate the "mystery" with "sacrament"
is the *Catechism of the Council of Trent*.[19]

Scheeben pointed out the Ephesians 5:32 does not simply mean that Marriage is a symbol of the supernatural union between Christ and his Church, because, "in that case marriage itself would not be mysterious, but would only be a figure, itself empty of content, that would serve to call up before our minds a mystery extrinsic to it, that is, the union of Christ with the Church. Hence matrimony would be the sacrament of a mystery rather than a mystery, and a barren sacrament at that."[20] Christian Marriage truly participates in the "great mystery," and thus, each Christian marriage is a "great mystery" of union with Christ, through the union and communion of married life and love.

In the light of Ephesians 5:32, all of Saint Paul's words in his exhortation on Marriage describe this human, nuptial, participation in Christ's "great mystery." We have already examined headship — but it also comes into the "great mystery" of the risen Lord, who is head, hence source of all Grace, in and for his beloved Church. Comment on each of the verses around Ephesians 5:32 will bear out the sacramentalism of Saint Paul.

Verse 25: "Husbands, love your wives, as Christ loved the church, and gave himself up for her. . . ." There is an echo here of Paul's cry of love and faith, ". . . the life I now live in the flesh I live by faith in the Son of God, who loved me and gave himself for me" (Gal 2:20). In the light of our earlier study of the "great mystery," the giving-up in self-sacrifice on the Cross is not only the ultimate model for husbands, but the birth of the Church from the side of Christ crucified. He dies for her that she might have life. The new Eve is presented to the new Adam, only after she is taken from his pierced side, in the deep slumber of his death.

Verse 26: ". . . that he might sanctify her, having cleansed her by the washing of water with the word, 27. that he might present the church to himself in splendor, without spot or wrinkle or any such thing, that she might be holy and without blemish." The redemptive death of Christ is both the obvious Baptism, "washing of water with the word," and the sanctifying of the Spirit. Christian initiation is here superimposed on the Jewish and pagan Greek custom of the pre-nuptial ablutions of the bride.[21] Even the presentation of the bride may reflect the presentation of neophytes, after Baptism and Confirmation, for the offering and reception of the Eucharist. Thus the imagery in Ephesians moves back and forth between Christian initiation and Marriage customs. This is an interesting inter-play in the light of Paul's baptismal case for unity "in Christ" in Ephesians, an inter-play of significance in establishing the baptismal basis for the sacramentality of Christian Marriage.

There is a parallel in Saint Paul's second letter to the Corinthians where he takes on the role of *paranymphus*, the male attendant of the bridegroom. Admitting the incongruity of his role, he wished to present the church of Corinth to Christ "as a pure bride to her one husband." He feared a recurrence of Eden, the deception of this bride by the serpent of false preachers (11:1-4). But in Ephesians we do not find the eschatological implications as clearly suggested, the presentation of the baptized to Christ at the end of time (as also in Rm 14:10, 2 Cor 4:14, and Col 1:27-28).[22]   In Ephesians, Paul does not put himself forward as the *paranymphus*, nor does he propose John the Baptist in this role.

Jesus Christ is his own *paranymphus* in Ephesians 5:27. He presents his bride to himself. He is faithful to his own word of power and promise uttered in his dying for her, in the washing and sanctifying. Paul drew on a Jewish tradition of Yahweh presenting Eve to Adam, like a bridegroom's attendant (interpreting Gn 2:22).[23]   But now, in Christ, God is not only the attendant, but the Bridegroom. We touch upon the incarnational basis of the "great mystery." God Incarnate gave himself up for the men and women who are his spouse, the Church, re-creating them in Baptism and Confirmation, joining them to himself in the Eucharist, so that their own Marriage unions will re-capitulate his self-giving.

This sacrificial theme is suggested in the description of his spouse, after her redemptive washing and sanctifying (see also Tt 3:5, the washing of regeneration and renewal in the Holy Spirit). Now she is "in splendor," like the apocalyptic bride "adorned for her husband" (Rv 21:2). But this is not the splendor of the jewelled Jewish bride (cf. Ps 44:14). The splendor of the bride of Christ is her purity and holiness: ". . . without spot or wrinkle or any such thing, that she might be holy and without blemish." Again, she is like the apocalyptic bride, "clothed with fine linen, bright and pure. . .," which linen is "the righteous deeds of the saints" (Rv 19:8). The perfection of the Church, "without spot or wrinkle," was recognized in Our Lady by the Fathers of the Second Vatican Council.[24]

In the term "without blemish" the purity and holiness of the washed and sanctified bride is taken into sacrifice. The male lamb of the Passover was to be "without blemish" (Ex 12:5); likewise the victims in Leviticus, for example, the female lamb of sin offering (Lv 4:32). Saint Paul seems to move through cleansing, sanctifying and sacrifice, the three steps of Christian initiation: Baptism, Confirmation, Eucharist. The bride is "presented" only to be united to Christ in his self-offering, in his priesthood and victimhood. And this bride is the Christian people — in this letter, at Ephesus, in this context, husbands and wives. So, already in Saint Paul we see the "great mystery" coming into the lives of men and women.

Verse 28: "Even so husbands should love their wives as their own bodies. He who loves his wife loves himself. 29. For no man ever hates his own flesh, but nourishes and cherishes it, as Christ does the church." The sacrificial, eucharistic, nuances are reinforced by these verses. The bride united to Christ in his sacrifice, the bride who is a victim "holy and without blemish" is one with Christ, his own body, the Church. Saint Paul speaks to both husbands and wives in these verses, remembering his balances in the headship question, the mutual rights over one another's bodies in Marriage (cf. 1 Cor 7:3-4). Behind these verses is Christ's teaching from Genesis (2:24) about the "one flesh" or "one body" of the indissoluble bond of Marriage. Christ's indissoluble bond with his spouse is the source of the love of Christian spouses.

Verse 30: ". . . because we are members of his body." This clause qualifies the preceding verses, with the "we" widening the exhortation to include wives as well as husbands, the implicit mutuality. The "body," the espoused Church, is cherished and nourished because (in virtue of further eucharistic nuances) it is "his" body. Husbands and wives who are cherished and nourished by the Bridegroom, are to cherish and nourish one another. Their love may even be seen in the light of proper love of self: "He who loves his wife loves himself" in terms of "Love your neighbor as yourself," the *agape* "in Christ" of husbands and wives at Ephesus, who are brothers and sisters in the Lord, all "members of his body." Thus, spousal love for Christians is modelled on Christ cherishing his Church, his own body, "one flesh" with him.[25]

Verse 31: " 'For this reason a man shall leave his father and mother and be joined to his wife, and the two shall become one.' " Saint

Paul cites Genesis 2:24, just as Our Lord quoted it in his own Marriage
teaching (Mt 19:5 and Mk 10:7), but without Genesis 1:27. Did Saint
Paul know the teaching of Our Lord on Marriage? Certainly, as can be
inferred from his own distinction when he teaches the Corinthians
about Marriage: "To the married I give charge, *not I but the Lord*, that a
wife should not separate from her husband . . ." (1 Cor 7:10), as distinct
from what follows: "To the rest *I say, not the Lord* . . ." (1 Cor 7:12). Thus,
Paul echoes Our Lord and Genesis, but with his own purpose.

We may discern his intention in quoting Genesis 2:24 when we
consider how abrupt it sounds, unless immediately qualified by the
"great mystery," not simply in the verse that follows the quotation, but
the verse which precedes it, ". . . because we are members of his body.
For *this reason* a man shall leave his father. . . ."[26] In Genesis, Adam's
reason for leaving father and mother was the creation of Eve, "bone of
my bones and flesh of my flesh" (2:23), Adam here representing all his
descendants with human parents. In the new dispensation, the Son
leaves his Father to seek the new creation, his spouse, the Church, one
with him because of his solidarity with us, in the flesh, in the Incarnation. In the Church, husbands and wives leave their parents to become
one in Marriage, because they are "members of his body" — thus a new
kind of Marriage is revealed "in Christ," a Marriage not of creation but
of the new creation, not of the created order only, but with a
supernatural goal and purpose, the extension of Christ's body, the
Church.

We are at the core of the teaching in Ephesians as it marks the
transition from the "great mystery" of Christ espousing his Church to
the "great mystery" of the Marriage of Christians. Because the Ephesians are "members of his body" they can recapitulate in their Marriages
Christ's spousal union with themselves. A textual variant which has
passed from the Greek into the Vulgate is significant in this regard
insofar as it reinforces Genesis 2:24 by echoing Adam's cry of delight on
beholding Eve: ". . . because we are members of his body," to which the
Vulgate adds, "of his flesh and of his bones" (*de carne eius et de ossibus eius*;
cf. Genesis 2:23, "This at last is bone of my bones and flesh of my flesh;
she shall be called Woman. . . .")[27]

Adam is a type of Christ. As Bridegroom of the Church, Christ is
the paradigm for Christian spouses. But does Saint Paul want an exact

parallel between Jesus Christ and husbands, and the Church and wives?
In terms of the hierarchy, priority and source of life, headship certainly
suggests a precise parallel, in Paul's mind. But the passage taken as a
whole presents the balance of gender, as perceived by a theologian of
our times commenting on Ephesians 5: "The decisive parallel of that
text is not that of the husband representing Christ and the wife the
Church. It is rather the unity of love in one flesh." Noting the typology,
which includes all spouses in Adam and Eve, all Christian spouses in
Christ and his bride the Church, he adds: "It is clear that Paul sees in
Genesis 2 that the order of creation is contained within the order of
redemption, so that even Adam's marriage foreshadows the Church."[28]

Saint Thomas sees the created reality of Marriage raised to a
sacrament as he comments on this passage. He does not leave the "great
mystery" up in some celestial realm for, as a type of Christ, Genesis 2:24
is meant to be lived out and fulfilled in Christians. The "great mystery"
thus refers to other people.[29]

Verse 32: "This is a great mystery, and I mean in reference to
Christ and the church; 33. however, let each one of you love his wife as
himself, and let the wife see that she respects her husband." Verse 32
has already been commented on at length; the following verse is a
simple repetition of Saint Paul's exhortation to spousal love in the "great
mystery," in Christ. The verb for "love" is the same as that in the
imperative form in v. 25: *agapate*. Paul's command to love is a command
to live in *agape*, the ultimate form of love. But this love is God's gift:
"God's love has been poured into our hearts through the Holy Spirit
who has been given to us" (Rm 5:5).

The nuances of sacramentality are found in this *agape* which is to
be God's gift to husbands and wives. Without the divine gift such
Christian love is impossible, yet Paul requires it in the married state. But
it is given to those reborn "in Christ," to those espoused by Christ, now
called to recapitulate his espousal of the Church in their marriages. Paul
can command this ultimate form of love knowing that God will grant it
in Christian Marriage. He can command wives to "respect" their
husbands or, to put it better, to "reverence" them, repeating in verse 33
his headship teaching of priority and hierarchy.[30]   But this union of
complementary genders is always for unity, the underlying theme of
Ephesians, unity based "in Christ," a union in Christ's sacrificial *agape*,

lived out in the Grace of one's Baptism. So we bring together the themes in Saint Paul's teaching on the new kind of Marriage, "in Christ."

THE BASIS OF THE SACRAMENT

Saint Paul's theology of Marriage, centered on Ephesians, must be developed in the light of the tradition of the Church. In this way we can discern the basis for the sacrament of Marriage in Christians who, as the baptized, have the capacity to minister the sacrament to one another. In turn, this prepares the way for a study of the development of the Church's awareness of the sacramentality of Marriage, which is inextricably bound up with the question of the place of human consent in the sacrament.

I. CHRISTIANS, ESPOUSED BY CHRIST

Just as God conferred the created reality of Marriage on man and woman in the act of creation, so, in Christ, he confers the sacramental reality of Marriage on man and woman in re-creating them. In terms of the "great mystery," Jesus Christ prepares his people for earthly nuptials by incorporating them into his own nuptials, by the "washing of water with the word," holy Baptism. The instincts of the Eastern liturgies are vindicated once more as the baptismal waters of the Jordan are recalled both in the Syro-Oriental rite of Marriage and in the blessing of rings in the Maronite rite of Marriage.[31]

At the ecclesial level, human beings are taken into the divine nuptials, a recapitulation of the Incarnation. Writing late in the fourth century, Saint Pacian of Barcelona perceived the spousal implications of Christ taking our flesh from Mary, thus making it his own flesh: "And these are the nuptials of the Lord, of one flesh joined, that according to that great sacrament they might be two in one flesh, Christ and the Church. From these nuptials is born a Christian people, the Spirit of the Lord having descended from on high. . . ."[32] Saint Pacian described the sacrament of Baptism as Christ's continuing espousal of his Church.

At the personal level, the espousal of each Christian may be seen in Our Lady, sign of the Church, according to Blessed Isaac of Stella, a Cistercian abbot of the twelfth century. Each faithful soul is a "spouse of the Word of God" because Christ espoused the Church, Mary and thus each faithful Christian.[33]   We find this same awareness of the baptized, justified Christian as espoused by Christ in Newman's perceptive novel of the third century Church, *Callista*. Newman puts on the lips of the priest Caecilius a cry of ardent faith and love: "There is but one lover of souls . . . and he loves each one of us as though there were no one else to love. He died for each one of us, as if there were no one else to die for. . . . The nearer we draw to him, the more triumphantly does he enter into us; the longer he dwells in us, the more intimately have we possession of him. It is an espousal for eternity."[34]

Saint Paul's own cry of faith adds the dimension of the Cross to the justifying Grace of Baptism. In Christians, "as members of his body," the Bridegroom draws his bride into his sacrificial espousals. "I have been crucified with Christ; it is no longer I who live, but Christ who lives in me; and the life I now live in the flesh I live by faith in the Son of God, who loved me and gave himself for me" (Gal 2:20). Newman cited these words of Saint Paul, insisting on a participation in the Cross as part of the process of our justification.[35]

However, does baptismal justification confer on Christians the capacity to enter sacramental Marriage? If considered broadly as sinners being raised to a state of Grace and adoption as sons and daughters of God, justification suggests a capacity to enter a higher form of Marriage for those who have been regenerated, sanctified and made pleasing to God. Hence our justification suggests the sacramentality of the Marriage of Christians. We still remain in the ambit of Saint Paul, an implicit sacramentality; that Christian Marriage is different from pagan Marriage because Christians are different people, re-born by Baptism, living "in Christ," united as "members of his body," the Church. Thus those who live "in Christ" are married "in Christ."[36]

If justification is considered more precisely, as our inner renovation and the objective infusion of God's own justice, then two lines of argument are possible. Each suggests the sacramentality of the Marriage of the justified in a different way.

Marriage, entered honestly and without impediment, is always a good act. The natural Marriage of pagans, as a created reality, is a good act. But this good natural act is elevated to the supernatural order when Christians marry, as they signify and participate in the "great mystery." The good deeds of those regenerated in the Holy Spirit are truly meritorious, transformed in the Holy Spirit and welcome in God's sight. Therefore, God ratifies the union of two Christians in Marriage as a meritorious act.

True as this may be, such an argument only seems to leave the difference between a "natural" Marriage and a Christian Marriage at the level of the moral order. Christian Marriage differs from "natural Marriage" because it is meritorious. This could have the further repercussion of limiting "true" sacramentality only to those virtuous souls living out the *res tantum* of their Baptism, that is, Christians in a state of Grace. Other Christians could perhaps enjoy such "true sacramentality" in their Marriages, if we applied a theology of revivification, that their recovery of Sanctifying Grace by way of a return to the sacraments would make their Marriage sacramental. It is evident that this understanding of sacramentality is Donatist, making validity depend on worthiness, reducing an *ex opere operato* sacramental act to a level only qualitatively different from the *ex opere operantis* form of "natural" Marriage — assuming, for the time being, that even this adequately describes a "natural" Marriage.

A second line of argument resting on justification would be to propose the justified who enter Marriage as people who can lay a claim to God's Grace for their Marriage. This is not to argue that nature can lay any claim on Grace, for it is those *already* "in Christ" by Baptism who seek Grace in Marriage. This "already" is a key to all other sacraments which may follow Baptism, for the baptismal espousal, as we have seen, is presupposed as the fundamental union with and in Christ, making possible Christian Marriage.[38]

Such a line of argument takes us beyond implicit sacramentality, but on its own is only the case that God "ought" to impart a special Grace to the baptized when they marry. If we link this argument to the place of the Cross in the life of the justified, we may make the argument more morally compelling; that God will grant special strength for married

Christians, because they themselves are called to heroic *agape*, the love
of the Bridegroom who "gave himself up" for his spouse on the Cross.

Such an argument is morally compelling. It develops Saint Paul's
teaching in Ephesians. But it needs to be strengthened further by the
foundation of Paul's teaching, the sacred signification of Marriage: that
Christian spouses recapitulate and reproduce in their Marriages that
sublime union between Christ and his Church. The true *agape* of Christ
crucified is signified in the Marriages of those justified, "in Christ." If it
is truly signified then God grants spouses the ability to signify it, to
practice his own *agape* in their shared lives. The signification of the
"great mystery" is therefore God's assurance that he will grant Grace to
Christian spouses to put into action what he intends their union to
signify.

Once more the principle of being "already" united to Christ is the
basis for this spousal *agape*. God has already given the capacity for this
kind of love to all Christian men and women in their Baptism. As
"brothers" and "sisters" begotten by the Father in Christ, as fellow
"members" of Christ's body the Church, they can love God and one
another long before they even consider Marriage. But their specific
human love for one another is transformed into a spousal love, a
spousal form of *agape*, in Marriage. Grace is required for such a transformation, hence a special sacrament to provide a spousal form of love,
always God's gift, "poured into our hearts by the Holy Spirit who has
been given to us" (Rm 5:5).

"The lover is perfectly and truly one with the beloved only if he
loves the latter with the same love as that with which he is loved, but this
is impossible unless both are already united to each other in a different
way."[39]   Scheeben's insight concerning Christ and the soul, like the
poetry of Saint John of the Cross, rebounds on the source of the
analogy, Marriage itself. By the Incarnation, Jesus Christ, "the lover," is
already united to "the beloved," the Christian, making possible a capacity to love as Christ loves. Jesus Christ has not only united men and
women to himself, by the Incarnation, but in himself, in his Church, "as
members of his body." Thus they are already united to one another in
such a way as to make the human spousal union a further means of
Grace — within the Church and for the sake of the unity and growth of
the Church.

We already move beyond arguments which depend on the *res tantum* of Baptism, hence Marriage. We move beyond arguing that it is appropriate to grant Grace in Christian Marriage, or that Christian spouses can claim such Grace. We even move beyond the morally compelling argument that God in fidelity to the "great mystery" signified will grant to spouses the Grace to live together in the *agape* they are meant to signify in Marriage. We enter the domain of the organic objective reality of the Church, the ecclesial meaning of the justification of the baptized.

There is within each Christian a reality anterior to the *res tantum* of Baptism, a reality which cannot be lost, unlike the *res tantum* of justifying Grace which can be lost by mortal sin. This reality is at once personal and ecclesial. It is the *res et sacramentum* of Baptism, the indelible sacramental character. In seeking to understand this mysterious objective reality, in its ecclesial and personal aspects, we can establish the sacramentality of Marriage, at least in terms of the capacity of Christians to confer on one another a unique kind of Marriage. Such a task centers on the work of the Holy Spirit whose action in Marriage will be considered in the light of the baptismal character, his own consecration and sacred seal.

II. CHRISTIANS, SEALED BY THE HOLY SPIRIT

In the order of objective reality, what distinguishes a baptized person from an unbaptized person is the indelible character of Baptism. Without defining the precise nature of this mysterious divine modification of each baptized person, the Magisterium affirms the reality of this "created grace."[40] Three sacraments impart an indelible character: Baptism, Confirmation and Orders. However, in theology after the Second Vatican Council, little attention has been given to the character, except to challenge its existence in Orders, explaining it simply as an outward sign. This error properly provoked correction by the teaching Church, in accord with the Council teachings which recognize the reality of sacramental character.[41] Some extensive analysis of the theology of the character was available before the Council, in particular a recovery of the biblical and patristic understanding of the Seal of the Holy Spirit and a development of Saint Thomas' ecclesial interpretation.[42]

What then is the place of the character of Baptism in the sacramentality of Marriage? The reality of this mysterious and irrevocable consecration is already implicit in the two references to the "seal" of the Holy Spirit in Saint Paul's ecclesial and nuptial letter to the Ephesians: "In him you also, who have heard the word of truth, the gospel of your salvation, and have believed in him, *were sealed* (*esphragisthete*) with the promised Holy Spirit, who is the guarantee of our inheritance until we acquire possession of it, to the praise of his glory" (Ep 1:13-14). "And do not grieve the Spirit of God, in whom you *were sealed* (*esphragisthete*) for the day of redemption" (Ep 4:30). But Saint Paul addresses the Ephesian Christians, to whom he imparts the Marriage doctrine. Thus, his specific Marriage teaching only applies to those who have been "sealed" in Baptism, those who bear the permanent seal (*e sphragis*) of the Holy Spirit (cf. 2 Cor 1:21-22).

Prescinding from the patristic development of the seal,[43] and from its eschatological meaning (cf. Rv 7:2-8; 9:4; 14:1; 22:4), we find Saint Thomas to be a sure guide in relating this baptismal reality to Marriage. He provided the basis for an ecclesial understanding of the character of Baptism, Confirmation and Orders. Each character places a person in the organic hierarchy of the Mystical Body of Christ, not only for the purpose of final glory among God's permanently sealed faithful ones, but for the purpose of offering worship in different ways within the Church.[44]   This empowerment for worship is a true participation in the Priesthood of Christ. It is not only a passive ability to receive Grace, but the power to minister Grace to others, according to one's place in the ordered organism of the Mystical Body.

Following this ecclesial understanding of the character, the Fathers of the Second Vatican Council cited Saint Thomas as they taught: "Incorporated into the Church by Baptism, the faithful are appointed by their *baptismal character* to Christian religious worship; reborn as sons of God, they must profess before men the faith they have received from God through the Church."[45]   But such appointment is by a divine gift, at the visible, organic, structured level of the Mystical Body. This is not the gift of Sanctifying Grace; rather, it is the basis for that Gift of the Holy Spirit, an objective basis which is also the work of the Holy Spirit, but a permanent gift which can never be effaced by the human will or by human sin. As baptized, confirmed or ordained Christians, by these very characters, members of the Mystical Body are configured to Christ the Head of the Body. At the same time, in his or her appointed ways as "member" of the Body, each Christian bears the image of Christ who himself "reflects the glory of God and bears the very stamp of his nature (*character tes hypostaseos autou*)" (Heb 1:3).

Ordered to acts of worship, in different ways Christians can receive and minister the sacraments "as members of his body." They live and act "in Christ," not depending on their own moral or spiritual worthiness, but with the assurance that their sacramental actions are the actions of Christ to whom they are configured. Therefore, the baptized man and woman who enter Marriage are agents of Christ, already raised to the supernatural order and empowered to act for a supernatural end.[46]

Even granted that the validity of Marriage can depend on true consent, human intentionality, human capacities, the power of the baptismal character within spouses is God's assurance that he will ratify their union. He confers on it a binding permanence of his espousal of our nature in the Hypostatic Union of the Incarnation. But we must locate this objective sharing in the "great mystery" within the Church, because the baptismal character constitutes the Body of Christ, making true "members of his body."

By the baptismal character, sacramental Marriage is an ecclesial act — with ecclesial consequences and an ecclesial end. This is not only a social observation, that Marriage extends the Church through the family. It rests on a sacramental understanding of the Church as the Mystical Body of Christ, the divine-human society constituted and extended in time by the three character sacraments. No character is imparted in Marriage, so Marriage does not constitute the Mystical Body as does Baptism, Confirmation or Orders. But even if Marriage cannot establish the organic essential hierarchy of the Church, it is still essential to the complete societal structure of the earthly Church. Marriage is the sacramental union of the baptismal characters of two members of the Body, a union constituting the "*ecclesiola*," the family unit of the Church. The baptismal participation of a man and woman in the worship and ministry of Christ's priesthood is reordered by their ecclesial union as "one flesh," nothing less than the "great mystery" in the humblest Christian home.

Therefore, in the baptismal character of spouses, we see why Saint Paul emphasized the unitive love of Marriage in his epistle on unity at Ephesus. The spousal consent of Christians is an ecclesial consent, determined by the baptismal character to become a consent not only for the union of husband and wife but for the unity and growth of the Church. Even if it does not constitute the hierarchy of the Church, Marriage is of the "*esse*" rather than "*bene esse*" of the Church.[47]

The baptismal character is the source of ecclesial rights and duties. As "members of his body," configured to Christ and "one flesh," married Christians can live up to their baptismal character or fail to respond to it, redirected as it is by their sacramental union. But always, they succeed or fail as organic "members of his body."

This is the sacramental reason why the Church regulates the circumstances for the exercise of her members' right to marry. The baptized still enjoy the "natural right to marry," but their baptismal character makes their matrimonial consent the consent of Christ and his Church, an ecclesial consent — hence subject to the higher morality of the Kingdom and the archetype for that new life of selfless *agape*, the "great mystery." Called to live as true images of Christ, their spousal union is of a higher order, the sublime supernatural order of the baptismal life. But God responds to human frailty, granting to his own what he commands, imparting to baptized men and women the spousal consecration of the Holy Spirit.

III. SPOUSES, CONSECRATED BY THE HOLY SPIRIT

The sacramental character is a consecration by the Holy Spirit, that is, a permanent setting-apart which imparts objective holiness to a person, irrespective of his or her moral worth or intensity of subjective faith. In a less defined sense we use the term "consecration" to describe the work of the Holy Spirit in sacramental Marriage, *in fieri* and, by extension, *in facto esse*. Proposed by Scheeben,[48] the Magisterium has accepted this terminology. The Fathers of the Second Vatican Council echoed the teaching of Pope Pius XI in *Casti Connubii*. Called to be faithful to one another, to live the *agape* of "authentic married love," and to be parents, "Spouses, therefore, are fortified and, as it were, *consecrated* for the duties and dignity of their state by a special sacrament. . . ."[49]

The term "consecrated" is qualified by "as it were," making it clear that "consecration" in the sacrament of Marriage is not the imparting of objective holiness by way of an indelible character, as in Baptism, Confirmation and Orders. The use of "consecrated" to describe Christian spouses is also distinct from the use of the term applied to the eucharistic Species or holy Chrism. Because it is used of persons, it is closer to the meaning of "consecrated" religious men or women, but with an important difference: consecrated religious are "consecrated" *ex opere operantis*, whereas Christian spouses are "consecrated" by the sacrament of Marriage, *ex opere operato*, consecrated to be married Christians in the Church.

This mysterious spousal consecration will be examined later in terms of the bond of Marriage.[50]   At this stage, it seems best to consider it as the work of the Holy Spirit, divine Agent of all consecration in the Mystical Body. But this immediately suggests the practical question: how are spouses consecrated in Marriage? This raises the further question of the way in which the sacrament *in fieri* is imparted, by the consent of the spouses or by a blessing.

Assuming that consent is the efficient cause of Marriage, the accepted understanding of causality in Marriage today, we see what further distinguishes spousal consecration from other consecrations in the sacraments or rites of the Church. As active agents in the sacrament, men and women are more than "apt subjects" for Marriage. As spouses in Christ, as persons already consecrated as "members of his body" by thei ➤ aptismal character, they consecrate the union; the union does not consecrate them.

This emphasis on the role of spouses is only a development of Saint Paul's doctrine of Marriage, which locates the difference between Christian Marriage and "natural" Marriage in the difference between Christians and the unbaptized. In no way do I imply that the lived sacrament, as union, does not "consecrate" husbands and wives with its blessings day by day. But the spouses themselves provide the consecration of that union by being Christians, by being God's new creation, sealed forever with the Spirit. By the spousal consent and consummation, they claim as their right the strength of the mysterious spousal consecration by the Holy Spirit. This is strength to reproduce the "great mystery" in their shared lives, strength to be faithfully "one flesh," strength to be fruitful as parents, strength to remain "in Christ," strength for the *res tantum* of Marriage.

As both strength and challenge to live out Baptism, Confirmation or Orders, the permanent sacramental character is reflected in the bond of Marriage, likewise the *res et sacramentum*. As parallel to the character in those three sacraments, the bond in Marriage is the focus for the work of the Holy Spirit in spousal consecration. Moreover, in itself, and in their fidelity to one another as "one flesh," the bond is consecrated because it signifies the "great mystery" of Christ's union with his Church. But these further considerations must wait until we examine the place of the bond in sacramental Marriage.

IV. SPOUSES, SANCTIFIED BY THE HOLY SPIRIT

The Spirit not only consecrates Christians in a unique spousal way in their Marriage; the Spirit *sanctifies* them in Marriage.[51] In considering this second work of the Holy Spirit in the sacrament, we look more to the lived sacrament than to the sacrament *in fieri*. It is significant that the Fathers of the Second Vatican Council chose to introduce their famous teaching on the universal call to holiness with reference to the "great mystery" in Ephesians 5. The Church is holy because Jesus Christ ". . . loved the Church as his Bride, giving himself up for her so as to sanctify her (cf. Ep 5:25-26); he joined her to himself as his body and endowed her with the gift of the Holy Spirit for the glory of God. Therefore all in the Church, whether they belong to the hierarchy or are cared for by it, are called to holiness."[52] Truly, those called to recapitulate this "great mystery" are called to holiness, "as members of his body," sanctified by his self-giving in which they were cleansed and re-born.

The strength of the Spirit may be claimed because, by spousal consecration, Christian spouses are appointed to be married members of the Mystical Body. But they can reject that strength of God, for we are within the domain of the living out of the *res tantum* of Marriage. In spite of this possibility, God continually offers himself, in the sanctifying Spirit, in order to help them to live in the *agape* which Saint Paul proposed as the way the "great mystery" is fully realized. But that "great mystery," in itself, was completed in Pentecost. The Church thus wants those entering Marriage to be confirmed if at all possible.[53] This seal of the Spirit may not pertain to validity, but is surely to be insisted on today if we are to draw those preparing for Marriage through a pre-matrimonial catechumenate, so that the Pentecost which completed the "great mystery" may be poured out in their married life.

Always, it is through the Holy Spirit that Christians are raised into the "great mystery." Père Humbert Clérissac could thus propose Pentecost as the ecclesial completion of the "great mystery": "These are the crown jewels of the Spouse. It is the contractual alliance entered into at the hour of the Supper and sealed by the Eucharist, which determines the royal dowry of the Church awaiting the bloody nuptials of the Cross and the nuptial embrace of Pentecost."[54]

As the Church was raised into the loving embrace of her Bridegroom at Pentecost, so men and women called to Marriage in the Church are granted the presence of Jesus Christ, through the Holy Spirit. He abides with them in their married life, through the Holy Spirit. He empowers them to love as he loves, through the Holy Spirit. Rightly, Pope John Paul II linked the work of the Spirit in Marriage with the Cross, which Newman saw within the continuing life of justified believers: "The Spirit which the Lord pours forth gives a new heart, and renders man and woman capable of loving one another as Christ has loved us. Conjugal love reaches that fullness to which it is interiorly ordained, conjugal charity, which is the proper and specific way in which the spouses participate in and are called to live the very charity of Christ who gave Himself on the Cross."[55]

The "conjugal charity," the *agape* which Saint Paul emphasized in his letter to the Ephesians, provides a positive understanding of holy Marriage as a remedy for concupiscence (*remedium concupiscentiae*). The Holy Spirit poured forth into the hearts of husbands and wives, is the Spirit of selfless love, the only remedy to the selfish sensuality which is concupiscence. Through this sinful effect of the Fall, sexuality is disintegrated and disintegrating, "the inner disintegration and fragmentation of human existence caused by sin — human sensuality as it is opposed to the whole orientation of the person."[56] Marriage is not a remedy for concupiscence simply by providing a permitted "outlet" for sexual drives, for many Marriages falter and fall through unbridled eroticism, especially in our times. Marriage, as a sacrament, redeems sexuality by re-directing it, refining it and elevating it in conjugal love, which is the mutual *agape* of Christian spouses.

The love which the Holy Spirit gives husbands and wives was described by Pope Paul VI in *Humanae Vitae*. It is a fully human love "of the senses and the spirit at the same time." It is total love, a complete sharing and mutual gift of self. It is faithful and exclusive love, fidelity unto death which is noble, meritorious, but often difficult. It is a love which is fruitful, open to the transmission of human life because conjugal love of itself is ordained towards the begetting and education of children.[57]

Within the wider and deeper context of this generous conjugal love, sexuality is re-directed, refined and elevated, because it is made to serve the three goods of matrimony (*boni matrimonii*): the shared procreation of children, the mutual fidelity of spouses and the unbreakable bond of the sacrament. When spouses love one another with mutual reverence, respecting these "goods" of Marriage, sexuality is freed from concupiscence. But it is only through the strength of the Spirit who consecrates them to their married status in the Mystical Body that husbands and wives can learn the redeemed meaning of their sexuality. It is only through this wisdom of the Spirit who sanctifies them that they can find the strength to live in chaste love.

Sanctification is not a once-and-for-all event, but a process of living out sacramental Marriage day by day. Just as the Holy Spirit works through the baptized, so that they consecrate the union by consent and consummation, so the Holy Spirit works through them in the lived sacrament so that they sanctify one another. This mutuality is essential to any spirituality of married life, a way of putting into practice the mutual "giving way" of Ephesians 5:22-24 and 1 Corinthians 7:3-4. The Eucharist and Penance are the central and supreme moments in mutual spousal sanctification, because they are received by spouses, by Christians appointed by the Holy Spirit to be responsible for one another in the Mystical Body, unto death. Saint Paul's words to

Christians married to non-Christians may be extended to all Christian spouses: "Wife, how do you know whether you will save your husband? Husband, how do you know whether you will save your wife?" (1 Cor 7:16).

With the urgency of our times and the scandal of Christian Marriage degraded and defiled before them, the Fathers of the Extraordinary Synod of 1985 called for a specific spirituality for Christian spouses.[58]   Sanctification is not merely some noble ideal for the few. It is a universal call of God, and thus all husbands and wives are called to holiness. But that call, and the dynamism of their mutual love in the nuptial meaning of their bodies, draw us to complete this development of Saint Paul's sacramentality of Marriage by looking to the final end for which all Christians are consecrated, healed and sanctified in the sacraments.

Marriage "in Christ," is the union of man and woman recreated in Baptism, already raised into the "great mystery." Even as they live that "great mystery" of Christ giving himself up for the Church, even as they give way to one another in true conjugal *agape*, so their tender regard for one another can never consume or distract them from a tender regard for eternity. Their eyes are raised together towards that destiny for which they were created, for which they have been redeemed. Together, through the struggles and joys of family life, they move towards the Kingdom in its fullness. Together, they are drawn to the fulfillment of the "great mystery" into which they have been raised by the Holy Spirit, through the sacraments.

Married "in Christ," consecrated by the Spirit to form families within the great family of the Mystical Body, they have been espoused by God, so that they might espouse one another, and be raised to an ultimate espousal in the nuptials of heaven. Already they taste the timelessness of divine love, in their love for one another. Already they know the eternal youthfulness of the Bride of Christ, washed and sanctified, presented to her Bridegroom, holy and without blemish. Already, in this sacrament of the "great mystery" they hear the voice of the Spirit and the Bride blending in one nuptial invitation to the eternal Supper of the Lamb.

CHAPTER THREE

The Quest For The Sign

De esta manera decía:	To the Son His thought displayed:
Ya ves, Hijo, que a tu esposa	"You see how Your beloved bride
A tu imagen hecho había,	After Your image has been made.
Y en lo que a ti se parece	In what she most resembles You
Contigo bien convenía.	Her loveliness I have arrayed,
Pero difiere en la carne,	"Though differing from You by that flesh
Que en tu simple ser no había;	Your finer nature never knew;
En los amores perfectos	There is in every perfect love
Esta ley se requería. . . .	A law to be accomplished too. . . ."

Saint John of the Cross, *Romance VII, Continues the Incarnation*

Before we examine the consent and the bond of the sacrament of Marriage, we should understand something of the history of its sacramentality which is inseparable from the questions regarding the place of consent and consummation in the sacrament. This need not be a complete history of Christian Marriage, its laws, customs and rites. Others have already provided ample information on the wider history of Christian Marriage.[1]   Our purpose here is simply to trace the awareness of *sacramentality* and how it developed in the Church from the post-apostolic age to our own.

Such a brief overview is not a history of how the sacramentality of Marriage "developed" or "emerged." That would imply the error that the doctrine that Marriage is a sacrament of the New Law is a relatively recent teaching of the Church imposed in the light of scholastic sacramental theology.[2]   We have already seen how the "great mystery" and its sacred signification in the teaching of Saint Paul was the way Christians understood Our Lord's elevation of Marriage to the supernatural order in the era of the New Testament. This implicit sacramentality in Saint Paul's understanding of Marriage is both maintained and developed in the patristic age, in the theology of the schoolmen and in the high scholastic and post-Tridentine ages. Saint Augustine and Saint Thomas Aquinas were key figures in affirming the sacramental nature of Christian Marriage.

This developing understanding of the sacrament — which continues in our own time — can well be called "The Quest for the Sign." Our Lord instituted no visible new sign for the Marriage of Christians. Saint Paul saw what we call "sacramentality" in the persons of the baptized spouses themselves. But this subtle and unique ground for the sacramentality of Marriage has often clouded the theologians' awareness of Marriage as a sacrament. In distinguishing the consent of the baptized as the cause of the sacrament in its making (*in fieri*), and in striving to find the sacred meaning of consummation, theologians were actually engaged in a quest for the sacred sign, the "*sacramentum*," of the "great mystery" which they always knew was signified in the Marriage of believers. The quest continues, in its own way, even in our times, though now it is mostly a quest to articulate better the sacramentality already wisely discerned by others and affirmed by the Magisterium. To evaluate the continuity of this task, the tests for the development of doctrine proposed by Cardinal Newman have been appended to this brief history of the awareness of the sacramentality of Marriage.

THE PATRISTIC AGE

The earliest reference to Christian Marriage beyond the letters of Saint Paul is to be found in the *Letter to Polycarp* of Saint Ignatius of Antioch, written around 110 A.D. This is also the earliest claim by the Church to take control of the celebration of Marriage, assuming therefore that Christian Marriage is different from pagan Marriage, even if at this time it was entered into with the accepted Roman family and civil customs, shorn only of their pagan cultus to the household gods.[3]   Asserting the episcopal jurisdiction which he saw as essential to the Church, Saint Ignatius said that it was proper that men and women who wished to marry should be united "with the consent of the Bishop," so that Marriage would be not according to lust, but "according to the Lord (*kata Kyrion*)."[4]

His context is typical of patristic references to Marriage. The virtues of virginity and continence are praised, and Marriage is subordinated to celibacy. As with his so-called "monarchical episcopacy," we may assume that Saint Ignatius urged on Saint Polycarp what was already the accepted Eastern practice. In the West, such distinctively Christian procedures for Marriage emerged only gradually, perhaps because Christians were such a small minority in a society which followed Roman family Marriage rites. In the East, gathered together from so many ethnic and religious backgrounds, Christians rapidly formed their own distinctive Marriage practices. We even see implicit in Ignatius' wish for episcopal "approval" the seeds of another divergence between the Christian East and the Christian West; the East celebrating Marriage by way of an episcopal or sacerdotal blessing, the West maintaining the Roman civil consent as the essence of the celebration.

Saint Ignatius also echoed Saint Paul's words in Ephesians, that husbands should love their wives as Christ loved the Church, but as with other Fathers, we do not find him developing the "great mystery" in connection with what we term the "sacramentality" of Marriage. As Fr. G. H. Joyce points out, Ephesians was never used as a proof-text by the Fathers in defense of the sacramentality of Marriage.[5]   The Fathers remained in the Pauline tradition, but were more concerned about how married Christians should live out the "great mystery" day by day.

Early in the Third Century, before he fell into heresy, Tertullian described Christian Marriage as that which "is joined together by the Church, strengthened by an offering, sealed by a blessing, announced by angels and ratified by the Father."[6]   These words need not be taken at face value to describe a fully developed celebration of Marriage with Nuptial Mass and priestly blessing.[7]   As with the Fathers, Tertullian was more interested in how God blesses the married life of Christians; married within the community of the Church, sharing in her liturgy, blessed by domestic prayer and the presence of the angels. Yet he indicated Marriage as a state of life endowed with its own Grace. In this same letter to his wife, he described a mixed Marriage between a Christian and a pagan as having "in part, the support of divine grace."[8]

Tertullian's later Montanist rigorism against marrying again after the death of a spouse, digamy, suggests his sacramental view of Marriage. His Montanism led to contempt even for a first Marriage. We should not take Montanist religious celebration of Marriage as evidence that Catholics in Northern Africa only celebrated Marriage with ecclesiastical rites.[9]

Writing at the same time as Tertullian, Clement of Alexandria saw the presence of Jesus Christ in the family as caused by a wife being joined to her husband by God, a fulfillment of Christ's promise, "Where two or three are gathered in my name, there am I in the midst of them" (Matthew 18:20).[10] Against the Gnostics who denied the holiness of Marriage, Clement affirmed that Marriage is a holy estate, even commanded by the Old Law.[11] The Gnostic threat to Marriage was twofold; either excessive asceticism which forbade all Marriage, or excessive sexual license, which undermined all Marriage.[12] The Fathers responded to this threat by maintaining the Pauline balance of chaste and faithful Marriage in Christ.

In the mid-Third Century, Origen referred explicitly to the Grace of Marriage, commenting on the Gospel of Saint Matthew. Because God makes the man and woman one in Marriage, ". . . in this joining there is Grace for those who are joined by God."[13] Origen cleverly related this to Saint Paul's wish concerning his own celibacy and married life: "I wish that all were as I myself am. But each has his own special gift from God, one of one kind and one of another" (1 Corinthians 7:7). Origen perceived that Saint Paul was saying that if celibacy is a gift of God, so Marriage is a gift, hence graced by God.

Late in the Fourth Century, Saint Ambrose of Milan, writing to Bishop Vigilius, decried the Marriage of a Christian to a pagan: ". . . if Marriage itself needs to be sanctified by the priestly veil and blessing (*velamine sacerdotali et benedictione*), how can that be called Marriage where there is no agreement in the faith?"[14] By his time, the practice of adapting the Roman veiling of spouses in a blessing ceremony in church was well established, if not universal. He also refers to Christian

Marriage as "sanctified by Christ," in a synodal letter to Pope Siricius.[15] The context of this is also a praise of virginity.

Pseudo-Ambrose, or Ambrosiaster, in the pontificate of Pope Damasus (366-384 A.D.), is aware of the sacramental signification of Christian Marriage in this era. Commenting from Rome on the "great mystery" in Ephesians 5:32, he said that Saint Paul meant that "the great sign (*sacramentum*) of this mystery is in the unity of man and woman."[16]

In the East, the Fathers placed much emphasis on Christ's presence and miracle at the Marriage Feast of Cana. They saw this as his radical transformation of Marriage into a sacred estate, the healing and sanctifying of sexuality. Saint Epiphanius, late in the Fourth Century, described the changing of water into wine as the eradication of the carnality of Marriage.[17] Saint Cyril of Alexandria, commenting on Saint John's account of Cana, saw Christ sanctifying the very beginnings of human generation in Marriage by his presence at the wedding feast.[18] In the Fifth Century, writing against heretics who opposed Marriage, Theodoret saw the new wine of Cana as the Lord's own gift of Marriage.[19] This emphasis on Christ's presence at Cana may well have helped consolidate the Eastern practice and belief that the presence and blessing of a priest was what effected a Christian Marriage.

The evidence for a sacramental understanding of Marriage up to, or apart from, Saint Augustine is admittedly fragmentary and imprecise. What we can conclude is that Saint Paul's understanding of the radical difference between Christian Marriage and pagan Marriage was maintained in the thought, practice and discipline of the Church of the first five centuries. The "great mystery" is seen as signified in the Marriages of Christians, but in the West this "*sacramentum*," this sacred sign, does not have the precise meaning later developed by theologians as they sought to discern the exact number of the sacraments. Pope Saint Leo the Great distinguished Christian Marriage from *de facto* concubinage by describing Christian Marriage as "from the very beginning instituted in such a way that over and above the union of the sexes it should include in itself the sacred symbol of Christ and the Church." A bond-woman living as a concubine with a Christian lacked this nuptial mystery (*nuptiale mysterium*), and was not truly married.[20]

The Fathers show greater esteem for virginity than for Marriage because of the eschatological meaning of celibacy for the sake of the Kingdom which was especially relevant to them in the face of late imperial Roman society in its last stages of decadence and decline. This, coupled with the emergence of monastic life, explains a certain reticence about sexuality in Marriage. Long before Saint Augustine's theology of concupiscence, the ascetical tradition maintained great reserve about sexual intercourse in marriage, as for example in the views of Didymus the Blind in Alexandria during the Fourth Century. Significantly, he was a teacher of Saint Jerome.[21]

The Marriage of Our Lady and Saint Joseph was already a matter of much discussion. Speaking of this sublime union, Saint Ambrose laid down the famous principle that it is "not the deflowering of virginity but the nuptial compact which makes a Marriage."[22]   Thus we see that the development which emphasized the consent rather than consummation in Marriage was based not only on the later Roman legal tradition but on the sublime Marriage of Nazareth. But how consent and consummation related to the sacrament was not regarded as a question needing to be resolved. Thus the patristic understanding of what we term the "sacramentality" of Marriage was an extension of Saint Paul's doctrine of the distinctive nature of the Marriage of Christians, "in Christ," thus graced by Christ. It remained for Saint Augustine of Hippo to take the doctrine further.

SAINT AUGUSTINE

Working as a bishop in Northern Africa from 395 until his death in 430, Saint Augustine faced many practical pastoral problems in caring for his flock at Hippo. In that unstable era, Marriage was always an important part of the work of a bishop. The Roman Empire was collapsing. The certainties and stability of family life were less secure. The Church was challenged, not only by barbarian invasions, but by heresies in the East and West. In that era, the basis of Saint Augustine's writing on Marriage was Christ's gift of stability to Christian Marriage, indissolubility.

Saint Augustine took up and developed what the Fathers and other Christian writers had always assumed or defended, Our Lord's definitive teaching which looked back to Eden, which raised Marriage to the status of an unbreakable, permanent, life-long union. In Augustine, we find emphasis not so much on the Grace-imparting mutual consent of Marriage in the making, "*in fieri*," but on what consent establishes, that is, the unbreakable union caused by sacred signification, the "sacrament" as it may describe Marriage "*in facto esse*," the "lived sacrament."

Against the anti-Marriage views of the Manichaeans, Saint Augustine defended Marriage as a created reality. Even before Jesus Christ raised it to a new dignity, Marriage enjoyed three intrinsic "goods": *proles*, that is, the procreation of children; *fides*, that is, the mutual fidelity of the spouses; and *sacramentum*, the permanence of the union. He repeatedly referred to these three goods of Marriage. Significantly, in his commentary on Genesis, he shows what he meant by "*sacramentum*" in this context of Marriage as a created reality: ". . . the 'sacrament' means that a marriage is not to be broken apart, not even so that the party who abandons, or the abandoned party, may marry again in order to have children."[23]

Clearly in this context his meaning of "sacrament" is the standard understanding of his own time and culture, viz. a religious commitment or a binding sacred oath. In that sense, even pagans ought to remain married to one another until death since the Creator instituted Marriage and even the absence of the first "good" of Marriage, offspring, cannot justify abandoning a sterile spouse. But this is not the only meaning of "sacrament" in his writing on Marriage. As a binding, sacred commitment, causing indissolubility, it provides the ground for his more developed, and specifically Christian, use of the word. We must be careful, however, not to equate it with the second of the goods of Marriage, *fides*, as may happen if we apply our modern subjective understanding of "commitment" to "sacrament," a defect in Schillebeeckx' analysis of Augustine's use of the term.[24]

The binding indissolubility is what interested Augustine, that which he termed, in the different context of explaining Christian Marriage and the problem of concupiscence, as "something belonging to the conjugal state."[25] This bond is not to be broken for any reason, even when a spouse commits adultery. In his defense of the goodness of

Marriage, *De bono coniugali*, he distinguished Christian Marriage as excelling "in sanctity as a sacrament" which does not allow for remarriage even for the sake of having children because the marriage bond (*vinculum nuptiale*) remains intact until death. He immediately compared this to the ordination of the clergy, in whom the sacrament of orders remains even if they have no congregation or are degraded for some offense because, once received, the sacrament of the Lord remains, even for judgment.[26]

In comparing Christian Marriage to Holy Orders, Saint Augustine is clearly using "sacrament" with a deeper meaning than the binding religious commitment of the third of the three goods of Marriage. He has built on that meaning, but the excellence of Christian Marriage, distinct from "natural" Marriage, lies in the holiness of the "sacrament." Returning to his *De nuptiis et concupiscentia*, where he discerned a mysteriously binding "something" in Marriage, we can see further what he meant.

He explained that Marriage is to be commended to the faithful, not only because of the "goods" of children and mutual chaste fidelity, but also because of a certain "sacrament." He immediately referred this to Saint Paul's "great mystery," by citing Ephesians 5:25: "Husbands love your wives, as Christ loved the Church." Then he went on to describe the essence of the sacrament, the "*res sacramenti*," as indissolubility. He compared those who separate or remarry to the soul of an apostate, "walking out, so to speak, on its espousal to Christ," which even after the loss of faith does not lose that sacrament of the faith which it received in the washing of regeneration.[27]

In Christian Marriage, Saint Augustine saw the human, religious commitment raised to a sacred signification of Christ's love for his spouse the Church, the "great mystery." And this signification brought about an indissoluble life-long bond, more binding than the natural bond of pagan Marriage.[28]   His comparison with Baptism, with its implicit theology of the indelible character, shows that his understanding of the permanent causality and of the work of God in Marriage was a sacramental objectivity, later to be systematized and developed by the scholastic theologians. His thought in both the *De bono coniugali* and the *De nuptiis et concupiscentia*, comparing Marriage to Orders and Baptism, is a marked development which goes well beyond the concept of "sacrament" as a binding religious commitment. It is strengthened in objectivity and imbued with a supernatural quality because "sacrament" means a sacred symbol which causes what it represents, namely the indissoluble union between Christ and his Church.

While we should never read back into Saint Augustine the theology of those who inherited his teaching, his sacred symbol which causes an indissoluble union between spouses, no matter what their level of "commitment" may be, is much closer to the scholastic and magisterial understandings of the sacramentality of Marriage than is at first apparent. Three questions may make this clearer: (1) whether Augustine was consciously aware of the "great mystery"; (2) whether he not only saw the causality of the sacred symbol as the sacrament of Marriage "*in facto esse*," but of the consent as Marriage "*in fieri*"; (3) whether he saw Marriage as imparting Grace to the spouses in a way similar to the sacraments of Christian initiation.

The "great mystery" is evident in Saint Augustine's writings. Preaching on the Marriage Feast at Cana, he said that Our Lord came to the wedding feast to affirm conjugal chastity (to give his divine approval of Marriage), and to "reveal the sacrament [the sacred symbol] of Marriage." Moreover, he added that the bridegroom at Cana was a type of Christ to whom it was said, "You have kept the best wine until last," viz. the wine of his Gospel.[29]

Granted that "sacrament" here means "sacred symbol," we see a different emphasis from the other patristic references to Cana which saw the miracle as the symbol of a new kind of Marriage for Christians. Augustine implicitly maintains the symbolism of the "best wine," but the archetypal Bridegroom is Jesus Christ. Also in his preaching on Saint John's Gospel we find him describing succinctly how the Church was formed from the pierced side of Christ, just as Eve was formed from the side of Adam: "Adam slept that Eve might be; Christ died that the Church might be."[30]   Furthermore, preaching on the first epistle of Saint John, he saw the "great mystery" of "one flesh" in the espousal of the Church in the Incarnation: "The spouse of Christ is the whole Church, whose principle and first fruit is the flesh of Christ: there the bridegroom is joined to the bride in bodily union."[31]

But did Saint Augustine relate this "great mystery" to Christian Marriage in a *causal* way? We return to the passage in the *De nuptiis et concupiscentia,* where he compared indissolubility to the baptismal character. He points to the causality of the "great mystery" in three ways: (1) He cites Ephesians 5:25, "Husbands, love your wives as Christ loved the Church," and then goes on to affirm that the "effect of this sacred symbol (*sacramenti res*)" is indissolubility. (2) He adds that this indissolubility "is safeguarded in Christ and the Church which, living with Christ who lives forever, may never be divorced from him." In "Christ who lives forever," he saw the eternity of the Resurrection in the "great mystery" imparting divine indissolubility to the union of Christ and his Church, and hence to Christian Marriage. (3) He goes on: "The observance of this sacred symbol is such 'in the city of our God, even on his holy mountain' (Ps 47:2), that is the Church of Christ, by the married faithful, who without doubt are members of Christ . . .," that they cannot separate and remarry even in order to have children. He sees the participation in the "great mystery" by married Christians as being based on their being "members of Christ" (cf. Ephesians 5:30).[32]

Clearly Saint Augustine saw the "great mystery" encompassing the Incarnation, Passion and Resurrection as the cause of Christian Marriage.

In answer to the second question, it is not so clear that he saw sacramental causality in the human consent of the spouses, Marriage *"in fieri."* Praising the Marriage of Our Lady and Saint Joseph, he discussed their Marriage of consent, without consummation. By mutual consent they abstained from intercourse yet were truly married, a model for those who so choose to live. Mary "is called a wife from the first plighting of their troth, although he neither had nor would ever have married relations with her."[33]   In an earlier work on the way the Evangelists agree with one another in their Gospels, he used the Marriage of Our Lady and Saint Joseph to show that a Marriage can be a true Marriage "not by the physical union of the sexes, but by maintaining the affections of the mind."[34]

All we may infer from these passages is that he maintained the principle of his spiritual father, Saint Ambrose, that consent rather than sexual union constitutes a Marriage. He did not develop the causality of consent in the celebration of the sacrament, a task taken up later by the canonists and scholastic theologians.

The third question was whether Saint Augustine saw Marriage imparting Grace to the spouses as in the celebration of the sacraments of Baptism, Confirmation and the Eucharist. All that can be said is that his emphasis on indissolubility, on the sacred symbol of the "great mystery" as the source of indissoluble Christian Marriage, implies some divine Grace granted to spouses to persevere in the three "goods" of Marriage. Again it remained for later theologians to develop a theology of Grace granted in Marriage.

Father Joyce politely suggests that Saint Augustine overlooked the obvious harmony with Baptism and Orders which would logically suggest Grace imparted in Marriage.[35]   It is more likely that he could not reconcile the sexual act with a rite which imparted Grace. His theology of concupiscence was the probable source of his silence concerning Grace imparted to spouses. Yet, as with his theology of the "sacrament," even concupiscence may suggest Grace imparted in order to make Marriage an effective "remedy for concupiscence." By proceeding along that line of reasoning, later theologians were able to move beyond the limits of his evident thought in this matter. Augustine's *De bono coniugali* is really a defense of holy virginity, skillfully including an exaltation of Marriage, so as to give answer to the Jovinian heretics who, in a lewd and unstable age, exalted Marriage over virginity. We should not pass judgment on him for requiring heroic virtue in Marriage as a true remedy for concupiscence.[36]   But it is a matter of regret that he was unable to outline a theology of the Grace which alone makes such heroic virtue possible.

To summarize his development of the sacramentality of Marriage, we must return to the "great mystery" of Saint Paul and the Gospels. Whether or not the Old Latin text of Ephesians 5:32, which Saint Augustine used, translated *mysterion* as "*sacramentum*," he was well aware of the mystical symbolism of Marriage in Ephesians.[37]   Guided by his own Platonic philosophical formation, he could take the "great mystery" in Saint Paul and the Gospels that step further. It became the celestial archetype for the earthly "sacrament," hence the cause of indissolubility in the lived Marriage of Christian spouses. In Platonic terms, Christ's union with his Church could be the divine "form" for the earthly, created and redeemed, reality of Marriage between Christians. Guided by the practical categories of Aristotle, later theologians would be able to analyze and systematize what Augustine had achieved: the natural "sacrament" of Marriage as its third good, indissolubility, is raised by the "great mystery" to become a "sacrament" for Christians, a sacred symbol which signifies that mystery of Christ's deathless love for his spouse the Church, a sacred symbol which, therefore, causes what it signifies, an indissoluble bond between Christian husband and wife.

AFTER SAINT AUGUSTINE

The period of almost seven hundred years, from the early Fifth to the Twelfth Century, may justly be described as "After Saint Augustine" in terms of the sacramentality of Marriage. There is little clear development beyond his thought. Various factors combined to emphasize the stricter elements of his thought on Marriage and sexuality. As what remained of late Roman imperial society collapsed in the West under barbarian invasions, so in the East the rise of Islam isolated the Christians who looked to Constantinople and the older patriarchal sees.

In the West, monasticism became the vital heart of the Church, expanding and civilizing the new peoples and cultures. The monastic penitential systems and attempts to order society along godly lines treated Marriage with severity, largely to turn the peoples of the North from their pagan heritage of concubinage and infidelity. In his commentary on the first epistle of Saint Peter, Saint Bede dissuaded husbands from sexual intercourse in Marriage, as it was a hindrance to prayer.[38] His views show the monastic development of Saint Augustine's theology of concupiscence, early in the Eighth Century. But we cannot expect high development of a theology of sacramental Marriage in centuries when the monasteries were struggling to preserve or extend Christian civilization in the face of barbarism and violence.

Wherever it remained under the sway of the Byzantine Empire, society in the East was guided by the Justinian Code which did not require ecclesiastical Marriage for all citizens. But in practice Christian Marriages were always church rites, presided over by a bishop or priest who imparted the nuptial blessing. The holy mystery of Marriage was regarded as a sacrament, but at this stage not all Eastern Christians regarded the nuptial blessing as the sacrament because the Roman tradition of mutual consent still lingered.[39]

In the West, different challenges to Christian Marriage provoked a development in the discipline of matrimony, thus strengthening reverence for Marriage as a "sacrament" in Saint Augustine's sense of an indissoluble bond and sacred symbol. New cultures from the North brought with them their own laws and Marriage customs which were different from the Roman "consensus." These Northern laws and customs made much of the taking of the bride into the bridegroom's house, hence of consummation. Marriage was also seen as a tribal or family contract, with emphasis on a dowry, or even a bride-price, among the Celts and Anglo-Saxons.[40]

These practices were Christianized by balanced inculturation, accepting customs and correcting abuses. By developing Marriage liturgies, the Church sought to control the celebration of Marriage "in fieri."[41] By formulating Marriage laws, the Church sought to go beyond Marriage "in fieri" so as to maintain indissolubility, to reprove abuses and guard family life. The Pseudo-Isidorian Decretals of the mid-Ninth Century included laws to regulate both the celebration and the security of Christian Marriage.

In the mid-Ninth Century we find an important example of this Christianizing process. In 866, Pope Nicholas I gave a directive to the recently converted Bulgars, requiring rites and defining an essential for Christian Marriage. As opposed to what the Greeks had told the Bulgars, the Pope maintained that simple consent is sufficient and all that is required to make a Marriage. To rule out the view that consummation brings about a Marriage, he cited pseudo-Chrysostom: "The will, not coitus, makes a Marriage."[42] The Pseudo-Isidorian Decretals of this same period also rested on spurious sources, being falsely attributed to Pope Anicletus and Saint Isidore. They were not put together, however, by way of an innocent mistake but were rather formulated through imprudent clerical zeal for Christian order in the face of challenges to indissolubility and monogamy.

In the East, the Church had long since succumbed to a different challenge, the power of the civil order. The Byzantine emperors so dominated the clergy that indissolubility had collapsed and remarriage after divorce was permitted in some cases.[43] Sacramentality might have been maintained in the rites, but not securely in the law. On the other hand, in the West, no universal law or custom required Church rites for Marriage, but the sacramentality of Marriage was maintained by Church law and theology.

Nonetheless, in the year after his ruling "*Ad Bulgaros*," Pope Nicholas I, too, had to face the challenge of the state. Lothaire, King of the Franks, supported by some prelates, sought to divorce and remarry. Until his death in 867, the Pope stood firm in vindicating Lothaire's wife, Teutberga. This defence of indissolubility set a precedent for papal authority over Marriage, which would later face such challenges as the matrimonial matter of Henry VIII of England.[44]

Another case in this era was the subject of the treatise, *De nuptiis Stephani* by Hincmar of Rheims. The union of Stephen, a noble of Aquitaine, with the daughter of Count Regimund was deemed invalid by Hincmar because it was never consummated.[45] He mistakenly declared that this Marriage lacked the "*fidei sacramentum*," the faith that was required "in every saving action," thus also in the "mystery of Marriage, through which man and wife are one flesh . . .," even though the ecclesial "*fidei sacramentum*" of Baptism was greater than that of Marriage.[46] Except for his Frankish view of consummation, Hincmar followed Saint Augustine. But he went further in describing Marriage as one of the "saving actions" involving faith, the sacraments. In commenting on the matrimonial matter of King Lothaire, though, he relied strictly on Saint Augustine.[47]

The Northern view that consummation is essential to Marriage later passed into the decretals of Gratian, himself a Lombard. Various authorities took different sides on this question: the Bologna school for consummation as essential, the Paris school for consent as essential. Abandoning his personal views, Pope Alexander III ruled in favor of the classical patristic and Roman tradition that consent makes a Marriage.[48] But this very debate shows that, by the early Middle Ages, the Augustinian reserve about sexuality in Marriage had faded, whatever place canonists or theologians assigned to consummation in Marriage. Gratian described only a consummated Marriage as valid or "ratified" (*ratum*) and matrimonial consent as the beginning of a Marriage (*coniugium initiatum*), thus reflecting the Northern bias in favor of sexual union as making a Marriage.[49] Reflecting the outcome of this debate, our Code describes the essential consent as the ratifying element. While normally required for indissolubility, consummation cannot make a Marriage.

THE SCHOOLMEN

The development of scholastic theology in the Twelfth Century marked the major stage in the systematization of the sacraments. The final identification of seven sacraments, the "*septenarium*," including Marriage, was not the work of one person, but a consensus among theologians quickly taken up by the teaching Church.[51]

In this gradual process of defining the sacraments as such, Hugh of Saint Victor (1079-1141) provided significant development in awareness of the sacramentality of Marriage. He remained in the tradition of using the term "sacrament" in a broad way to include rites, ceremonies and doctrinal mysteries, listing eighteen of these in his *De sacramentis*. But he went beyond the understanding of "sacrament" as a sacred symbol to the concept of a "sacrament" as a representation of something sacred which, in itself, contains sanctification.[52] This definition is vague enough to include vessels, vestments, holy water, vows, virtues and dogmas, but Hugh explicitly, and in detail, included and emphasized Marriage.

In his doctrine of Marriage, Hugh of Saint Victor was one of those shooting stars which appear from time to time in the development of doctrine. He anticipated various modern developments. He taught that in Marriage there are two "sacraments." The greater "sacrament" is spiritual married love, the "*dilectio mutua animarum*" of the spouses, signifying the union in love between God and the soul. The lesser "sacrament" was sexual union, signifying the "great mystery" of Christ and his spouse, the Church.[53] His "greater" and "lesser" distinction made virginal Marriage possible, since the "greater sacrament" could exist by itself, but the lesser could only be included within the greater signification. Apart from the high value he placed on married love, Hugh's awareness of the union between the soul and God reveals his deep understanding of the "great mystery" of Christ the Bridegroom and our union with God in the espousal of Baptism, which is our participation in the Incarnation, Passion and Resurrection.

Behind his theology of the "great mystery" on two levels was a theocentric understanding of Marriage as a created reality. He used "sacrament" to designate non-sacramental Marriage, the bond which Saint Augustine saw as the third of the "goods" in all Marriages. But Christian Marriage was God's gift to his elect, a signification of that loving election. Christians entered Marriage by mutual consent, not consummation. Moreover, Marriage was a covenant of conjugal love, thus spouses were called to become spiritually one in the communion of heart and spirit in their shared lives.[54]   In Hugh of Saint Victor, we are looking at a modern, almost personalist, understanding of the sacrament — at least as the lived sacrament, Marriage "*in facto esse*."

Putting to one side his Augustinian view which did not properly integrate sexual union with married love, we can see the great advance he made in developing what is implicit in Saint Paul's insistence on mutual *agape* in Ephesians 5:25, which is grounded in the spouses' baptismal participation in the "great mystery" of Christ, as "members of his body." But he did not say that the sacred symbol of Marriage confers Grace on the spouses. Hugh developed a deeper understanding of signification. He maintained the essential role of consent and produced a theology of married love derived from God. Like Saint Augustine, though, he did not see the sacrament as a means of Grace.[55]

Peter Abelard (1080-1143) included Marriage in his list of five sacraments along with Baptism, Confirmation, the Eucharist and Extreme Unction. But, in the Augustinian tradition, he separated Marriage from the other sacraments, seeing it not as a means of Grace but as the remedy for concupiscence for those unable to remain celibate.[56] He saw "spousal consent" as the "sacrament" of Christ's union with his Church, whereas other theologians at this time found that sacred symbol in sexual union.[57]

Peter Lombard (1095-1160) included Marriage in his list of the seven sacraments. His definition of a sacrament included causality, saying that a sacrament ". . . exists as a sign and cause of God's grace, the form of invisible grace, such that it begets the image itself [of God] in the soul."[58]

However, Peter Lombard also remained in the tradition of Saint Augustine. He set Marriage apart in a category of its own so that it only fulfilled the first part of his definition. It existed as a sign but not a cause of Grace. Marriage was purely remedial, against concupiscence.[59] But this Augustinian view may also have been influenced by an opinion he may have shared with others, that Marriage and Penance were already sacraments under the Old Law.[60] At the same time he was clear that consent makes Marriage.[61] In the developing awareness of the sacramentality of Marriage, Peter Lombard's importance lies in his *IV Sententiae* which became the starting-point for the youthful Aquinas' study of Marriage.

At this time, Gandulf of Bologna stated that Grace was given in Marriage, as in all of the sacraments, but he did not elaborate.[62] Later, commenting on Peter Lombard, Alexander of Hales went further and described matrimonial Grace as growth in the "spiritual union of love." But with a strictly "occasional" view of Grace, he saw the sacrament only as the occasion or sacred circumstance making such a union possible. Even Saint Bonaventure adhered to the tradition of marriage as a remedy for concupiscence, but he recognized "Grace as the remedy." This Grace would only be given to those who were strictly disposed to reverence the three "goods" of marriage in a chaste way. He also placed value on mutual consent, but saw it as the sacramental event together with the priestly blessing.[63] It is a matter of dispute as to what extent Saint Bonaventure also favored "occasional causality," but his view of Marriage would indicate that he held this position.[64]

Saint Albert the Great brought together a variety of scholastic interpretations of the sacramentality of Marriage. In his own commentary on Peter Lombard, he set out three positions on Grace in marriage: (1) sacred signification without Grace, the Augustinian view, (2) a development beyond this to find Grace in the remedy for concupiscence in those who are rightly disposed, (3) the further position that Grace is imparted to the spouses. He favored the third view as "highly probable."[65] This view was also favored by his student, Saint Thomas Aquinas, and, as we shall see, later developed by him in his writing on sacramental Marriage.

The Magisterium responded rapidly to the systematization of the seven sacraments, including Marriage. In 1184, at the Council of

Verona, Pope Lucius III listed Marriage with the other sacraments against the Cathari who denigrated Marriage.[66] In 1208, Pope Innocent III included Marriage among the seven sacraments in a profession of faith required of Spanish Waldensians returning to the Church.[67] In 1199, out of respect for the "sacrament of faith" which makes the "sacrament of Marriage" truly valid, he refused to allow a spouse to seek a second marriage when the true spouse had apostatized.[68]

We may summarize the influential work of the schoolmen as a consensus that Marriage belongs to the seven sacraments and, therefore, that in some sense Marriage is a means of Grace for the spouses. But the definitive synthesis of this ground gained was made by the Angelic Doctor himself.

SAINT THOMAS AQUINAS

The critical and central moments in the Church's developing awareness of the sacramentality of Marriage are found in the writings of Saint Thomas Aquinas. His work had undeniable influence, not only on the Magisterium but on subsequent theology and law as well. Today, his work continues to provide ways forward in deepening our understanding of the sacramentality of Marriage.

His most extensive work on Marriage is found in his *Scriptum* on the *Sententiae* of Peter Lombard, an early work probably written in Paris between 1252 and 1256 with the encouragement of Saint Albert the Great. This writing on Marriage is more accessible in an edited form as the *Supplementum* to his unfinished *Summa Theologiae*. Saint Thomas died before he treated Marriage in the Sacramental Questions of the *Summa*, therefore we cannot assume that the *Scriptum* or the *Supplementum* accurately convey what he might have written, particularly on the subtle question of the sacramentality of Marriage, had he lived to complete his opus magnum. To round out our consideration of his views on this matter we must also refer to his *Summa Contra Gentiles*, his various commentaries on the epistles of Saint Paul and to those areas in the *Summa* which treat of sacramentality or touch upon Marriage.

In the mind of Saint Thomas, the healing, sanctifying and elevating work of the sacraments ought to be understood in the light of his anthropology. Going beyond the negative elements in Saint Augustine, Saint Thomas sees man within the whole of creation as the supreme creature, the rational being for whom all other creatures exist. Man is the ultimate reality of the visible universe, not merely a part of creation, but able to comprehend, discover and "contain" the whole of it within his unique being.[69] This optimistic and confident view of human nature is reflected in Saint Thomas' approach to Marriage which he first considered in its natural state and then in a nature deprived by the Fall but not inherently corrupted. Grace, he says, can build on such nature. It can go far beyond being a remedy for concupiscence. Grace can transform and elevate Marriage as a "good natural state," made up of significant rational and affective human acts. Marriage as a "created reality" is potentially sacramental.

In his *Scriptum*, citing Aristotle's *Ethics* 8, he dismissed Marriage as "natural" because of necessity, and saw it as "natural" in terms of its goodness, using the natural virtues as an analogy.[70] Procreation, forming a family, was evident in Genesis. Thus Marriage did not emerge from some form of savagery but was created as the original, familial, mode of human existence.[71] Later, in his *Summa Contra Gentiles*, he developed indissolubility as something required for the unity and stability of the family, the dignity of the wife, and the deep friendship which ought to exist between the spouses who share their lives.[72]

His view of sexuality in Marriage was positive. He set out the goodness of creation as the basis for his argument that the sexual act is not always sinful, an error spread in his time by the Cathari or Albigensians. Moving beyond the Augustinian preoccupation with concupiscence, and beyond Peter Lombard, he saw married intercourse, not as a grave sin "excused" by a divine blessing, but as "excused" only because concupiscence gives it the "semblance of an inordinate act."[73] He will be able to include sexual love within sacramentality, because Marriage as a "natural state" already anticipates sacramentality. In his anti-Islamic apologetic in the *Summa Contra Gentiles* there is a sense of incompleteness in his arguments for indissolubility and against polygamy. The "natural state" seems almost to demand elevation by Christ to the supernatural order as the sacrament of his union with his Church. The human race may have mismanaged, betrayed and distorted the original created reality of Genesis, but the sacrament will give it a perfection far beyond a remedy for concupiscence.

In understanding Saint Thomas' specific contribution to our awareness of the sacramentality of Marriage, it seems best to proceed in two stages: (1) his use of signification, (2) his perception of the Grace imparted in the sacrament.

I. SIGNIFICATION IN SAINT THOMAS

In the *Scriptum*, Saint Thomas worked Marriage into his framework of sacramentality based on the teachings of Peter Lombard. Aristotelian categories had helped provide theologians with the "matter" (the material element or action) and "form" (the words which accompany the matter) distinction in the sacraments. But it was not easy to define this distinction in Marriage. Saint Thomas only faced the problem of this visible signification (the *"sacramentum tantum"*), for without it Marriage could not be a sacrament. He proposed the consent, not the priestly blessing, as the form and the "sensible acts" of Marriage as the matter of the sacrament.[74]   This position is close to our modern view that both matter and form are within the words and action of mutual consent, mutual self-donation.[75]

From Peter Lombard's principle, later evident in his own *Summa*, that the sacraments derive their efficacy from the Passion of Christ, Saint Thomas faced the problem of how Marriage can be conformed to the Passion since it involves pleasure rather than pain. His reply shows an awareness of *agape* in the "great mystery" in Ephesians: "Although Matrimony is not conformed to Christ's Passion as regards pain, it is as regards love whereby He suffered for the Church who was to be united to him as his spouse."[76]

In a fourth objection to the sacramentality of Marriage, he posed a problem regarding signification. Granted that Marriage signifies the union between Christ and his Church, nevertheless it does not cause that union. Yet all the sacraments cause what they signify. To meet this objection, he distinguished three elements in every sacrament: (1) the *"sacramentum tantum,"* the visible sacred sign; (2) the *"res et sacramentum,"* that reality which is both contained and signified in a sacrament; and (3) the "*res tantum*," the Grace granted, requiring a response of faith to be efficacious and fruitful.[77]

In Marriage, Saint Thomas perceived that the union between Christ and his Church is not the reality contained. This sublime union is the "thing signified though not contained" (*res significata non contenta*). Obviously no sacrament can cause a reality of that kind. But each sacrament has another reality, both contained and signified, which it does cause. He added that Peter Lombard did not hold this view because he was of the opinion that there was no contained reality in Marriage.[78] Saint Thomas had clearly moved beyond Peter Lombard at this point.

In reply to a fifth, closely related objection, that there is no such "*res et sacramentum*," or contained reality and sign, in Marriage because Marriage does not imprint a character, he affirmed his three-fold distinction once again. The acts are the "*sacramentum tantum*"; the bond (*vinculum*) between husband and wife is the "*res et sacramentum*"; the effect of the sacrament is the "*res tantum*," an ultimate contained reality. He accepted Peter Lombard's "reality not contained" as the signification of Christ united to his Church.[79]

In signification, Saint Thomas thus discerned two contained realities: (1) the bond, analogous to the indelible character in the three character sacraments; (2) the Grace of the sacrament given to the spouses who, as we shall see, are disposed to receive it by the created Grace of the bond. So, by way of distinctions, he moved beyond Saint Augustine's concept of Marriage as a sacred symbol which only effects indissolubility and beyond the schoolmen who did not see Grace as being caused by the mutual consent of the spouses.

The signification of "one flesh" (Genesis 2:24; Ephesians 5:31), he explained when commenting later on the epistle to the Ephesians. Spouses were "one flesh" in three ways: (1) by love, "*per affectum dilectionis*"; (2) by shared lives, "*per conversationem*"; and (3) by sexual union, "*per carnalem coniunctionem*."[80] He used "*coniunctio*" also to describe the union of Christ and his Church. In his *Scriptum* he had already made it clear that sexual union is not essential to Marriage, and is thus not essential for strict sacramental signification causing the bond and the Grace. Rather, sexual union in Marriage is within that encircling signification, the "great mystery" of Christ's union with his Church.[81]

While maintaining that sexual union was not essential to Marriage, he still stressed that it was integral to it as a complete sign of the union of Christ with his Church.

As with Hugh of Saint Victor — but only within one "sacrament" and not as two sacred symbols — Saint Thomas saw two forms of signification in Marriage. Through consent, before consummation, Marriage signifies "that union of Christ with the soul through Grace." Through sexual union, consummation, Marriage signifies Christ's union with the Church. The union of Christ with the soul (as Justification it would seem in his context) can be broken by sin, but the union between Christ and his Church cannot be broken, for it is his union with the Church "insofar as it is his assumption of human nature in the unity of his person which is completely indissoluble."[82]

Saint Thomas thus proposed the basic espousal of the "great mystery," the Hypostatic Union in the Incarnation, as the source of indissolubility in Marriage which is both "ratified" and "consummated." He allowed the "spiritual bond" caused by consent to be dissoluble before consummation for some higher spiritual reason such as entering religious life, a situation not unknown in his time when there could be a lapse of time between consent and consummation. He did not allow the "carnal bond" caused by consummation to be broken at all, not only because it signifies the Hypostatic Union, as Christ joined to his Church, but also because it completed the translation of the body of one party to the control of the other. Only fleshly death could end the bond of the flesh.[83]   Implicit in this reasoning is Saint Paul's advice on mutual conjugal rights; that the husband rules over the wife's body, and the wife rules over her husband's (cf. 1 Corinthians 7:3-4).

However, mutual consent in itself does not signify the "great mystery" in Marriage, according to Saint Thomas. It is the efficient cause of Marriage. It makes present the signification of the "great mystery," which is the ultimate cause of the sacrament. But he added a lesser signification for nuptial consent: ". . . nor does consent, properly speaking, signify the union of Christ with his Church, but his will by which it happens that the Church is united to him."[84] Consent signifies the will of Christ whereby his union with his Church was brought about. The implications of this insight will be examined in the next chapter.[85]

In Saint Thomas' theology of Marriage, signification may be summarized as serving several functions. It provides the accepted rationale for Marriage as one of the seven sacraments. It encircles the whole sacrament informing its three dimensions as: mutual consent (*sacramentum tantum*), the bond (*res et sacramentum*), and the Grace for married life (*res tantum*). Outside these essential elements, signification is the locus either for married sexual union to achieve procreation, or the locus for a Marriage like that of Our Lady and Saint Joseph which lacked this sexual form of completion.[86]   The signification of Christ and his Church imparts not only indissolubility but also a positive value to sexuality within the majority of Christian Marriages where spouses consent to exercise their rights to bodily union.

In his *Summa Contra Gentiles*, Saint Thomas attacked a threat of his times, the error of the Cathari, or Albigensians, that all sexual intercourse is sinful.[87]   Commenting on the first epistle to the Corinthians, he deemed sexual union in Marriage to be an "act of religion," with the procreation and education of children in view. With the caution of possible venial sin through concupiscence, he drew upon the selfless love of the "great mystery" of Christ and his Church, signified in the "act of justice" in rendering the Marriage "debt" in sexual union. *Agape* makes every act of virtue meritorious, including sexual union: "Every virtuous act is meritorious if it is performed with love."[88]

This more positive attitude towards the physical dimension of the vast majority of Christian Marriages does not lessen the need for Grace. It underlines the great need of spouses for the sacrament if they are to live faithfully in the true love of Christ, the faithful Bridegroom.

II. THE GRACE OF MARRIAGE IN SAINT THOMAS

Saint Thomas identified two contained realities in the order of Grace in sacramental Marriage: the bond and God's Grace. When consent is properly made, the bond is established and made indissoluble by consummation. If the spouses do not place any obstacle in the way, they receive Grace in Marriage for the task of procreation and education, for mutual fidelity and the sharing of their lives. When we look

closely at these two contained realities, we see how they relate to one
another in the lives of married Christians.

Following Saint Augustine, Saint Thomas compared the created
Grace of the bond to the indelible character of Baptism, Confirmation
and Orders. He referred to this comparison in his *Scriptum* when asking
whether the third of Saint Augustine's "goods" of Marriage, the "sacrament," is the chief good of Marriage, even beyond the goods of children
and fidelity. He observed that power is given in the character sacraments to perform spiritual deeds, but in Marriage power is given to
perform bodily actions. As compared to the character sacraments,
Marriage imparts indissolubility but, insofar as this bond pertains to
physical acts, it differs from a sacramental character and is terminated
by bodily death.[89]   Earlier, in the *Scriptum*, he made it clear that
spouses are tied together formally, not effectively, by this bond which is
signified and effected in their mutual consent.[90]   To see the ultimate
causal role of the bond, however, we must examine the second contained reality, the Grace of married life.

As noted, Saint Thomas went beyond Peter Lombard in the
Scriptum, seeing a reality both signified *and* contained in Marriage. That
reality is the bond (*res et sacramentum*). In that same passage, though, he
rejected the view that Marriage is only a sign of Grace but confers no
Grace, or that Grace means only a remedy for concupiscence. In this
context he explained the role of the bond, pointing towards the Grace
given to spouses (*res tantum*) so that they can live out what their Marriage
signifies. He taught that, as the water of Baptism imprints a character
but does not result immediately in an infusion of Grace (meaning here
the baptismal Grace of justification), ". . . so the outward acts and the
words expressing consent directly effect a certain tie (*nexum quendam*)
which is the sacrament of Marriage; and this tie by virtue of its divine
institution works dispositively to the infusion of Grace (*dispositive
operetur ad gratiam*)."[91]

This was a cautious, but firm, step to say that the "tie," which is
established by the bond, "works dispositively to the infusion of Grace."
Spouses are thus disposed for the further full Grace of Marriage (the *res
tantum*) by the bond (or *sacramentum*) as indissolubility granted by God.

If this affirmation of dispositive Grace in Marriage was cautious
in the context of a "more probable opinion" that Grace is given in

Marriage, in his later thought Saint Thomas went even further. In his *Summa Contra Gentiles*, we find a clearer, more confident and definite statement: "And because sacraments bring about that which they signify, it is believed that grace is conferred on the spouses by this sacrament. . . ." Then he immediately adds this note regarding the signification of Marriage: ". . . to which the union of Christ and his Church pertains." And in an interesting ecclesial way, he also added the following regarding indissolubility, ". . . which is of utmost importance to them so that in an earthly and fleshly way they may determine not to be disunited from Christ and the Church."[92]

The shift from Peter Lombard's paradox of a sacrament which did not confer Grace was complete. But his wording was precise. He was not so naive as to require any "*ex opere operato*" infusion of Sanctifying Grace through the bond. But, as the dispositive means of Grace, the bond works as the strengthening gift of indissolubility, forming the secure basis whereby married Christians "may determine not to be disunited from Christ and the Church." The ecclesial nuance is important. The bond disposes for a special, close, married participation in the unity of the Mystical Body, thus fulfilling Saint Paul's vision of Marriage in Ephesians, spouses as "members of his body."

Even in his *Scriptum* we find a further intimation of his developed thought. In asking whether the "sacrament" is the chief of the three goods of Marriage, he described procreation as the first good and primary end in the natural practical sense, but that the "sacrament" was the "more excellent," because, for man it is more excellent to be in Grace, even if natural life is essential before we can be raised to Grace.[93]

A further intimation of sanctification through the bond is found when he explains how sexual union is "excused" by the three goods of Marriage. Offspring and fidelity bestow virtue on sexual union in Marriage, but Saint Thomas goes further with the effect of the third good, the "sacrament," which makes the act not only good but also holy. The signification of the "union" between Christ and his Church through the indissoluble bond is the source of this goodness.[94] Placing this teaching in the context of married life in the *Scriptum*, Saint Thomas, as an acute observer of human experience, was already moving beyond the third good, the "sacrament," as the "bond" or as Saint

Augustine's "indissolubility" to the "*res tantum*," the graced life of the spouses, the elevation and redemption of sexual love.

His broader view, from the bond to the graced life of the spouses, is evident when he explains that, as a good of Marriage, the "sacrament" is not only indissolubility, but all those things which come from the Christ-Church signification.[95]   Going further, he gently corrects Peter Lombard's Augustinian definition of "sacrament" as the good of indissolubility. Marriage, in its own right, is a "natural undertaking" before it is a sacrament, and the sacramental aspect is a condition added to it from which it derives its goodness. This broader meaning he even describes as "sacramentality": "Therefore, its sacramentality (*sacramentalitas*), if I may use the word, is reckoned among the goods which justify Marriage; accordingly, this third good of Marriage, the sacrament, denotes not only its indissolubility, but also all the things which pertain to its signification."[96]

The move from "sacrament" as bond to what the bond disposes in spouses, "sacramentality," is a move from the bond, "*res et sacramentum*," to the Grace of married life, "*res tantum*." Because he did not complete his *Summa*, we do not know exactly how he would have developed this Grace of married life, which includes "all the things which pertain to its signification." In commenting on Ephesians, he moved beyond the mystical meaning of the "great mystery" to the tangible reality of Marriage. Genesis 2:24 may provide a type of Christ the Bridegroom, but this is meant to be translated into the fidelity of married people. The sacramental signification demands a response that it be fulfilled in the lives of married Christians as types of Christ (*de aliis vero in figura Christi*). Married people are the "others" (*aliis*) who signify the Christ-Church bond in Marriage.[97]   His comments on Ephesians also broadened the idea of "sacramentality," thus leaving the way open for a developed theology of the continual mutual ministry of Grace in Marriage, Grace as *lived* sacramentality.

One final aspect of his thought indicates the direction he would have taken in a completed *Summa*. Saint Thomas held that sacramental Grace, like an infused habit, flows from Sanctifying Grace, but is distinct from it, just as the infused virtues are distinct from it. He differed from the Scotists who held that sacramental Grace is an aspect of Sanctifying Grace.[98]   He thus moved beyond the position that sacraments impart Sanctifying Grace, with a right or title to actual graces for the state of life derived from each specific sacrament. He recognized distinctive sacramental Grace, intrinsic to each sacrament, depending on its specific healing and elevating end in the life of the individual Christian and in the whole life of the Mystical Body of Christ. If he argued that the Grace of Baptism differs from the Grace of Confirmation, we may infer that he would have set forth the distinctive Grace of Marriage, the dispositive bond and the lived Grace of married life and love.[99] But the *Summa* was not completed. It remained for others to develop the *"res tantum"* of Marriage, to meet more forceful challenges to the sacramentality of Marriage than the fanaticism of Albigensians or the unimaginative caution of theologians.

In his *Summa*, however, we already have a rich and poignant hint of his developed mind, had he written the projected Questions on Marriage. He was discussing the supremacy of the Eucharist among the sacraments. He perceived how the Eucharist shares signification with Marriage. His words suggest the deeper spiritual union of spouses, given Grace to be parents, lovers, friends, Grace to signify and share in the "great mystery." "Marriage at least in its signification touches upon this sacrament (the Eucharist) insofar as it signifies the union between Christ and the Church, which unity is formed through the sacrament of the Eucharist: hence the apostle says, 'This is a great mystery, and I mean in reference to Christ and the Church.'"[100]

AFTER SAINT THOMAS

Saint Thomas died while on the way to the Second Council of Lyons, held in 1274. Saint Bonaventure died during the Council. The emperor of the shrinking Byzantine Empire, Michael VIII (Palaeologus) was pressing for reunion with Rome to heal the Photian Schism and gain European political support. Therefore, he commanded his legates to concede all doctrinal points so as to gain hasty reunion.[101] Ultimately, the project came to nothing, but the "profession of faith" required of the emperor shows that Marriage was firmly established as a sacrament, listed second to the last in the *"septenarium,"* before Extreme Unction.[102] This would pose no problem for even the most anti-papal of the Greeks, but there was also pointed emphasis given to indissolubility.

By the Thirteenth Century, the idea that mutual consent makes Marriage was almost universally accepted in the West, resting on Peter Lombard and the greater authority and influence of Saint Thomas. The form of the sacrament was recognized as the words of consent, "and not on the priest's blessing, which is a certain sacramental."[103]   To describe this joining-together by consent as the human form of the sacrament, Saint Thomas went on to describe it as a contract, not made as a betrothal, a consent regarding the future, but as consent in the present.[104]   This practical description of sacramental consent as a contract has provided the working basis for much Canon Law, the reality of the contract being determined in terms of true or defective consent.

But contractual consent also allowed for the continuation of a serious pastoral problem in the Middle Ages, clandestine Marriages. Without a universal law requiring witnesses or the presence of a priest at every Marriage and by identifying the valid contract with a valid sacrament, the Church allowed people to enter valid sacramental Marriage by themselves, not "before the Church," that is, in a "clandestine" manner. This clandestinity not only allowed for valid secret Marriages, with problems of alleged Marriages and claims for maintenance, etc., but also for the "Romeo and Juliet" problem of elopement and Marriage without even the blessing of an obliging friar.

While the Church stood for the right to marry, for the dignity and freedom of men and women making a unique contract which is a sacrament, the abuses of clandestine Marriage had to be checked. The Fourth Lateran Council had tried to curb clandestinity with little success.[105]   Local council rulings could be thwarted when courts recognized clandestine unions. The ease with which the sacrament could be contracted was a continual pastoral problem, only to be resolved later at Trent.

Early in the Fourteenth Century, the bold Dominican pioneer of Nominalism, Durandus of Saint-Pourçain, flatly denied the sacramentality of Marriage, but the immediate Thomist reaction against him forced him to retreat to Lombard's position.[106]   Slightly later, an ascetical attack on Marriage by schismatic Franciscans, the Fraticelli, prompted Pope John XXII to respond by describing Marriage as the "venerable sacrament of the spouses."[107]

In the following century, the Magisterium again spoke of the sacrament, once more in the context of efforts to achieve reunion with the East. In 1439 the decree of the Council of Florence setting out doctrinal requirements for the Armenians, included statements on Marriage, listed last among the seven sacraments. After a reference to the "great sacrament" in Ephesians 5:32, the words echoed Saint Thomas. Mutual consent is the ordinary efficient cause of Marriage: "The efficient cause of matrimony is the mutual consent duly expressed in words relating to the present." The Armenians were not allowed the Eastern belief that the blessing confers the sacrament. Moreover, as with the "profession of faith" of Michael Palaeologus, indissolubility was affirmed, "since the bond of a marriage legitimately contracted is perpetual."[108]

THE COUNCIL OF TRENT

Less than a century after the Council of Florence, the sacramentality of Marriage was attacked directly. In his *Babylonian Captivity* (1520), Martin Luther flatly denied that Marriage is a sacrament.[109]   In the following year, King Henry VIII of England replied with a defense of the seven sacraments, including a defense of Marriage, incongruous in the light of his own later matrimonial exploits. But this question of the "seven sacraments" was the immediate issue on which the first Protestants denied the sacramentality of Marriage.

Their arguments rested primarily on the "scripture alone" principle. Luther claimed that the Gospels do not show Christ instituting Marriage as a sacrament, like Baptism or the Eucharist. Use was also made of Erasmus' point that *mysterion* does not mean "sacrament" in Ephesians. But there was another framework constructed behind assertions such as that the marriages of patriarchs and pagans do not differ from Christian Marriage. This was Luther's theology of "justification by faith alone." Luther proclaimed God's non-imputation of sin to certain chosen members of the totally corrupted race of Adam. He completely changed the theology of Grace and sacraments. Grace becomes God's imputed justification by faith, granted to certain chosen people. And since a "reflexive faith" (believing that *I* am saved) is the center of the life of Grace, the sacraments are no longer "means of Grace." Luther and the early Protestants therefore found it difficult to see any form of Marriage as a means of Grace or as having any bearing on the salvation of the believer.[110]

In this system, Marriage was also set aside as a sacrament because such theology sharply separates nature from Grace, secular from sacred, State from Church. If Christ gave no new sign for a sacrament of Marriage, it therefore comes under civil jurisdiction. Thus Marriage was also drawn into Luther's doctrine of separation of Church and State. Selective interpretation of the Bible and the loss of sacramentality involved the loss of indissolubility. In the West, this was the first major step towards secularized Marriage.

Luther recognized Marriage as a created reality. But, in his understanding of a fallen fleshly creation separated from the spiritual order of Grace, Marriage is only a necessary or obligatory remedy for concupiscence. As a help for the fleshly nature of fallen man, Luther could esteem Marriage, even insisting on it against the "impossibility" of celibacy. He entered a form of Marriage himself, and spent the latter part of his life as a husband and father. As with various elements in his teaching, his later followers of a more "high Church" tendency do not in practice deny the sacred and even sacramental nature of Marriage.

Although Marriage came under the "godly order" of the theocratic state at Geneva, Calvin's views were close to Luther. Being married was no different from being a farmer or a shoemaker. Calvin made much of the "error" of the use of the term "sacrament" in Ephesians 5:32.[111]   In England, Anglican theology reflected the Reformers' doctrines, with the equivocation in the *Thirty-Nine Articles* that Marriage may be counted as a "lesser sacrament."[112]

The Council of Trent had to meet this Protestant challenge to the sacramentality of Marriage. This was foreshadowed in the definition of the "seven sacraments" in the first Canon on the sacraments in general.[113]   But debate on sacramentality had to wait until 1563, the final year of the Council, when the Fathers sought to find the most effective way of defining sacramentality while prudently avoiding side issues.

In 1563, a work by Melchior Cano, O.P. appeared, challenging the view that, because consent makes a Marriage, so the matter and form of the sacrament are found in some way within mutual consent. Cano argued that the words of consent are the matter, but the priestly blessing is the form of the sacrament. The minister of Marriage is the priest, not the spouses. His blessing is like the form of absolution, a word of faith, not of nature.[114] Unwittingly, Cano opened the way to an extrinsic theology of nuptial Grace, superimposed on consent.

But the Council Fathers were not distracted from their essential task of meeting the Protestant challenge by internal Catholic disputes. Faced with such questions in debate, they resolved not to define the matter and form, nor the minister of the sacrament, nor whether the contract is the sacrament.[115]

Avoiding such issues, they prepared a series of definitive Canons, anathematizing those who held specific errors concerning Marriage. The debates of late July, 1563, show us that not only were they responding to the Protestant denial of sacramentality, but that they were also haunted by the memory of Durandus of Saint-Pourçain. Therefore they expanded the wording of the first Canon, defining the sacramentality of Marriage so as to give Marriage full status as one of the seven sacraments of the New Law, and not a "lesser sacrament" as Anglican doctrine allowed. Although they argued as to whether Scripture or tradition should be the ground of sacramentality, there were no problems over the institution of the sacrament by Our Lord, or that, in some sense, it confers Grace.[116] Moreover, the Fathers were aware that by defining Marriage as the sacrament of the unbreakable union between Christ and his Church, sacramentality itself would be the surest defense against the Protestant denial of the indissolubility of Marriage.[117]

Accepted by a virtually unanimous vote at the Twenty-Fourth Session, November 11, 1563, the first Canon states: "If anyone says that matrimony is not truly and properly one of the seven sacraments of the Law of the Gospel, instituted by Christ the Lord, but that it was devised in the Church by men and does not confer grace, *let him be anathema.*"[118] In the categories we use today to determine the "note" of a doctrine, the Fathers of Trent raised the sacramentality of Marriage from being the teaching of the Ordinary Magisterium to the status of a solemn, infallible definition of the Extraordinary Magisterium of a

General Council of the Church, a "defined dogma of the divine and Catholic faith."[119]

The doctrinal *Preface* to the Canons describes the Grace of the sacrament as being derived from the Passion of Christ who instituted and perfects the sacraments. This Grace perfects the natural love of Marriage and strengthens the indissoluble unity of the couple. Thus Christ himself sanctifies the spouses.[120] There follows a citation of Ephesians 5:25, 32, but not as a *proof* of the sacramentality of Marriage, simply "as Saint Paul implied." The Fathers limited themselves to defining the truth in its essentials and made no attempt to defend or explain the truth by interpreting Saint Paul.[121]

In contrast, the pastoral problem of clandestine Marriages presented a more protracted matter for debate at Trent. The final outcome was the decree, *Tametsi*, which declared past clandestine Marriages to be "valid and true," though deplored and prohibited by the Church. Henceforth, without the presence of the parish priest (or another delegated by him) and two or three witnesses, the Council rendered those attempting Marriage in this way to be "unfit" and decreed that such contracts would be "null and void."[122]

The decree effectively ended the abuse of clandestinity, but the debates leading to it were heated.[123] Not a few Bishops doubted whether the Church had power over the matter and form of the sacraments, even when Our Lord had not left us specific matter and form. But in the decree the Church exercised her right to determine diriment impediments and to change the way in which consent is to be manifested.[124] Through *Tametsi* the simple contract of Marriage became a solemn contract "in the eyes of the Church." The Church in the West thus secured control over the public celebration of the sacrament of Marriage.

However, on the issue of whether a priestly blessing is essential for the sacrament, *Tametsi* could be read in two ways. By recognizing clandestine Marriage before the decree, the Council Fathers favored consent as essential for the sacrament. But, by requiring the presence of a priest after the decree, they gave some encouragement to those who held to the view of Cano, that the priest is the minister of the sacrament. Taken as a whole, *Tametsi* assumes the contrary view, that the consenting couple are the ministers of the sacrament. The fact that *Tametsi* was not universal law (for example, inapplicable in Protestant regions), and the fact that canonists allowed exceptions to its solemn contract, cannot be said to make the priest into the minister of sacramental Marriage.[125]

AFTER TRENT

As we would expect, the sacrament of Marriage was included among the seven sacraments in the *Tridentine Profession of Faith* or "Creed of Saint Pius V."[126]   In the pastoral sphere, the *Catechism of the Council of Trent* proposed the sacramentality of Marriage, echoing Saint Thomas' teaching on nature perfected by Grace, mutual consent made "in the present" as the external cause of the sacrament and the three "goods" of Marriage which make sexual union right and honorable. Marital fidelity requires a love which is "special, holy and pure."[127]   Those preparing for Marriage are to be disposed so that they regard it as a sacrament, a work not human, but divine.[128]

However, after Trent, we do not find a widespread development of sacramentality among theologians. The Council's definition was accepted by theologians, but pastoral exigencies led to an emphasis on moral or canonical problems in what remained of Catholic Europe and in the new world.

Saint Robert Bellarmine (1542-1621) was a major exception to this tendency.[129]   His experience in teaching at Louvain made him aware of the Protestant challenge to sacramental Marriage. In his famous *De controversiis christianae fidei*, the treatise *De sacramento matrimonii* shines out as an example of his reasoned application of Thomism to the questions of his time.

His role in developing a deeper awareness of the sacramentality of Marriage in the Church may be seen in two areas: (1) the way he took Saint Thomas' "*res tantum*" to a further stage by presenting Marriage "*in facto esse*" as a permanent sacrament; (2) his authoritative stand for the inseparability between the contract and the sacrament. The first area shows a new development, and the second is an example of the crystallization and organization of the work of others. Both matters are treated, not in the context of argument against the Protestants, but in denying the opinion of a Catholic, Melchior Cano, who saw the contract as the matter and the priestly blessing as the form of sacramental Marriage. As already noted, the Fathers of Trent did not seek to resolve the question of the matter and form of Marriage.

The theme of the permanent sacrament emerges in Saint Robert's resolution of the question of the matter and form of the sacrament. Against Durandus' denial of the sacramentality of Marriage, Saint Robert Bellarmine emphasized the Grace of the mutual consent, forming a sublime union: ". . . the union which the sacrament of matrimony brings about is a union not of bodies alone but also of souls, not out of just any but out of true and divine love." He then referred to the "great mystery" in Ephesians, adding, ". . . hence it is a union which sanctifies souls and makes them holy unless an obstacle is placed in the way."[130] He saw what Marriage signifies as effected in the sacrament, a "union" infused with divine "charity," Saint Paul's *agape* in Ephesians 5:25, 28, 33.

Saint Robert went on to consider Marriage as a "sacrament" in two ways, not only as a contract entered into by mutual consent (Marriage "*in fieri*") but also as a lived union (Marriage "*in facto esse*"). With inspired insight he compared this second way of considering Marriage to the second way in which the Eucharist is a sacrament, the permanence of the Real Presence effected by transubstantiation.[131]

Thus married Christians "sacramentalize" the "great mystery," not only in the consent which establishes married life but in their very lives themselves. This is the key to further understanding the continuing Grace of the sacrament (the "*res tantum*") and, as such, these words of Saint Robert were taken up over three centuries later by Pope Pius XI.[132]   But Saint Robert added a further reflection on Marriage as a permanent sacrament. "If Marriage already entered into and celebrated is truly considered, one cannot deny that those couples who are living together in a conjugal society and union are an external material symbol representing the indissoluble union between Christ and his Church; in a similar way, in the Sacrament of the Eucharist, after the consecration has taken place, the consecrated species remain, which are a sensible and external symbol of internal spiritual nourishment."[133]

This remarkable analogy drawn from the sacramentality of the Blessed Eucharist, points to the "consecration" of the spouses by the sacrament of Marriage. But it must be balanced with the caution he added when referring to the visible sacrament of their union, from Ephesians: "unless an obstacle is placed in the way." The Eucharistic Species are consecrated, transubstantiated, "*ex opere operato*," and, of themselves, can raise no obstacle if the correct matter and form is used. The "consecration" of the nuptial union is "*ex opere operato*" insofar as the bond is concerned if the parties are free and make true consent. But spouses can place an "obstacle" to the visible signification of their lived permanent sacrament, for example, by separating and not maintaining a visible "conjugal society." Yet, even in spite of this, the analogy holds, for in the face of such an obstacle to the Grace of the sacrament, the bond remains intact.

The second area in which Saint Robert contributed to a deeper awareness of sacramentality was in the context of his view of the permanence of the sacrament, that is, in his argument against Cano where he insisted that the contract and the sacrament are inseparable. To this end he cited Hugh of Saint Victor, Saint Thomas, and the Council of Florence on the effectual power of consent in the sacrament, together with inferences from *Tametsi* at Trent.[134] He concluded, "From all this we can reason that the opinion of Cano is altogether singular and new," and that either the argument of Cano separating the contract from the sacrament is false or the Church is in error.[135]

The inseparability between contract and sacrament has a bearing on sacramentality, clearly in the value of consent which will be examined in the next chapter but also in terms of creation and its sacramental renewal in Christ. The "created reality" of Marriage was raised by Our Lord to be a sacrament, described by Saint Robert in the words "elevated by Christ to the sacred, supernatural, order."[136] Saint Robert's influential stand on the sanctity of the Marriage contract would be very important in the problems which lay ahead for the sacrament of Marriage.[137]

In the Seventeenth and Eighteenth Centuries, the problem was aggressive royal absolutism, or Regalism. The French jurist, J. Launoy (1603-1673) saw Marriage as a civil contract, regulated by the State, which determines diriment impediments, leaving only the "blessing" to the Church.[138] Cano's theology was used eagerly to promote matrimonial Regalism, pastorally dangerous because it devalued the sacrament, leaving spousal morality to the State — the dilemma of Protestant society. Fueled by anti-papal Febronianism, the apogée of Regalism was the legislation of Emperor Joseph II of Austria between 1780 and 1790, reducing the clergy to instruments of State law.[139]

In spite of the authority of Bellarmine, some theologians were swayed by Regalism, hence uncertain on the question of the minister of the sacrament. Cardinal Prospero Lambertini allowed separation of contract from sacrament as a probable opinion, but later, as Pope Benedict XIV, in 1758, he recognized matter and form within the contract made by mutual consent.[140] Saint Alphonsus Liguori (1696-1787) noted his changed views when he set out the various opinions and favored Bellarmine in his *Theologia Moralis*.[141]

After the French Revolution and Napoleon I, the new challenge of the secular state emerged, with parallel civil and ecclesiastical systems of matrimonial practice. In the Nineteenth Century, the Church had not only to defend her rights, but to strengthen the faithful with a better understanding of Christian Marriage as an inviolable and wondrous sacrament.

THE NINETEENTH CENTURY

The theology of Matthias Scheeben (1835-1888) marked a further synthesis and development in a deepening awareness of Marriage as a sacrament. His thought is already evident in this work, therefore only major themes are singled out rather than a synopsis of his theology which reaffirms Saint Thomas' doctrine of Grace as intrinsic to nature, perfecting nature, and not "tacked onto" nature.[142]

Scheeben set the sacrament of Marriage in its proper ecclesial context. Having explained the sacramental characters as consecrations which form the Mystical Body of Christ, he presented Marriage as "the fourth consecratory but non-hierarchical sacrament." He added that the character is the source from which matrimony derives its whole supernatural consecration, as well as the bond connecting it with the mystical Marriage of Christ and the Church, showing that it is not merely the image, but the offshoot of that mystical Marriage. In matrimony, further, the character clearly manifests the full range of its power and meaning, since it brings out the fact that those who possess it belong completely to Christ, body and soul, as his members.[143]   Here we find the whole continuity of the doctrine of the *intrinsic* sacramentality of Marriage; from Saint Paul's "members of his body," and Marriage "in Christ," through Saint Augustine, Saint Thomas and Trent — but now to be found in the theology of the Church as the Mystical Body, a theology of which Scheeben was a major pioneer.

Although, according to Scheeben, the holy state of sacramental Marriage "is not a constitutive element in the mystical organism of the Church, but only its offshoot," nevertheless, the God-Man receives spouses "and consecrates them as active organs in His mystical body."[144] In this ecclesial context, Scheeben saw the fruitful Grace produced by the sacrament founded upon the inner mystical nature of sacramentality. Marriage he considered as the "figure and organ of the marriage between Christ and the Church."[145]   As fruitful Grace, sacramentality must be defined and clarified in terms of the "great mystery." Theological exegesis of Ephesians 5:25-32 may yield a proof that Marriage is a sacrament by showing that Christian Marriage has the power to produce Grace.[146]   This is the method followed in Chapters One and Two of this work.

Scheeben proclaimed the dignity and sanctity of the sacrament as the consecrated life of married laity in a century when the secular State and the forces of anti-clerical liberalism, masonry and socialism were assailing Christian Marriage. But the depth of his mystical and ecclesial sacramentality would not be influential until the era of Pope Pius XI and Pope Pius XII. The Magisterium in Scheeben's era contended with the secularist assault by utilizing what weapons had been handed on from the past. In 1864, in his *Syllabus of Errors*, Pope Pius IX condemned propositions haunted by the ghost of Cano.[147]   By the separation of contract from sacrament, like the regalists before them, the secularists of the Nineteenth Century claimed the contract, hence Marriage, for themselves, leaving the "prayers" to the priest.

In 1880, Pope Leo XIII met the growing challenge of civil Marriage and divorce with his encyclical *Arcanum Divinae Sapientiae*. Reinforcing the sacramental dignity of Marriage, he cited the Tridentine affirmation of the sacramentality of Marriage taught by the Fathers, the Councils of the Church and Tradition ". . . that Christ our

Lord raised Marriage to the dignity of a sacrament; that to husband and wife, guarded and strengthened by the heavenly Grace which his merits gained for them, he gave power to attain holiness in the married state. . . . Through the 'great mystery' of Christ's union with his Church, such sacramental Marriage is indissoluble."[148]

Leo XIII also opposed and condemned the false distinction between contract and sacrament, describing the sacrament of Marriage as a "holy sign which gives Grace."[149]   But the major emphasis of his teaching was against divorce, a modern problem already evident in his pontificate.

THE TWENTIETH CENTURY

To meet the problems of Marriage in rapidly changing and more complex societies, the Church could not rely only on better canonical procedures or new legislation, such as the decree *Ne Temere* of Pope Saint Pius X, 1910, or the *Codex Iuris Canonici* of Pope Benedict XV, 1917. Early in our century, among canonists and moralists we find a stronger awareness of Marriage as a permanent, lived sacrament, in Bellarmine's second sense of "sacrament," not the making of the contract but a state of graced life.

Adolphe Tanquerey (1854-1932) prefaced his analysis of Marriage with observations on the sacrament. From its signification, Marriage cannot be a supernatural union without Grace, nor can it be *permanently* a supernatural union without Habitual Grace, to which actual graces are added as the right of those who share in the sacrament. Tanquerey thus saw it as "highly probable" that Marriage not only signifies but causes Grace.[150]

Also writing before the First World War, Dominic Prümmer (1866-1931) described the sacrament in a wider sense than contractual consent. Although it is a lesser state of life than holy virginity, sacramental Grace is given in Marriage, as a sacramental state of life.[151]   With Sanchez and Prümmer, Fr. Leeming listed Palmieri, Ojetti, Billot and Hugon as other authorities who agreed with Bellarmine that Marriage is a permanent sacrament.[152]

Christian Marriage came under more pressure after the First World War. The era of the 'Twenties was one of skepticism and hedonism, the age of the totalitarians of the Left and the Right, culminating in the crisis of the Depression. In 1930, fifty years after *Arcanum Divinae Sapientiae*, on the last day of the year after the Anglican Lambeth Conference had surrendered to contraception, Pope Pius XI issued his encyclical on Marriage, *Casti Connubii*. In the Magisterium, this was the most significant moment since Trent in the Church's developing awareness of the sacramentality of Marriage.

Pius XI strongly reaffirmed that Marriage is a sacrament instituted by Christ. He included in *Casti Connubii* a specific emphasis on the Grace of the sacrament: ". . . this sacrament not only increases Sanctifying Grace, the permanent principle of the supernatural life in those who, as the expression goes, place no obstacle (*obex*) in its way, but it also adds particular gifts, dispositions, seeds of Grace, by elevating and perfecting the natural power."[153] He added that this Grace gives spouses the understanding and ability to succeed in married life, and the right to actual graces when they are needed.

Therefore, according to Pius XI, spouses enjoy a threefold Grace in Marriage as a permanent, lived sacrament: (1) increased Sanctifying Grace; (2) a special Grace elevating and perfecting natural power; (3) the right to actual graces.[154] While affirming an increase of Sanctifying Grace, as in all sacraments rightly received, Pius XI favored the Thomist theology of a specific sacramental Grace of Marriage, "elevating and perfecting" nature.

In a further reference to sacramentality, later echoed at the Second Vatican Council, he said of spouses, "By such a sacrament they will be strengthened, sanctified and in a manner consecrated."[155] He immediately cited Saint Augustine's comparison of the sacramental bond with the characters of Orders and Baptism, adding a little later, that spouses are "not fettered but adorned by the golden bond of the sacrament."[156] From such authoritative words, reflecting Scheeben, we will see how "consecration" is integrated with the bond.[157]

Confronted by the modern collapse of Marriage, morality and the family, this wise Pope saw that not only did he have to maintain the constant emphasis of the Church on the indissoluble bond of the sacrament, but he had to move from, and through, this bond to the

Grace of the permanent, lived sacrament. He accomplished such a move by endorsing Bellarmine and drawing conclusions.

In the latter part of *Casti Connubii*, seeking good pastoral remedies for the matrimonial malaise, he said of spouses: "Let them constantly keep in mind that they have been consecrated and strengthened for the duties and for the dignity of their state by a special sacrament, the efficacious power of which, although it does not impress a character, is undying. To this purpose we may ponder over the words full of real comfort of holy Cardinal Robert Bellarmine, who with other well-known theologians with deep conviction thus expresses himself. 'The sacrament of Matrimony can be regarded in two ways: first in the making and then in its permanent state. For it is a sacrament like to that of the Eucharist, which not only while it is being conferred, but also while it remains, is a sacrament; for as long as the married parties are alive, so long is their union a sacrament of Christ and his Church.' "158

To this "undying" "efficacious power" of Marriage as a permanent sacrament, Pius XI added an exhortation. Spouses must cooperate with God "in order that the grace of this sacrament may produce its full fruit." Just as natural powers are to be used well, "so also men must diligently and unceasingly use the powers given them by the grace which is laid up in the soul by this sacrament. Let not, then, those who are joined in Matrimony neglect the grace of the sacrament which is within them." The Pope specifically cited 1 Timothy 4:14, "Do not neglect the gift you have. . . .," echoed in these words. Assuring spouses that "they will find the power of that grace becoming more effectual as time goes on . . .," he also cited 2 Timothy 1:6-7, ". . . the gift of God that is within you."159

The citing of two passages used to demonstrate the indelible character of Orders, and his reference to Orders as analogous to Marriage, shows that Pius XI had not only endorsed Marriage as a permanent sacrament, infusing "grace which is laid up in the soul." He had also developed the idea of the permanent bond, the *"res et sacramentum,"* as analogous to a character, and as the ground and source of all the sacramental Grace, the *"res tantum."* This unique Grace of Marriage grows as spouses cooperate with the gift they have received. Thus, from the sacrament itself, "they will find the power of that grace becoming more effectual as time goes on."

By this development of the continuous sacramental efficacy of the sacrament, Pius XI reinforced the moral teaching in his encyclical against divorce, contraception and abortion. *Casti Connubii* also encouraged and inspired the development of modern apostolates of preparation for Marriage, to form future spouses for the fruitful mutual ministry of Marriage.

In the midst of the Second World War, in his encyclical on the Church as the Mystical Body, *Mystici Corporis Christi*, Pope Pius XII described the contracting parties of Marriage as "ministers of Grace to one another."[160] But some took the objective value of the sacrament too far. In 1954, in his encyclical on holy virginity, *Sacra Virginitas*, Pius XII curbed an exaggeration of the *"ex opere operato"* sacramentality of Marriage, which proposed Marriage as a "fitter instrument than virginity for uniting souls with God."[161]

Yet Pius XII strongly encouraged a richer understanding of the married life of Catholics. The widow of Dietrich Von Hildebrand recounted her husband's discovery of Marriage as a sacrament at the time of his conversion. She described how Pius XII, when he was Nuncio in Munich, encouraged Dietrich in his view of love as the *meaning* of sacramental Marriage, a major theme in his work *Marriage, the Mystery of Faithful Love*.[162] However, in 1944, in the face of more extreme opinions, the Holy Office had to take a stand in favor of procreation as the primary *end* of Marriage.[163]

In the post-War decades, the effects of the world's steadily accelerating assualt on Marriage and the family were evident within the Church. The secularist reduction of Marriage to a contract little different from other contracts, hence easily voidable, hastened the spread of divorce. The new technology of contraception hastened the moral decay which would later be termed "the sexual revolution." In the pluralist societies, Catholics were not immune to these assaults on Marriage, just as in missionary regions pre-Christian Marriage practices raised their own problems. Therefore, we find the Fathers of the Second Vatican Council addressing "polygamy, the plague of divorced, so-called free love . . ." and "selfishness, hedonism, and unlawful contraceptive practices."[164] In this world of the latter decades of our century, they reaffirmed the sacramentality of Marriage.

"Just as of old, God encountered his people with a covenant of love and fidelity, so our Savior, the spouse of the Church, now encounters Christian spouses through the sacrament of marriage. He abides with them in order that by their mutual self-giving spouses will love each other with enduring fidelity, as he loved the Church and delivered himself up for it."[165]   Thus, the Second Vatican Council encompassed the developing awareness of the sacrament, from Saint Paul through to *Casti Connubii.*

When Pope Paul VI reaffirmed the constant teaching against the inseparable foes of Marriage, abortion, sterilization and contraception, in *Humanae Vitae,* he included sacramental Marriage as a doctrinal principle of conjugal love.[166]   In the controversy which erupted over *Humanae Vitae,* few paused to reflect on the contraceptive effect on the lived sacrament, a problem which will be introduced later in this work.[167]   But the effects of the sexual revolution were evident in the decade after *Humanae Vitae,* not only in continuing efforts to deny that procreation is the primary end of Marriage, but also in tribunal practice, in some places, which called into question the indissolubility of the sacramental bond.[168]

With the post-conciliar liturgical reform came a stronger emphasis on the faith of those entering the sacrament of Marriage, reflected in the introduction to the new Roman rite of Marriage.[169]   Pressure for solutions to the problem of Catholics with little or no faith entering sacramental Marriage came from the 1980 Synod of Bishops to which Pope John Paul II responded in *Familiaris Consortio,* 68. This question of faith is the most immediate problem in the sacramentality of Marriage today. It will be introduced in Chapter Seven together with ecumenical and contraceptive problems related to Marriage.

But in *Familiaris Consortio,* 13, we find a compact and rich restatement of the sacramentality of Marriage, already embodied in this work. Within the "great mystery," John Paul II sets out God's work, in and through spouses, as they minister the sacrament by mutual consent, bodily union and shared lives.

CARDINAL NEWMAN'S TEST

Having surveyed the "quest for the sign" in the developing awareness of the sacramentality of Marriage in the Church, from Saint Paul to John Paul II, we face a question. Is this an authentic development of Christian doctrine? The question has important pastoral and ecumenical implications. As a way of resolving the question, let us turn to the seven marks of authentic development proposed by Cardinal Newman in his *Essay on the Development of Christian Doctrine*. The marks of a true development are: (1) preservation of type, (2) continuity of principles, (3) assimilative power, (4) logical sequence, (5) anticipation of its future, (6) conservative action on its past, and (7) chronic vigor.[170] Immediately we can see that these marks need not be applied laboriously as some test of the development of the Church's awareness of the sacramentality of Marriage. They accurately and simply summarize the "quest for the sign."

In ever maintaining the "great mystery" of Ephesians 5:32 as the source of the radical difference between Christian and non-Christian Marriage, there is constant "preservation of type," grounded in the awareness that Jesus Christ raised the created reality of Marriage to a new dignity by requiring indissolubility and mutual fidelity. By consistently keeping before them the principles of indissolubility, mutual fidelity and fruitful and chaste love, the Popes, Councils, Fathers and theologians maintained a harmonious "continuity of principles," unshaken and indeed strengthened by the recurring challenges of paganism, heresy, secularism and the demands of the State.

An "assimilative power" is evident in absorbing what was good in rival systems or cultures, while rejecting what was corrupt and incompatible with the principles of the sacrament. Thus the simple and logical Roman understanding of Marriage made by mutual consent was absorbed and raised by stages, through its contractual sacramental reality to become the solemn contract of *Tametsi* at Trent. Likewise, the customs of the pre-Christian North were adapted and incorporated in various Marriage rites, while such false elements as sexual union being regarded as the cause of Marriage were rejected. In terms of the history of ideas, we also see the assimilative power of spousal sacramentality in Saint Augustine's Platonic view of the "great mystery" as the source of indissolubility and in Saint Thomas' Aristotelian analysis of the dimensions of the sacrament, further developed by Saint Robert Bellarmine.

We see the "logical sequence" in the steps from the basis, Our Lord's teaching on indissolubility and Saint Paul's discernment of the "great mystery" as source of unity and love, on to the identification of the caused reality, the bond, by Saint Augustine. In turn, the schoolmen sought to work out how mutual consent effects this bond, and how such a unique work of Grace ranks Marriage among the seven sacraments. Their work was completed in the next step, the synthesis and analysis of Saint Thomas, recognized and accepted by the Council of Florence and the Council of Trent, then taken beyond the consent and bond to the grace of the lived sacrament by Bellarmine, Scheeben, Pius XI, the Fathers of Vatican II and the Popes of our era.

Always within the development, it is easy to detect a clear "anticipation of its future," especially by the constant return to the "great mystery," and by perceiving within the espousals of our creation and Redemption the sources of a later, fuller, awareness of Marriage as a sacrament. Nothing novel was ever introduced in a process always marked by caution, reverence for its sources and traditions. Thus we find the "conservative action on its past." The two moments where accusations of novelty were made, naming Marriage as a sacrament and regulating its celebration through *Tametsi*, may both be explained in terms of this conservation of the past. Marriage was always seen as a "sacrament" in the practice of the Church, centuries before the term was applied to the seven great mysteries of Christian life. *Tametsi* could lay down rules for the mode of celebration only because Our Lord left us a new kind of Marriage for Christians, without any specific mode of celebration. But where do we discern "chronic vigor"?

We find the "chronic vigor" of this evidently authentic development in the obvious tenacity of thought; in the decisions of Popes and Councils, made in the face of heresy or the immoralities of princes; in the distinctions and arguments of theologians, made within an act of faith in the teaching of Jesus Christ on Marriage. But there is another form of "chronic vigor" found in a wider area where Newman himself discerned a marvellous "sense of the faith."

All along, while Popes and Councils decided, and theologians argued, millions of Catholic men and women celebrated sacramental

Marriage and lived sacramental Marriage in millions of Christian families. This is why we turn now from the "quest for the sign" in history, to the sign discerned and lived, to the human actions and words which are the visible fabric of this sacrament of the "great mystery" of Christ and his beloved Church. In three stages, following Saint Thomas, the human dynamism of the sacrament will be studied: (1) the consent, or *"sacramentum tantum"* which establishes the sacrament, (2) the bond, or *"res et sacramentum"* which is rendered indissoluble by sexual union, and (3) the covenant, seen as a broad description of the *"res tantum,"* the Grace of the state of Marriage.

CHAPTER FOUR

The Sacramental Consent

Entrádose ha la Esposa
En el ameno huerto deseado,
Y a su sabor reposa,
El cuelo reclinado
Sobre los dulces brazos del Amado

Now, as she long aspired,
Into the garden comes the bride, a guest:
And in its shade retired
Has leant her neck to rest
Against the gentle arm of the Desired:

Debajo del manzano,
Allí conmigo fuiste desposada,

Beneath the apple-tree,
You came to swear your troth and to be
mated,

Allí te dí la mano,
Y fuiste reparada,
Donde tu madre fuera violada.

Gave there your hand to me,
And have been new-created
There where your mother first was violated.

Saint John of the Cross, *Songs between the soul and the bridegroom*

In the silence of a parish church, in the presence of a priest, their families and friends, a baptized man and a baptized woman face each other and exchange the consent of Marriage. The simple words they address to one another are words of great power, words which change reality. Their consent is the form of a sacrament. Within that form is the mutual giving of oneself to the other, which is the matter of the sacrament. And they themselves are the ministers.

Their sacramental consent will be considered in three stages which reveal Jesus Christ acting within this human act or, in other words, its sacramentality. First, consent is the effectual form of Marriage. Second, as such it causes the contract which is a more precise, human way of seeing the "joining together" of the sacramental covenant. Third, spousal consent is meant to be a consent of love, infused with the Love of the archetype which is signified in this sacrament of the "great mystery" of the Love of Jesus Christ for his spouse, the Church.

CONSENT, THE FORM OF THE SACRAMENT

As the visible "*sacramentum tantum*" of Marriage, this sign is described by the Church as "an act of will by which a man and a woman by an irrevocable covenant mutually give and accept one another for the purpose of establishing a marriage."[1]   Although in practice, and even by definition, matrimonial consent is reduced to a simple "yes," it is much more than a mere assent. Consent in Marriage is a personal, intimate agreement, with the understanding and concord of two minds and wills implicit in the Latin words "*consentire*" and "*consensus*." In the context of Marriage, it seems tautologous even to say "mutual consent," although the adjective is added for emphasis, to underline the mutuality of this unique kind of consent.

The specific end of the consent is Marriage, the end determining the nature of this consent. The consent cannot be varied so as to determine the nature of Marriage, for example as some temporary arrangement. This defined matrimonial consent establishes an "irrevocable covenant" for the mutual giving and accepting of the spouses.

However, this is not a canonical treatise. For the purposes of this work on sacramentality, let us assume that consent is made normally, properly, as the Code requires — and as it is made in most Marriages. The consenting parties are at least not ignorant of the fact that Marriage is a permanent partnership between man and woman, ordered to the procreation of children through some form of sexual cooperation.[2]   In this valid sacramental consent, there is no deceit,[3] no force or fear,[4] and the consent is unconditional, free from some future condition being placed upon the Marriage.[5]   Moreover, the parties maintain an internal consent of the mind, in conformity with the words and signs of consent.[6]

Free from defects which would destroy its end, this consent is the mutual giving and accepting of persons: "I, John, take you, Catherine, for my lawful, wedded wife. . . ."; "I, Catherine, take you, John, for my lawful, wedded husband. . . ." But this "taking" is "giving" and the acceptance of the gift of the other.

I. THE SACRAMENTAL WORD

As we have seen, in their quest for the sign and in their developing awareness of the sacramentality of Marriage, theologians of the West identified the human words of consent as the efficient cause of Marriage. Christ our Lord had added nothing new, in human word or act, to the created reality of Marriage. Therefore, in a tradition aware of the diverse customs of various peoples, yet also aware of the freedom and dignity of spouses, the theologians saw the "sacramental word" in the human consent.

In the East, a different practice and belief took hold. The effective "sacramental word" was identified in the blessing imparted by the priest as minister of the sacrament. Yet this is not to say that consent is lacking. For example, in the Byzantine rites of Marriage, consent has been already expressed, *"de futuro,"* in the engagement rite which is celebrated before the sacrament is celebrated. But this consent is sealed, as it were, by the blessing, evident in the coronation of bride and groom at the heart of the celebration of the sacrament. The priest, crowning the groom, says, "The servant of God, N., marries (literally "is crowned for . . .") the handmaid of God, N., in the name of the Father, and of the Son, and of the Holy Spirit." This formula is repeated as the bride is crowned.[7]   In the Russian rite, there are questions and answers before the blessing and crowning, seeking the intentions of the spouses to take one another in Marriage, without any commitment to another party.[8]

Therefore, even in a different mode of celebration in the East, we find the consent of spouses assumed and respected. From our point of view, it would be the willing presence of bride and groom before the priest, indicating their consenting intentions, which would effect the Marriage rather than his solemn benediction. Thus the "sacramental word" is present even in the rites which do not articulate it clearly.

If consent is the "sacramental word" how is it effectual as the form of the sacrament? Pope John Paul II, in *Familiaris Consortio*, teaches: "The communion of love between God and people, a fundamental part of the Revelation and faith experience of Israel, finds a meaningful expression in the marriage covenant which is established between a man and a woman. For this reason the central word of Revelation, 'God loves His people,' is likewise proclaimed through the living and concrete word whereby a man and a woman express their conjugal love."9   Where is this "living and concrete word whereby a man and a woman express their conjugal love" to be found first and foremost, but in the consent of the spouses?

The source of Marriage, as we have found, lies in the Love of the Holy Trinity, God himself. Proceeding forth from his Father, the Son, the Word, is generated in the unity of Love, the Holy Spirit. In that "divine decree" of the eternal Word we find the ultimate Consent which is the source of the human, though sacramental, consent of that bride and groom giving themselves to one another in a parish church. In two ways this man and this woman are caught up into the eternal Word himself: in their creation and, yet more wondrously, in their Redemption.

This man and woman are human beings created in the image of God, endowed with his "likeness." They are part of the whole creation which is the work of the Trinity, yet a creation made through the Word, for "all things were made through him, and without him was not anything made that was made. In him was life, and the life was the light of men . . ." (John 1:3-4). In the words of God, "Let there be light . . .," and "Let us make man in our image, after our likeness . . ." (Genesis 1:3, 26), Adam and Eve were formed. From the hand of God, Adam accepted Eve in a consent of delight, a consent in human words: "This at last is bone of my bones and flesh of my flesh; she shall be called Woman, because she was taken out of Man" (Genesis 2:23). Now, in human words, a man and a woman consent to become "one flesh."

The man and woman, in Marriage, thus act as the "image and likeness" of God in their words, in consent itself. By creation, in "imaging" the divine decree, they become co-creators with God, in the Marriage consent, in their "one flesh" for the procreation of the human race. Thus, in consent we find a "primordial sacrament" of Marriage,

signification of the divine creative decree, effecting a new reality —
Marriage, "one flesh."

In the Redemption, in the healing of what the Fall impaired in
Marriage, we find the second, more wondrous "image" of God, the
elevation of the human words of consent to become the efficient cause
of a sacrament. Now the words of consent are significant and effectual
in the Word-made-flesh, in the divine decree of the Incarnation. In the
Hypostatic Union of the divine and human natures in Jesus Christ we
have the source of a human nuptial union, indissoluble, faithful. In the
figure of Mary Immaculate we have the perfect spouse, the Church,
sought by this Bridegroom, espoused already in his incarnate nuptial
union with us. Her spousal consent, her "Fiat," mutually complements
the divine "Fiat!" And the "Word became flesh. . . ."

In the consent of the enfleshed Word to die for his spouse, in his
words of turning to Jerusalem, of setting his course at the supper table,
supremely in his Eucharistic self-giving, we have the consent of the
"great mystery." Now, in human words, a man and a woman give
consent as the new Adam and new Eve, baptized to become the new
creation, espoused already by God, "in Christ." Thus, their human
words are raised to participate in the re-creating Word Himself, words
infused with his undying love for his spouse, the Church. "I, John, take
you, Catherine"; "I, Catherine, take you, John. . . ." As Pope John Paul
II has pointed out, these words are the language of the body, first
produced in Genesis and Ephesians before they come to the lips of
spouses in this sacrament.[10]

How easily we say that these words of consent are the form of the
sacrament. But that statement places this language of the body, "I take
you. . .," on the same level as, "I baptize you. . .," "Be sealed with the
Gift of the Holy Spirit. . .," "I absolve you. . .," and supremely, "This is
my Body . . . this is the cup of my Blood." All these effectual sacramental words are spoken in union with the Word-enfleshed. He acts in and
through this human language, and behold, a new creation — baptized,
sealed, absolved, nourished, and thus married "in Christ," the
Bridegroom.

II. WORDS OF FAITH AND OBEDIENCE

In all the sacraments the uttered forms are words of faith, words of prayer, invocation, worship. They are all spoken as consent to the divine Will, that God will effect what he wills in each sacrament. The consent of Marriage involves faith, a matter of current debate in the Church, for what degree of faith should we require of those entering sacramental Marriage?[11]   Deferring that problem till later, we can still say that we find faith, as a "human faith," in the consent itself.

The consent of Marriage is an act of faith in "the other." To be married entails this act of faith, for a spouse can only say, "I take you. . ." in the nuptial sense because he or she believes in the value of "the other" as a spouse. It is interesting to note that all the conditions which we find in the Code regulating true spousal consent are determined by this human faith. This basic faith is only possible when it is free from ignorance concerning Marriage, free from deceit, force or fear, and especially when it is open to the future, the risk of the unconditional gift of self, made with internal sincerity. Under these conditions of human freedom, "I take you . . ." means, in some degree, "I believe in you."

In the sacrament, this human faith is elevated, suffused, as it were, with the virtue of Faith imparted in Baptism. "I believe in you . . ." becomes a word of worship, "I believe in the God who makes us one." This faith may be explicit, with a strong awareness of the sacrament, or implicit, simply embodied in a partner choosing sacramental Marriage, "because I'm a Catholic." But whatever "degree of faith," in the sacrament the partners draw upon their shared Baptism, on the character which places them within the Mystical Body of Christ, on that permanent consecration which makes their consent the cause of a permanent union.

Such sacramental consent, as an act of faith, is graced by God, a consent seeking divine help in the risk of believing in the unknown future of two lives surrendered to one another. But in the "created reality" or "primordial reality" of the human faith in one another, do we not see an implicit seeking of divine help? The act of faith in the other is part of that "preparation for the Gospel," that "whatever good or truth" found among non-believers of which the Fathers of the Second Vatican Council spoke.[12]   As such, in our secularized societies, for a non-believer even to choose Marriage in the face of other options may well represent that implicit faith through which God offers salvation. If this is so in the case of non-believers, how much more is offered explicitly to those who make the consent of faith in sacramental Marriage.

Obedience is essential to faith. We even find it in the implicit faith of the non-believer who chose to submit himself or herself to the binding consent of Marriage. But obedience is explicit in the sacraments, flowing from the obedience of the crucified Son of God. Furthermore, all sacraments are acts of obedience to the commands of the Son to enter his New Covenant by these specific chosen acts. "If you love me, you will keep my commandments" (John 14:15). His sacramental commands are clear: "Go! Baptize . . .," "Do this in memory of me," and, for Marriage, his prophetic word on indissolubility, "So they are no longer two but one (flesh). What therefore God has joined together, let no man put asunder" (Matthew 19:6).

In *Familiaris Consortio*, in the context of faith and sacrament, John Paul II also returned to Genesis to find obedient faith. Because "it is the very conjugal covenant instituted by the Creator 'in the beginning' . . . the decision of a man and a woman to marry in accordance with this divine plan, that is to say, the decision to commit by their irrevocable conjugal consent their whole lives in indissoluble love and unconditional fidelity, really involves, even if not in a fully conscious way, an attitude of profound obedience to the will of God, an attitude which cannot exist without God's grace."[13]

However, the Pope's teaching suggests obedience to the three "goods of matrimony" which, as it were, stand over against both partners as they make their consent. Their obedient faith is to be obedience to the procreative will of God, to the exclusive fidelity he expects of them, to the indissoluble bond established by their consent and sexual union. Yet, to achieve this, husband and wife must be open to the *agape* of Jesus Christ, following Saint Paul's advice in Ephesians, on how they conform themselves to the "great mystery." They will set their hearts on children, fidelity and the bond if they "give way to one another" in the mutual obedience of faith in one another. Let us not hear any fine talk of "the vocation of Christian Marriage" without this obedience to God, embodied in mutual obedience to one another.

The sacramental consent is a surrender of wills, by an act of intellect and will, to be "one flesh," one will, or rather, a harmony of two wills, because the freedom to be one's self is not crushed by obedience to one another.[14] "See, I come to do your Will!" is uttered by consenting spouses, accepting God's vocation and his Grace, that they may do his Will in making their consent a word to "the other": "See, my beloved, I come to do *your* will."

III. MALE AND FEMALE CONSENT

In sacramental consent, each spouse makes consent in differing ways as male and female. In his creation, the Triune God has inscribed reciprocity of gender into the human person, ". . . male and female he created them." Gender is not a function, an accidental quality of a person. Gender is the created condition of being a man, being a woman, through which, at once, the Creator fashioned Marriage. Thus the words of consent, "I take you . . .," constitute this *sacramentum tantum*, in which we find expressed the spousal significance of masculinity and femininity.[15] The unique capacity of man and woman for complementing one another is the sign in the union of Marriage of God's Covenant. He brings together the difference of gender, to make "one flesh," signifying the union and communion between the God-Man and his spouse, the Church, the union and communion of the New Covenant.

In putting an end to the tension and conflict between fallen man and fallen woman through Baptism, God does not do away with gender. When the baptized marry, the groom consents as a husband, the bride consents as a wife. The wording of most forms of consent may be identical, but the giving and receiving is different — yet complementary. It is a dialogue of different genders which are not only physical, but spiritual realities.[16] It is the forming of a unity between persons meant for one another, as male is meant for female, and female is meant for male. It is a unique consent because only between male and female, relating as spouses, can we find this complementary communion of persons.[17]

If that was given by God, in his very act of creating man and woman, so it continues in his act of Redemption. The divine Consent of the Father and the Son is welcomed in Mary's feminine consent, the condition required in creation itself for the Incarnation. Her consent is that of the espoused Church, the bride whose fulfillment is the final eschatological welcome and consent to the Bridegroom, "Amen. Come, Lord Jesus!" (Revelation 22:20).[18]

Therefore, according to the signification of the "great mystery" in the sacrament, the groom is by Baptism an ikon of Jesus the Bridegroom, the second Adam; the bride is by Baptism an ikon of Mary-Church, the second Eve. His consent is the active, dynamic, sacrificial and priestly word of power. Her consent is the receptive, peaceful, welcoming and fruitful word of power. The states of being feminine and being masculine are both necessary for the harmony, equilibrium and unity effected by consent.[19]

We need not be intimidated by those whose ideology reduces gender to a "role," so that masculinity and femininity become interchangeable functions. Gender is canonized by the "great mystery" of the Bridegroom and his bride, the Church; hence the complementary difference between male and female is vindicated by Divine Revelation. But by observing gender, we may discern the differing psychologies of male and female, the differing male and female expectations with which the bride consents to the groom and the groom consents to the bride. They both consent to Marriage, but in differing male and female ways of consenting.

Nevertheless, gender difference is not to be taken to any exaggerated emphasis on the male "active" consent and the female "passive" consent. The bride of Christ is "one flesh" with him, his own body, the Church, endowed by Grace with the capacity to give back to him the love with which he loves her. Thus, Divine Revelation gives Christian spouses an equality in mutual consent, mutual love, while preserving the mystery of gender in the sacrament.

IV. CONSENT AS CHOICE

Finally, let us consider consent as the form of the sacrament under the aspect of human choice. The seeking and finding of a spouse becomes definitive choice in consent. The Popes have emphasized

careful preparation in making this choice for life.[20]   But the choice in
the sacrament signifies a divine choice, made with all the divine patience
of salvation history. God has chosen us in Christ, chosen us in our
creation, in our Baptism. This mystery of our personal "election" is his
choice of a bride, the Church, for his Son, for we become "members of
his body," his spouse, in Baptism. The seeking, finding, and choosing of
his spouse is part of Christ's "great mystery" of spousal love.

In creating us in his own image and likeness, God has given us the
power to choose, to be moral agents, capable of "knowing and choosing
the good." Man and woman were created for the specific good of
Marriage, for that unity towards which their gender complementarity
tends, the "good" of spousal unity written into human gender.[21]   This
good is chosen in the selection of "the other." "I take you . . ." means "I
choose you, and you alone, to be my spouse." It is for this choice of the
good that "a man leaves his father and his mother and cleaves to his
wife, and they become one flesh" (Genesis 2:24). This choice is the
specificity of exclusive spousal love.

At the same time, the choice in the form of Marriage is a choice not
only of the "good" of "the other" but of "us," husband and wife as "one
flesh." It is an effectual choice which changes the isolation of two
individuals into that unique unity. Therefore, in that choice to become
one, both husband and wife choose all that is inherent in Marriage, as
"our" Marriage.

The three "goods" of matrimony are chosen in sacramental consent. An accurate interpretation of Saint Thomas shows us that he saw
the three "goods" not as adjuncts (fines per accidens), but essentials (fines
per se) of Marriage.[22]   In choosing "the other," in the shared choice of
"ourselves" as "one flesh," the form of the sacrament is a commitment to
fidelity and the indissolubility of the sacrament. But if it is commitment
to the most noble end, indissolubility, it is also a commitment to the
primary, natural end, the procreation of children, the gift of life,
nurture and education.

In the sacramental consent, this natural "good" of fecundity is
chosen. For human beings this is not the free fecundity of God who
creates life by his word, nor is it the determined fecundity of animals. It
is the chosen, responsible fecundity of the personal choice of man and
woman.[23]   The consent to become "one flesh" is a choice to be fruitful,

to be open to God's act of his fruitful creation of new persons through the nuptial union. In consenting to give themselves, spouses consent to transmit human life, for, "By means of the reciprocal gift of self, proper and exclusive to them, husband and wife tend towards the communion of their beings in view of mutual personal perfection, to collaborate with God in the generation and education of new lives."[24]

Yet the whole "good" of Marriage, and the "goods" inherent in Marriage, is the gift of God. The sacramental choice is thus an acceptance from God of all that he offers. Unless consent is seen as definitive choice, made under divine Providence as a moral human act, it can be reduced easily to a conditioned response, a social necessity, calculated self-interest or a random possibility, all ways of seeing consent outside of God's Providence, hence outside of a sacrament. By encouraging young men and women to pray for guidance in making the choice of a life partner, so we dispose them to make their sacramental consent as a choice before God. Then indeed, in their consent they will recognize the effectual sacramental word, in words of faith and obedience, in words spoken as man and as woman, in words which choose Marriage and effect its binding contract, which we will now examine.

CONSENT AND CONTRACT

The sacramental consent of Marriage is irrevocable. We have already seen how the scholastic theologians recognized the contractual nature of this irrevocable consent. When dismissing betrothal "*de futuro*" as not being true matrimonial consent, Saint Thomas compared Marriage to "other contracts."[25] He made it clear that words of consent were necessary in Marriage because "there can be no material contract unless it is at the same time accompanied by words which express the will of those who are contracting," taking for granted that the joining-together of Marriage entails obligations, just as in material contracts.[26]

In the contract of sacramental Marriage we find the matter of the sacrament, a mutual exchange of the gift of self, the rights to the body of one another. In saying, "I take you . . .," this giving of rights is a mutually binding agreement. Thus the form of the sacrament expresses what is happening, the giving over of rights and the acceptance of obligations.

In the light of a reaction against the contractual nature of sacramental Marriage, it is interesting to observe the way married people
express the contractual nature of their union. They speak of "Marriage
vows" or "promises" or "tying the knot." Unlike some theologians, they
are not uncomfortable with the human dimension of contract in this
sacrament. If Our Lord can use bread, wine, oil, water, words, why can
he not incorporate the human contract into a sacrament? It is obvious
that Marriage is a *unique* contract, but it is like other contracts because it
establishes the mutual obligations of commutative justice. While we
would want to widen these mutual obligations beyond "rendering the
Marriage debt," including a community of life and especially procreation, the contract keeps before us the binding force of sacramental
consent. By playing down or denying the contract, we not only eliminate the objective standard required by canonists in their work, but we
also damage sacramentality, by weakening the solemnly binding obligations entailed in procreation, fidelity and indissolubility.

I. CONSENT AS EFFICIENT CAUSE

In the contractual dimension of Marriage, we find a more precise
understanding of the effectual power of the "sacramental word" of
consent. The contract is caused by the free and expressed consent of
spouses. Thus consent is the efficient cause of the contract and, through
the binding contract, consent is the efficient cause of Marriage. This
basic *human* causal denominator was identified and defended by the
Magisterium and the theologians of the West.

Consent is the efficient cause of Marriage *through* the binding
contract. The contract is not Marriage. When spouses consent, they
establish the contract as the effective bond, Marriage "*in fieri*," leading
to, and making possible, the *union*, the formal bond of the shared lives in
a consummated Marriage "*in facto esse*."[27] Thus, in the making of Marriage, the contract effects binding unity, but the contract has as its own
final cause the ends of Marriage: procreation in a shared community of
life and love, mutual fidelity, and indissolubility. As effective bond, the
contract has its finality in married life which it establishes.

The contract is the means whereby consent informs the whole of married life. It places a binding obligation on the daily, unspoken but lived, renewal of "I take you. . . ." It sets up the standard of Christ's "great mystery," "giving way to one another" as Saint Paul taught.

In the same context as his linking consent to contract, Saint Thomas stated that the consent is not the Marriage. The consent does not signify the union between Christ and his Church, but it does signify his will, by which it happens that the Church is united to him.[28]   It is this will of Christ whereby his union with the Church was brought about that is to be lived by Christian spouses in their Marriage.

In binding them to one another, the contract binds spouses mutually to the enduring fidelity willed by the Divine Word, in taking our flesh, in espousing us, in dying out of love for his spouse. The making of a human contract seals consent in a human way, yet that contract is raised into the binding power of the Grace of the "great mystery" when Marriage is a holy sacrament of the baptized. Their will to exchange rights and accept obligations is henceforth derived not only from Natural Law principles of commutative justice. In the sacrament, their will is derived from the Justice of the Cross, the salvific will of Christ, sealed in his blood of a new and eternal Covenant, the blood shed for his spouse. Christian spouses can say to one another, "And by that will we have been sanctified through the offering of the body of Jesus Christ once for all" (Hebrews 10:10).

Even though it is God's gratuitous gift to creatures, the New Covenant is contractual. Rightly may Canon 1057, 2 propose "an irrevocable covenant" as a synonym for the contract caused by consent as "an act of will." In his Covenant, Jesus Christ imparts a kind of equality to his spouse, "one flesh" with him, "members of his body." In humble service, he binds himself to her, as in a human contract, requiring obligations of her yet "giving way" to her, by lovingly honoring his will, his promises to be with her always, to sustain her and to come at last to take her to himself.

II. AN ECCLESIAL CONTRACT

The signification of a binding contractual relationship between Christ and his Church is found in the three sacraments which constitute

the Church: Baptism, Confirmation and Orders. In these character
sacraments we accept the obligations and Jesus Christ honors the
promises of his Covenant. But in Marriage, the contractual signification
is clearest, because it comes from *within* the visible *"sacramentum tantum"*
of Marriage itself.

Aware that Our Lord provided no new form for sacramental
Marriage, theologians recognized that Christian Marriage is an already
sacred "created reality" which at its very roots as consent and contract
has been made into a sacrament. Marriage was transformed into a
sacrament not by having something added to its good "created reality"
from outside it; rather it was transformed *from within*, because the
parties who make Christian Marriage have already been transformed
by Baptism. Their sacred contract binds members of the Mystical Body.
Intrinsically transformed, the contract of Christian Marriage is always a
sacrament, always ecclesial. "Nowhere does the mystical life of the
Church penetrate more deeply into natural relationships than in
matrimony. In this sacrament the Church clasps to her heart the first of
all human relationships."[29]

Thus in history the Church insisted on the inseparability of contract and sacrament. At Trent, in *Tametsi*, the Church made the simple
contract into a solemn one, witnessed "by the Church" (*in facie Ecclesiae*)
and registered. But in admitting the validity of clandestine Marriages
up to that time, the Council Fathers recognized that the simple contract
was a sacrament.

After Trent, the Church faced the challenge of those who wished
to bring Marriage under State control, a threat to every dimension of
the morality and stability of Christian Marriage. The Church, resting on
the Council of Florence which spoke of consent as the "efficient cause,"
and on what we inferred from *Tametsi* at Trent, drew on the "more
probable" view regarding the inseparability between contract and sacrament. For Christians, the contract rightly made the sacrament. There is
no alternative lesser degree of "marriage" under civil auspices.
Through the teaching of Pius IX and Leo XIII, this inseparability
between contract and sacrament has the status of *proxima fidei* in
Catholic doctrine.[30] This teaching was well established before the
political struggles with Regalism and liberal secularism.

What the Code of 1983 provides is the same working principle as

that in the Code of 1917.[31]   The sacrament is always a contract, thus
the canonist's question is whether *this* specific contract is or is not a
sacrament. The inseparability between contract and sacrament certainly keeps Marriage within the care of the Church, providing objective standards for canonists and pastors. It places a clear option of faith
before the baptized when they choose to marry — Marriage on the
terms of the Church, as a sacrament, or another kind of union outside
the Church. This is not a denial of religious freedom or a form of
"coercion," as a modern critic has claimed.[32]   It is a challenge to faith,
to decision, to some degree of commitment in pluralist societies where
other options may be freely chosen. But Catholic spouses are meant to
know that Marriage as sacrament is only available within the family of
the Church, and on the terms determined by the Church.

The solemn contract required normally by the Church in the
public mode of celebration is a reminder to spouses that their consent is
never a private act, not even an act between themselves and God alone.
It is the consent of two "members of his Body," to be made in the
community of his Body, the Church, in the celebration of her various
Marriage liturgies. Tertullian rejoiced in the witnessing of Christian
Marriage by the community of the Church and the holy angels. The
Eastern liturgies celebrate Marriage with the blessings, witnessed by the
Mother of God, the saints and angels. Thus the ecclesial witnessing of
this spousal contract extends beyond time to the Church in glory.

To maintain the public ecclesial nature of consent before God and
the whole Church, the sacrament should truly be celebrated before the
Eucharistic altar, in the heart of the parish community, visibly linked in
place and symbol to the other sacraments of God's People. With the
welcome of patient pastoral preparation, such insistence on a sacred
contract made in a sacred place may be, for those of minimal faith, a call
to deeper faith and thus to a serious attitude towards Marriage as a
sacrament.

That the normal, binding consent and contract occurs in a church
further signifies the ecclesial meaning of the "great mystery" of Christ
who ". . . gave himself totally by giving his life for his beloved community; he was and is totally faithful to his community. Husband and wife
are united not just because they are 'one flesh,' that is created for
one another, complementing one another as human persons but also

because they are Christians who are loved by Christ and united in their love for Christ. They are therefore, married 'in the Lord.' "[33]

CONSENT AND LOVE

In considering consent and contract, we have anticipated the bond of Marriage which will be developed further in Chapter Five. In considering consent as a way to understand spousal love in a sacramental way, we have anticipated the Grace imparted in "getting married" and being married. Up to this point our concentration, though, has been on consent as the visible, effectual sign of Marriage. Through its causality, that visible dimension of mutual consent informs the love of husband and wife, the love infused with the Love of God, Source of all love.

To be truly "fruitful," the sacrament is meant to include love, a love which Pope Paul VI proposed as fully human, total, faithful and exclusive, and fruitful in procreation.[34]   All sacraments are challenges insofar as they set up ideals of Christian life. Marriage certainly sets forth ideals. Even as pastoral sense lays down a minimum for sacramental Marriage, so let us never cease to proclaim and propose the ideal of married love, especially as it can be realized through the Grace of this sacrament of Christ's love for his Church.

I. IN THE HEART OF CHRIST

Let us return now to the Source of Love, to the "eternal decree" of the Word proceeding from the Father, to the Consent of the Incarnate Word, to Mary's "Fiat," to the consent of Christ to "go up to Jerusalem" and die for his spouse. This loving consent is more than a simple model for Marriage. "The faithful love existing between Christ and his Church is more than an example for Christian marriage. The self-giving of husband and wife is more than an image of Christ's giving of himself to the Church. In effect, the mutual love of husband and wife is a sign that makes present the self-giving love of Christ, a sacrament which communicates and realizes the saving love which Christ has for his Church."[35]

The self-giving love of Christ, his *agape*, though, may seem too exalted, too spiritual, to be involved in the love of Marriage, friendship, *philia*, and especially sexual love, *eros*. Concerning erotic love, the reproach has been leveled: "The spiritualizers always want to transform it into *agape*."[36] But that would make Saint Paul become the first of these so-called "spiritualizers," for this *agape* is the spousal love he proposed in Ephesians! Yet this love is not up in some spiritual realm; it is among us as Love Incarnate in Christ.

As model or source of this love for spouses, this Love Incarnate has been expressed accurately by Pope Pius XII in his encyclical on the Sacred Heart of Jesus, *Haurietis Aquas*, May 15, 1956. Through the Incarnation, we see the joining and harmony of divine and human love, for "Nothing, therefore was lacking in the human nature which the Word of God joined to Himself. Indeed He assumed a human nature in no way diminished or changed in its spiritual or bodily capacities, that is, a nature endowed with intelligence and will and the other internal and external faculties of perception, with sense appetites and all the natural impulses."[37]

Pius XII found a threefold love in the Heart of Christ. He first found "that divine love which He shares with the Father and the Holy Spirit, but which in Him alone, in the Word namely that was made flesh, is manifested to us through a frail, mortal human body, since 'In Him dwells the fullness of the Godhead bodily,' (Colossians 2:9)."[38] Then he found "that most ardent love which, infused into His soul, enriches the human will of Christ, and whose action is enlightened and directed by a twofold most perfect knowledge, namely the beatific and infused."[39] Finally, he found "sensible love, since the body of Jesus Christ, formed by the operation of the Holy Spirit in the womb of the Virgin Mary, has a most perfect capacity for feeling and perception, much more than the bodies of other men."[40] Thus, in the Heart of the Incarnate Word, we see divine and human love in united harmony.

This is the Heart of the Bridegroom. Pius XII saw the Heart of Christ, a human instrument assumed in the Incarnation as "the true symbol of the boundless love by which our Savior, through the shedding of His blood, contracted a mystical marriage with the Church." At once he cited Saint Thomas, "Through charity He suffered for the Church who was to be united to Him as His spouse."[41] He saw this union also as the birth of the Church and the outpouring of the sacraments from Christ's wounded Heart.[42]   Finally, he recognized in the Resurrection triumph the eternal love of the Bridegroom for his spouse: "After our Savior ascended into Heaven — his body adorned with the splendor of eternal glory — and sat at the right hand of the Father, He did not cease to bestow upon His spouse, the Church, that ardent love with which His Heart beats."[43]

To those who are "in Christ," to those married "in the Lord," the Bridegroom imparts this same love. Because spouses participate in this Love Incarnate, in the love of the Hypostatic Union, their human love can be taken up into his *agape*. Their sexual love and their spousal friendship is not quenched by this love of his Heart, for this is the Heart of flesh in which the Marriage of divine and human love has already been accomplished. Their human love is redeemed, elevated and brought to its generous ends: the procreation and education of children in the Church, the fidelity which endures all trials, the indissolubility derived from the higher unity of the divine and the human in Christ.

In their mutual consent, "I take you . . .," husband and wife place themselves in the Heart of Christ, not only to learn the art of loving, but to draw from his Heart the Grace to love. Rightly indeed is that glorious Heart of flesh enthroned in so many Christian homes.

II. IN HUMAN HEARTS

Jesus Christ imparts the love of his Heart to the hearts of those who are married in the sacrament of his love. We can give this more concrete meaning by reflecting on the human heart in the Jewish, biblical tradition, where the heart is not the passive symbol of Western romanticism. In its popular sensual and sentimental form, that romanticism encourages a narrow, subjective and irrational understanding of love, which is not the sublime love to which spouses consent, and towards which their consent is directed in sacramental Marriage.

In the Jewish biblical tradition, the heart is the center of intellect and will. It is thus the central organ which integrates the whole person, a rational and volitional center for intentionality and commitment: ". . . where your treasure is, there will your heart be also"

(Matthew 6:21). The heart is the source of the commitment of the
whole person.[44] Pharaoh's heart was "hardened" against the children of
Israel, and hearts are likewise described as fearful, blind, stubborn,
veiled, pure, and gentle. Mary's heart pondered on the events in the life
of her Son (cf. Luke 2:19; 2:21). In fulfillment of prophecy (Jeremiah
31:33-34), the new Law is written in people's hearts (cf. Hebrews 10:16).
Thus, in the heart, the Scriptures present the total commitment of a
person, rational, volitional and emotional.

In nuptial consent, spouses make that commitment of the heart to
one another. Their consent initiates Marriage, thus it is meant to initiate
a total commitment of two hearts to one another. In living that commitment, they will need generous hearts for the procreation of children, in
a love which is not only a consent to live for themselves. They will need
to share the custody of the heart, to maintain fidelity, the one to the
other. They will need strength of heart to persevere in the indissolubility of this sacrament. In the realities of married life, they need the Grace
of the generosity, custody and strength of the Heart of Christ, which is
what he offers in the sacrament, as their mutual consent places them
both within the self-sacrificial consent of his Heart.

Let a young married Catholic couple place the realities of this total
commitment before us: "The total self-giving of marriage . . . is primarily an attitude of mind and heart, the total commitment of each spouse's
whole personality to the other. It would be foolish to pretend that this is
something easy, and even more foolish to pretend that the sensation of
'being in love' in a starry-eyed way, though very delightful, will be
sufficient to last through all the difficulties of life." Then they take us
into the "great mystery," as they make their own act of faith: "Christ's
own act of commitment to us led him to the cross; his covenant was
sealed with the sacrifice of his life. So too the covenant of marriage will
sometimes have to take part in the pain and agony of the cross. But, as
St. Paul in another context could say, 'Christ's grace is enough for us.'
Christ committed his spirit into the hands of the Father and in marriage
the spouses commit their lives to the Author of Life. The sacrament of
marriage gives us the 'grace of state,' the spiritual gifts which come from
sharing in Christ's redemptive power."[45]

If ". . . where your treasure is, there will your heart be also," so in
sacramental consent each spouse sets his or her heart on "the other," on

the beloved, as his or her "treasure" or "pearl of great price." The poetry
of the Song of Songs aptly expresses their mutual intention to persevere
in love in the life they will share from this moment of consent: "Set me as
a seal upon your heart . . ."(8:6). In this great sacrament, these words
may likewise become a prayer they address together to Christ the
Bridegroom: "Set *us* as a seal on your Heart." Then, indeed, he will
become the hidden Treasure of their Marriage.

III. CONSENT FOR CONSUMMATION

Marriage is not the coming together of two minds. It is the union
and communion of two persons, consummated and expressed in sexual
union. Consent is not only a consent for the mutual pleasure of sexual
union. It is a choice for "one flesh," expressed and made permanent by
sexual union.[46]

The right to sexual union, the right "over the body" of the other
partner, is not to be parodied as if this is reducing the consent and
contract to a dealing in flesh. The right to the body of the other partner
is a profound right, normally inherent in the mutual consent. In that
mutual consent, the specific choice of "the other" is exclusive, so that
henceforth no one else may ever claim sexual union with "the other,"
but the one who says, "I take you. . . ."

Let us not forget the sexual meaning in that particular formula, "I
take you. . . ." The "taking" in words of consent is to be fulfilled and
completed in the mutual "taking" of bodily union. The words of consent
cause, by solemn contract, a Marriage that is valid, ratified before God
and his Church. But the fulfilling and completion of this natural bond is
by the bodily enactment and expression of the words in sexual union.
This consummation is the mutual accomplishment of what consent
initiated, and the Marriage becomes ratified and consummated (*ratum et
consummatum*). The natural bond is perfected and becomes the indissoluble bond of Marriage which no human power can dissolve.

Consent is thus revealed in consummation, not merely as consent
to sexual intercourse, but as consent to the total giving of self in an
exclusive and absolutely binding way. The next chapter will develop
the meaning and purpose of sexuality and its sacramental nature in

Marriage.[47] Here, while we remain in the area of spousal consent, consummation is necessary to throw further light on the deeper meanings of the choice, already outlined as: (1) reflecting our baptismal "election" in Christ, (2) an exclusive ethical choice of *this* partner (the good, specificity), (3) a choice to become "us" in "one flesh," and (4) a choice of the "goods" of Marriage, especially procreation. The providential nature of this spousal choice under the guidance of God was also underlined. It is, therefore, a choice to be made in a responsible way, with prayer. This act of the will is the heart of conjugal love.[48]

However, if consent is made in love and for love, then consent for consummation is a choice to give oneself in love. This consent for consummation may be understood at two levels: (1) choosing to give the self to "the other," (2) choosing to receive the other, acceptance. The giving is well-known, and in the sacrament, it signifies the self-giving of Jesus Christ. His consent to give himself to the Church and for the Church, was accomplished with his cry, "It is consummated!" In her consent, perfectly expressed in Mary, the Church receives his gift of himself, and is taken into his immolation, which is the Eucharistic sacrifice, his sacrifice made the sacrifice of the espoused Church giving herself back to her Bridegroom.

In the next chapter we will develop this Eucharistic "consummation" further, in the more precise context of the sacred bond. However, in the context of consent, that second level of consent for consummation ought to be appreciated in its sacramental dimension. To choose to accept "the other" is a mutual realistic love, accepting the self-gift of the beloved. In their consent, Christian spouses are called to recapitulate the acceptance of the Heart of Christ, welcoming sinners with all their faults, weaknesses and blemishes. Thus each spouse accepts the beloved not as some imaginary ideal figure, but as he or she is. Without that reasonable honesty, there can be no sure foundation for married love, for a love which will be called upon again and again not only to say, "I'm sorry," but, "I forgive you." That is the absolving love with which the Bridegroom accepts his beloved Church.

Let us take that to a further, more subtle level. If consent is for consummation, meaning not sexual union in itself, but the completeness and exclusive love accomplished by union, then even in the moments of mutual consent acceptance may be experienced and

expressed. Hearing "I take you . . .," the beloved may marvel with the
wonder of love, "How wonderful that you exist — for me!" But the
Christian spouse is called precisely to marvel with the humility of being
accepted in love, "You chose me! But you could have chosen someone
else." The response of the beloved, uttered or unspoken, is always the
specific choice of the good, the choice of "the other" for his or her value
and self-worth — "But I chose *you!*"

IV. THE CONSENT OF THE CHURCH

In all the sacraments we are chosen and accepted by Jesus Christ.
The fruitfulness of each sacrament is intensified by the loving awe of the
experience of this acceptance. Each of us voices the continual consent of
the espoused Church, the wonder of the Bride in the sacramental
embrace of her Bridegroom who died for love of his beloved.

In Marriage, the sacrament is likewise fruitful in a literal re-
enactment of this "great mystery" of the mutual acceptance of Christ
and his Church. "But I chose you!" may well be echoed by a rhetorical
question, "But why did you choose *me?*" In being chosen, in being
accepted, the beloved is humbled. Thus the first fruit of sacramental
consent is a mutual putting on of the humility of the espoused Church.

This ecclesial consent is fruitful in both forms of self-giving love, in
Marriage and holy virginity. Hans Urs Von Balthasar has observed that
"The 'yes' of the Marriage vow and the 'yes' of the counsels correspond
to what God expects man to be in imitation of Jesus Christ who, on the
Cross, gave all he possessed, body and soul, for the Father and the
world. In the state of election, the Christian gives his body and soul to
God, and God dispenses the fruit of his sacrifice to his brethren,
conferring on the one who has made the sacrifice a mission within the
Church. In the married state, the Christian, by his sacramental 'yes,'
gives his body and soul to his spouse — but always in God, out of belief
in God, and with confidence in God's bountiful fidelity, which will not
deny to this gift of self the promised physical and spiritual fruit."[49]

Through the spiritual fruitfulness of giving and accepting in nuptial consent, spouses are open to God. They consent to be the Church of
the married Christians, to form the "domestic church," the family unit

of the greater Family of God. Thus, the love they express in the choice to give and receive is not only a consent to love one another, "for better, for worse, for richer, for poorer, until death do us part." It is a love which goes beyond themselves to seek fruitfulness in children.

By the divine will, inscribed into gender in creation, there is a continuity in the physical fruitfulness of married love: "Be fruitful and multiply, and fill the earth . . ." (Genesis 1:28). In Israel this fruitful love was cherished and valued: "Your wife will be like a fruitful vine within your house; your children will be like olive shoots around your table" (Psalm 127:3). In the New Israel, the sacramental consent is openness to God, the Author of life, that he will increase the Family of the Church in granting the gift of children.

Therefore, in two ways we may see this consent for fruitfulness in the sacrament. As ikon of Christ, the husband consents to give himself to his wife, who accepts his gift of fruitful life, as the Church accepts her Lord, for she is the Marian ikon of openness to divine fruitful love. But, in a second way, as Christians choosing to be "one flesh," consenting spouses place themselves at the disposal of God, offering their "one flesh" to his creativity, offering their consent for consummation as a consent for a further accomplished love, the procreation of children, the making of the domestic church.

V. THE SIMPLICITY OF CONSENT

To draw out the implications and meanings of sacramental consent may seem to make this human act complicated and subtle. Does not this range of fruitful ideals raise spousal consent to a level which demands acute spiritual and intellectual awareness? Do we not demand a precise and refined sacramental intention of those who enter this sacrament? But the Church keeps this sacramental consent simple and thus accessible to all her members who intend to marry.

The Code is clear that, "Provided it does not determine the will, error concerning the unity or the indissolubility or the sacramental dignity of marriage does not vitiate matrimonial consent."[50]   Provided they are free and have a general intention to marry as Christians marry, mistaken notions of Marriage do not prevent Christians from becoming the ministers of this sacrament to one another as they make their consent.[51]   While we must propose and proclaim the deeper sacred meanings of this consent and solemn contract, we dare not complicate the celebration of the sacrament so as to make it a pious Pelagian exercise in subjective faith and subtle intentionality. Then Christian Marriage would be only accessible to an elite, holy minority. Obviously, when they make their consent, many couples are not aware of every dimension of Marriage and the graces offered to them. But sacraments are for our weakness, and the operation of this sacrament is ultimately the work of the Holy Spirit.

The simplicity of consent is a call to unconditional faith, open to the unknown future, to risk, even to suffering. Facing one another in that quiet parish church, a man and a woman place their simple human consent into the great Heart of Jesus Christ, and he, the unseen Guest at their Cana, joins their vows to the undying love he has for his spouse, the Church. At that moment the sincere gift of their two hearts may seem uncertain, frail and small, but in the years which lie ahead, they will learn that ". . . God is greater than our hearts" (1 John 3:20).

CHAPTER FIVE

The Sacramental Bond

En sus brazos tiernamente
Y allí su amor la daría;
Y que así juntos en uno
Al Padre la llevaría.

Tenderly in His arms He'll take her
With all the love that God can give
And draw her nearer to the Father
All in unison to live.

Donde del mismo deleite
Que Dios goza, gozaría;
Que, como el Padre y el Hijo,
Y el que de ellos procedía.

There with the single, same rejoicing
With which God revels, she will thrill,
Revelling with the Son, the Father,
And that which issues from Their Will.

El uno vive en el otro,
Así la esposa sería,
Que, dentro de Dios absorta,
Vida de Dios viviría.

Each one living in the other;
Samely loved, clothed, fed and shod
She, absorbed in Him forever,
She will live the Life of God.

Saint John of the Cross, *Romance IV*

We are at the heart of the sacrament, which is the work of God according to the definitive teaching of Jesus: " '. . . and the two shall become one.' So they are no longer two but one. What therefore God has joined together, let no man put asunder" (Mark 10:8-9). It is God who joins husband and wife in this sacred bond as they exchange their mutual consent and consummate their solemn nuptial contract by sexual union, the sign of their total giving of self to one another.

We have already seen that Saint Augustine perceived that joining together which is the indissolubility of Christian Marriage as a "conjugal thing," a "nuptial bond."[1]   Saint Thomas further identified this bond as the contained reality, *"res et sacramentum,"* of Marriage, analogous to the permanent character of Baptism, Confirmation and Orders, but not eternal, rather indissoluble as long as bodily death does not separate the spouses.[2]

From this bond, based on it, guarded by it, and in a sense, responding to it, true married love grows in a ministry of Grace to one another within the family. Pope John Paul II observed: "Like each of the seven sacraments so also marriage is a real symbol of the event of salvation, but in its own way. The spouses participate in it as spouses together, as a couple, so that the first and immediate effect of marriage (*res et sacramentum*) is not supernatural grace itself, but the Christian conjugal bond, a typically Christian communion of two persons because it represents the mystery of Christ's Incarnation and the mystery of His Covenant.' "[3]

John Paul II makes it clear that supernatural Grace is not the immediate effect of Marriage. The bond (*res et sacramentum*) is the immediate effect of Marriage. We may infer from his words that it is because of this bond that we refer to spouses "together" as a "couple." This is the familiar way of referring to those who are "one flesh" in a Marriage that is both ratified by mutual consent and consummated through sexual union. John Paul II proposes this bond in a rich, personalized way as a "typically Christian communion of two persons," adding at once why it is both "typically Christian" and "binding" — "because it represents the mystery of Christ's Incarnation and the mystery of His Covenant."

The bond is derived from the "great mystery" which is signified and extended in the "one flesh" of husband and wife. Because it comes from God, signifying the "great mystery" of Christ the Bridegroom, it is a supernatural bond, a divine gift. It is an abiding and effectual gift when two persons already raised to supernatural life in Baptism minister Marriage to one another by their consent and sexual union.

We return again to consent as it is directed towards consummation. The words of consent initiate the "language of the body," so that man and woman become an unrepeatable, permanent sign "for all the days of my life," a sign of permanent, interpersonal communion based on the New Covenant of Jesus Christ.[4]   This coupling, however, must actually take place to make the bond indissoluble. Consent may be said to establish the beginning of a Marriage (*matrimonium initiatum*) since it effects the sacramental bond. Consummation, though, is what renders that bond indissoluble. Canon 1141 in the Code states that such a Marriage (which is ratified and consummated) cannot be dissolved by any human power or any cause other than death. Canon 1142, however, does provide for the dissolution of the *non*-consummated Marriage between baptized persons at the request of both or either party, even if one party is unwilling. The Pope can exercise this power for a just reason.

In *Casti Connubii*, Pius XI pointed out that the Church can dissolve a Marriage which is ratified but not consummated, adding, "However not even this power can ever affect for any cause whatsoever a Christian marriage which is valid and has been consummated, for it is plain here that the marriage contract has its full completion (*maritale foedus plene perficitur*) so, by the will of God, there is also the greatest firmness and indissolubility which may not be destroyed by any human authority."[5]

Consent thus establishes a sacramental Marriage but consummation perfects the bond. To use a translation of *"foedus"* in Pius XI more in keeping with post-conciliar language, the bond is the perfection of the marital "covenant." In understanding better this abiding center of Christian Marriage, let us reflect: (1) on the Holy Spirit, true Author of the bond which makes spouses one, (2) on the "sacramentality" of the body in Marriage as spouses become "one flesh," and (3) on indissolubility, that quality of the bond which links spouses together "until death do us part." In such a reflection, the binding strength and challenge of true married love is revealed.

THE BOND OF THE HOLY SPIRIT

All the sacraments include a specific operation of the Holy Spirit. In Baptism, we find the Spirit of regeneration, justification and sanctification. Confirmation is itself the seal of the Holy Spirit. In the Eucharist the Holy Spirit is invoked in the *epiklesis* upon the gifts and, after the consecration, on those who will receive the Body and Blood of Christ, sanctified in the Spirit: ". . . and all were made to drink of the one Spirit" (1 Corinthians 12:13). In Penance, the Spirit is sent among us for the forgiveness of sins. In Holy Orders, men are consecrated by the Holy Spirit. In the Anointing of the Sick, the Spirit imparts strength and healing. Indeed, in all the sacraments, apart from these specific operations, we recognize the operative power of the Holy Spirit through whom all the works of God are accomplished among us. But how is the Holy Spirit operative in a specific way in Marriage?

We may distinguish two closely related ways in which the Holy Spirit is effective in Marriage: (1) the Spirit of unity effects the bond (*res et sacramentum*), his objective consecration wrought through the spouses in their consent and consummation; and (2) on the basis of this indissoluble bond, the Spirit of Christ's love, his *agape*, is poured into the hearts of spouses in their lived *koinonia*, the interpersonal unity of the lived bond, the Grace (*res tantum*) of married life as fidelity to the bond.

I. ONE FLESH IN THE SPIRIT

The first and fundamental operation of the Holy Spirit may be derived from the "great mystery" itself. The Spirit was operative in our creation when the Creator God breathed his spirit (*ruah*) into Adam. Marriage, as the "primordial sacrament" and "created reality" was "from the beginning" the work of the Spirit through human beings. Every Marriage recapitulates the creation and purpose of gender and is a "sacrament of creation," the work of the creating Spirit.[6]

In the Incarnation we find the Spirit overshadowing Our Lady, thus effecting the Hypostatic Union in the Person of Jesus Christ, the Word made flesh. Consummated sacramental Marriage represents in its indissoluble bond the higher, eternal and absolute unity between the divine Nature and human nature in Christ. We have seen how Saint Thomas saw the union between Christ and his Church as the Incarnation, one ground of indissolubility. This union between Christ and his Church cannot be broken "insofar as it is his assumption of human nature in the unity of his person, which is completely indissoluble."[7] But if the Holy Spirit effected *that* Hypostatic Union — our espousal by

Christ as his Church — and if that is what is signified in the bond of consummated Marriage, then the Spirit effects that bond between the spouses.

In the conscious espousals enacted by Christ the Bridegroom we also find the Holy Spirit promised by Christ as his gift of unity and truth to the Church. In the deeper mystical espousal of the Church on the Cross we saw the Spirit breathed forth into the Bride, the "*Spiritus de Spiritu*" or "*Spiramen*," recapitulation of the nuptial act of creation, for from the side of the pierced Second Adam comes forth the Bride.[8]   So she who is "one flesh" with Christ, his body, is created in his "It is finished!" ("*Consummatum est!*") when he breathed forth his Spirit which, on Calvary, anticipated Pentecost. Because this Bride of Christ is joined to her Spouse by the Spirit, so human spouses who signify and recapitulate this "great mystery" are likewise made "one flesh" by the Holy Spirit.

The Prophet who promised the Spirit, and the Priest-Victim breathing forth the Spirit in his death of love, is also the King, the risen Lord, Head of his Bride, Head of the Mystical Body. In his Resurrection (raised for our justification), the Bridegroom is the eternal undying Spouse of the Church. Eternally one with his Father, he imparts the Holy Spirit to his Bride. Saint Augustine perceived this dimension of indissolubility within the "great mystery" when he wrote, "for the Church living with Christ who lives for ever may never be divorced from him."[9]   Christ Jesus, raised in the Spirit, imparts the Spirit to human spouses as they enter the bond of Marriage, called to represent his same eternal, deathless love and constant communion with his Church.

Therefore, returning to the archetype, we find the signification of the "great mystery," the "*sacramentum tantum*," forming the "*res et sacramentum*," the indissoluble nuptial bond. From each major phase of the "great mystery" the Holy Spirit may be rightly appropriated as the effectual cause of the indissoluble nuptial bond. This will become even clearer when we consider the role and work of the Holy Spirit within the Mystical Body.

II. THE SPIRIT OF UNITY IN THE CHURCH

When we related the "great mystery" to an analysis of Saint Paul's exhortation on Marriage in Ephesians 5, that exhortation had to be placed in its important context — a call to unity within the Church at Ephesus. Saint Paul's words point directly to the unifying work of the Holy Spirit in the Church: "I, therefore, a prisoner for the Lord, beg you to lead a life worthy of the calling to which you have been called, with all lowliness and meekness, with patience, forbearing one another in love, eager to maintain the unity of the Spirit in the bond of peace. For there is one body and one Spirit" (Ephesians 4:1-4). These words introduce his detailed exhortations to unity, where we find the teaching on Marriage and the "great mystery."

Within the Church, the "unity of the Spirit in the bond of peace" is the work of the Holy Spirit, especially through the sacraments whereby Christ's faithful grow in faith, hope and charity. Moreover, the Holy Spirit may rightly be described as the "soul of the Mystical Body," or ". . . that vital principle by which the whole community of Christians is sustained by its Founder."[10]   The unity of the Holy Spirit rests on our Baptism, "For by one Spirit we were all baptized into one body . . ." (1 Corinthians 12:13). The work of the Holy Spirit is likewise that of the "Organizer" of the Church, effectively and intimately directing, guiding, correcting and bringing into harmony and order all the living members of the Body of Christ, as we see vividly described by Saint Luke in the Acts of the Apostles.[11]

Christian spouses were reminded by Saint Paul that they too are "members of his body." How then are they to signify the "great mystery" of "one flesh" if not through the power of the Holy Spirit? Saint Paul, in the very context of advising Christians that their Marriage bond does not hold if a pagan partner wishes to separate, also reminded husbands and wives that "God has called us to peace" (1 Corinthians 7:15). But how can there be any abiding bond of Christian Marriage, unless it is through "the unity of the Spirit in the bond of peace"?

The ecclesial nature of the Marriage of Christians indicates an ordered basis for the contention that the bond, the "*res et sacramentum*," between the spouses is the work of the Holy Spirit.

To take this work of the Spirit further, into the bond itself, it would be useful to develop certain points of Matthias Scheeben. In discussing the Marriage of Adam and Eve in the state of innocence and how this may well have led to the generation of children in a state of Grace, Scheeben said: "When our first parents contracted their union with each other, they also entered into union with the Holy Spirit as the principle of supernatural grace, so that He cooperated with them not only with his creative power, but with his divine generative power. Thus the Holy Spirit, the source of supernatural blessing in the consummation of the union, became also the pledge and seal of the union in its very formation."[12]

Nevertheless, in spite of the Fall, by being raised to become members of the Mystical Body of Christ, Christians enjoy a more sublime Marriage than this primordial union sealed by the Spirit. Their fruitfulness in procreation has the higher goal of extending the Mystical Body, for their union is that of "two consecrated members of Christ's Body," bearing the indelible character of Christ. "They can unite with each other only on the basis of their oneness with Christ; the union of each with the divine head is carried over into the union which they contract with each other. The former union transfigures and consolidates the latter."[13] We return to the principle of the inner transformation of natural Marriage into sacramental Marriage because the partners are already transformed, in Christ by Baptism, before they come together in the sacrament.

Citing Saint Bernard of Clairvaux, Scheeben set out the prior espousal by God of each soul, using nuptial imagery: "The real indwelling of the Spirit of the bridegroom in His bride is to the spiritual marriage of the Son of God with the soul what corporal union is in corporal marriage, a union to which bride and bridegroom aspire in their reciprocal love. Hence it can be regarded as the consummation and sealing of the affectional union between the Son of God and the soul."[14] Now if we are thus united to Christ in an indwelling of the Holy Spirit, it is evident that the nuptial bond completed by the "corporal union" of Christian spouses is likewise the work of the Holy Spirit, albeit not in the same sense of indwelling, but rather as effecting an indissoluble unity, just as he effects the eternal realities of the characters in Baptism, Confirmation and Orders. In giving their very selves to one another in consummated Marriage, Christians receive this gift of indissolubility from the Spirit who is himself the gift of Love between the Father and the Son.[15]

In a bodily way, through sexual union and shared lives, they participate to some degree in the Unity of the Spirit which is within the Holy Trinity. We will return to this in the context of the bond as love. But we may learn this from the "great mystery," as Christ breathes forth his Spirit from the Cross, becoming "one flesh" with his bride, the Church, with us. As Christian husbands and wives are to show forth this great archetype in which they already share, they receive the Spirit as unity, as it were, imparting the Spirit of unity to one another in mutual consent and the self-surrender of consummation.

But can the flesh in sexual union be an instrument or means of such a sublime and sacred bond? Again we turn to Scheeben, applying his principle of the Incarnation in a way he did not apply it to Marriage: "Material nature, which ordinarily tends to draw the spirit itself down from its native eminence, was raised so high by the Incarnation that henceforward, endowed with divine energy, it was to cooperate in effecting the supernatural elevation of the spirit. So great was the blessing which the Incarnation of the God-man shed over matter, that the flesh could become, and was made to become, the vehicle of the Holy Spirit."[16]

This is the sacramental principle. But it renders sexual union in Christian Marriage a part of the sacramental order. The indissoluble bond is perfected by consummation, accomplished by two members of the Mystical Body of Christ. Thus consummation in sexual union is "the vehicle of the Holy Spirit," and he is the true source of the sacred and inviolable bond. Moreover, the Spirit abides in Marriage on the basis of this bond, for if each Christian family is the "domestic church," a miniature Mystical Body of Christ, then the Spirit abides in each family as the Soul of that "domestic church." Yet he abides only because Christians have first become "one flesh," made one in the "unity of the Spirit in the bond of peace."

III. CONSECRATION

We have already introduced the "consecration" of the sacrament of Marriage in considering how the "great mystery" can enter the lives of a

Christian man and woman as they celebrate Marriage.[17]   Because they are already permanently consecrated by Baptism to their organic place as "members of his body," so they are consecrated as married members of that same Mystical Body of Christ. The consecration of sacramental Marriage is not the permanent setting-apart for worship within Christ's Priesthood which is the consecration of the indelible characters as outlined by Saint Thomas.[18]   But it does bear comparison insofar as the permanent element in Marriage, the bond (res et sacramentum) bears comparison with the permanent gift of the Spirit in Baptism, Confirmation and Orders. Moreover, the bond has a binding ecclesial power, for by consent and sexual union, husband and wife not only form the permanent bond for the unity of their shared lives and growth of their family, but for the unity and growth of the Church. This is why the consecration wrought in Marriage, like the strictly organic consecrations of the character sacraments, renders Marriage part of the being (esse) rather than the well-being (bene esse) of the Church.[19]

But what did Scheeben, Pope Pius XI and the Fathers of the Second Vatican Council mean by qualifying the consecration of Marriage by "as it were consecrated . . ."?[20]   The sacred bond of the Holy Spirit would seem to provide the answer if we ask the question: In what sense can a bond between husband and wife be a "consecration"?

Jesus Christ, Priest and Bridegroom of the Church, consecrated himself at the Last Supper as Priest and as Victim. He set himself apart for the sacred duty of obedient love, his self-immolation on the Cross. As the God-Man, Son of the Father, he was already consecrated as Priest by the Hypostatic Union, "a high priest, holy, blameless, unstained, separated from sinners, exalted above the heavens" (Hebrews 7:26), a Priest by the divine decree of his generation as the Son (cf. Hebrews 1:5; 5:5-6). As Bridegroom seeking his beloved spouse, he consents to die out of love for her, to become her Victim-Spouse. Thus at the Last Supper, his nuptial consent is offered to the Father: "And for their sake I consecrate myself, that they also may be consecrated in truth" (John 17:19). He sets himself apart as Victim for his beloved spouse, a consent fulfilled in "my body which will be given up for you . . .," "my blood which will be shed for you and for many," and in the "Consummatum est!" of the Cross. This consent and self-giving was specific, exclusive and total for his beloved spouse. He set himself apart in consecration for her.

Likewise, by consent and self-surrender in consummation, a Christian husband and a Christian wife set themselves apart, in consecration for one another. They do not do this by their own power; rather, they provide the human consent and the bodily union through which the Holy Spirit binds them together as "one flesh." As they do not effect this by their own power, neither they nor any other human power can eradicate or dissolve this mutual consecration. What they purposed in consent is accomplished by bodily union; henceforth, as Saint Paul taught, ". . . the wife does not rule over her own body, but the husband does; likewise the husband does not rule over his own body, but the wife does" (1 Corinthians 7:4). Each belongs to the other through that specific choice of the beloved, "the good" which we found in sacramental consent, through the exclusive and total self-giving of sexual union.

That which is consecrated is set apart in a sacred way for sacred purposes. Just as Christ Jesus set himself apart for the sacred, exclusive union with his beloved Church — with us — so husband and wife are set apart in this sacred bond of the Spirit for an exclusive union. As the Bridegroom was "one flesh" with his beloved spouse, so she could belong to no other party, and rightly could she claim his fidelity in return. Thus the setting-apart of nuptial consecration is for one another, set apart to be together, to be "ourselves" in the "one flesh."

This bond is consecrated because it is complete in the union of two bodies of two baptized persons, each a "temple of the Holy Spirit" (1 Corinthians 6:19). Already belonging to the Holy Spirit, already flesh and blood consecrated by him, they can only be "one flesh" through him. Now, in the bond of the Spirit, they form one "temple of the Holy Spirit," never to be violated by infidelity. If adultery is a sin against this sacred bond of the Spirit whereby spouses consecrate one another in "one flesh," likewise to be ruled out is a termination of shared life without just grounds, or a preference of common life with some other person, even without sexual union. By the sacred and exclusive nature of this consecration, Christian husbands and wives are bound to fidelity (*fides*), the second "good" of Marriage, the fidelity of Christ Jesus who gave his body and blood so as to become one flesh with his Bride.

A sublime truth is, therefore, both expressed and sealed when the new spouses receive the Body and Blood of their Lord in the Nuptial Mass. The first Food of these two lives bound together underlines the

mutual consecration of their bodies, their selves. His Holy Communion
with them shows forth the "great mystery" to which they are raised by
the bond of the Spirit. His Holy Communion with their new "temple of
the Holy Spirit," their "one flesh," invites them to live in a perpetual
communion of life and love, which will likewise be the work of the
gentle Paraclete.

IV. THE BOND OF LOVE

Two hearts set on one another in the consent were raised into the
loving consent of the Heart of Christ. Now that consent is consummated in sexual union, what the consent initiated and established is
permanent, "until death do us part." They have consented and united
to be open to the love, the *agape*, of Jesus Christ which the Holy Spirit
pours into their hearts (cf. Romans 5:5).

Because the bond is not a "thing," but a permanent union and
communion of two persons, it distinguishes Marriage from "living
together." "Love always aspires to permanence. To love another totally,
but only for a time, is a contradiction in terms."[21]   In the bond of the
Spirit, husband and wife renounce the "freedom" of cohabitation, a
relationship which is based on the temporary kind of sexuality because
no act of sexual union can have anything but a transitory meaning
where there is always freedom to depart. In the bond of the Spirit,
nuptial consummation and every act of sexual union thereafter means
"forever," because this "one flesh" is the temple of the Spirit and can
only cease to be "one flesh" when death allows that temple to cease to be.

In renouncing the "freedom" of cohabitation, spouses choose the
higher freedom of Marriage, the freedom of the son and daughter of
God. This is the freedom of stable, secure, abiding, and hence, true love.
The bond of the Spirit is the firm basis for such continuing love in the
lived sacrament, in the "*res tantum*" of shared lives recognized, as we saw,
by Saint Robert Bellarmine and Pope Pius XI.[22]   John Paul II likewise
recognized the work of the Spirit in such stable love: "The Spirit which
the Lord pours forth gives a new heart, and renders man and woman
capable of loving one another as Christ has loved us." Having affirmed the profound need man and woman have of the Holy Spirit in

Marriage, he went on to show how married love is likewise developed to perfection in the *agape* of the Spirit. "Conjugal love reaches that fullness to which it is interiorly ordained, conjugal charity, which is the proper and specific way in which the spouses participate in and are called to live the very charity of Christ who gave Himself on the Cross."[23]

The "being together" of Christian spouses is "being together" in the bond of the Spirit — his fellowship, communion, or *koinonia*. This is the practical and loving basis for the family, again derived directly from the bond of the sacrament. That consecrated exclusiveness sets up the security of the Christian home, where man and woman are free to become parents, extending their love for one another in the generous procreation and education of their children. As the "domestic church" this family circle is encompassed in the High Priestly Prayer of Christ, ". . . that they may be one even as we are one, I in them and you in me, that they may become perfectly one" (John 17:22-23). Thus the self-consecration of Christ included his priestly pleading for the unity which can only come from God.

We return once more to the ultimate Source, to the Holy Trinity recognized in sacramental Marriage as the Source of the "great mystery" and through the bond of the Spirit as the Source of unity. Within the Trinity, Saint Thomas perceived the Holy Spirit as the Bond of Love. As Love proceeding from both Father and Son, the Holy Spirit is the "bond" of their unity.[24]   The liturgy also proclaims this unifying Love of the Spirit in the doxology of the Canons of the Mass and the impetratory doxology which concludes the oration of each Mass: ". . . in the unity of the Holy Spirit. . . ."

The Spirit is always Gift. In creation it is bestowed as Gift; and in the sacraments of the new creation, it is bestowed as an "outpouring of love,"[25]   again a Gift. In Marriage this love is for unity and permanence, the bond of love, communicating to the husband and wife something of that Unity which is in the Holy Trinity by the gratuitous self-giving of the creating and redeeming Trinity. God thus imparts to them the ability to love in a selfless, even heroic way. Such is his free offer, which they remain free to accept or reject. Today, that acceptance or rejection seems to depend, in so many instances, on whether they recognize the bond of the Spirit as a divine challenge to love, in a fidelity which truly says "forever."

THE SACRAMENTALITY OF THE BODY

The place of sexual union in Marriage as a sacrament is not only consummation, which completes and seals the contractual bond established by consent. Through the sacrament, sexual union has its own sacramental meaning and value. Because it is the bodily union of spouses, sexual union in Marriage is best described by the words "spousal union."

In his catechesis on sexuality, Pope John Paul II pointed out that in its masculinity and femininity, the body assumes the value of a sign, in a way, a sacramental sign. In Marriage, we thus see the redemption of the body (cf. Romans 8:23), the recovery of the original and clear "nuptial meaning of the body," in an interior mastery and freedom of the spirit, expressed in spousal union free from lust.[26]

All seven sacraments are bodily actions, instituted by Jesus Christ so that henceforth they would contain and effect divine actions. In Marriage, no new sign was given, but the existing realities of consent and spousal union were restored to the original "one flesh" of creation and raised to the sacred significance of the "great mystery" of Christ espousing his Church and becoming "one flesh" with her. Thus we may explore the dynamics of sacramentalized sexuality to deepen our understanding of the sacred bond.

I. SPOUSAL UNION, AN EFFECTUAL SIGN

The body is a "sacrament" of the self. This ought not to suggest a sharp separation between body and soul; on the contrary, a person is made and re-made by his or her bodily acts, because of the unity between body and soul. Our embodied morality of acts, our belief in bodily Resurrection, our belief in the Incarnation, our sacramental actions, all these dimensions of the Catholic Faith lead us away from any false dualism. Therefore, spousal union is to be understood within a sacred understanding of the body, expressed by Saint Paul in his words against fornication (cf. 1 Corinthians 6:12-20).[27] Bodily actions not only unite husband and wife to one another; in the lived sacrament of

Marriage, they become a means of ministering Grace to one another as "one flesh."

The nuptial meaning of the body is the "given" meaning of the body in creation, that capacity inscribed by the Creator in the human person to become a self-gift. John Paul II saw the original innocent nakedness of male and female as signifying this nuptial capacity to give one's self in a gift which has intrinsic value — the value of the person in and for himself or herself.[28] The "language of the body" is thus uttered in the bodily self-giving of spousal union. The "I choose you — and you *alone!*" of consent is now fulfilled in the "taking," which is a gift of self *to* the beloved, a receiving of the gift of self *from* the beloved, and at that third most intensely humbling redemptive level, the experience of *being received* by the beloved: "But . . . why did you choose *me?*"

By the self-giving of spousal union, the man and the woman make this total, mutual, exclusive surrender to one another. This gift of self for another is found in the almost ecstatic utterance by Saint Paul: ". . . and the life I now live in the flesh I live by faith in the Son of God, who loved me and *gave himself* for me" (Galatians 2:20). We may apply these words to the sacrament of Marriage, to two lives lived "by faith," the mutual fidelity sealed by the exclusive meaning of "for you alone" in their spousal union. Thus the sublime self-giving of Jesus Christ, the Bridegroom, informs and ennobles what is already a natural good, the spousal union of two embodied persons, giving themselves in that "high-point" of their Christian married life together. Each act of sacramentalized spousal union is thus a sign of the self-giving of Christ the Bridegroom.

Called to mutual self-effacing *agape*, man and woman lay down their lives for one another as they give themselves to one another. Here, in its spousal, sacramental, form is that "greater love," seen when one lays down his life for a friend (cf. John 15:13). Obeying Christ's new law of Marriage, spouses are the truest friends in their "one flesh" bond, willing to obey the Lord by loving one another as he has loved (cf. John 15:12-14). The Eucharistic self-giving of the Body and Blood of this Bridegroom, ". . . my body, given up for you," is recapitulated in the quality of generous love in each act of spousal union which is open to the fruitfulness of new life, of forming a wider family.

That underlying efficacy of the sacrament, the remedy for concupiscence, may be understood in this redemptive giving and laying
down of one's life for the beloved. The Semitic "knowing" of spousal
union is now an awareness of self, as a male, as a female, as a person
"given" by the Creator to be a "gift." Thus, the tendency to lust which
makes another person into an object, an instrument to be used for
pleasure, is healed in the redemptive giving of self which treats the
beloved as a subject, a person of inherent worth, another self.[29]

Pleasure is natural and good in spousal union, but the greater
pleasure in the self-giving of sacramentalized sexuality is to please the
beloved by love which affirms again and again, ". . . you and you alone."
However, in an age drenched in a false eroticism, let us never forget
that, in practice, many sound and stable Marriages do not reach their
"high-point" in spousal union. Helping with the dishes or preparing a
small meal or some other apparently minor signs of affection may *mean*
more than spousal union. Nevertheless, there is inherent in spousal
union the meaning of total self-giving and exclusive fidelity to the bond
which imparts value and meaning to all other signs of love in married
life. If some other moments seem to mean more, they are only given this
value by the exclusive love affirmed and embodied in spousal union.

Moreover, as in the Marriage of Our Lady and Saint Joseph, a man
and woman, by mutual consent, can refrain from consummation and
any spousal union in their Marriage. Only if we place this within the
ultimate "nuptial meaning of the body" can we understand how this can
be a Marriage. Our common calling is to give ourselves completely to
God. Within that universal vocation we may discern two specific vocations: the chaste self-giving of Marriage, and the chaste self-giving of
virginity. Our Lady and Saint Joseph combined both vocations. They
gave themselves to one another by mutual nuptial consent, and by a
mutual consent they shared the gift of their virginity, offering
themselves to God. That gift was embodied, in shared lives lacking only
spousal union, but imbued with tender love. This way of love by
consenting not to exercise that mutual right over one another for
spousal union is understood well today by many couples using natural
means of planning their families. They share in something of the love
between Our Lady and Saint Joseph, a love which points to the ultimate
nuptial meaning of our bodies, union with God forever in his Kingdom.

II. SPOUSAL UNION AS WORSHIP

In the medieval English Marriage rites which passed from the Sarum Rite into the Anglican Prayerbook, as the groom places the ring on his bride's finger, we hear him say: "With this ring, I thee wed, with my body, I thee worship. . . ." What is this bodily "worship"?

The time-honored words capture a further dimension of the sacramentality of the body in Marriage. This worship obviously does not refer to "*latreia*," which may only be given to God. It is a form of "*dulia*," profound veneration and reverence, but in a spousal sense as a deep respect for the sacred body of the beloved. It underlines the holiness which the sacrament imparts to sexuality in Marriage, by making sexual union become spousal union.

This "worship" also signifies the self-surrender of spouses. The gift which a man and a woman offer to one another as their "worship" is nothing less than the gift of self, a sacrifice of self, such that giving *to* the beloved, receiving *from* the beloved, and being received, is a redemptive gift *for* the beloved. Thus spousal "worship" is taken up into the sublime action of worship, Christ the Bridegroom immolating himself for his spouse, the Church.

A Eucharistic quality may be discerned in the loving awe with which spouses ought to offer such "worship" to one another. In spousal union they should give thanks for the gift of the other, and even give thanks that they have been called into being as persons, with such a unique capacity to give. Thus the redemptive and Eucharistic "giving thanks" dimensions of the Sacrifice of the Mass are reflected in two members of the worshipping Mystical Body, made "one flesh" in this sacrament.

From such considerations, those who share the nuptial bond may recognize the need for a "total devotion," similar to that which God himself shows to the one he loves. The "worship" of bodily reverence must affect all the small moments of cherishing in daily married life, so that "worship" is "giving worth" to the beloved as a person, to whom one is committed permanently by the sacred bond of the Holy Spirit. Enlightened by that Spirit, spouses recognize that: "The person to whom one makes love is made in God's image and likeness, and remade in the likeness of Christ. This is why, in the marriage service, we have the words, 'With my body, I thee worship'."[30]

III. A CATHOLIC TRADITION

In our survey of the history of the sacramentality of Marriage, we have come across instances of the negative attitude to sexuality within Marriage, from the Manichaeans, Montanists, Cathari, and even within the ascetical monastic tradition, for example, Saint Bede.[31]   But this must be balanced by a prevailing tradition which recognized the dignity and sacred value of spousal union.

Saint John Chrysostom preached on 1 Corinthians 12:21-24, on the interrelated parts of the body. He used this as an opportunity to point out the sacred dignity of the sexual organs of male and female.[32]   Preaching on the Epistle to the Colossians, he proclaimed the decency and sanctity of spousal union, within the sacrament of Christ and his spouse, the Church. In the context of denouncing the infidelity and immorality of men and women in Constantinople, he propounded a healthy, balanced Christian sexuality, based on the mutual reverence and respect of the sacrament, but free from any shame or a rejection of the body.[33]

Among the scholastics, the prevailing view was in this positive tradition, giving value to spousal union.[34]   Saint Thomas, as we have seen, saw that spousal union could be sacred and meritorious.[35]   His attitude rested on his doctrine of creation; sexuality was part of the natural created order, and our bodily nature was established by God for good ends.[36]

In our age this tradition is so well established as to need no detailed apology, as was necessary in the past.[37]   If the bond was once threatened by a negative "Jansenistic" attitude to sexuality, today the bond is threatened by inordinate and manipulative sexuality, the legacy of the "sexual revolution." Separated from procreation and self-giving, this depersonalized sexuality is a lust which can invade Marriage. In the face of this threat, the Catholic tradition can strengthen the bond in two ways.

First, we need to rediscover the meaning of the unchanged teaching of the Magisterium on the higher value of virginity.[38] We saw Saint Augustine uphold virginity by placing value on Marriage, but today Marriage needs the selfless example and sign of the Kingdom which virginity offers. The spousal bond can only benefit from a confident affirmation of virginity, based on a deeper understanding of this other "nuptial meaning of the body," in the context of vocation, in the light of the Magisterium.

Second, we need to remind spouses and those preparing to enter the spousal bond, that Marriage is a school of love. The complete "making of love" needs to be learned, not in a worldly hedonistic sense, but within the school of the sacrament.[39] The *agape* of the Bridegroom is learned by "giving way to one another," learning the meaning of the bond of "one flesh," which today includes responsible fidelity in the face of widespread adultery.

IV. THE SACRAMENTAL BOND AND ADULTERY

The first sin against the sacrament is adultery. It is the "adulteration" of the "one flesh," thus a rejection of the truth revealed in the "language of the body" and the "nuptial meaning of the body." Adultery sins against total and exclusive self-giving by attempting to impart that gift to another partner, outside the bond. It falsifies the sign of "one flesh."

Saint Paul vividly and accurately depicted this falsification of the "one flesh" when he declared: "The body is not meant for immorality, but for the Lord, and the Lord for the body. And God raised the Lord and will also raise us up by his power. Do you not know that your bodies are members of Christ? Shall I therefore take the members of Christ and make them members of a prostitute? Never! Do you not know that he who joins himself to a prostitute becomes one body with her? For, as it is written, 'The two shall become one.' But he who is united to the Lord becomes one spirit with him" (1 Corinthians 6:13-17).

The "members of his body," later evident in Ephesians, show us that adultery is a sin against the Mystical Body of Christ and, as such, a sin against the sacrament of Marriage. Those whose bodies have become the "temple of the Holy Spirit" are no longer their own property: "You are not your own; you were bought with a price . . ." (1 Corinthians 6:19-20). When we combine this ecclesial, baptismal and Eucharistic meaning of the body of the Christian with the mutual "ownership" of Marriage, the sin against the bond is revealed as also a rejection of that "giving way": "For the wife does not rule over her own body, but the husband does; likewise the husband does not rule over his own body, but the wife does" (1 Corinthians 7:4). True love, drawn from the Heart of the Bridegroom, gives way in considerate fidelity to the bond, because the true spouse knows that he or she is not self-owned, but bound to God in Baptismal character, and bound to the beloved in the bond of sacramental Marriage.

This awareness of being bound to the other is undermined by concupiscence in its sexual form, in three dimensions: as fleshly lust, as the desire of the eyes and as pride (cf. 1 John 2:16). The weakness of the first two dimensions of sexual concupiscence may be subject to pressures from within or without the Marriage bond. But the third dimension is the depth of adultery, that proud defiance which seeks self and violates the bond which God has made. In the name of "my freedom" the spouse pretends not to be the spouse and lies with his or her body, simulating that self-gift which can only occur within Marriage.

The breaking of the Sixth Commandment is thus not only a sin against justice, a sin of deception, lust and infidelity to spouse and the family. It is a sin against the sacrament which signifies that faithful union between Christ and his Church, because it is a breaking up of the unity of the Mystical Body. Realized in the community of life and love, Marriage as a lived sacrament is meant to be open to the *agape* of the Bridegroom. In losing that *agape*, the adulterer has lost Grace, rejecting the sacrificial truth of Christ, that "love demands that otherness comes before self — always."[40]

But just as love is to be learned in the school of Marriage, so fidelity is to be learned by practice. Our Lord internalized adultery when he taught that ". . . every one who looks at a woman lustfully has already committed adultery with her in his heart" (Matthew 5:27). Pope John Paul II warned of this "looking" which reduces a person to an object and a means.[41] From this "looking" comes that infidelity which devalues and impairs the self-giving of the bond, no longer seeing in the other, the spouse, the true worth and dignity of a man or woman to be valued for himself or herself. Even within Marriage, this devaluing of the body of the other becomes an adultery in the heart, perceived by the Pope as a descent into Manichaean error, the separation of the body from the person, so that it becomes a thing to be used.[42]

Spouses who begin to regard one another as sexual objects have already entered the divisive domain of adultery. The bond of two persons in a communion of self-giving is reduced to harlotry. Saint Paul's harsh image of "one flesh" with a prostitute replaces the loving unity of Christ and his Church. The signification of the sacrament is falsified. In so many cases, it is evident that formal adultery often results from such subtle infidelity within Marriage, when all meaning, hence all Grace, is drained from the sacrament.

However, those who recognize the sacramentality of the body in their Marriage will remain faithful to the bond of the Holy Spirit. Their love for one another will remain exclusive; a way which is unrepeatable, a way reserved only for the beloved, a way which no stranger may ever traverse. Such faithful spouses will fulfill the advice of the Fathers of the Second Vatican Council, speaking of this embodied spousal self-giving: "Outstanding courage is required for the constant fulfillment of the duties of this Christian calling: spouses, therefore, will need grace for leading a holy life: they will eagerly practice a love that is firm, generous, and prompt to sacrifice and will ask for it in their prayers."[43]

Thus the love of faithful spouses is formed by and directed to a greater Love, to the Triune God himself. Together, they journey as "one flesh," knowing that these bodies, through and in which they love each other will be dust one day, when the bond between them has ceased. But their shared hope is in the Resurrection of these bodies, when the self-giving they exchanged in this life will be perfected in the nuptial gift of eternal life.

INDISSOLUBILITY

Caused by mutual consent, consummated and sealed by spousal union, the bond of Marriage is indissoluble. This is the constant teaching of the Catholic Church. The Council of Trent taught infallibly that the

Church is not in error in having taught and in teaching that the bond of Marriage cannot be dissolved or that any partner may remarry while the other partner lives.[44] In the face of social, political and religious pressures, even at the cost of the English schism, the Church has maintained the indissolubility of the bond, according to Our Lord's teaching, "So they are no longer two but one (flesh). What therefore God has joined together let no man put asunder" (Matthew 19:6 and Mark 10:8-9).

In concluding our reflections on the bond effected in the sacrament of Marriage, it is important to understand indissolubility in the context of sacramentality. In turn, this leads to conclusions concerning modern attempts to weaken or destroy indissolubility within the Church.

I. INDISSOLUBILITY WITHIN THE SACRAMENT

The history of sacramentality, outlined in Chapter Three, shows us a principle: *Indissolubility is inseparable from the sacrament.* From this principle we may derive a further position, that a sacramental Marriage must be indissoluble.

Our Lord's teaching in the Gospels was clear, even though there has been much debate over his allowing separation or divorce in Matthew 5:32 and 19:9 in the case of *porneia*, variously translated as "unchastity," "adultery," or "lewd conduct." As Saint Paul received this teaching there is no sign of such an exception, at least as allowing remarriage: "To the married I give the charge, *not I but the Lord*, that the wife should not separate from her husband (but if she does, let her remain single or else be reconciled to her husband) — and that the husband should not divorce his wife" (1 Corinthians 7:10-11). As Saint Paul received the teaching, so the Church received it, such that we even find the curious negative witness to indissolubility in the early centuries of extreme ascetical doubts about remarrying after the death of a partner[46] thus implying that remarriage after divorce is clearly forbidden.

Saint Augustine's understanding of sacramentality focussed on this indissoluble quality of the bond of Christian Marriage.[47] Such a view persisted among the scholastics. Saint Thomas, having provided prudential Natural Law arguments in favor of indissolubility as serving the goods of stable procreation and education of children and mutual fidelity, likewise sees the "good of the sacrament" in Saint Augustine's sense as the better argument for indissolubility: ". . . indissolubility befits marriage inasmuch as it is a sign of the perpetual union of Christ and his Church, and inasmuch as it is required as an obligation of nature itself for the good of the children."[48]   In accord with his concept of nature and Grace, there is perfect harmony between the prudential and the sacramental requirement of indissolubility.

The sacramental theologian sees indissolubility within the "great mystery," Jesus Christ the Bridegroom united to his beloved spouse forever. This sublime archetype is derived, as we have seen, from the Unity of the Holy Trinity and realized in the Hypostatic Union, the inseparable unity of the Divine Nature and the human nature in Christ. The divine espousal with us was effected in the Incarnation, consummated on the Cross, revealed as indissoluble in the eternity of the Resurrection.

If Christian spouses recapitulate that divine espousal in the sacrament of Marriage, the inherent "good of the sacrament" of indissolubility is the divinely imparted quality of their bond. Just as the first sin against the bond, adultery, is a sin against the sacramental good of fidelity, *"fides,"* so the second sin against the bond is divorce — a sin against the sacramental good of indissolubility. Those who divorce (not in any merely legal sense allowed by the Church in some cases), are falsifying the signification of the sacrament, saying, as it were, that Christ can separate himself from his Church, or that his spouse can separate herself from this Bridegroom. Just as the "language of the body" is falsified in adultery, a denial of Christ's abiding fidelity to his Church, so the "one flesh" of the bond is apparently sundered by human power in the act of divorce. This sin against the sacrament takes its most anti-sacramental form when a partner then proceeds to contract an invalid marriage, a further falsification of the "one flesh." If some religious rites are used for such a union, this may suggest that Christ the Bridegroom can find some new spouse, other than his beloved for whom he sacrificed himself.

No human power can dissolve a sacramental Marriage which is

ratified and consummated. Indeed, "The Church cannot have any power over the reality of a conjugal union that has passed into the power of him whose mystery she must announce and never hinder."[49] In the West, there is a mainstream of consistent papal policy in favor of indissolubility, evident from the Fifth to the Twelfth Centuries, when this "good of the sacrament" was under cultural and political threat.[50] Much of this policy may be explained in terms of law based on fidelity to the teaching of Our Lord on Marriage. But the policy was reinforced by the growing awareness of the sacramentality of Marriage, more evident after the Twelfth Century in the age of the scholastic theologians.

This sacramental understanding of the papal policy is borne out by the Reformation when the rejection of the sacramentality of Marriage was at the same time a rejection of indissolubility. That the Reformers and their successors gave way to social and political pressure must be balanced by their loss of the sacramental understanding of man and woman. In their view of fallen human nature, male and female did not have the capacity or dignity to be able to signify and recapitulate the indissoluble bond of Christ the Bridegroom. This pessimism concerning our nature also struck out celibacy as "impossible." It allowed for concessions towards divorce, surrendering to that "hardness of heart" which led Moses to grant the right of divorce (cf. Matthew 19:8). But today we should be careful lest we gradually take the same path, because indissolubility, hence the sacrament, is being undermined.

II. INDISSOLUBILITY THREATENED

Under the influence of those societies where divorce is prevalent even among Catholics, various attacks are being launched against indissolubility. In the name of the Second Vatican Council, the contract of Marriage is replaced by a subjective understanding of the covenant of love, allowing wider scope for dissolution of Marriages.[51] By defining them in a literalist, organic way, Marriages can "die" and thus easily be dissolved. But the more subtle attack on Marriage is to attempt to undermine Our Lord's teaching by the rash use of methods of biblical criticism, and then to propose the Eastern Orthodox policy in favor of remarrying the innocent party of a divorce as the future direction which the Catholic Church should take.[52]

As to the use of methods of biblical criticism, the Church stands secure in her Magisterium, which faithfully transmits and maintains the teaching which Saint Paul recognized as from the Lord. In her practice, the Church has not allowed the exceptive clause in Saint Matthew's Gospel to permit anything more than the "separation from bed and board," defined at Trent as permissible.[53] That the Church in various situations allows a civil divorce to accompany such a separation of the spouses in no way implies recognition of divorce. The other "divorces" allowed by the Church are for unions which are null in her eyes, when civil arrangements are necessary to dissolve such unions together with her own decree of nullity.

For those who make use of the historical and form-critical methods of analyzing the Scriptures, there is a probable answer in interpreting whether Our Lord's teaching on indissolubility is as absolute as the Church maintains. Using these methods, Descamps concluded that Our Lord took a radical course in the face of Jewish permission for some divorces, "that Jesus absolutely condemned remarriage is the almost unanimous conviction of commentators," and that "These agree also in general in thinking that Jesus at the same time condemned divorce itself."[54] To raise the old canard that Our Lord's words concerning a woman putting away her husband cannot be genuine, in no way sets aside his teaching. In Jewish practice a man could initiate a divorce, but not a woman, yet Our Lord said, ". . . and if she divorces her husband and marries another, she commits adultery" (Mark 10:12). But a woman could initiate divorce proceedings if her husband was a leper, and in the time of Christ, under Roman influence, Herod the Great's sister and granddaughter had changed husbands.[55] Moreover, an unduly critical approach to this text assumes that Our Lord's knowledge was not only inadequate concerning the changes in his own culture but limited only to that culture.

The other subtle approach of favoring Eastern Orthodox practice in the remarriage of innocent parties stands or falls on the arguments put forward to justify it. These will be examined in the context of the ecumenical problems of the sacramentality of Marriage.[56] In the next Chapter, we will see how "covenant" far from weakening indissolubility, in the sacramental context, only reinforces the teaching of Christ which remains the constant teaching of his spouse the Church.

III. THE GIFT OF INDISSOLUBILITY

Our final reflections on the sacramental bond return to the work of the Holy Spirit in this "*res et sacramentum*," this inviolable core of the sacrament, not a "thing" but a bond of persons who give themselves to one another in spousal union. Indissolubility shows us the abiding nature of this personal bond, a gift of the Spirit to those whose consent is raised into the salvific will of Jesus Christ, a gift of the Spirit to those whose consent is consummated in spousal union.

By presenting indissolubility as a divine gift, we affirm a positive understanding of this quality of sacramental Marriage. It is most important in an age which values freedom to present the bond in a positive way. Spouses are not bound to one another in such a way as to lose their individual identity; we may note Saint Thomas pointing out that the bond joins spouses formally, not effectively.[57]   Pope Paul VI put this eloquently in pastoral terms: "The gift does not involve a fusion. Each personality remains distinct, and far from losing itself in the mutual gift, flourishes, improves, grows, affirms and is affirmed, for the length of married life according to this great law of love: the giving of oneself to one another for the giving of selves together."[58]

The freedom bestowed in the bond is the freedom to give oneself exclusively, to give as a member of the Mystical Body. The dynamic unity of that living, working Body of Christ rests securely in the families which are formed out of this self-giving. Thus the stability of the bond makes spouses become witnesses before the world of the indissoluble love of Christ, his unity with the Church, and the coherent unity within that visible Church. The Second Vatican Council endorsed this "witness value" of matrimonial indissolubility as part of the most important aspect of the apostolate of the laity.[59]   The world desperately needs to see revealed in this sacrament of Marriage visible evidence of a love which says,"Forever!"

The gift of the Holy Spirit who effects unity within the Mystical Body is that tendency towards unity which Saint Paul encouraged at

Ephesus. This specific gift of the indissolubility in the Marriage bond is always to be seen in the context of the Church, where the Spirit who is the Bond of Love in the Holy Trinity ". . . is the one who consummates and seals all in unity."[60]   The bond whereby spouses are "one flesh" calls them to learn the art of nuptial unity and to reveal this to the world.

Whether they know it or not, they are not only strengthening and witnessing to the unity of the Church in that nuptial bond. They are also pointing beyond themselves to the future, to that unity which is to be our destiny, that final, ultimate nuptial meaning of all our bodies. Saint Augustine wrote of this eschatological meaning of the indissoluble bond of monogamous Christian Marriage. He looked back to the polygamy of the old order, finding some mystical symbolism in it, the coming subjection of many to the reign of God on earth. But, in the signification of Christian Marriage, he looked forward to the perfect unity of the celestial city: "Just as the sacrament of the multiple marriages in those times pointed to the future multitude of all the people on earth subject to God; so the Sacrament of single Marriage in our times points to the future unity of all of us subject to God in the one celestial city."[61]

Thus the bond of spousal consent consummated in spousal union points beyond an earthly sacramental union to the nuptials of the Lamb of God. In his beloved spouse, the Church, we seek the perfect unity and harmony to be revealed finally in her glory as the Jerusalem above, the mother of us all.

CHAPTER SIX

The Sacramental Covenant

Mucho lo agradezco, Padre,	*"Thanks to You, Almighty Father,"*
El Hijo le respondía;	*The Son made answer to the Sire,*
A la esposa que me dieres,	*"To the wife that You shall give Me*
Yo mi claridad daría.	*I shall give My lustrous fire.*
Para que por ella vea	*"That by its brightness she may witness*
Cuánto mi Padre valía.	*How infinite My Father's worth*
Y cómo el ser que poseo,	*And how My being from Your being*
De su ser le recibía.	*In every way derived its birth.*
Reclinarla he yo en mi brazo	*"I'll hold her on My arm reclining*
Y en tu amor se abrasaría,	*And with Your love will burn her so*
Y con eterno deleite	*That with an endless joy and wonder*
Tu bondad sublimaría.	*Your loving kindness she may know."*

Saint John of the Cross, *Romance III, Of the Creation.*

The visible effectual sign of Marriage is the mutual consent of man and woman, the *sacramentum tantum*. This action of man and woman establishes the bond, perfected and made indissoluble by their spousal union, and this bond is the abiding and indissoluble *res et sacramentum*. But there is a third dimension to the sacrament of Marriage, the continual Grace offered to spouses, the *res tantum*. This is the lived sacrament.

"Covenant," it would seem, is the best way to understand and describe the lived sacrament. It provides an inclusive description of sacramental Marriage, derived from the "great mystery" of Christ and his spouse, the Church. Before proceeding to consider the covenantal Grace offered to spouses in the sacrament, it is important to clarify what we mean by "covenant," and how this term can be applied accurately, and inaccurately, to Marriage today.

COVENANT

In English, the secular meanings of "covenant" do not seem promising if applied to the sacrament of Marriage. In legal usage, "covenant" may refer to the "last will and covenant," more commonly "testament," ordering the estate of a deceased person. It may also be the "deed and covenant" in property transactions. And, in the same area, it may have a minor, restrictive meaning, for example, a "covenant" placed on an apartment house forbidding the presence of what is natural and good — children and animals.

In these secular meanings of "covenant," it is difficult to discern the alleged personalism of the term. To assert that contracts deal with things and covenants deal with people is a naive simplification of reality. Although often impersonal, contracts may involve personal duties, mutual rights, terms of employment, whereas, in British Law, covenants cover material things, property and the uses to which it may be assigned.

However, personalist meanings of "covenant" may be found in the religious sphere of Christianity and Judaism. These meanings are derived from, but developed beyond, treaty relationships in the ancient Near East, pacts between persons, groups or nations. To clarify the accurate use of "covenant" in Marriage, we must investigate the developing meaning of "covenant" in Scripture. On this basis, we may interpret the use of the term *"foedus"* by the Fathers of the Second Vatican Council.

I. THE OLD COVENANT

The term *berit, é diathéke*, in the Old Testament, describes the divine agreements made especially with Noah, Abraham, supremely with Moses, and with David, agreements of divine conditions and promises.[1] The Hebrew word *berit* has two major meanings: (1) a political or economic alliance or pact between equals (parity treaty) or between a superior and inferior power (vassal treaty), (2) an alliance with God. The *berit* may also mean a law (cf. Deuteronomy 4:13).

Even as the great Covenant with Moses bears comparison with a vassal treaty, because God requires observance of the Law from his People, its religious nature set it on a different plane than vassal treaties such as those of the Hittites. Covenant and cult were closely associated, as we shall see, on Sinai.[2] The Covenant was thus not a simple contract; rather, it was a defined sacred relationship between God and his People. It included certain contractual terms, and penalties or "curses" for those who violated the sacred Covenant. But the Lord God was a merciful King. Infidelity was a serious violation of the relationship and an affront to the patient and faithful God who had established a binding familial *union* with his People.[3]

In the Covenant terms of the Ten Words of Yahweh, the Commandments, we find "family law" directly bearing on Marriage. Adultery, desire for adultery and parents' rights are included in the Commandments. But within Marriage itself as an institution in Israel, as we have noted,[4] we do not find any sacred tendency towards what we know as "sacramentality." The seeds of sacramentality for Marriage come from beyond Marriage, from the whole covenantal relationship of God and Israel. This explains descriptions of Marriage in terms of "covenant" in Proverbs 2:17, Jeremiah 31:32, Ezekiel 16:8 and Malachi 2:4. "Covenant" was not a conventional term for Marriage. Rather, these passages take Marriage in its best Jewish form and apply it to the great Covenant.[5]

Love in Marriage gave the prophets, tested by the infidelities and tragedies of the nation, a more personal and intimate way of proclaiming the Covenant. Marriage gave the people a more personal and intimate understanding of God bonded with his people. This is the rationale of the nuptial imagery of Yahweh seeking Israel his spouse, for example Hosea 2:16-23. In some non-Jewish treaty covenants, the gods could be involved with humans in what was almost a bilateral covenant, benign and reasonable.[6] But even if Yahweh remained the Lord and King of the Covenant, he was still the benign Father of his family, Israel. In Deuteronomy, the penalties or curses were balanced by a love of God's Law and a sense of trust in God and his Law.[7] To this reasoned awareness of the wisdom of the Covenant, the prophets added the dimension of hope for a new and better Covenant, which Jeremiah proclaimed would be engraved on human hearts (cf. Jeremiah 31:31-32 and 40:38-42).

As it made Israel God's adopted family, the Covenant suggested a tender vision of God. Thus the New Covenant in the love of Christ is implicit in the Old Covenant. God's covenantal love was his *hesed*, a steadfast, patient love (cf. Deuteronomy 7:9; Jeremiah 2:2; 31:2; Hosea 2:21). His justice, *sedaqa*, was to be trusted for he would honor his promises.[8] In this later prophetic and Deuteronomic understanding of the Covenant as the future hope of Israel, we find a development far beyond a conditional pact laid down by a severe superior power. But God's gratuitous gift of peace and happiness to his people is best expressed as a new, intimate relationship, like that of bridegroom and bride.[9] Already we see intimations of indissolubility and fidelity.

But why can Marriage be applied to the Covenant so as to reveal the God of promise, hope and love? Because Marriage was within God's act of creation, "from the beginning," when God and man were in perfect harmony. Marriage represents a "primordial sacrament," a reality derived from creation itself. In creation there was the primordial covenant between God and man, within which male and female found harmony in their own spousal "covenant." By presupposing this created reality, Marriage can be related to the great Covenant with Yahweh, highlighting the meaning of infidelities against that Covenant.[10] In turn, the way lay open for Christ Jesus to apply the new order of his New Covenant to Marriage, expressed by Saint Paul in terms of the archetype of the "great mystery."

If the slave girl and prostitute represented status below the Covenant or infidelity to the Covenant, so virginity emerged as true fidelity to Yahweh. The "virgin daughter of Sion" is faithful in being espoused and virginal, even as she fails and suffers (cf. 2 Kings 19:21;

Isaiah 37:21; Lamentations 1:15; 2:13). But she is only truly "virginal" in fidelity to her God.[11] Therefore, the perfection of the Old Covenant was ultimately found in Mary Immaculate, the faithful Daughter of Sion, whose espousals to God brought forth Christ the Lord in whom a new Covenant would be established with a New Israel, his bride the Church.

This covenant symbolism of the bond of love between God and his people finds a place in the Coptic rite of Marriage. The rings are exchanged by bride and groom, as signs of binding love. But the people responding to the words of the priest, address those who wed: "Do not forget the Covenant established with our Fathers, Abraham, Isaac and Jacob, your holy Israel."[12]

II. THE NEW COVENANT

The institution of the Blessed Eucharist at the Last Supper gives us the terms "New Covenant," *é kainé diathéke*. In his own blood, offering himself for us, Christ the Lord gives up his shed blood of this new and eternal Covenant, blood poured out for the many so that their sins may be forgiven (cf. 1 Corinthians 11:25; Matthew 26:28; Mark 14:24; Luke 22:20). In the Cross, in the Eucharist as the sacramental *anámnesis* of the Cross, the sacrifice of blood seals the New Covenant, just as Moses sealed the Old Covenant in blood, from animals offered as "peace offerings" (cf. Exodus 24:3-8).

Writing to the Galatians, Saint Paul compared the Covenant promise in Israel to an abiding last will and testament (cf. Galatians 3:15-18). In Hebrews we also find a play on this symbolism of the last will and testament coming into effect after death, or through the shedding of blood (cf. Hebrews 9:16-18). But this is no longer the favored interpretation of *é diathéke*, or *"testamentum"* in the Vulgate.[13] Covenant conveys the idea of a wider and richer relationship between God and his people, not merely a legal device or inheritance.

Moreover, the New Covenant in Christ is "new" not in the sense of being a reproduction of the old, but as a new dispensation between God and man. Hence the use of the richer Greek term for "new."[14] Writing to the Romans, and able to assume knowledge of the Old Law among them, Saint Paul used the prophecy of Isaiah 59:20-21, fulfilled in

Christ's Covenant but now open to the Gentiles (cf. Romans 11:25-29). But this New Covenant is God's free gift, a gift of Grace and freedom which he contrasted with the "slavery" of the Old Covenant, identifying this with the burden of the Old Law which Judaizing Galatians favored (cf. Galatians 4:21-31). Writing to the Corinthians, he can assume less awareness of the concept of "covenant," but he contrasted the New Covenant with the old; the former represented the Spirit and life, whereas the latter represented a written code (cf. 2 Corinthians 3:4-6). The author of the Letter to the Hebrews was able to assume a clear understanding of the Old Covenant and contrasted the new and "better covenant" with the old (cf. Hebrews 8:6, 8) and presented Jesus Christ as the Priest and Victim, mediator of this new and better Covenant (cf. Hebrews 9:15; 12:24 and 13:2).

In the new dispensation of Jesus Christ, the free gift of Grace replaces the burden of the Law, and fidelity to God is how members of his Church find freedom, children of the new Jerusalem "above" (cf. Galatians 4:26).[15]   However, we may discern the problem with the concept of "covenant" in the early Church. Already, in the apostolic age, there were Gentile Christians for whom the concept meant little. This would explain why "mystery" replaced "covenant" in Saint Paul's letters to Colossae and Ephesus. As we have seen, the "great mystery" is deeper and wider than the New Covenant, for it is through the Incarnation and work of our Redemption that God raises his New Israel into the new covenantal dispensation of Grace.

Therefore, the New Covenant may be seen within the context of the "great mystery" of God's mighty acts in and through Jesus Christ and his Mystical Body, the Church. The tender steadfast love, *hesed*, of Yahweh becomes the sacrificial love of God Incarnate, the *agape* of the Redeemer. The nuptial metaphor of the prophets becomes a hope fulfilled. God chooses his beloved, and in a new Eve, the new Adam brings forth and weds his spouse, the virgin-mother Church, personified in the Virgin Mother Mary. The New Covenant relationship is one of faith — again personified and perfected in Our Lady's "fiat" and in her ecclesial obedience at Cana.[16]   Thus the life of fidelity, the faith of the New Covenant, is contained within the "great mystery" of the espousal of the Church, our espousal in Grace as a people and as baptized individuals.

What we see in the nuptials of the "great mystery" is thus not only the fulfillment of the prophetic metaphor of hope for Israel, but the birth of the universal New Israel, the Church. In the dispensation of the New Covenant, which is the Redemption of mankind, not only is the relationship with God transformed and elevated to faith and Grace. The relationships between the members of this People of the New Covenant are transformed. Now they enjoy union with God, in Christ, "members of his body," capable of receiving and living in his *agape*. Therefore the relationship of Marriage is transformed. John Paul II perceived this as the restoration of the "primordial sacrament," the perfect harmony of the "covenant" in creation in Eden — a covenant with God and between man and woman. In the Covenant of Grace and election, God choosing us and espousing us, Saint Paul in Ephesians revealed Marriage as the "Sacrament of Redemption."[17]

The Church is central to the New Covenant relationship in a way that is established more firmly than the status of Israel under the Old Covenant. The divine Marriage has been accomplished. The New Israel is espoused forever. Her status, thus the status of each of the "members of his body," is assured: ". . . and lo, I am with you always, to the close of the age" (Matthew 28:20). This bond of the Bridegroom's love for his spouse was also expressed by Saint Paul: "For I am sure that neither death, nor life, nor angels, nor principalities, nor things present, nor things to come, nor powers, nor height, nor depth, nor anything else in all creation, will be able to separate us from the love of God in Christ Jesus our Lord" (Romans 8:38-39).

Within the Church of this spousal Covenant, the seven sacraments are "sacraments of the New Law," the covenantal description of the sacraments, including Marriage, used repeatedly at Trent.[18] Pope John Paul II echoed this in *Familiaris Consortio*: "Receiving and meditating faithfully on the word of God, the Church has solemnly taught and continues to teach that the marriage of the baptized is one of the seven sacraments of the New Covenant." Then he continued, bringing together the new baptismal and ecclesial meanings of the new, redemptive, Covenant: "Indeed, by means of baptism, man and woman are definitively placed within the new and eternal covenant, in the spousal covenant of Christ with the Church. And it is because of this indestructible insertion that the intimate community of conjugal life and love, founded by the Creator, is elevated and assumed into the spousal charity of Christ, sustained and enriched by His redeeming power."[19]

Thus the papal teaching brings together all the "new" elements in the New Covenant and places the covenant of Marriage within that Covenant of Christ's spousal *agape*. Later, in the last, sacramental, phase of his Marriage catechesis, he described Marriage as "the sacrament of the New Covenant" because, as the sacrament of the "great mystery" of Jesus Christ and his Church, Marriage signifies God's loving "election" of people, realized in Christ and in the Church. As such, it is described as "great" in Ephesians, in the context of Saint Paul's exhortation to a redemptive quality of Christian life.[20]

From this understanding of Marriage as a covenant within the New Covenant, we may infer that "covenant" provides us with an inclusive and descriptive frame of reference for Marriage. This may be summarized in a simple way. The sacrament of Marriage is derived from the "great mystery." Within the "great mystery," the New Covenant is established, a new relationship between God and his people. Therefore, Marriage reflects that permanent Covenant relationship in its own abiding structure as a personal covenant relationship between man and woman.

III. "FOEDUS" IN THE TEACHING OF VATICAN II

The third stage of understanding the meaning of "covenant" in Marriage is to see what the Fathers of the Second Vatican Council intended when they chose *"foedus"* as their descriptive word for Marriage. *"Foedus"* can mean an agreement, compact, pact, treaty, or alliance. It implies some more personal relationship than *"contractus,"* and is a more suitable and personal term for "covenant" than the biblical Latin term *"testamentum."* As such we see why "covenant" as *"foedus"* is rendered as *"l'alleanza"* or *"il patto"* in Italian and *"l'alliance"* in French. Already within the Latin term itself, we see a good reason for its use in *Gaudium et Spes*, 48 and 50.

"Foedus" is introduced in *Gaudium et Spes*, 48: "The intimate partnership of life and the love which constitutes the married state has been established by the creator and endowed by him with its own proper

laws: it is rooted in the contract (*foedere*) of its partners, that is, in their irrevocable personal consent." Then there is a general description of Marriage as established by "a conjugal covenant" (*foedere coniugali*) whereby a man and woman become "one flesh." Then this "*foedus*" between husband and wife is related to the Old Covenant and to the "great mystery": "Just as of old God encountered his people with a covenant of love and fidelity (*foedere dilectionis et fidelitatis*), so our Savior, the spouse of the Church, now encounters Christian spouses through the sacrament of marriage." Finally, in the same place, the Christian family is described as springing from Marriage, ". . . which is an image and a sharing in the partnership of love between Christ and the Church (*imago et participatio foederis dilectionis Christi et Ecclesiae*)." "*Foedus*" also appears in *Gaudium et Spes*, 50, in a description of the indissoluble nature of Marriage, with or without children where it speaks of ". . . its nature as an indissoluble compact between two people . . . (*indoles foederis inter personas indissolubilis*)."

Although it would be an exaggeration to depict the choice of this term as a complete re-definition of Marriage, its choice by the Fathers of the Council was deliberate. It was not a novel term in the area of Marriage, for it may be found in *Casti Connubii*.[21]   That it ought to be translated as "covenant" is also in accord with the intentions of the Fathers, although the better English translation of the Council documents renders it, as we have seen, apparently according to context, successively as "contract," "partnership," "covenant," and "compact."[22]   This variable translation does not seem to be in accord with the intentions of the Fathers of the Council, even as it may be a reaction against attempts to make "*foedus*" as "covenant" into a loose, interpersonal, juridical *definition* of sacramental Marriage.

The Fathers, though, did not seek to define Marriage in a juridical way. Definition was not the purpose of a pastoral Ecumenical Council, least of all in *Gaudium et Spes*, a Pastoral Constitution. Moreover, Marriage was included in Part II, where ". . . the subject matter which is viewed in the light of doctrinal principles consists of elements, some of which are permanent and some of which are contingent."[23]

Gaudium et Spes, Part II, chapter 1, "The Dignity of Marriage and the Family," was the outcome of a process which continued for the duration of the Second Vatican Council. In 1962, the Council Fathers were presented with a draft schema "On Chastity, Virginity, Matrimony and the Family."[24]   This draft of a separate Constitution on these matters was rejected by the Central Preparatory Commission, and in stages replaced by a chapter within *Schema 13*, which finally took the form of *Gaudium et Spes*.[25]   On November 16, 1965, the Fathers voted their approval of this chapter "On Marriage and the Family."

The choice of *"foedus"* must first be put in the context of the document, a pastoral presentation of the role of the Church in response to the hopes and problems of the modern world. Marriage was thus not primarily presented as a sacrament, but introduced in terms of its universal "sacred value" to encourage not only Christians but all people, nevertheless presenting certain key points of the teaching of the Church in order to reinforce all Marriages.[26]   But *"foedus"* was not chosen as some general term to assist this dialogue with the world. It was chosen as a Christian, biblical, term, to provide God's binding basis for "the intimate partnership of life and love which constitutes the married state."[27]

Moreover, in the *Relatio de particularibus* put before General Congregation 132 of the Council, we find an ecumenical justification for the choice of the biblical term *"foedus"* rather than *"contractus."* The term was favored because it would provide less difficulty for the Eastern Churches, presumably those in communion with Rome as well as those who are separated.[28]   The Theological Commission later responded to last minute attempts to modify *"foedus,"* in the form of *"contractuali foedere"* (a contractual covenant) by pointing out that this was not necessary. The Commission also cited *Casti Connubii*, 37, to support their pastoral emphasis on Marriage as it is lived, rather than as it is contracted, Marriage as the secure and stable, intimate relationship between spouses and as the stable unit of the family in society.[29]   Attempts to return to *"contractus"* may also have been rejected because contracts were regarded as breakable in the modern world.[30]

Taking these pastoral reasons into account, *"foedus"* was seen as a useful biblical term, widely acceptable and yet suggesting the sacred stability and indissolubility of Marriage. But "the intimate partnership of life and love," Marriage as a lived reality, remains central to *Gaudium et Spes*, leaving the way open to see *"foedus,* covenant," as a stable description of Marriage as a relationship modelled on the eternal fidelity of God.

The Council's use of *"foedus"* as "covenant" has been maintained by Pope John Paul II as we have seen both in *Familiaris Consortio*, 13, and in his catechesis on Marriage. But the Pope carefully integrates the spousal covenant with the New Covenant, in turn placing this Christ-centered relationship between God and man within the "great mystery" of Christ and his Church. But does *"foedus"* weaken indissolubility?

In the post-conciliar reform of Canon Law, *"foedus"* was chosen as the best descriptive term for Christian Marriage: "The matrimonial covenant (*foedus*) by which a man and a woman establish between themselves a partnership of their whole life, and which of its own very nature is ordered to the well-being of the spouses and to the procreation and upbringing of children, has, between the baptized, been raised by Christ the Lord to the dignity of a sacrament."[31]   But the second part of the descriptive Canon maintains the juridical place of the valid "contract" between the baptized as being inseparable from the sacrament: "Consequently, a valid marriage contract (*contractus*) cannot exist between baptized persons without its being by that very fact a sacrament."[32]   In Canon 1057, *"foedus"* takes on a slightly different meaning: "Matrimonial consent is an act of will by which a man and woman by an irrevocable covenant (*foedere irrevocabili*) mutually give and accept one another for the purpose of establishing a marriage."[33]

This personalist emphasis in the Council and in the Magisterium of John Paul II has entered the new *Code of Canon Law*. Marriage is a "covenant," by which a man and woman establish a partnership of their whole life. The consent establishes a covenant which is irrevocable as the mutual self-giving of the two persons. The contract retains its juridical place within this covenant relationship of a life partnership and mutual self-giving.

It is false to claim that contract has been replaced by covenant so as to give us a more flexible and less binding understanding of Marriage.[34] "Covenant" marks a distinct development, a stronger God-centered understanding of Marriage as it is "covenanted" (Canon 1057) and as the lived "Marriage covenant" (Canon 1055). A juridical and sacramental understanding of indissolubility will not be weakened if "covenant" is kept within the biblical meanings envisaged by the

Council and Pope John Paul II. The binding spousal covenant is embodied within the *irrevocable* New Covenant of Jesus Christ, who is espoused *forever* to his Church, the new Israel, in the "great mystery."

This binding biblical meaning of "covenant" must be maintained in sacramental and pastoral theology. But "covenant" is not simply a synonym for indissolubility or the bond. It is not an exclusive term. It need not exclude that human dimension of the sacrament, the "contract." Indeed, if the Council Fathers in 1965 saw "contract" as a weak term, an arrangement which could be broken, in the years after the Council the "sexual revolution" swept away even the concept itself of contract in Marriage, with so-called "family law" and "no fault divorces," and various kinds of "open marriages" and "relationships." By paradox, in our times, the "contract" at least maintains the idea of a humanly binding, legal union. As such it should be retained, even in sacramental and pastoral theology. However, "contract" must be subordinate to "covenant" because the spousal covenant is a stronger, richer framework for Marriage. It is the gift of God who "joins together" in a more binding and sacred way than any voidable human contract.

Therefore the covenant of love *includes* the consent and the human contract, the bond, and the community or partnership of life and love which makes a family. However, this inclusive word is best used to describe Marriage as it is lived day by day, *"in factum esse."* Since it is such a strong, descriptive scriptural term, "covenant" provides us with a key to that third dimension of the permanent sacrament, Saint Thomas' *res tantum*, the Grace which God offers and gives within a covenant of love which is Christian married life. Day by day, as the baptized ministers of Grace, intrinsic to their consent and consummation, spouses are ministers of this covenant of love and its special graces.

THE GRACE OF THIS COVENANT

To those he calls and chooses, God our Father never denies the Grace they need to live in their own Christian state of life. This has been the experience of countless Christians, called to the state of married Christian life. But married life is not easy. The inner division in our very selves so often frustrates the harmony and communion which is a covenanted way of life. Thus, the abiding reality of the Grace of Marriage is God's constant offer to spouses of a healing and elevating work, never separate from their cooperation, from their actions.

A practical realism, balanced with the sacramental vision, can guide us to look for the priorities required in this covenant lived within the New Covenant. These priorities of the Grace of Marriage are not only what is demanded of Christian spouses, but what they can expect God to provide if they seek to live up to what the sacrament signifies, his own Covenant fidelity.

I. BELIEVING IN MARRIAGE

The first priority is to believe in the sacrament. The specific capacity for belief in the sacramental nature of Marriage will vary widely, even between partners in the same Marriage in some instances. If we see preparation for Marriage as catechesis for a sacrament, much can be accomplished in making men and women aware of the truth that Marriage does not depend only on the resources and skills of the couple, but on God.

Believing in the sacrament means believing that the gracious Bridegroom of the Church continues to uphold married Christians with the strength of this sacrament, not only in the moments of consent, but in the years which follow. This faith in the Grace of Marriage, however, must rest securely on some awareness of the dignity of being baptized as "members of his body," an awareness of the basic espousal which Saint Paul set forth in Ephesians.

When explaining this dignity and power of Christians, pastoral sense would suggest that some other model be used in place of our mystical espousal in Baptism, for example, our adoption by God. Those who are members of Christ's Body are children and heirs of God, Christ's fellow heirs filled with the Spirit, able to cry, "Abba! Father!" (cf. Romans 8:15). Such is the strong Trinitarian Love with which our good God enfolds his own people. Spouses should know that this is the same love which enfolded them when they set their hearts on one another in mutual consent, when they thereby formed a bond as indissoluble as the bond of love of the crucified Bridegroom, when they purposed to live in a covenant community of life and love until death, when they became "those whom God has joined together."

In all the sacraments of a state of life, God calls us, he empowers us, and he sends us forth to bear fruit. A husband and wife should know that there is a Grace of state imparted to them as they consecrate one another in Marriage, implicit in Bellarmine's teaching on the lived state of Marriage as a sacrament.[35]   The Church, and the world, will then see in such a lived covenant what Pope John Paul II described as memorial, actuation and prophecy.[36]   God calls and empowers and sends forth spouses as "one flesh" to be living "sacraments," effectual signs of what he has done, what he is doing now, and what he promises. But to be fruitful in such a way in our times, this lived sacrament must be taught, defended and proclaimed. Christians entering Marriage have the right to know and believe that Marriage is taking up and using the Sanctifying Grace of their Baptism in a unique way.[37]

The pastoral wisdom of the *Catechism of the Council of Trent* remains valid in our different post-conciliar era. Men and women preparing for sacramental Marriage should be disposed so that they regard their Marriage as a sacrament, "a work not human, but divine,"[38] a God-given covenant.

II. THE CROSS AND RESURRECTION

To set out the generous Grace of this lived covenant of love, we must look to the Bridegroom, Jesus crucified and risen, in his "great mystery" of deathless love. But in the light of the Cross and Resurrection, and reading the "signs of the times," we must ask a question: What is the basic actual Grace for which spouses are disposed by this sacrament? Is it perseverance? At once we see what Marriage shares with any chosen state of Christian life, the need for "steadfast determination of the will," the need "to stand fast to the commandments of God in all things that matrimony demands."[39]

The children of the Old Covenant struggled to remain faithful to the way of life of their Covenant relationship with God and with one another. For the children of the New Covenant the struggle continues, but it has been resolved in the perfect fidelity and perseverance of

Christ crucified and risen. Therefore, as Christian spouses pray for perseverance in a world where Marriage so often fails, they need not only the realism of the Cross, the will to self-giving and self-sacrifice. They also need the hope of the Resurrection, in a world where married life and forming a family are beset with profane pessimism.

The God of the Covenants calls his people forward to a promised land, a promised eternity. In this Covenant journey, faith is "the assurance of things hoped for, the conviction of things not seen" (Hebrews 11:1). The synthesis of faith and hope in Hebrews is a good description of the faith of spouses as they begin their covenant journey of married life. They consent to become "one flesh," not knowing what is ahead of them, thereby not only recapitulating the Covenant journey of Israel but participating, through their own covenant, in the Covenant journey of the pilgrim Church.

The human faith, hope and love of spouses is raised by the sacrament into the strength of the divine virtues, Faith, Hope, and Charity. We have already seen how the human faith involved in consent is the natural basis for a life of fidelity. But for the sacrament to be fruitful through its Grace, spouses are called to put their faith in God who made them one and who keeps and honors his promises. In imparting his own spousal love, his *agape*, the Bridegroom elevates their own human love to become the self-giving of his Cross. But the hope of Marriage is to persevere in the union, to live the bond in fidelity, whatever sufferings come, whatever sin and human frailty may bring, "until death do us part."

Baptized into the Cross and Resurrection, spouses learn the realism and hope of the Bridegroom who persevered, who went forward to Jerusalem to die for his bride, to make of her a new and eternal Jerusalem, the resplendent Mother, pure and spotless, bathed in his risen glory. They will learn the generosity of the Cross, seeing the gift of procreation as not only a share in the Creator's work but a share in the extension of the Mystical Body of the Redeemer. They will make the sacrifices of the Cross, persevering in the task of forming a family, seeing in their children new heirs to the promise of the Covenant. But they can only persevere "in the mystery of the spiritual fecundity of faith, hope and love," in faith in the God revealed in the Cross, who "has first revealed himself as the eternally faithful one in whom man must believe, in whom he must hope, and whom he must love."[40]

III. CALLED TO PEACE

Following the teaching of John Paul II that Marriage as sacrament takes up and makes specific the Sanctifying Grace of Baptism, we may discern in the spousal life of the Virtues, something of the distinctive Grace of Marriage envisaged by Saint Thomas. The baptismal Virtues in Marriage can be seen in their new spousal form as the divinization of the natural faith, hope and love of any good Marriage. Baptism is more clearly recognized as the basis of this sacrament in the new, "one flesh," form of the Virtues of Faith, Hope and Charity, as well as in the making of Marriage by the consent and spousal union of those who are "in Christ," a "new creation" and "members of his body."

Marriage, as a lived covenant of love, depends on two other sacraments, Penance and the Eucharist. Let us begin with Penance, for penitence is the prerequisite for any sacramental action to be fruitful.

Within Marriage there is a reconciling unity, to which Saint Paul called the Ephesians. In resolving Marriage problems at Corinth, Paul made an incisive comment about married life, setting forth in a few words his own philosophy: "God has called us to peace" (1 Corinthians 7:15). Clearly this applies to the Pauline Privilege and similar permitted resolutions of some matrimonial situations.[41]   But peace is within Marriage, in the covenant, the "pact." The Grace of peace is founded on the security of the indissoluble bond which, even as it is a communion of persons, stands over against every Marriage as a point of reference for, or a judgment on, the behavior of spouses. The peace of the Cross binds man and woman together as "one flesh," the reconciling "unity of the Spirit in the bond of peace" (Ephesians 4:3). This peace of the Cross, however, is known only in forgiving and being forgiven, in the mutual "giving way" to one another at its most costly level.

"See, my beloved, I come to do *your* will!" That is the reconciling love which "gives way" to the beloved. In its perfect form in the love of the Bridegroom for his Church, it was his acceptance of her hidden will, to be accepted, cleansed, re-born and taken to him forever, that yearning for saving union imprinted in our created nature. But the bride responds to her Beloved with penitent love, marvelling at her election and acceptance, humbled in being accepted by One who gave himself for her.

In this school of the forgiving, accepting love of the Bridegroom, spouses learn the capacity to forgive and impart peace. The cruel betrayal of the bond by infidelity is the ultimate test, the supreme invitation to forgive and to share in the Divine Mercy and the beatitude of the merciful. The peace of reconciliation after any argument or rift shows us how this sacrament of the "great mystery" is lived. The consoling, comforting arms of the beloved become a harbor of peace, reflecting One whose arms embraced his spouse in loving immolation for her on the Cross. We also see this reconciling love, not so much in forgiveness, but in the way spouses live the sacrament by imparting peace to a sick, fearful, despairing or confused partner. Spousal union itself can be a sacramental sign of forgiveness or healing, just as the sacrifice of spousal union can be an equal sign of acceptance, for example in those Marriages where one partner can no longer engage in physical love.

The peace of the sacrament may be discerned especially when disparate personalities become "one flesh." Over the years of quiet service and persevering love, the turbulent partner is gradually pacified, or at least given the capacity to understand himself or herself. A toleration is acquired which confounds the world. It confronts the intolerance of difference which is concealed in our "liberal" societies, which pay lip service to public pluralism and distrust personal differences. This hypocrisy conspires to drive men and women to divorce, especially when they are challenged either by differences between their personalities, or that turbulent kind of Marriage between two energetic personalities. This latter kind of union of two non-passive partners challenges them to higher levels of reconciliation, when it is much harder to "give way," but that reconciliation will be as colorful and dramatic as the rift, for such people relate to their God in the same shades of color and contrast. He is always greater than our hearts.

Only penitents can find this forgiving love, because they know themselves in the sacrament of Penance where they are accepted again and again by the merciful Lord. Spouses, as parents, sustained by the sacrament of Penance which always expresses the repentance and mutual pardon which is so much a part of daily life, can thus bring the peace of Marriage into the home, into the heart of the Christian family.[42]   Here the sacrament of Marriage becomes not only the sign of the love of Christ for his Church but of the victory he grants to spouses when they have to cope with forces which would deform and destroy their love. Thus, through Marriage, sustained by Penance, the family can become a sign of the reconciled and reconciling Church.[43] This is not an ideal. It is visible in countless Christian homes today.

IV. IN THE EUCHARISTIC COVENANT

Pope John Paul II placed the covenant of Marriage within the Eucharist, the Sacrifice of the New Covenant: "The Eucharist is the very source of Christian Marriage. The Eucharistic Sacrifice, in fact, re-presents Christ's covenant of love with the Church, sealed with His Blood on the Cross. In this sacrifice of the New and Eternal Covenant, Christian spouses encounter the source from which their own marriage covenant flows, is interiorly structured and becomes continuously re-newed. As a representation of Christ's sacrifice of love for the Church, the Eucharist is a fountain of charity."[44]

As there is a need for spouses to be penitents, regularly coming to confession, so there is a need for them to receive the Eucharist fre-quently, and together if possible, as "one flesh," as a family. The Eucharistic way in which their Marriage covenant is structured and continuously renewed can be understood as the strengthening of their "one flesh," by becoming together "one flesh" with the Eucharistic Lord. In turn, this unifies the family, so often the experience of families today, and thus unifies the wider Church. A married lay theologian, Germain Grisez, father and grandfather, has expressed this unity: "This real unity of the marital covenant symbolizes the unity of Our Lord Jesus and the Church (see Ephesians 5:32), for the Church is his fullness (Ephesians 1:23) and he fulfills the Church (see Colossians 1:19-20). The unity of the new covenant which marriage signifies is accomplished in Jesus' sacrifice and actualized for us in the Eucharist."[45]

What then is the Eucharist but the Bridegroom giving himself in love continually for, and to, his bride, the Church? Personified in Mary, is not the Church able to give herself, and be offered, to the Father in union with the Spirit, in Christ's nuptial oblation? What else is the nourishing of the Eucharist but the Bridegroom nourishing and cherishing his own flesh "as Christ does the Church, because we are members of his body" (Ephesians 5:29-30)? Therefore, when Christian spouses come to Mass and share in the Eucharist, they draw once more on the "great mystery," and so they can rediscover the Grace of their own covenant of love. Their love becomes that of the self-giving Bridegroom whose broken Body and outpoured Blood seals the Eternal Covenant. Within that Covenant, their own nuptial covenant can become a self-giving union and communion, leading them to eternal life.

The sacrament which signifies the "great mystery," as a lived sacrament, should be enfolded continually in the Eucharist, the sacrament which contains the "great mystery." As it is celebrated, Marriage should be enfolded visibly in the celebration of the liturgy. This is vividly set before us by the post-conciliar practice of bride and groom making their consent after the Gospel and before the Liturgy of the Eucharist. The Word of God calls them to Marriage, and the Word and Marriage calls them further, to the Eucharist, as "one flesh." Therefore, what the liturgy symbolizes should be the rule of life for this Christian state of life — the regular, frequent and mutual return to the source and summit where the Lamb gives himself up for his bride and grants us a foretaste of his nuptial banquet.

V. PERSEVERING IN LOVE

The years pass so quickly. The children are given by God and reared and educated. And, one by one, they go forth to find their state of life. The years pass, and does love pass with those years? The fervor of the seeking, choosing and self-gift may well fade with time. The trials of life together, its tensions and troubles, may test love as that first fervor becomes but a memory. But has love itself been lost? Need it be lost? Are

Christians to succumb to that cold *ennui* which breaks so many Marriages in our times? We turn to the sacrament, abiding ever, a lived covenant community of shared life and love.

In the making of the sacrament, the Holy Spirit bound two hearts together in the Heart of Christ. He continues to work in the children of the Father, members of the Son. Through the Spirit, the faithful Bridegroom abides with his Church. So he abides, through the Spirit, in each sacramental microcosm of the Church, each Marriage. The Bridegroom who consecrated himself in the truth promises the "Spirit of truth" to those whose consecration in truth is Marriage, whose love is derived from the Triune Source of all love.

What then is the quality of the "truth" of love in which spouses are "consecrated," in which they are set apart and established "until death do us part"? It is a kind of "beholding in love," firmly based on the truth of Christian anthropology, revealed in a unique way in Marriage. This "beholding" of the beloved in a way which does not fade is much more than respect. It is the perpetuation of what Josef Pieper expressed in the words, "How good it is that you exist!"[46]

Those words can be the ecstatic cry of the young bridegroom or bride. But they may also be the silent, unuttered "beholding" of love between aged spouses who have made the journey together over many years and whose persevering love is that visible and permanent sacrament of Marriage recognized by Saint Robert Bellarmine. When family and friends are with that aged couple, they do not need to hear them utter protestations of love, for they can see the "beholding" of steadfast love, the Covenant *hesed*, the *agape* of Jesus, love which is two bodies, two selves, mutually laid down in sacrifice for one another. They see spouses who are true friends.

There may or may not be a romantic quality in this steadfast perseverance in love. There will be the capacity to suffer, to enter the divine and human compassion of the Heart of Christ. Love is not simply to gratify oneself by happiness. There is a loving sorrow and pain.[47]   In the "great mystery" we see the crucified Bridegroom suffering for his Church, yet the suffering penetrates the Church, personified in Mary, Mother of Sorrows. Both the Bridegroom and his spouse were obedient to the law of suffering which mysteriously penetrates our cosmos. They shared suffering in their love. And if the Church in the earthly pilgrimage of her espousal with Christ must suffer, it is because she loves and is accepted in love for who she is. Her "beholding" of her Bridegroom is a perpetual contemplation and adoration: "How good it is that you exist!"

The "great mystery" in Marriage reveals the Christian anthropology which is the basis for a love which is willing to suffer. The beloved is loved, not for any qualities he or she may possess, but for his or her inherent and unrepeatable value as a person. This is the truth of love, the truth of love as an acting being's response to the given reality of existence, of the creation in which he or she is embodied.[48] In the affirmation of the being of the other, the beloved, each spouse can never treat that unique person as an instrumental means to some end, my happiness . . . my pleasure . . . my comfort.

Whatever the cost, spouses will persevere in such love, finding in their sacrament a taste of the freedom and joy of the timeless eternity. Not only will they choose and will the good of the beloved, they will choose and will the good of Marriage, "until death do us part." Not burdened by the bond, but free, the Eucharistic quality of their love will be a gratitude to the beloved, and in the beloved to God, for the gift of "being there."[49] Thus, "How good that you exist!" becomes a prayer of thanksgiving, woven into the shared life of prayer, which is the surest way to persevere in the living of this sacrament in an abiding covenant of love.

Called to peace, finding peace in this love, spouses can look back and reflect on the dignity and trust which God gave them in their baptismal capacity to make sacramental consent, to form the holy bond and its covenant community of life and love. They can look back on the making of the sacrament and refresh their abiding fidelity to one another which is their married way of living in the New and Eternal Covenant. They chose this Christian state of life and yet they know that they were chosen for it, under the Providence of God who orders all things to the good.

That death will end this earthly, sacramental way of life together does not bring fear to their hearts. Perfect love has cast out fear. Having ministered faithfully to one another as the best of friends, in the humble actions and ways of family life, they look beyond the brief parting of death to the end, the *telos*, for which God created them, redeemed them and made them "one flesh." Their journey together has been God's chosen means for their salvation. They have found the peace of their covenant, and they can wait in hope for the glory of the celestial nuptials. They know that "Love bears all things, believes all things, hopes all things, endures all things. Love never ends. . . ." (1 Corinthians 13:7-8).

CHAPTER SEVEN

Sacramental Problems

Y dice el Pastorcico: ¡Ay, desdichado De aquel que de mi amor ha hecho ausencia, Y no quiere gozar la mi presencia, Y el pecho por su amor muy lastimado!	*"Alas! Alas! for him," the Shepherd cries,* *"Who tries from me my dearest love to part* *So that she does not gaze into my eyes* *Or see that I am wounded to the heart!"*
Y a cabo de un gran rato se ha encumbrado Sobre un árbol do abrió sus brazos bellos, Y muerto se ha quedado, asido de ellos, El pecho del amor muy lastimado.	*Then, after a long time, a tree he scaled,* *Opened his strong arms bravely wide apart,* *And clung upon that tree till death prevailed,* *So sorely was he wounded in his heart.*

Saint John of the Cross, *Other songs concerning Christ and the soul.*

In the field of sacramental Marriage, there are certain practical, pastoral, problems which may be clarified and even resolved in the light of a theology of Marriage as a sacrament of the New Covenant. A study of the sacramentality of Marriage would not be complete without an examination of some of these problems. For our study, four areas which may benefit from a deeper understanding of

Marriage as a sacrament have been selected: (1) the pastoral problem of what degree of faith should be required of baptized persons who seek the sacrament of Marriage, (2) whether Marriage between a Christian and an unbaptized person is in some way "sacramental," (3) the ecumenical problem of the attitude of other Churches and ecclesial communions to Marriage as a sacrament, (4) the problem of the effect of contraception on a sacramental Marriage.

Each of these is in itself a theme for a separate work. Our purpose here is thus only to introduce the problem and suggest some ways in which the sacramentality of Marriage may help resolve the issues.

FAITH AND SACRAMENT

Especially in the years following the Second World War, when there was growing awareness of "de-christianization" in Western Europe, pastors began to reflect seriously on the problem of "faith and sacrament" in Marriage. What degree of faith are we to require of those who seek sacramental Marriage, and yet who have little or no connection in commitment or practice with the Catholic Church into which they were baptized? Are we to refuse sacramental Marriage to these men and women because their lack of faith may render the sacrament invalid, or lay upon them a burden of indissolubility which they cannot bear "until death do us part"? Are we to send them away to seek a civil marriage and wait until they are ready to enter a sacramental Marriage?

The liturgical and catechetical revival of our century placed more emphasis on the dispositions of faith with which people should fruitfully receive sacraments. This only served to draw more attention to the question of admitting lapsed or careless Catholics to sacramental Marriage. In the Constitution on the Sacred Liturgy, *Sacrosanctum Concilium*, the Fathers of the Second Vatican Council emphasized the importance of faith in receiving sacraments. The Fathers taught that sacraments "not only presuppose faith, but by words and objects they also nourish, strengthen and express it. That is why they are called 'sacraments of faith.' They do, indeed, confer grace but, in addition, the very act of celebrating them most effectively disposes the faithful to receive this grace to their profit, to worship God duly, and to practice charity."[1]

A comparison between the text of the proposed schema at this point, and the text finally accepted, shows that the Fathers did not seek to weaken the *ex opere operato* principle affirmed at Trent.[2] But they did seek to promote the more *fruitful* participation of the faithful in the celebration of sacraments. They did not define any precise degree or form of faith required for receiving sacraments, and it is clear that they did not make the validity of sacraments depend on any defined form or degree of faith.

The publication of the new Rite of Marriage, for the Roman Rite in 1969, encouraged demands for a stricter control of those seeking sacramental Marriage. Citing *Sacrosanctum Concilium*, 59, the introduction to the rite declared: "Pastors are first of all to encourage and nurture the faith of the prospective spouses, for the Sacrament of Marriage supposes and openly expresses faith."[3] In the following decade some theologians pressed the demand for the need for explicit faith before entering sacramental Marriage.[4]

The problem was a major concern of the International Theological Commission, in its published *Propositions on the Doctrine of Christian Marriage*, evident in Proposition 2.3. Noting that the validity of Marriage does not necessarily depend on whether or not the sacrament is "fruitful," the Commission raised the dilemma of baptized non-believers. The Commission maintained the inseparability between contract and sacrament: "The intention of carrying out what Christ and the Church desire is the minimum condition required before consent is considered to be a real human act on the sacramental plane. The problem of the intention and that of the personal faith of the contracting parties must not be confused, but they must not be totally separated either." Here we see that the Commission was itself divided over the problem, for the doubt was raised,"Where there is no trace of faith (in the sense of *belief* — being disposed to believe), and no desire for grace or salvation," whether such a situation rendered the sacrament invalid. The uncertainty of the Commission was evident: "As was noted, the personal faith of the contracting parties does not constitute the sacramentality of matrimony, but the absence of personal faith weakens the validity of the sacrament."[5] The curious phrase "weakens the validity of the sacrament" show us the uncertain mind of the Commission.

Among the Position Papers of some members of the Commission, Karl.Lehmann maintained the distinction between the objective reality of the sacrament and the fruits of Grace, which presuppose a proper disposition. And he went on to discuss the problem of varying degrees of membership in the Church among the baptized, according to their commitment.[6]

In the light of his detailed historical study of the inseparability between contract and sacrament, Carlo Caffarra opposed allowing non-sacramental celebrations or Marriage "celebrated in stages" for baptized non-believers, declaring, ". . . these pastoral proposals strike us as a mistaken response based on erroneous arguments to a *real* problem, namely, evangelization in general and the evangelization of marriage in particular."[7]

It was inevitable that the problem would be raised at the 1980 Synod of Bishops on the family. Before voting, Proposition 12 (in 6. *De Fide et Sacramento*) was modified. From being an extreme statement suggesting that *Sacrosanctum Concilium*, 59, requires explicit faith for validity, it became a call for investigation as to what extent faith is required for validity.[8] As *Sacrosanctum Concilium*, 59, concerns faith in the *fruitful* reception of sacraments, it cannot be used to require explicit faith for the validity of sacramental Marriage. The *Relatio* after the discussions of the Synod Fathers favorably noted the call of some Italian Bishops for a catechetical attitude towards preparation for Marriage, so that spouses may persevere in Marriage.[9]

In *Familiaris Consortio*, Pope John Paul II responded to the problem as raised by the Synod. Facing the contemporary reality of the problem of marriage with baptized non-believers, the Pope went to the very roots of Marriage as a created reality "in the beginning." The decision to marry "really involves, even if not in a fully conscious way, an attitude of profound obedience to God, an attitude which cannot exist without God's grace." He noted the familiar social motives for seeking to be married in a church, but he put the objective reality of Baptism above these motives, which he would not denigrate.

The Pope refused to provide "further criteria for admission to the ecclesial celebration of marriage." This would involve the risk of "making unfounded and discriminatory judgments" (as to the "degree" of faith in each party). It would risk raising doubts as to the validity of Marriages already celebrated. It would raise the danger of calling into question the sacramentality of Marriages between non-Catholic Christians. Therefore, he said that Marriage can only be refused to those who "reject explicitly and formally what the Church intends to do when the marriage of baptized persons is celebrated." In such cases, the obstacle is not raised by the Church but by those still seeking Marriage in a church. The Pope concluded with a call for "evangelization and catechesis before and after marriage."[10]

I. RESOLVING THE PROBLEM

The Pope takes us back to the roots of Marriage, to that "obedience to God" involved in the choice to marry. Today, even this choice to marry is significant. There are other options to Marriage. We have already examined the element of obedient faith involved in mutual consent.[11]   This suggests the first way to resolve our problem. We may investigate faith, how it can be lost, how it is possible for all to have some faith in God.

Faced with the indifferentism and rationalism of the Nineteenth Century, the First Vatican Council would not allow for parity between Catholics with faith and those who follow false religions or who suspend their assent until scientific proof is provided.[12]   Implicit in this teaching is the moral culpability of willfully rejecting revealed truth.[13]   This tradition explains the provisions in Canon Law forbidding sacramental Marriage to a notorious apostate, except under certain conditions.[14]

But the loss of faith was not seen only in terms of rejection of doctrine or the loss of the virtue of faith. Even if losing the faith is not like losing one's keys, through ignorance, pastoral neglect or family circumstances, Catholics often "fall away" or "lapse." This was already apparent in the late Nineteenth Century.[15] We may also ask to what extent such people have "lost" the faith, for vestigial faith in God may be evident in the good will of seeking or agreeing to be married in a Catholic church.

If it is possible to acknowledge good will among those who have lapsed, but are not notorious apostates, we may also draw upon the First Vatican Council for a positive view of the human capacity to believe in God. The Council also taught that God can be known by reason from what he has created.[16] However, granted this possibility of belief in God, one can yet resist God's Grace.[17] Each person has the possibility of belief, even if in fact each person does not exercise this capacity for various reasons.[18]

In the face of fideism or the pessimism of Calvinism or Jansenism, the Church holds out the optimism of any person being able to believe in God through the exercise of his or her reason. The same principle applies to knowledge of the moral law. In 1860, the Holy Office sent an instruction on how to deal with polygamy to the Vicar Apostolic of the Gallas people in Southern Ethiopia. The instruction affirmed that these "savage" people have the innate capacity to discern the moral law of Marriage, and can be expected to make the transition from polygamy to monogamy as part of their conversion to the Catholic Faith.[19] When we link this high, but reasoned, expectation of moral awareness with the teaching of the Second Vatican Council on the potential of those non-believers who "not without grace strive to lead a good life,"[20] then how much more confident can we be that God can work through lapsed Catholics who seek sacramental Marriage?

The objection may be raised that the real issue is the faith required to have an adequate intention to receive a sacrament. We turn now to sacramental theology.

The Church has never defined precisely what intention is required of adults to receive sacraments validly. In a purely negative way we can see that only a deliberate major obstacle could make an adult Baptism invalid, for example rejecting being baptized. A very weak or impenitent faith would hamper the effects of justifying Grace of which Baptism is the instrumental cause.[21] But the

character would be imparted nonetheless, disposing the new Christian for the Grace to live faithfully the gift received. Moreover, Baptismal Grace would "revive" were the impenitent or careless convert to turn to God at some later stage with a deeper faith.[22]
A similar model of faith-intentionality applies to Marriage. People can marry with weak or faithless motives and later be subject to a conversion, which enriches their Marriage so that the reality of the bond is able to be lived in such a way that they become ministers of Grace to one another. But their weak or faithless motives or vague or confused intention did not invalidate their Marriage. God, who is greater than our hearts, is able to bring to fruition what he begins in even his most "unpromising" children.

But is this not "expecting too much" of people, binding them to an indissolubility for which they may not be "ready"? Once this pastoral concern suggests civil marriage or some religious rite in place of the sacrament as a "stage" leading to a later sacramental Marriage, we should note what has happened. We have reverted to the separation of the contract from the sacrament. Cardinal Felici drew attention to this danger in the faith and sacrament issue when speaking at the opening of the academic year of the Lateran University in 1976.[23]   Carlo Caffarra perceived it in his Position Paper for the International Theological Commission in 1978.[24]   By celebrating Marriage in "stages," what Cano foreshadowed and the Regalists wanted would be achieved: a civil contract first, separated from a sacrament, added later for those who are "ready" for it.

But if, as ministers of the sacrament, the spouses who contract Marriage thereby effect the sacrament, what is their "intention of the Church" envisaged for all sacraments by the Council of Florence?[25] It can only be the simple guidance for true consent set out in Canon Law.[26]   This pertains to validity. To be fruitful, the sacrament requires a response of faith to what God has effected. This response cannot be limited only to the moments of consent, for there is a further danger in placing too much scrupulous emphasis on how Marriage is celebrated "in fieri" and forgetting the lived sacrament "in facto esse" where the real development of married life occurs.[27]

To be married according to the "intention of the Church" is defined in a minimalist way, that those marrying "are at least not

ignorant of the fact that marriage is a permanent relationship between a man and a woman, ordered to the procreation of children
through some form of sexual cooperation."[28] To go beyond this
sacramental consent and demand deep faith or correct awareness,
even of indissolubility or the dignity of the sacrament,[29] leads subtly
in another direction — towards Jansenist sacramentalism.

The Jansenist danger suggests a useful parallel in sacramental
theology: contrition and attrition. The Jansenists demanded a heart-
felt loving penitence, a profound contrition, before absolution could
be validly imparted. They rejected the minimal disposition required
for validity, attrition, confessing because one fears the reality of
hell.[30] Their position effectively kept many people from confession, because these people either felt they could not come up to the
high spiritual standards required by the Jansenists, or because they
were not prepared to undergo repeated refusal of absolution, when
the priest judged the penitent to be lacking in perfect loving penitence. In Marriage we could fall into the same disastrous pastoral
position by refusing to grant sacramental Marriage to those whose
disposition was minimal, like attrition in Penance, simply an ac-
knowledgment of the reality of the permanent relationship of Marriage and its procreative function.

As with Jansenism in France, the pastoral consequences of
refusing Marriage to baptized non-believers would be to advance the
process of de-christianization by closing off the Church to the ignorant and weak. Once Marriage is reserved for the "committed" or
devout, an elitist model of the Church emerges, a Church only for
those who have the piety or intellect to enter a "true" sacramental
Marriage.

Also, what happens to the sacrament once we demand such high
standards of faith? It is no longer a healing, strengthening *means* of
Grace, but a reward for those who are faithful, or a decorative
accessory to Marriage, or the outward sign of the Pelagian achievement of two people who were able to rise by virtue of their own
efforts (*ex opere operantis*) into the Christian married elite.

But the Catholic Church is for all people, for the weak and
sinful, all of us who need sacraments and who receive them imperfectly, relying on the God who acts in the sacraments. Because

sacraments are for people in need of Grace, we ought to welcome all who seek sacramental Marriage. Following the pastoral common sense of *Familiaris Consortio*, we should only refuse Marriage to willful apostates who, in most cases, would not seek this sacrament to begin with. But the Church must provide catechesis before Marriage and pastoral care afterwards. Whatever its pitfalls, the faith and sacrament problem has called us all, clergy and laity, to that task, to help even the weakest nominal Catholics to marry well and to persevere in their covenant of love.

MARRIAGE WITH AN UNBAPTIZED PERSON — A SACRAMENT?

Aware that many Catholics are marrying unbaptized persons, including members of other religions, Pope John Paul II asked for respect for the religion of the other partner, and that Bishops "ensure that there are proper pastoral safeguards for the faith of the Catholic partner and for the free exercise of his faith, above all in regard to his duty to do all in his power to ensure the Catholic baptism and education of the children of the marriage."[31] Let us assume that we are dealing with a Marriage where this mutual respect has been achieved, a Marriage where the Pauline Privilege cannot be invoked, where, for example, a Catholic and an unbaptized person married according to Church law, or where the conversion to Christianity of one partner was accepted peaceably by the unbaptized partner. What is the *sacramental* status of such a Marriage?

In his apostolic letter on inter-Church Marriages, *Matrimonia Mixta*, Pope Paul VI said, "Neither in doctrine or in law does the Church place on the same level marriage between a Catholic and a baptized non-Catholic, and one between a Catholic and an unbaptized person." He also added, "Undoubtedly there exists in a marriage between baptized persons, since such a marriage is a true sacrament, a certain communion of spiritual benefits which is lacking in a marriage entered into by a baptized person and one who is not baptized."[32] That these Marriages are non-sacramental is implicit in the Pope's words. Writing in 1978, Karl Lehmann accepted this same view as that of "most contemporary writers."[33]

However, the problem remains unresolved. We are not considering "natural" marriage between two unbaptized persons; rather, a Marriage beyond this "created reality," when one partner has the Christian, baptismal, capacity to marry. Even if we start with the "created reality" of natural Marriage, we recognize that in itself this is blessed by God, "at the beginning," in creation. As God's work, with the goodness of creation, natural Marriage is potentially sacramental, blessed by God to signify and effect his fruitfulness and fidelity. Natural marriage is "pre-sacramental" Marriage.[34]

Peter Lombard regarded Marriage as a sacrament, in creation and under the Old Law, before Christ, an opinion which may well have influenced his limited, remedial, view of Marriage, for he also listed Penance as a sacrament under the Old Law.[35] Discussing whether unbelievers could marry validly, Saint Thomas argued for the reality of their Marriages. But even as he did not regard these Marriages as sacraments of the Church, but simply a "natural state," he added, ". . . and still such a marriage is in some way potentially (*habitualiter*), though not actually (*actualiter*), a sacrament, since it was not an act entered into in the faith of the Church."[36]

To see how such a Marriage between the unbaptized can be "in some way" a sacrament "potentially," we turn to John Paul II. In his Marriage catechesis, which included such depth of insight into the "created reality," he described Marriage as the "primordial sacrament," the "sacrament of creation." Even as Marriage was damaged by the Fall and needed to become the "sacrament of Redemption," in its natural state it never lost that primordial signification, nor the capacity to be a figure or type of what it would, and could, become through the "great mystery."[37]

If the Marriage of the unbaptized retains this dignity as a sacrament of creation, expressing and effecting God's first blessing, then at least we can say this of our Marriage between a Christian and an unbaptized person. Can we say more? When we turn to Saint Paul and reflect on the role of the baptized partner, this union which already signifies and perpetuates creation may be seen to signify something more specific, *within* the "great mystery" of Christ and his spouse the Church.

I. DRAWN INTO THE "GREAT MYSTERY"

Writing to the Corinthians, Saint Paul said: "To the rest I say, not the Lord, that if any brother has a wife who is an unbeliever, and she consents to live with him, he should not divorce her. If any woman has a husband who is an unbeliever, and he consents to live with her, she should not divorce him. For the unbelieving husband is consecrated through his wife, and the unbelieving wife is consecrated through her husband. Otherwise, your children would be unclean, but as it is they are holy" (1 Corinthians 7:12-14).

Saint Paul discerned a true Marriage in this union, if consent to cohabit peacefully is granted in some way. The family is blessed through the Christian partner, so that the children are "holy" not "unclean," which may mean they are catechumens or even baptized because the Christian saw to this without opposition from the unbaptized partner, and they are certainly not illegitimate. But the way the Marriage is raised to some special status is through the Christian partner.

The unbaptized partner is "consecrated" through his or her Christian spouse. The Greek verb used for "he is consecrated" (*égiastai*) is the same used by Christ the Bridegroom, consecrating himself, and thus his spouse through him, at the Last Supper (cf. John 17:19). Thus the Christian partner is the minister of Grace in this Marriage, the Grace of Christ. In some way, he or she sets the unbaptized partner apart in the exclusive union of self-gift, bringing the *agape* of the Bridegroom to this Marriage. Therefore, at least from the side of the Christian, we are looking at a Marriage well beyond a natural union.

This Marriage lacks the *mutual* consecration by the exclusive self-gift in the love of the Bridegroom. But, from "one side" Christ the Bridegroom is seeking his spouse the Church by the ministry of a person "in Christ" by Baptism. The signification is incomplete, just as there is lacking the Christ-Church unity in "one flesh." The "one flesh" of creation, though, is here and more, because the unbaptized partner is being drawn into the "great mystery" through the ministry of the Christian partner. If Christ seeking his spouse is what is signified, then this Marriage vividly signifies the salvific will of God.

Let us not forget the unbaptized partner who may be a non-believer, an unbeliever, or a member of some other religion. This person does not come "empty-handed" to the Marriage. He or she stands to gain much in terms of the ministry of Grace which the Christian can, and should offer. But, in return, in loving and cherishing one who is "in Christ," the unbaptized person is able to love Jesus. This love may not be given with any conscious faith in Christ, or even belief in God, but it is "graced" by God.

The hidden working of Grace may become clearer by reflecting on Maritain's theory of the graced status of the free human act of choosing and willing the good, for example, in the case of the first free moral act of an unbaptized child.[38] If God imparts Grace in such a choice for the moral good, and this is an inchoate act of faith in him, how much more does he sustain the unbaptized man or woman who makes the nuptial gift of self to his or her Christian spouse. Therefore, the unbaptized ministers to the baptized, and brings himself or herself to this Marriage as one redeemed by Christ who "has in a certain way united himself with each man."[39]

The salvation of both partners may well be worked out in terms of how each of them lived their covenant of love in this Marriage which is an effectual sign of God's universal salvific will. But salvation is always and only mediated through Christ and his Church, that is, through the "great mystery." By being consecrated in a union of "one flesh" with a Christian, the unbaptized partner is associated with the mystery of the Church. Under the Old Covenant, "strangers and sojourners" enjoyed the spiritual hospitality of Israel. Under the New Covenant, the unbaptized are brought into the hospitality of the Church by way of Marriage to a Christian.

So much depends on the quality of the nuptial ministry of the Christian partner, because this association with the mystery of the Church is a call to enter the Church, to receive the gift of Faith in Baptism. Through the words and deeds of the Christian spouse, we would hope for this complete response to the call of the Bridegroom and his spouse the Church. But in his hidden ways, God may offer salvation as a Baptism of desire, in living the Marriage covenant. Fidelity to that covenant is always fidelity to God.

Therefore, we may discern even the salvific signification and causality of sacramental Marriage in these Marriages, which we should not dismiss hastily as "non-sacramental." A theological answer to this problem is less dogmatic than a legal answer and, in an established union under pressure, a theological answer would stand in favor of the bond.[40]

"SACRAMENT," AN ECUMENICAL QUESTION

The ecumenical question does not pertain to the intrinsic sacramentality of inter-Church Marriages, for these are truly sacramental.[41] The problem is to ascertain whether the separated Churches and ecclesial communities regard Marriage as a sacrament, not only in belief but in practice.

Among the Protestants, Marriage is not regarded as a sacrament of the New Law instituted by Jesus Christ. In spite of the diversity of Protestantism and, in some quarters, a better understanding of Baptism, the Eucharist and ministry, the Reformers' denial of the sacramentality of Marriage has been maintained.[42] Marriage is subject to civil laws and indissolubility is not accepted in practice. At the same time, many Protestants, especially in the Evangelical tradition, reverence Marriage and family life as blessed by God. They share our anxieties concerning Marriage and the family in the modern world.

On the other hand, the Eastern Orthodox and many of the Anglicans see Marriage as a sacrament. Let us, therefore, concentrate on the ecumenical question within Orthodoxy and the Anglican Communion.

I. THE EASTERN ORTHODOX

With the publication of *Crescens Matrimoniorum* in 1967, the Catholic Church sought to remove problems in law for Marriages between Catholics and the Eastern Orthodox.[43]   With the Orthodox, Roman Catholics share not only the apostolic succession and sacraments, but also a common faith in the seven sacraments and their efficacy. The Orthodox see Marriage as one of the seven "holy mysteries." Those who marry are raised into the "great mystery." Married life is a state of Grace, a vocation to be sharers in the three-fold office of Jesus Christ: Prophet, Priest and King.[44]   With their liturgical awareness of the "great mystery," the Orthodox can provide many insights into the sacrament as it is celebrated and lived.[45]

Do Roman Catholics and the Eastern Orthodox differ sharply over the question of how the sacrament is celebrated? The Orthodox maintain that the priest is the minister of the sacrament, imparted by way of a blessing. However, this was not the ancient tradition. Saint John Chrysostom saw consent as making a Marriage.[46]   A contemporary Orthodox author, even though not sympathetic to Catholicism, has stated that whoever accepts the contract, not the ceremony, makes the sacrament.[47]   But the blessing remains the form, to use the Roman Catholic term, of Marriage "*in fieri*" for the Orthodox.

The problem does not seem to be insurmountable since, as we have already suggested, mutual consent is implicit in the rite of betrothal which takes place at the church door, and the rite of Marriage celebrated at the ambo.[48]   The Christian East sees sacramental action with a different emphasis than does the West. The East's view is perhaps closer to the old "occasional causality" view, insofar as the celebrants and recipients of sacraments seem to be those who lay themselves open in a kind of passive way to the divine action within the context of liturgy. The indicative baptismal formula of the Eastern Churches expresses this view: "The servant of God N. is baptized in the Name of . . .," rather than our Western formula: "N., I baptize you in the Name of. . . ."

Although we would maintain consent and the ministry of the bride and groom as essential for the sacrament, we may learn something of the Eastern view of the sacrament from their understanding of the Holy Eucharist and Marriage. Although the practice of Nuptial Mass was lost in the Byzantine Rite, apparently the Marriage rite is to be seen in a Eucharistic context. As minister of the Eucharist, the priest is minister of Marriage. Those who are members of the Eucharistic community are married in Christ, within the ambit of the Divine Liturgy.[49]   Marriage is seen in an ecclesial way. It is a sacred, graced event within the Church, not considered in a juridical sense, but as the Mystical Body offering divine worship which incorporates this specific act of nuptial worship. Because of their abiding Eucharistic unity with Christ, as "members of his body," two Christians who marry have their Marriage transformed into a holy mystery by the blessing of the Church.

Considering the practice of multitudes of Eastern Christians united to the See of Peter, the question of blessing or consent does not seem to be an ecumenical barrier with our separated Orthodox brethren. Where the problems begin is over the question of indissolubility.

The Orthodox grant divorces and permit remarriage for specified reasons. The grounds for divorce include: adultery of a wife with any other person, of a husband with a married woman, attempted murder, abortion, impotence prior to Marriage, malicious abandonment of a spouse, leprosy, prolonged abuses or "shaking" of the union. Treason is no longer a major ground, and change of religion is a cause which may lead to divorce.[50]   In the last century, however, the grounds of divorce became even wider in practice through decisions of the patriarchal synod of Constantinople.[51]

In the light of Catholic adherence to Our Lord's teaching and his indissoluble union with his Church in the "great mystery," it seems difficult to reconcile such law and practice with a complete understanding of Marriage as a sacrament. It will not do to dismiss the problem with irenical words about this merely being a "different interpretation" of Our Lord's exceptive clause in Matthew 5:32. The Orthodox have moved far beyond allowing divorce for the innocent victim of adultery, even assuming that is what the exceptive clause means.

A theological argument for this practice seems specious when it describes love as a gift and adultery as a "gift refused," thus terminating a Marriage, or when it accepts indissolubility but never as legally absolute.[52]   The argument looks worse when set against a statement defending the paradox of Eastern Orthodox stern disapproval of Marriage after the death of a partner: "Christian marriage is not only an earthly sexual union, but an eternal bond which will continue when our bodies will be 'spiritual' and when Christ will be 'all in all'."[53]   If this is said against remarrying after the death of a spouse, does it not likewise apply to remarrying after divorce?

The root of the problem which produces such confusing exaggeration or denial of the bond is the Church-State relationship. Up until the Sixth Century, the East was at one with the West over indissolubility. A clear history may be set out describing the stages whereby the hierarchy in the East capitulated over divorce and remarriage to the Byzantine Emperors.[54]   But to be just, that interpretation must be placed in the context of the Eastern understanding of Christendom. In the hieratic State, the Emperor played a protective and a juridical role in Church affairs. For the clergy, it was often a matter of the "art of the possible" in return for protection from Islam and heresy.

There are two possible ways, however, for dialogue on this issue: (1) The patristic basis which the Orthodox cite to justify their practice and which is embodied in their Canons can be examined together; (2) the distinction between defined doctrine and practice can be considered.

If we look at the patristic basis for the Orthodox law and practice, much seems to depend on the interpretation of uncertainty in a letter of Saint Basil the Great to Archbishop Amphilochius of Iconium.[55] Father Joyce was on secure logical and historical ground. He interpreted Saint Basil as being uncertain, not as to whether a married man living with another woman is married to her or can be married to her, but as to whether they each incur the full canonical penance for adultery or only for fornication, since she seems to have been his concubine.[56]   But this case of uncertainty over a canonical penance was later used as patristic authority to allow remarriage, in a penitential kind of ceremony, after divorce.

Little value may likewise be given to Saint Basil's silence over remarriage when he prescribed a prolonged canonical penance for an adulterer who had left his wife.[57]   This becomes clearer in the light of his stated view that remarriage after divorce is not lawful.[58]   If the man had married again, Saint Basil would not prescribe a penance for one grave sin in the past, when a further phase of that sin had commenced. This must also be seen in the context of the severe penitential discipline of the time.

Nevertheless, let us enter into dialogue on the patristic basis for Orthodox law relating to divorce and remarriage. Because we share a common reverence for the holy Fathers of the East, this is an excellent starting point for an examination of the problem.

The second way for dialogue to proceed would be to examine the distinction between defined doctrine and practice. A point of reference could be the definition of indissolubility at Trent.

With the question of whether adultery dissolves Marriage and allows the innocent party to marry again, the Fathers at Trent faced not only the challenge of the Reformers but doubts raised by Erasmus in an extreme way and, cautiously, by Cardinal Cajetan and Ambrosius Catharinus.[59] Some Fathers, therefore, wanted what became Canon 7, on indissolubility, to be worded in guarded terms, stating that the Church has not erred in teaching that adultery does not dissolve a Marriage. But for a request from the Republic of Venice, this amendment would have passed into oblivion.

The Venetians at that time controlled Cyprus, Crete and various Greek islands where Greek rites were observed in communion with Rome. Marriage practice followed Greek ways. For the sake of pastoral patience in changing these ways, and no doubt to secure civil peace, the Venetians sought the modifying qualification of the wording of Canon 7.[60] After phrases were added ensuring that the Canon was a dogmatic decree, Canon 7 was accepted by the Council, with the modifying qualification in the opening words: "If anyone says that the Church is in error for having taught and for still teaching that in accordance with the evangelical and apostolic doctrine (cf. Mark 10; 1 Corinthians 7), the marriage bond cannot be dissolved because of adultery on the part of one or the other of the spouses. . . ."[61] Thus the evangelical and apostolic doctrine of indissolubility was defined by the Church, but the "anathema" only applied to those who said the Church had erred in teaching indissolubility. As the Orthodox also teach the doctrine, whatever may be their practice, the separated Churches of the East do not come under any censure in this Canon. The Venetian modification of the Canon is thus a useful ecumenical inheritance for our times.

Therefore, we did not and do not hurl recriminations of heresy at one another over this question. We do challenge the Eastern Orthodox to justify their practice. We do ask them to reflect on the historical situation in the past in which such practice developed. We may also ask them to consider how far that situation has changed. If the Greek Orthodox Church can challenge the government over abortion, surely the issue of stable married life in a changing world may require a revision of Church law and practice, without relying on civil approval.

Laws can be changed and reformed. The principle of indissolubility cannot be changed. It is inherent in the "great mystery" of the sacrament. If indissolubility is denied in practice, we can only believe a Marriage is indissoluble *post factum*, that is, if it ends with the death of a partner! But if our separated Orthodox brethren have apparently moved in that direction, we would do well to scrutinize the practice of our own Marriage tribunals, lest what Caesaro-Papism wrought in the East should penetrate the West by way of the best pastoral intentions.

II. THE ANGLICANS

No single attitude regarding the sacramentality of Marriage can be said to characterize the Anglican view. However, some ground for agreement was achieved in 1975 with the publication of a report on Marriage by the Anglican-Roman Catholic International Commission (A.R.C.I.C.).

Starting with a working principle that the unity of Marriage is sacramental in virtue of Baptism and is the work of God in Christ, the theologians involved in this project agreed that Marriage is "an effective sign of grace when it is celebrated between the baptized."[62] They did not find ground for disagreement over doctrine, and the Anglicans welcomed our post-conciliar use of "covenant."

While this joint report did not accept the Tridentine definition of Marriage as "one of the seven sacraments of the New Law, instituted by Jesus Christ," there is an evident development in Anglican consensus regarding the sacramentality of Marriage. If we contrast the two extremes within Anglicanism, this consensus in A.R.C.I.C. becomes clearer.

Evangelical Anglicans may not wish to describe Marriage as a sacrament. They may term it a "lesser sacrament," reflecting Article

XXIV of the Reformation-era *Thirty-Nine Articles of Religion.* According to Article XXIV, Marriage cannot be counted as one of the "sacraments of the Gospel," but is found among the "states of life allowed in the Scriptures," because, in accord with Luther, Marriage lacks "any visible ceremony ordained by God."[63]   Yet, Evangelicals participating in the A.R.C.I.C. group accepted the affirmation that Marriage is "an effective sign of grace when it is celebrated between the baptized."

Among the Anglo-Catholics, Marriage is regarded as one of the seven sacraments in the Catholic sense.[64]   Among more traditional Anglo-Catholics and high-churchmen, this belief is linked with a strong conviction that Marriage is indissoluble. A Catholic awareness of the sacrament of the "great mystery" has produced some sensitive and accurate theological writing, especially on the lived sacrament, graced by God.[65]   This view of sacramental Marriage developed during the Oxford Movement. As we shall see, some of the earlier high-churchmen were not of this opinion.

Between these extremes there is a wide range of Anglican views on Marriage. The problem is not so much the variety of views on the sacramentality of Marriage, which is to be expected in as comprehensive a body as the Anglican Communion. It is the same issue which separates us from the Eastern Orthodox — the indissolubility of Marriage.

Considering the matrimonial matters of Henry VIII and the strong influence of the European Reformers, the beginnings of Anglicanism did not favor indissolubility as integral to Christian Marriage. In 1553, Archbishop Cranmer's never-enacted code, the *Reformatio Legum Ecclesiasticarum*, included ample grounds for a Church divorce.[66]   But gradually two views on indissolubility emerged, not necessarily matching either the "high," Catholic tendency, or the "low," Protestant one.

In the Elizabethan age and early Seventeenth Century, the Reformation approval of Church divorce was matched by a strong disapproval of divorce and remarriage, due to the accelerating number of divorces in England. Later in the Seventeenth Century, however, the notable high-church ritualist, Bishop Cosin of Durham, rejected the indissolubility of Marriage when speaking in the House of Lords on the case of the divorce and remarriage of Lord Ros. This case set a precedent, allowing Parliament to grant civil divorces whereas until that year, 1670, the ecclesiastical divorce was technically only a separation "from bed and board."[67]

In 1857, the Church of England was divided over the Bill introducing civil divorce procedures. The Bill became law, and an Established Church found that it could not speak out officially against the new provisions. Anglo-Catholics and anti-rationalist Evangelicals were set against any Church concessions to the new law by way of remarriage. However, in 1888, the Lambeth Conference, representing all Churches in the world-wide Anglican Communion, left open the question of the remarriage of an innocent party after a divorce on the ground of adultery, and tacitly allowed clergy to admit such remarried persons to Holy Communion.[68]

We begin to see some Anglo-Catholics weakening after this Lambeth Conference, vehemently attacking divorce and maintaining indissolubility, yet allowing for exceptions on the ground that God's Law could not be fulfilled in certain cases.[69]   In 1930, the same Lambeth Conference which gave way over contraception, also allowed Bishops the right to admit remarried divorcees to Holy Communion, but did not allow Anglican rites for a second union.[70]   Six years later, the nation was divided over the issue of the abdication of King Edward VIII, who wished to marry Mrs. Wallis Warfield Simpson, an American divorcee. Social stigma still clung to those who had been divorced.

After the Second World War, some Anglicans demanded Anglican Marriage rites for the second union of an innocent party. In 1955, Princess Margaret's wish to marry Group Captain Peter Townsend raised the issue in the public forum. In spite of much agitation for her freedom to marry, she decided not to proceed, apparently under high-church guidance. In 1957, an Act of Convocation formally admitted remarried innocent parties to Holy Communion.

In 1964, Archbishop Arthur Michael Ramsey of Canterbury appointed a group to investigate further changes. In 1966, they produced a controversial report, *Putting Asunder*.[71] By the last years of the 'Sixties, pressure was building up for the remarriage in church of innocent parties.[72] A new commission produced a further report, *Marriage, Divorce and the Church*, relating Church practice to civil practice, and favoring the current Eastern Orthodox approach to divorce and remarriage.[73] The Anglicans not only had strong ecumenical contact with the Orthodox, but, as the Established Church in England, they hold a similar position to the Greek Orthodox, with similar problems.

In the midst of this steady process of change, we should never forget the difficult problem of authority in Anglicanism, and where it is ultimately located. Moreover, there is the complex problem of Anglican Canon Law and its relationship to British Law.[74] What may seem to be a giving way to social pressure may also be an attempt to retain established status, by adjusting to changing civil procedures in matrimonial matters.

Lady Helen Oppenheimer was a member of the *Putting Asunder* group, appointed in 1964. Taking what was characteristic of a middle-ground Anglican position, in 1976 she argued against both "rigorists" and liberals.[75] She favored a sacramental view of Marriage but asked, ". . . marriage may not melt like ice, but perhaps it might melt like gold?"[76] With such views predominating, what was already well-established in other parts of the Anglican Communion soon came to England. There were some Anglo-Catholic attempts to hold fast to the bond, but this was a rear-guard action.[77] The remarriage of the divorced, including some clergy, was gradually introduced. Even if many of the Anglicans see Marriage as a sacrament, in practice indissolubility is an ideal and no longer an inherent reality of the sacrament.

In the late 'Seventies and the 'Eighties, Anglicans were more preoccupied with other issues such as the ordination of women. This may partly explain the Anglo-Catholic failure to stop the remarriage of the divorced in church. It is interesting to note, moreover, that Anglicans who left official Anglican structures in various countries over the ordination of women, to form "continuing" Churches, often insist on the Catholic attitude on the sacramentality and indissolubility of Marriage.

In the midst of this process of change, the A.R.C.I.C. joint report of 1975 gained ground on sacramentality. But it included the frank admission that the Anglican and Catholic theologians could not agree on the question of divorce and remarriage.[78] In the light of this paradox of loss and gain, it is important that discussions on the sacramentally binding nature of Marriage should be resumed, even in the midst of discussions on more immediate problems of mutual concern. Our continuing interest in this manner should be motivated not only by the pastoral realities of inter-Church Marriages, but in an abiding respect for the mind of the Council that, among those separated communions "in which Catholic traditions and institutions in part continue to exist, the Anglican communion occupies a special place."[79]

THE SACRAMENT AND CONTRACEPTION

We have already referred to two sins against specific goods in Marriage: adultery, a sin against fidelity (*fides*), and divorce, a sin against indissolubility (*sacramentum* in the Augustinian sense). But there is also a sin against the first and natural good of Marriage, the procreation of children (*proles*). This is contraception. We begin with *Familiaris Consortio*.

All Marriages are undermined by contraception because it attacks that natural good by wresting from God his role as the Creator of life, in which role he is the giver of Marriage to man and woman. Through contraceptive acts a spouse is excluding God, determining the conditions for procreation without him. Spouses make themselves the "arbiters" of the divine plan and they "manipulate" and degrade their human sexuality.[80]

Once we place Marriage within the divine context, and see spouses as co-creators with the Creator, we begin to see what sterilizing spousal union means. But the problem of contraception in Marriage cannot be compartmentalized. Through the attack on the primary, natural, good of procreation, contraception attacks the other goods, fidelity and indissolubility. The three goods are closely related to one another. When you attack that which is "primary" in the sense of Marriage being naturally ordained towards a family, you likewise attack the "secondary" goods which Saint Thomas described in higher and broader terms than "offspring."[81] The noble fidelity and indissoluble covenant are not left unscathed when contraception becomes the determinant of procreation.

It is possible to argue in natural terms of the damaging consequences of contraception. Infidelity may be encouraged by the use of contraceptives: (1) because of the concentration on genital sexuality; (2) because of a weakening of respect for chastity and self-control; (3) by the reduction of a man or woman to an infertile sexual object or instrument, always available to the spouse — or any other partner. If infidelity is encouraged, so indissolubility is weakened.

We need, though, to take the argument further, into the supernatural dimensions of the great sacrament of Marriage. The covenant is the key to a better perception of this grave pastoral problem.

I. FIDELITY TO THE COVENANT?

Sacramental Marriage is meant to signify the mutual fidelity of Jesus Christ the Bridegroom and his spouse, the Church. But the sacrament causes what it signifies, that is, it gives the Grace to be faithful to one another in this covenant of love. In its dimension of fidelity, the Grace of the sacrament can only be effectual if no obstacle is raised against it.

The question arises: Do those who use contraceptives trust their Creator, the Author of their Marriage? This lack of faith in the Creator may be behind much of the skepticism concerning natural ways of spacing birth, even granted that ignorance and misinformation on these matters is widespread. The human technology is preferred to the divine economy, inscribed in the fruitfulness of each woman.

The lack of trust in God goes further in the sacrament, for here spouses are called by the Church to believe that Marriage is one of the seven sacraments. Resorting to contraception may mean that spouses do not trust the power of Grace. God is not seen as being able to sustain husband and wife so that they can be chaste in their periodic abstinence, required by the natural means of regulating one's family. As a rejection of what God offers, this is also a sin against the virtue of Faith, for it embodies doubt that Marriage is a true sacrament in terms of effectuality. Granted once again that ignorance or socially acceptable "fear of the child" may be at work in many instances, this lack of belief in the sacrament and trust in God must surely weaken confidence in the other dimensions of the Grace of Marriage.

The mutual love (*agape*) of the Bridegroom cannot flourish when the covenant laws of Marriage are broken, bent or weakened. The love which is "giving way" to one another must be directed to Jesus Christ and derived from his Cross, the love of his New Covenant. But once a couple stop placing their gift of fruitfulness at the disposal of God, they seek themselves, not God. A false anthropology emerges; man and woman declare their independent status, suppressing their partnership with the Creator and their sacramental dependence on the Redeemer and the work of the Holy Spirit. But that is not the male and female human nature revealed in the laws of the Marriage covenant — to become "one flesh," to be faithful to one another and to God, to live out the total self-giving of Jesus the Bridegroom. These laws reveal a dependence on God, raised to partnership with him in the order of creation and, in the Church, in the order of Redemption through procreation.

The sacrament they live comes from God. In gratitude it is meant to be returned to him, by living at his disposal as "one flesh." In withholding their fruitfulness by sterilizing it, a couple have not only redefined themselves as independent of God, they have redefined their covenant and taken it out of his New Covenant.

Their "new" covenant is a spurious compact to evade their responsibility to be ". . .'ministers' of God's plan," who ". . . 'benefit from' their sexuality according to the original dynamism of 'total' self-giving, without manipulation or alteration."[82]   Once they served God, and one another, as cooperators and co-creators; now they have become accomplices. Once they stood in the light of that nuptial Eden, generously open to Grace; now they seem to conceal themselves from the Lord, for they are naked, not in the innocent freedom of union with God, but naked in their self-contained, deliberately sterile, artificial sexuality. Again, culpability may be lessened by the fears and pressures of life in a society which bids them to suppress and manipulate the gift of fertility.

Perhaps they sought freedom in contraception. They cast off the "burden" of divine partnership, or responsible shared choice involved in the "giving way" of periodic abstinence. They freed themselves from the "burden" of a love which is chaste. But the "freedom" which they find is only a shared selfishness.[83]   What was easy, convenient, efficient, was chosen, and the choosing was "freedom," as libertarian society proclaims. But true freedom is to choose the good, to love the good, to find the beloved, not in the twilight of complicity, but in the light of the nuptial Eden. Here the Triune God gave man and woman to one another, and it was to this Eden of "one flesh" that the Bridegroom called spouses in his gift of the sacrament. In the light of this nuptial Eden, persons are revealed as to be loved for who they are, accepted totally, in a covenant love which includes and elevates the natural fertility inscribed into the gender of each person.

The freedom of a love which has cast out fear is found in the covenant of Marriage. Can the "fear of the child," or fearful lack of trust in the sacrament, co-exist with covenant love?

II. ONE FLESH?

The sacramentality of Marriage includes the self-giving of "one flesh" in spousal union. There are two ways of seeing contraception as a failure to become "one flesh," hence a further weakening of the covenant of love as it is taken out of its sacramental New Covenant context.

The "language of the body" is falsified in contraceptive intercourse. What is meant to be part of the whole encircling sign of the sacrament is being falsified. What is meant to say, "I give you myself, all of myself," is qualified by ". . . but not my fertility," or ". . . but not as a person who can transmit life." As the meaning of spousal union is falsified so "this leads not only to a refusal to be open to life but also to a falsification of the inner truth of conjugal love, which is called upon to give itself in personal totality."[84]   Thus the impaired sign of the sacrament can weaken the bond and strike at the Grace of married life. Just as the attack on the natural good of Marriage strikes at the goods of fidelity and indissolubility, so the same falsification of part of the sign of Marriage strikes at the reality and effect of the sacrament.

This falsifying of the sacramental language of total self-giving is better understood, however, if we ask what this new, falsified, "language of the body" is saying. It does not say, "I give you myself," but "I give you part of myself." A third "party" has intervened, the sterilizing agent. Both partners are aware that this has happened. This knowledge cannot vanish, with all the best motives, justifying reasons or loving intentions. That sterilizing agent has sundered the unitive and procreative aspects of their spousal union.[85]

We may take this falsification of the sacramental language of spousal union down to a further level. By suppressing the fertility of a married person, contraception has manipulated the personal giving of spousal union in such a way as to dissociate the body from the person. A contraceptive Manichaeism emerges. The body is separated from the person, so that spousal union is a sterile union. This takes spousal union in either of two Manichaean directions: either (1) "What we do with our bodies does not matter, for our sterile union is for a higher, spiritual love which justifies us in using our bodies as we choose, etc.," or, (2) "Our union is carnal sport, for we have taken measures to ensure that this recreation is as convenient as possible (no moralism, no side-effects such as pregnancy, etc.)".

This is disembodied sexuality because in (1) the body is reduced to an instrument to be used, and in (2) this is compounded by that instrument being further reduced to an end in itself. What has become now of the "one flesh" union which signifies the total self-giving of Christ and his Church? The rationalizing romanticism of (1) and the animal eroticism of (2) have falsified sacramental Marriage.

The incarnate Bridegroom did not exploit his Church; rather, he "gave himself up for her" (Ephesians 5:25), in embodied self-gift, in fruitful sacrificial union. Therefore, the sacramental "language of the body" can never make the beloved an instrument, or a pleasurable end in himself or herself. In the light of the considerate, embodied love of the "great mystery," we see again the value of the person affirmed for who he or she is as an accepted totality. One dimension of being a person cannot be chosen in a way which suppresses the other dimension, the capacity to transmit life as a co-creator. In the light of the selfless "giving way" in love of Christ and his spouse the Church, we see the wisdom of the warning of Paul VI in *Humanae Vitae* of the degradation, especially of women, once contraception enters Marriage. The person becomes an object. Two objects, or a subject and object, cannot become "one flesh."

III. UNITY

Another possible direction in understanding this problem is to consider the effect of "one flesh," which is the formation of a community of life and love. In that community, the very best of all friends share all that they have. The Marriage "vows" usually include words to this effect. Therefore, fertility is "our fertility," ours insofar as it belongs to God who shares it with the couple in his covenant, "ours" insofar as it is equally "our" gift from God.

This sharing of fertility is found in "one flesh" decisions as to how "we" dispose of that fertility before God. But contraception separates fertility into "mine" and "yours," as it opens the way for unilateral decisions not to procreate. Especially when one spouse decides to use contraception, which can always be a one-sided decision and act, then the "one flesh" interpersonal communion is broken. One party has arrogated the right to decide in the most intimate and fundamental area of spousal decision making, the formation of a family.

Just as the accomplice situation damages the Grace of Marriage, so does this rejection of Saint Paul's advice to "give way" to one another in mutual consideration. The sacred bond itself is weakened by this assault on unity.

IV. THE LIFE OF THE CHURCH

The union of Christ and his Church is always fruitful. Therefore, we cannot dissociate the problem of contraception from the healthy life and unity of the Body of Christ. Sin always weakens that Body in this world. One contraceptive example of this would be when "our fertility" is finally reduced to genitality. The fertile husband becomes only the virile man. The fertile wife becomes only the nubile woman. Their "one flesh" has changed into the pride of the flesh, and the way lies open to the sin of a kind of adultery within Marriage.

When Marriage is open to God, obedient in faith and trust in him, it is a ministry to God and to one another, and therefore fruitful in the life of the Church. Two "members of his body" build up the Church, and perpetuate the life-giving union of the Bridegroom and his beloved spouse. But if contraception is an obstacle to the Grace of Marriage, it harms not only the couple, but the Church as well, for all "members of his body" are interrelated. Likewise, the obstacles people put in the way of the fruitful reception of the sacraments may be compared to marital contraception.[86] When sacraments are received unworthily, when sacraments of a state of life are lived badly, then the Mystical Body on earth is weakened, divided, harmed.

Inseparable from this problem is the dissent from Church teaching involved in contraception, not only the influential dissent of some theologians or pastors, but the living dissent of spouses who use contraception. They cannot be unaware of the official teaching today. But they may be subject to pressures, bad advice, false information or the weariness of human weakness.[87] Nevertheless, as with all our frailties, the Church suffers from dissent, and her own "sacramentality" as the saving sign is obscured or compromised. Yet the sacrament can offer remedies for this weakening of the Church today.

V. A RESPONSE

Within the Church, dissent as opinion or action cannot be separated from the order of Grace. What spiritual fruit can dissent bring forth in the Body of Christ? But the healing of this problem is not an academic or disciplinary exercise. It must include the firm, but patient, proclamation and explanation of the binding teaching of the Church. The ground, though, must be prepared for this teaching, and this truth ought to be reinforced by a return to the sacrament of Marriage.

The preparation for Marriage ought to give future spouses a spiritual and theological vision of Marriage, as above all a great sacrament of the "great mystery." To raise men and women to seek the love, the *agape*, of Jesus the Bridegroom and his beloved Church, to show them the freedom of faith in God, trust in God, openness to God, to evangelize them with the promise and hope of the power this sacrament imparts to be chaste, considerate and strong — this is our task! Moreover, what begins in preparation needs to be refreshed again and again in the years of married life.

In this context we can effectively introduce the information of the natural ways of spacing birth which God has provided, so that spouses become "ministers" of life. Open to God, their awareness of the cycle of human fertility becomes a way of Christian life for them. Open to God, they already experience his Grace, as Von Balthasar has pointed out, and the distinction between the unitive and procreative aspects of Marriage is no longer important for them.[88] They have integrated themselves as loving, life-giving persons, able to make free, generous and responsible decisions in the question of their family. They have integrated their fertility into a spirituality of Marriage.

Their fidelity, itself built upon fidelity to God, has a redemptive quality. In that covenant fidelity we see the virtues taken up in the Grace of the sacrament. In their faith, Christian spouses offer our world the hope which contraception has torn from it. That hope, in turn, is lived in the supreme virtue, the love which "bears all things, believes all things, hopes all things, endures all things" (1 Corinthians 13:7).

To summarize and conclude this work, let us turn next to the achievement of this great sacrament, the Christian family. In the family life of sacraments and prayer spouses can find the strength to conquer fear and weakness.[89] Turning to the family is not turning away from the problems we have considered. Rather, it is where the problems are found, in the family community formed by the sacrament, that God can resolve all our human weakness.

CHAPTER EIGHT

The Sacrament Of The Family

La noche sosegada En par de los levantes de la aurora,	*Before the dawn comes round* *Here is the night, dead-hushed with all its* *glamours,*
La música callada, La soledad sonora, La cena, que recrea y enamora.	*The music without sound,* *The solitude that clamours,* *The supper that revives us and enamours.*
Nuestro lecho florido, De cuevas de leones enlazado, En púrpura tendido, De paz edificado, De mil escudos de oro coronado.	*Now flowers the marriage bed* *With dens of lions fortified around it,* *With tent of purple spread,* *In peace securely founded,* *And by a thousand shields of gold* *surmounted.*

Saint John of the Cross, *Songs between the soul and the bridegroom.*

In the mutual ministry of this great sacrament, as they make their consent, so husband and wife form that community of life and love which is the beginning of a Christian family. With the gift of children, this family attains its complete form. In the generosity of love open to God, open to the transmission of life, spouses find a further focus for their love in their children.

Their "one flesh" takes a new form as "flesh of our flesh, blood of our blood." The natural primary good of Marriage, children, becomes the "crown" of their Marriage. Therefore, the procreation, formation and education of children is the sacramental perfection of Marriage.[1]

In an age where pressure is brought to bear on parents to limit the size of their family, let us never forget that the Fathers of the Second Vatican Council commended "those who after prudent reflection and common decision courageously undertake the proper upbringing of a large number of children."[2]

Yet even a couple unable to bring forth their own children can be a family. Their Marriage "still retains its character of being a whole manner and communion of life and preserves its value and indissolubility."[3]   Their union extends the Mystical Body in its social visible form by bringing two members of that Body together, offering worship to God as "one flesh" in Christ, called to open their lives to others in the love of Christ, called to give witness in their lives to the fidelity of Christ.

The family is inseparable from the sacrament of Marriage. Whatever form that family takes, whatever cultural traditions mould the life of that family, for Christians, it always depends on the sacrament. The consent, indissoluble bond and covenant of Grace shared by parents, is, in a sense, their first gift to their children. The open quality of their consent has been crowned by children, thus making that consent an acceptance of each child. The indissoluble bond has become the secure basis for the growth and formation of the children. The covenant of Grace, the lived sacrament, draws each child into the *agape* of Jesus the Bridegroom. His love is imparted to children through their parents and, in fulfillment of their sacred duty, they bring their children to receive his Grace in Baptism, and to learn to love him within the family of the Church.

A SOCIAL SACRAMENT

The family reveals Marriage as a social sacrament. This is evident in the family partly forming the Church, providing the natural social basis, the incarnational, human dimension of the Church as a visible society.[4] The family is the place for the celebration of the sacraments which are usually initially received within the family circle, itself the normal unit of the family of the parish. The procreation of children is seen in this context in the ideal way envisaged by Saint Thomas, not only procreation and education, but the bringing-forth of children for the worship of God in the Church.[5]

The society of the Mystical Body grows through the Christian family. When Saint Thomas referred to the procreation and education of children "for the worship of God," he linked Marriage to Holy Orders, which is a fruitful sacrament in spiritual propagation. It is interesting to note that the family in Marriage provides this analogy for Holy Orders, the sacrament of the dynamic hierarchy of the Church. In the context of dialogue between Catholics and the Eastern Orthodox, this link between hierarchy in Orders and Marriage is set out clearly: "There is a profound communion between the bishop and the community in which the Spirit gives him responsibility for the church of God. The ancient tradition expressed it happily in the image of marriage."[6] This is seen in the simple, yet vivid, symbol in the Roman Rite of the episcopal ring.

Therefore we see a delightful interplay between the social sacraments of Marriage and Holy Orders. The nuptial role of Christ himself is reflected in his priests, each ordained male being an effectual sign of Jesus the Bridegroom, laying down his life, giving himself up for his beloved spouse the Church. At the level of sacramental sign, we see that only a man can be a priest, for the bride cannot be the bridegroom, and gender is inscribed into our very human nature in creation — and more wondrously elevated in the "great mystery" of Christ and his Church.

Marriage and family life also lead us back to the "great mystery," to an understanding of each person's vocation within the Church. Von Balthasar provides a key to this understanding by pointing out that "The absolute bond created by sacrament or vow is the fullness of Christianity. Until one chooses a state of life, one must continue in a *state of waiting*, which is far from being imperfect since it corresponds to the will of God."[7] If it is open to God's will, a state of waiting may not be imperfect, but it is incomplete, unresolved. Marriage and family show us a vocation found and fulfilled, God's plan for most of his pilgrim People. Marriage in the "great mystery" also gives us an understanding of celibate commitment — as a nuptial union, a fulfillment, as the forming of a new "family" in Christ.

In the tradition of the "great mystery," nuns see themselves as "spouses of Christ." The Second Vatican Council described priests in terms of this "great mystery," their task of "espousing the faithful to one husband and presenting them as a chaste virgin to Christ." The Council Fathers added, concerning priests, "They recall that mystical marriage, established by God and destined to be fully revealed in the future, by which the Church holds Christ as her only spouse. Moreover they are made a living sign of that world to come, already present through faith and charity, a world in which the children of the resurrection shall neither be married nor take wives."[8]

Yet, if the vocation of the priest or religious is a "Marriage" within the "great mystery," so too is the life of any single men or women who have resolved their vocations and are no longer in a state of waiting. All are called to *union* with God, a nuptial union, lived by most in this great sacrament of Marriage, lived by many others in the sacrament of Holy Orders or in vows, formal or private.

We are not called into the nuptial mystery of our Redemption only for our own good, however. We are called to union, hence to an active participation in the redeeming work of Christ the Bridegroom. In the world, for the sake of the world, the family formed by this sacrament gives the witness of "one flesh," of indissoluble unity, the sacrificial love of the Bridegroom, the joy and celebration of the community of life and love.

Each family which gathers at the altar to share in the Sacrifice of the Mass is a strong cell in the Mystical Body, the domestic church. But such a family is also the strongest cell in society at large. The natural unit of society is the family. When families are stable and united, so the society made up of those families will enjoy stability and peace. This social sacrament of Marriage is therefore "social" in the broadest sense, as the center of Christian ministry to human society. Would that the wider world could realize the service offered to mankind by the faithful lives of married Christians and the family circles they form through their covenant of love. People often remark on the witness value of the good Christian family as an example. But that witness goes beyond example to the very structure of society and the positive contribution offered to society by people who are mature and secure because they were formed in a Christian home. In such a domestic church we also find the transmission, not only of Catholic morality, but also of the rich heritage of culture and civilization which the Church has nurtured over the centuries.

In this context, we may find the work and witness of the Christian family in compassionate care for the poor, in that personal role of giving social service.[9]   This is one way in which the family, formed by this social sacrament, can counteract the plague of divorce, which so undermines society today.[10]   In such a role, we see the mutual ministry of spouses living their covenant sacrament. We see them taking up the Grace which God gives them and working in that divine strength for the sake of others beyond their own circle. So often we marvel because it is the family with many children, or afflicted with sickness or its own poverty, which shines forth in some street or small town as the family known and loved by those in trouble. In such a home, the love of the Bridegroom has been so assimilated by all members of this community of life and love that they cannot help extending their self-sacrifice to others. In such a home, people find the welcome of Christian hospitality, and see in a "sacramental" way that most warm and credible model of the Church — "the family of the families of God."[11]

PROPHETS, PRIESTS, KINGS

In the "great mystery" of our Redemption, Jesus Christ instituted sacramental Marriage by word and deed, as Prophet, Priest-Victim and King. His threefold office is imparted to those who minister sacramental Marriage to one another. In Christ, in their covenant of love, spouses are prophets, priests and the kings and queens of a Kingdom "not of this world." This is a way of understanding the graced life of the Christian family, taking from the sacrament itself the threefold office of Christ Jesus within the Church, for we are unable to separate Marriage and family from the Church.

We have already outlined the "kingly" role of spouses, their service of others, the royal mission of Jesus Christ in society for the sake of the world. John Paul II rightly perceived this as an exercise of the *agape* of Christ, a living out of his new commandment. In consent and the bond, in the lived covenant, we have seen spouses as the best of all friends, loving one another as Christ the Bridegroom has loved us, laying down

their lives as they lay down their bodies in mutual self-gift for the
beloved. In their "kingly" role, John Paul II saw the power of the
sacrament which spouses minister to one another: "Their guide and
rule of life is the Spirit of Jesus poured into their hearts in the celebration of the sacrament of Matrimony. In continuity with Baptism in
water and the Spirit, marriage sets forth anew the evangelical law of
love, and with the gift of the Spirit engraves it more profoundly on the
hearts of Christian husbands and wives. Their love, purified and saved,
is a fruit of the Spirit acting in the hearts of believers and constituting, at
the same time, the fundamental commandment of their moral life to be
lived in responsible freedom."[12]

The role of spouses as prophets is also evident in their call to be
open to all members of their own domestic church, the family, to all
members of the community of the Church and to the needs of society.
Their evangelical potential is often not realized, but the sacrament itself
is a call to a work of family evangelization. Again, John Paul II outlined
this role best in *Familiaris Consortio*: "The celebration of the sacrament of
marriage is the basic moment of the faith of the couple. This sacrament,
in essence, is the proclamation in the Church of the Good News
concerning married love."[13]

The Pope sees this call to prophetic work and witness in concrete
terms in the lived sacrament beyond the moments of faith in consent:
"God who called the couple *to* marriage, continues to call them *in*
marriage."[14] In the fabric of family life, the work of evangelization
begins, especially in the unity between parents and children, in all the
small but precious things which take the life of a family forward, day by
day, year by year. For some families this prophetic role will take an
explicit form in family catechesis, and in spreading the faith beyond the
family circle. Here the school of the sacrament teaches parents
themselves how best to impart the Faith of the Church, lived in their
own covenant of love.

The priestly role of parents in the family circle centers around
worship and prayer, the family within the parish, the altar of sacrifice
linked to the table of the home. The consent in love which we presented
as united to the consent of the Heart of Christ, to his sacrificial love,
means that Christ is to be present in each home. Only in prayer shared
together, led by the father as head of the family, or the mother as

receptive heart of the family, can we hope to find Christ present explicitly in a home. Only in prayer can the family fulfill its priestly call to sanctify and be sanctified, to perpetuate the work of the lived sacrament, that began in an act of worship and which continues to impart Grace so that spouses can make of their lives a spiritual sacrifice.[15]   Unless the Eucharist and Penance are ever present to nourish and to heal, this life of prayer and spiritual sacrifice cannot be attained.

The office of Jesus the Bridegroom, Prophet, Priest-Victim and King can best be understood in a return to the Cross which always stands at the heart of the "great mystery." Our very weakness, our failures, our sins, call us back to the Cross, to the way of Redemption through pain and suffering, to the path of reconciliation: "Christian marriage is marriage under the sign of the Cross. That means readiness for suffering; but it also means the promise of the Resurrection. It means assurance of the ultimate triumph of love."[16]

THE FAMILY, A "SACRAMENT"

To synthesize this Christ-centered vocation of the family, we may consider the dramatic moments of family life, for example, the grave illness of a small child, or a crisis in married love. But the little things in married life, in family life, also show a "sacramental" quality. The married Christian should never scorn these little things or disregard them. Even the small moments of married life, family life, are taken up into the lived sacrament of Marriage.

A spiritual guide of our century has summed up this value of the concrete realities of daily life in Marriage. Speaking of spouses, he said: "But they mustn't forget that the secret of married happiness lies in everyday things, not in daydreams. It lies in finding the hidden joy of coming home in the evening; in affectionate relations with their children; in everyday work in which the whole family cooperates; in good humor in the face of difficulties that should be met with a sporting spirit; in making the best use of all the advances that civilization offers to help us bring up children, to make the house pleasant and life more simple."[17]

That life should be "more simple" is a secret learned in the school of this great sacrament. The simplicity of spousal consent, the mysterious simplicity of the indissoluble bond of the sacrament, the simplicity of the Grace imparted by God to live the sacrament — all these aspects of the divine economy in sacramental Marriage flow on into the home. The moments of family life, meals together, little events such as the discoveries made by children and shared by all, the delight of being together and even the pain of parting, all these small elements have a "sacramental" quality. But this quality of lives lived in God and for God can only be appreciated by returning to the source, to the gift of sacramental Marriage, so majestic and yet so simple.

The sacrament makes the family into a "sacrament," a complex of human actions and relationships in which Christ is at work. If the whole Church is a saving sacrament, then the domestic church is itself a "sacrament." Its unity and stability come from the bond of Marriage. If the children can see their parents' fidelity to that bond of the Spirit, the family will remain united. In turn, this unity flows back into the wider unity of the whole Church, which is why Saint Paul integrated his Marriage teaching in Ephesians with the major theme of his epistle, the unity of the Church.[18]

Not only the children in the family can recognize the sacramental quality of the family, firmly established by the covenant of love between their parents. Often those outside a family circle, friends, relatives, are attracted to *that* particular family because, whether they know it or not, the presence of Christ the Bridegroom draws them to a little community of life and love, where the sacrament of Marriage is lived fruitfully. The Grace of the sacrament draws people together, because two people are "one flesh" in Christ, and in their married lives reproduce and signify the mystery of his Incarnation and Redemption. These are not distant ideals. I am describing here families I have known as a priest, and the home in which I was formed.

The open, attractive quality of the good Christian Marriage and its domestic sanctuary is a paradox. The love demanded by the sacrament is exclusive, demanding, specific. But it is at the same time open to others, inclusive, warm, hospitable. The reason for the paradox is this great sacrament. The love of the sacrament is the *agape* of Jesus Christ for his Body and bride, the Church. Never was there a love so "jealous" and yet so wide, and in this love, the consent, the bond and the covenant life of Marriage come together as the effectual sign of the "great mystery."

The sacramental family is not only "actuation" in living the Gospel well, it is a "memorial" of the mighty works of God and the heritage of the Church. But it is also hope for the world, a "prophecy" in itself of the potential of the history of our salvation. Pope John Paul II taught that "The future of humanity passes by way of the family."[19]   The future of the whole of humanity has passed already by way of the Family of Nazareth. In each sacramental family, Nazareth is perpetuated, as the past is celebrated, the present is lived in Christ and the future is our hope of eternal life. This is why there must always be a place in each sacramental home for she who is "our life, our sweetness and our hope," Mary immaculate, daughter of Sion, mother, virgin and spouse.

THE RETURN TO GOD

In concluding this work, let us return to the Source of all love, to the Triune God, Source of Marriage and family life. In the act of creation, God gave man and woman to one another in the "primordial sacrament." In their created capacity for self-giving, in their union and communion of "one flesh," man and woman are the image and likeness of the Creator. But this expression of God in married life and love is complete in their fruitfulness.

The family does show some "vestige" of the Trinity. As we have already observed in considering to what extent the family is a precise image of the Holy Trinity, we may never be able to provide a satisfactory family analogy of the Trinity.[20]   But Marriage and family life do share in the principles of union and communion, the principles of the Union and Communion of Persons in God. Perhaps the best way of attempting to appropriate roles in the family which reflect the Divine Persons is to see both parents as a single generative principle, analogous to the Father, and their children as analogous to the Son, and hence, the familial bond as analogous to the Holy Spirit, the personification of the mutual love of the Father and the Son.[21]

Even though this analogy of the Trinity is still imperfect, for parents do not generate their children as the Father generates the Son, this more refined family analogy draws us back to the divine Source. In the light of God, we see the dignity of human nature in the sacrament, in the capacities inscribed into that nature by the Creator, in the glory of divine Grace to which spouses are raised by the Triune God.[22]

Reflecting on this great sacrament as God's means of life and love, we propose one pastoral conclusion concerning the sacramentality of Marriage. In our world, Marriage and family are under pressure and in constant danger of being reduced to a functional, secular role. For the sake of our Catholic people, and for the wider benefits of Christian Marriage in society, we need to revise and reform our way of preparing couples for Marriage. Whatever else may have to be accomplished, preparation for Marriage should be *catechesis for a sacrament*.

The return to God, in a God-centered preparation for Marriage, includes and enhances our anthropology, our noble doctrine of human nature. Therefore, it will incorporate all the necessary practical and pastoral elements which experience has shown to be essential for a sound Catholic preparation for married life; for example, accurate guidance in natural ways of spacing children, prudent advice on inter-personal relations, sexuality and family economics. But let *the sacrament* be the sacred center of this preparation for married life — with emphasis, not only on the decisive choice and power of consent and consummation, but also on the Grace which God offers in the lived sacrament.

How this catechesis is to be carried out will vary according to different cultures and societies. For example, in highly secularized societies, couples may need a patient pre-catechesis in the very concept of "sacrament," beginning perhaps with the human values of the created reality of Marriage which is so little esteemed today. But there is a new hunger for God in the last years of this century. There is a search in life for "something more." There are grounds for hope that those who seek to enter Marriage within the Church are seeking to place their lives within the spousal gift of Jesus Christ our Redeemer.

He came to us, this loving Bridegroom, long promised in Adam's creation and Fall, prefigured in the spousal vision of the prophets of

Israel. He came to us, and took our flesh. He united himself to each of us, and so transformed all the ways of life which we had failed to live well. He taught explicitly and firmly of a new kind of Marriage, as part of his new way of life for us. He not only taught us as a Prophet, he lived out that teaching as Priest and King, taking to himself forever his bride, the Church, born, re-born, united to him forever in the water and Blood flowing from his pierced Heart. For love of her, he offered up his own Body, and made of her his own Body, "one flesh," sealed forever in his glorious Resurrection. This was, and is, his "great mystery."

Into that sublime mystery of redemptive, sacrificial Love, he raises men and women, by whose Baptism he has inwardly transformed the created reality of Marriage. In his Kingdom, it is a sacrament. Their human words effect a bond which lasts unto death. Their self-giving and accepting in love places them in the strength of his Grace, so that what they began in consent may be lived in the covenant community of life and love, a miniature Church, the sacramental family.

As they live their great sacrament, so they recapitulate the fidelity of their Savior, are one in the bond of the Holy Spirit, and enjoy the constant favor of the Father of all life. As they are open to the creative work of God, so their fruitfulness may be blessed in the gift of children, for the growth of the Mystical Body and the advancement of the Kingdom in human society. As the years pass, in joy, suffering, work and relaxation, they return again and again to Jesus the Bridegroom, nourishing his spouse the Church in the Eucharist, healing and accepting his spouse in Penance. In the home they make together they build a sanctuary of prayer, peaceful and secure under the mantle of Mary, perfect spouse of God, true image of the Church.

But this life of a sacrament is a journey, a pilgrimage. Ministers of a sacrament to one another, they journey together to a Kingdom. If it is God's will, they will rejoice in length of years and children's children, like the patriarchs of old. But the time for sacraments must pass, for sacraments belong to time, and must give way to that which they signify and that to which their Grace leads us. For faithful spouses, the parting of death is brief sorrow, for the Bridegroom has promised to come and take his beloved to himself forever.

Into that eternal nuptial feast each faithful spouse is called, and what each son of Adam and daughter of Eve lived on earth will be transformed in the Wedding Feast of the Lamb of God and his bride, the new Jerusalem: "Blessed are those who are invited to the marriage supper of the Lamb" (Revelation 19:9). Blessed indeed are those whose pilgrimage to that supper was made in Christian Marriage, this great sacrament.

Footnotes

Acknowledgments

1 See Norris, Thomas, "Why the Marriage of Christians is one of the Seven Sacraments," *Irish Theological Quarterly*, Vol. 5, No. 1, 1985, pp. 37-51.

2 See Corecco, Eugenio, "Il matrimonio nel nuovo Codex Iuris Canonici: osservazioni critiche," *Studi sulle fonti del diritto matrimoniale canonico*, Cedam, Padua, 1988, pp. 112-118.

Introduction: A GREAT SACRAMENT

1 Cf. Council of Trent, *Canones de sacramento matrimonii*, 1., Denzinger, H., Schönmetzer, A., *Enchiridion Symbolorum Definitionum et Declarationum de Rebus Fidei et Morum*, editio xxxvi, emendata, Herder, Freiburg, 1976, 1801: "*Si quis dixerit matrimonium non esse vere et proprie unum ex septem sacramentis Legis evangelicae, a Christo Domino institutum, sed ab hominibus in ecclesia inventum, neque gratiam conferre: anathema sit.*"

2 Cf. Leo XIII, *Arcanum Divinae Sapientiae*, 9, DS., 3142; Pius XI, *Casti Connubii*, 5 and 38, DS., 3700 and 3713; Paul VI, *Humanae Vitae*, 25; John Paul II, *Familiaris Consortio*, 13; Vatican II, *Lumen Gentium*, 11.

3 Cf. *Codex Iuris Canonici*, Libreria Editrice Vaticana, 1983, Canons 1055, 1056, 1057; Vatican II, *Gaudium et Spes*, 48.

4 For Marriage between a Christian and an unbaptized person, see Chapter Seven, pp. 199-203.

5 John Paul II, *Familiaris Consortio*, 13; English translation, Vatican Polyglot Press, Daughters of St. Paul edition, Boston, MA, 1981, p. 25.

6 Using Saint John of the Cross, *Poems of St. John of the Cross*, tr. by Roy Campbell, Collins, London, 1951; Spanish text with English translation.

7 Cf. *Ibid.*, the nuptial theology of the nine "Romances," pp. 48-77.

8 Cf. Council of Trent, *Doctrina de sacramento matrimonii*, DS., 1799; Vatican II, *G.S.*, 48: ". . . *ita nunc hominum Salvator Ecclesiaeque Sponsus, per sacramentum matrimonii christifidelibus coniugibus obviam venit.*"

9 Cf. Vatican II, *L.G.*, cap. v., 39-42.

10 John Paul II, *F.C.*, 16; see also Pius XII, *Sacra Virginitas*, 37, DS., 3911, 3912, condemning the error of those who set Marriage above consecrated virginity.

11 See also, Von Hildebrand, Dietrich, *Marriage the Mystery of Faithful Love*, Sophia Institute Press, Manchester, New Hampshire, 1984, pp. 60-63, for an excellent integration of Marriage with consecrated virginity.

12 See Saint Thomas Aquinas, *Summa Theologiae, Cum Textu ex Recensione Leonina*, ed. P. Caramello, Marietti, Roma, 1956, 3a. 60. 3., pp. 338, 339. The three dimensions of a sacrament are also expressed in his "O sacrum convivium."

13 John Paul II, *F.C.*, 13, citing his "Address to the Delegates of the Centre de Liaison des Équipes de Recherche" (November 3, 1979): *Insegnamenti di Giovanni Paolo II*, II, 2 (1979), 1032.

14 Cf. Saint Thomas Aquinas, *S.T.*, *op. cit.*, 3a. 66. 1., pp. 374, 375.

15 Cf. Saint Thomas Aquinas, *S. Thomas Aquinatis Opera Omnia*, 1., *In Quattour Libros Sententiarum*, curante Roberto Busa, S.I., Frommann-Holzboog, Stuttgart-Bad Connstatt, 1980; *In IV. Sententiarum*, 26. 2. ra. 5., p. 583 (*Supplementum* to his *Summa Theologiae*, 42. 1. ad 5) and *In IV.*, 31. 1. 3. ra. 5., p. 594 (*S.*, 49. 3. ad 5).

16 Cf. Saint Augustine, *De bono coniugali*, 24 (*P.L.*, 40, 394); *De nuptiis et concupiscentia*, 1. 10.11. (*P.L.*, 44, 420).

17 See Capello, Felix, *De Sacramentis, Tractatus Canonico-Moralis*, Vol. III, *De Matrimonio*, Marietti, Roma, 1933, pp. 3, 4, and Mackin, Theodore, SJ., *What Is Marriage?* (*Marriage in the Catholic Church*), Paulist Press, New York, 1982, p. 2.

18 See Chapter Seven, pp. 192-199.

19 This is implicit in Schillebeeckx, Edward, *Marriage: Human Reality and Saving Mystery*, Sheed and Ward, London, 1965, 1976; see pp. xxxi, xxxii, 338, 384, 385, 393, 394. The author wrote in the era of secularized theology when some theologians attempted to find God in "secularity." He also wrote before *Gaudium et Spes, Humanae Vitae* and *Familiaris Consortio*. Yet pp. xxxi, xxxii also anticipate his later "functional" Christology, which has raised the same problem.

20 Cf. Saint Thomas Aquinas, *Super epistulas S. Pauli lectura*, ed. Raphaelis Cai, OP., ed. viii revisa, vol. II, Marietti, Torino e Roma, 1953, *Ad Ephesios*, cap. v., lect. x, 334, p. 77.

21 Cf. *C.I.C.*, Canons 1055, 1061, 1068 and 1065 §1.

22 Cf. *Ibid.*, Canon 1065 §2.

23 Cf. Scheeben, Matthias, *The Mysteries of Christianity (Die Mysterien des Christentums)*, tr. Cyril Vollert, SJ., Herder, St. Louis, 1951, p. 599.
24 Cf. Tertullian, *Ad uxorem*, 2. 8. (*P.L.*, 1. 1302), but contested partly by Schillebeeckx, Edward, *Marriage: Human Reality and Saving Mystery, op. cit.*, pp. 251-255. He only denies that the Eucharist was part of the celebration of Marriage in the early Church.
25 See also, Grisez, Germain, *The Way of the Lord Jesus*, Vol. 1, *Christian Moral Principles*, Franciscan Herald Press, Chicago, 1983, pp. 801, 802.
26 Cf. Vatican II, *L.G.*, 11.
27 Vatican II, *L.G.*, 1.
28 Cf. John Paul II, *F.C.*, 55-62.
29 Saint John of the Cross, *Poems of St. John of the Cross, op. cit.*, Romance IV, p. 61.
30 Propositional Revelation, foundation of orthodoxy, is defended well in Grisez, Germain, *The Way of the Lord Jesus, op. cit.*, pp. 447-485, and Kevane, Eugene, "Apostolicity, Indefectibility and Catechesis," *Divinitas, Pontificae Academiae Theologicae Romanae Commentarii*, Rome, September, 1985, pp. 218-233. See also my own approach, Elliott, Peter, "The 'Propositional' View of Revelation," *Compass*, Chevalier Press, Sydney, vol. 4, no. 2, September-October, 1970, pp. 131-134.
31 See Chapter Three.
32 *Ibid.*, pp. 115-117.
33 John Paul II, *Apostolic Letter of Pope John Paul II on the Occasion of the International Youth Year*, 10; English translation, *L'Osservatore Romano*, English Edition, n. 13 (879), April 1, 1985, p. 5.
34 For example, Caffarra, Carlo, "Verità ed ethos dell'amore coniugale," in *Giovanni Paolo II, Uomo e donna lo creò, catechesi sull'amore umano*, Città Nuova Editrice, Libreria Editrice Vaticana, Roma, 1985, Introduzione generale, pp. 12-24.
35 Cf. John Paul II, "Nelle parole del consenso coniugale il segno del 'profetismo del corpo'," General Audience, January 19, 1983, *Insegnamenti di Giovanni Paolo II*, Libreria Editrice Vaticana, VI, 1, 1983, pp. 155-159, and "Corretto uso del linguaggio del corpo e testimonianza degna dei veri profeti," General Audience, January 26, 1983, pp. 247-249, especially 4, p. 249, the revelatory nature of the "language of the body," a "testimonianza degna di 'veri profeti'."
36 Cf. *Ibid.*, "Il matrimonio come sacramento secondo la lettera di Paolo agli Efesini," General Audience, July 28, 1982, *Insegnamenti di Giovanni Paolo II, op. cit.*, V. 3, 1982, 5, pp. 134, 135.
37 The General Audiences, April 16, 1980 to May 6, 1981.

38 Cf. Vatican II, *G.S.*, 13 and 47, the effects of Original Sin in Marriage.

39 Cf. John Paul II, "Santità e rispetto del corpo nella dottrina di San Paolo," General Audience, January 28, 1981, *Insegnamenti di Giovanni Paolo II, op. cit.*, IV. 1, 1981, pp. 177-181.

40 See Elliott, Peter, "Talking of Sacraments: A Case for Plain English," *Bulletin of Christian Affairs*, no. 21, April 1972, Holy Name Press, Melbourne, pp. 11-14.

41 See Leeming, Bernard, SJ., *Principles of Sacramental Theology*, Newman Press, Westminster, Maryland, 1956, p. 285, where Leeming indicates St. Augustine's Platonic assumption in using "sign." Leeming deals with the problem of sacramental causality, how sacramental signs "cause" Grace.

42 Cf. Saint Thomas Aquinas, *S.T.*, 3a. 66. 1.

43 See Grisez, Germain, *The Way of the Lord Jesus, op. cit*, pp. 729-733. This is an excellent vindication of "action" as the major corrective emphasis if sacramental theology is to maintain Catholic realism and causality. See note 40 above.

44 For a compact study of the schools of thought on sacramental causality, see Leeming, Bernard, *Principles of Sacramental Theology, op. cit.*, pp. 283-313.

45 Vatican II, *L.G.*, 11; English translation, Flannery, Austin, *Vatican Council II, The Conciliar and Post Conciliar Documents*, Costello, New York, 1975, p. 361.

46 Cf. *Ibid.*, *Sacrosanctum Concilium*, 7.

47 See pp. 124, 158-159.

48 Cf. Council of Trent, *Decretum de sacramentis*, Canon 8, DS., 1608.

49 See Leeming, Bernard, *Principles of Sacramental Theology, op. cit.*, pp. 5-7.

50 Cf. *Ibid.*, pp. 290-294, describing the "occasional causality" view.

51 *Ibid.*, p. 4.

52 Cf. Ratzinger, Joseph and Messori, Vittorio, *Rapporto sulla Fede*, Edizioni Paoline, Milan, 1985, p. 78. Cardinal Ratzinger shows how false Christology strikes at God, and no longer allows him access to the world of matter.

53 See Schillebeeckx, Edward, *Christ the Sacrament of the Encounter with God*, Sheed and Ward, New York, 1963, pp. 13-17.

54 See Grisez, Germain, *The Way of the Lord Jesus, op. cit.*, p. 746, n.13.

55 Saint John of the Cross, *Poems of St. John of the Cross, op. cit.*, Romance IV, p. 61.

56 Newman, John Henry, *Select Treatises of St. Athanasius*, Longmans Green, London, 1895, vol. II, pp. 192-195.

57 Newman, John Henry, *Parochial and Plain Sermons*, Longmans Green, London, 1891, vol. V, pp. 10, 11.

Chapter One: THE "GREAT MYSTERY"

1 John Paul II, *Apostolic Letter of Pope John Paul II on the Occasion of the International Youth Year*, 10, English translation, *L'Osservatore Romano*, English Edition, n. 13 (879), April1, 1985, p. 5.

2 On the background of "mystery," see, Brown, Raymond E., *The Semitic Background of the Term "Mystery" in the New Testament*, Fortress Press, Philadelphia, 1968.

3 International Theological Commission, *Propositions on the Doctrine of Christian Marriage*, Commentary 2, *Sacramentality of Christian Marriage*, in *Contemporary Perspectives on Christian Marriage*, ed. Richard Malone, John R. Connery, SJ., Loyola University Press, Chicago, 1984, pp. 17, 18.

4 *Ibid.*, Lehmann, Karl, "The Sacramentality of Christian Marriage," *I.T.C.*, pp. 93, 94.

5 To the extent that one may wonder whether they are separate accounts.

6 Cf. Vawter, Bruce, *On Genesis: A New Reading*, Doubleday, New York, 1977, pp. 55, 56.

7 Cf. Tosato, Angelo, *Il matrimonio israelitico, una teoria generale*, in *Analecta Biblica*, 100, Biblical Institute Press, Rome, 1982, pp. 114, n. 13 and 54.

8 See, John Paul II, *F.C.*, 11.

9 Cf. Ausin, Santiago, "Matrimonio y designo di Dios, anotaciones exegéticas a Gen 2, 4-25," Il Simposio Internacional de Teología de la Universidad de Navarra, *Cuéstiones Fundamentales sobre Matrimonio y Familia*, ed. Augustino Sarmineto, Eloy Tejero, Teodoro López, José Manuel Zumaquero, Ediciónes Universidad de Navarra, S-A, Pamplona, 1980, pp. 146, 147.

10 Cf. John Paul II, "Nel secondo racconto della creazione la definizione soggetiva dell'uomo," 4, General Audience, September 19, 1979, *Insegnamenti di Giovanni Paolo II, op. cit.*, II, 2, 1979, p. 325.

11 Cf. John Paul II, "La creazione come dono fondamentale e originario," General Audience, January 2, 1980, *Insegnamenti di Giovanni Paolo II, op. cit.*, III, 1, 1980, p. 11.

12 Cf. John Paul II, "L'unità originaria dell'uomo e della donna nell'umanità," 9, 10, General Audience, November 7, 1979, in *Insegnamenti di Giovanni Paolo II, op. cit.*, II, 2, 1979, pp. 1073-1076, and on Adam's sleep, pp. 1073, 1074.

13 Cf. John Paul II, "Radicale cambiamento del significato della nudità originaria," General Audience, May 14, 1980, *Insegnamenti di Giovanni Paolo II, op. cit.*, III, 1, 1980, pp. 1365-1369.

14 See Joyce, G.H., *Christian Marriage*, Sheed and Ward, London, 1948, pp. 31-36 for a rebuttal of the evolutionist theory of Marriage, and note Paul VI, *Humanae Vitae*, 8.

15 Cf. Scheeben, Matthias, *The Mysteries of Christianity, op. cit.*, pp. 595-598.

16 See Saint Thomas Aquinas, *Summa Contra Gentiles*, cura Ceslai Pera, OP., Marietti, Torino e Roma, 1961, Lib. III, cap. cxxiv, 2969-2976, pp. 185-186.

17 See Saint Thomas Aquinas, *S.C.G., op. cit.*, Lib. III, cap. cxxiii, 2959-2968, pp. 183-185.

18 Cf. De Vaux, Roland, *Ancient Israel*, Vol. I, McGraw Hill, New York, 1965, pp. 39, 40.

19 Cf. Mackin, Theodore, *What is Marriage?, op. cit.*, pp. 46-50.

20 Cf. Schillebeeckx, Edward, *Marriage: Human Reality and Saving Mystery, op. cit.*, pp. 76-81. See also Grelot, Pierre, *Le couple humain dans l'Écriture*, Les éditions du Cerf, Paris, 1969, pp. 46-55.

21 John Paul II, *F.C.*, 12, English translation, p. 24.

22 For a useful summary of the "Daughter of Sion" theology and writings, see De La Potterie, Ignace, "La donna e il mistero della Chiesa, principi ermeneutici per l'interpretazione della visione biblica sulla donna," *La donna nella Chiesa oggi*, a cura di Adriano Cafriolo e Luciano Veccaro, Edizioni Ella Di Ci, Torino, 1981, pp. 108-116. Also, see Ratzinger, Joseph, *Daughter Sion (Die Tochter Zion)*, tr. Charles McDermott, Ignatius Press, San Francisco, 1983.

23 Cf. Saint Irenaeus, *Adversus haereses*, 3, 21, 10 and 3, 22, 4 (*P.L.*, 7,955 and 7,959) and in a developed form, Saint John Chrysostom, *De coemeterio et de cruce*, 2 (*P.G.*, 49,396). See also Vatican II, *L.G.*, 56.

24 Cf. Sorci, Pietro, "Il tema della Chiesa-sposa nelle liturgie nuziali," in *Ho Theologos*, Facoltà Teologica di Sicilia, Nuova Serie, Anno 1, num. 1, 1983, p. 72.

25 Cf. Saint Thomas Aquinas, *In IV, op. cit.*, 27.1. 3b. ra. 1, p. 586 (S. 61. 3. ad 1). ". . . *sed per carnalem copulam significat conjunctionis ad ecclesiam quantum ad assumptionem humanae naturae in unitatem personae, quae omnino est indivisibilis.*"

26 Cf. Saint Thomas Aquinas, *S.C.G., op. cit.*, Lib. IV, cap. 34, 3695, 3696, pp. 310-313.

27 Cf. Saint Thomas Aquinas, *S.T., op. cit.*, 3a. 64. 7, p. 366, ". . . *a passione Christi derivatur, quae est Christum secundum quod homo.*"

28 Cf. Saint Thomas Aquinas, *Ad Ephesios, op. cit.*, cap. v, lect. x, 334, p. 77.

29 Vatican II, *G.S.*, 22; English translation, *V.II., op. cit.*, pp. 922, 923.

30 Saint Augustine, *In epist. Ioannis*, 2.2. (*P.L.*, 35, 1990).

31 John Paul II, *F.C.*, 13.

32 Saint Gregory the Great, *In Evangelica*, lib. II. hom. 38, no. 3 (*P.L.*, 76, 1283), cited in Scheeben, Matthias, *The Mysteries of Christianity, op. cit.*, p. 373, n. 15.

33 Maintained by Martelet, G., "Sixteen Christological Theses on the Sacrament of Marriage," in *I.T.C., Contemporary Perspectives on Christian Marriage, op. cit.*, p. 276, and see Vatican II, *G.S.*, 22, Christ the new Adam.

34 For the identification of Mary as the Church-bride figure, see De La Potterie, Ignace, "La donna e il mistero della chiesa," *La donna nella Chiesa oggi, op. cit.*, pp. 116-122.

35 Cf. Schillebeeckx, Edward, *Marriage: Human Reality and Saving Mystery, op. cit.*, pp. 109, 110.

36 Cf. A Lapide, Cornelius, *Commentaria in Ioannem*, cap. iii, in *Commentaria in Scripturam Sacram*, Tom. XVI, Editio nova, Vivès, Paris, 1977, p. 349.

37 Cf. Sorci, Pietro, "Il tema della Chiesa-sposa nelle liturgie nuziali," *Ho Theologos, op. cit.*, pp. 81, 82.

38 For a concise summary of the Jewish wedding customs, see Schillebeeckx, Edward, *Marriage: Human Reality and Saving Mystery, op. cit.*, pp. 97-101.

39 See Schillebeeckx, Edward, *ibid.*, p. 143, for the rabbinical context of the debate with the Pharisees.

40 John Paul II, *F.C.*, 13. English translation, p. 24.

41 For a modern mystic's profound insight into Marriage and the Cross, see Von Speyr, Adrienne, *The Cross, Word and Sacrament*, tr. Graham Harrison, Ignatius Press, San Francisco, 1983, pp. 29-35.

42 Cf. Durrwell, F.X., *In the Redeeming Christ: Towards a Theology of Spirituality*, tr. Rosemary Sheed, Sheed and Ward, New York, 1963, p. 283.

43 Cf. Definition of the Dogma of the Immaculate Conception, DS., 2803.

44 See Vatican II, *L.G.*, 63, 64, Mary, sign of Mother Church.

45 *Missale Romanum, ex Decreto Sacrosancti Oecumenici Concilii Vaticani II Instauratum Auctoritate Pauli PP. VI Promulgatum*, Typis Polyglottis Vaticanis, 1971, p. 654.

46 Cf. Durrwell, F.X., *In the Redeeming Christ, op. cit.*, pp. 284, 285.

47 Vatican II, *Sacrosanctum Concilium*, 5. English translation, *V. II, op. cit.*, p. 3.

48 *Missale Romanum, op. cit.*, p. 379.

49 Cf. Scheeben, Matthias, *The Mysteries of Christianity, op. cit.*, pp. 181-189, and especially pp. 185, 186.

50 Cf. Von Speyr, Adrienne, *The Cross, Word and Sacrament, op. cit.*, pp. 32, 33.

51 Wojtyla, Karol (John Paul II), *Sign of Contradiction*, tr. Mary Smith, Hodder and Stoughton, 1979, from "The Bridegroom is with you," cap. xi, pp. 97, 98.

52 John Paul II, *F.C.*, 13; English translation, p. 25.

53 For reference to the spousal implications of the Resurrection, see Durrwell, F.X., *The Resurrection: A Biblical Study*, tr. Rosemary Sheed, Sheed and Ward, New York, 1960, pp. 168, 169, and 177, 178, as well as Saint Augustine (see below, p. 134).

54 Saint Thomas Aquinas, *S.T.*, *op. cit.*, 3a, 48, 1, pp. 274, 275, and 3a, 62, 5, p. 352.

55 *Ibid.*, 3a, 56, 1, ad 4, p. 320.

56 *Ibid.*, 3a, 56, 2, ad 4, p. 321.

57 Wojtyla, Karol (John Paul II), *Sign of Contradiction*, *op. cit.*, p. 98.

58 *Missale Romanum*, *op. cit.*, p. 597.

59 For Resurrection as "birth," in the context of Mary's place in the Book of Revelation, see Feuillet, André, *Johannine Studies*, Alba House, New York, 1964, pp. 260, 261.

60 See Sorci, Pietro, "Il tema della Chiesa-sposa nelle liturgie nuziali," *Ho Theologos*, *op. cit.*, pp. 93, 94.

61 Cf. Saint Thomas Aquinas, *S.T.*, *op. cit.*, 1a, 31, ad 3, Vol. I pp. 164, 165.

62 Cf. *Ibid.*, 1a, 37, 2, pp. 189, 190.

63 Explained well in Ratzinger, Joseph, *Introduction to Christianity*, tr. J.R. Foster, Herder and Herder, New York, 1969, pp. 131, 132.

64 For an excellent statement of the way the Trinity is open to us in self-communication, see Grisez, Germain, *The Way of the Lord Jesus*, *op. cit.*, pp. 578-580.

65 Saint John of the Cross, *Poems of St. John of the Cross*, *op. cit.*, Romance III, p. 57.

66 Vatican II, *G.S.*, 48; English translation, *V.II.*, *op. cit.*, 950.

Chapter Two: MARRIAGE "IN CHRIST"

1 Kasper, Walter, *Theology of Christian Marriage*, Burns & Oates, London, 1980, p. 34.

2 He refers to them in their pagan sinful ways as "children of wrath" (Ep 2:1-3) and in their Gentile status as "strangers to the covenants of promise" (Ep 2:11-12).

3 Cf. 2 Cor 1:22; 1 Cor 6:11 and Scheeben, Matthias, *The Mysteries of Christianity*, *op. cit.*, pp. 572-576 and 590-591.

4 Cf. Scheeben, Matthias, *ibid.*, pp. 168-172.

5 Cf. Kasper, Walter, *Theology of Christian Marriage*, *op. cit.*, pp. 48-49.

6 From Rome, describing himself as a "prisoner" (Ep 3:1 and 4:1).

7   See Mackin, Theodore, *What Is Marriage?*, *op. cit.*, pp. 63-64 and his note 12, pp. 67 and 68, critical of Saint Jerome for providing a verb in verse 22 and for translating that verb too emphatically (*hypotassesthosan* as "*subditae sint*"). Even if Greek manuscripts vary as to whether this verb is there in an implicitly imperative subjunctive, Colossians 3:18 favors Saint Jerome.

8   Cf. Bover, José M., *Teología de San Pablo*, cuarta edición, Biblioteca de Autores Cristianos, Madrid, 1967, p. 634.

9   See Wojtyla Karol (John Paul II), *Sign of Contradiction*, *op. cit.*, p. 97.

10 Cf. Mühlen, Heribert, *Una Mistica Persona, la Chiesa come il mistero dello Spirito Santo in Cristo e nei cristiani: una persona in molte persone*, Città Nuova, Roma, 1968, pp. 160-162, and Schillebeeckx, Edward, *Marriage: Human Reality and Saving Mystery*, *op. cit.*, pp. 191-192.

11 As argued in Schillebeeckx, Edward, *ibid.*, p. 199, "There is no equality of nature between man and woman in society, but an all-embracing equality in dignity of the sexes 'in the Lord'."

12 Saint Thomas Aquinas, *S.T.*, *op. cit.*, 1a, 92, 1, ad 2, Tom. 1, p. 451.

13 Cf. Laroche, Michel, *Une Seule Chair, l'aventure mystique du couple*, Nouvelle cité, Paris, 1984, pp. 84-85, and Christ's servant headship, pp. 80-81.

14 Cf. Grisez, Germain, *The Way of the Lord Jesus*, *op. cit.*, p. 580.

15 Von Hildebrand, Dietrich, *Marriage the Mystery of Faithful Love*, *op. cit.*, p. 11.

16 Cf. A Lapide, Cornelius, *Commentaria in Scripturam Sacram, Commentaria in epistolam ad Ephesios*, Editio nova, Vivès, Paris, 1880, Tom. XVIII, in cap. v., p. 666.

17 Cf. Prat, Fernand, *The Theology of Saint Paul*, (*La Théologie de Saint Paul*) tr. John L. Stoddard, Newman, Westminster, Maryland, 1927, Vol. II, pp. 272-273, n. 1.

18 Council of Trent, *Doctrina de sacramento matrimonii*, DS., 1799; Council of Florence, *Decretum pro Armeniis*, DS., 1327.

19 Cf. *Catechism of the Council of Trent*, tr. John A. McHugh, OP., and Charles C. Callan, OP., Wagner, New York, 16th edition, 1962, p. 246.

20 Scheeben, Matthias, *The Mysteries of Christianity*, *op. cit.*, p. 601.

21 See Robilliard, J.S., "Le symbolisme du mariage selon Saint Paul," in *Revue des Sciences philosophiques et théologiques*, 21, 1932, pp. 243, 244 and 246.

22 Cf. Cerfaux, Lucien, *Christ in the Theology of Saint Paul*, Herder, Freiburg, 1962, pp. 349-350.

23 Cf. Schillebeeckx, Edward, *Marriage: Human Reality and Saving Mystery*, *op. cit.*, p. 110.

24 Cf. Vatican II, *L.G.*, 65.

25 See also Aranda, Gonzalo, "Relación entre los conyuges y valor del matrimonio a luz de Ef 5, 22-33," in *C.F.M.F.*, *op. cit.*, pp. 123-125.

26 As in O'Callaghan, Denis, "Marriage as Sacrament," in *Concilium* (English) May, 1970, p. 105.

27 The variant to Ephesians 5:30: *"de carne eius. . . .": auton ek tes sarkos autou kai ek ton osteon autou*; see *Novum Testamentum Graece et Latine*, ed. Augustinus Merk, SJ., Sumptibus Pontificii Instituti Biblici, Romae, 1984, p. 646.

28 Rahner, Karl, SJ., "Marriage as a Sacrament," in *Theology Digest*, 17, 1969, p. 7: ("Die Ehe als Sakrament," *Geist und Leben*, 40, 1967).

29 Saint Thomas Aquinas, *Ad Ephesios, op. cit.*, cap. v., lect. x., 335, p. 77: ". . . *de aliis vero in figura Christi*," moreover, "*et implemendum est in aliis in figura Christi.*"

30 The Vulgate and the Greek have "let her fear" ("*timeat*," *phobetai*) as the verb for a Christian wife's respect for her husband.

31 Cf. Sorci, Pietro, "Il tema della Chiesa-sposa nelle liturgie nuziali," *Ho Theologos, op. cit.*, pp. 80-81.

32 Saint Pacian, *Sermo de baptismo*, 6 (*P.L.*, 13, 1093).

33 Cf. Blessed Isaac of Stella, *Discursus* 51 (*P.L.*, 194, 1865).

34 Newman, John Henry, *Callista, a Tale of the Third Century*, Longmans Green, London, 1855, new impression, 1928, p. 222.

35 Cf. Newman, John Henry, *Lectures on the Doctrine of Justification*, Longmans Green, London, 1838, new impression, 1924, pp. 176-178.

36 Cf. Delicado Baeza, José, "El matrimonio en el mistero de Cristo," *C.F.M.F., op. cit.*, p. 93.

37 Cf. Council of Trent, *Decretum de iustificatione*, cap. xvi, DS., 1546.

38 As in Scheeben, Matthias, *The Mysteries of Christianity, op. cit.*, pp. 602-603.

39 Scheeben, Matthias, *Nature and Grace*, tr. Cyril Vollert, SJ., Herder, St. Louis, 1954, p. 139.

40 Cf. Council of Trent, *Decretum de sacramentis*, Canon 9, DS., 1609, and Council of Florence, *Decretum pro Armeniis*, DS., 1313.

41 Cf. Vatican II, baptismal character, *L.G.*, 11; priestly character, *Presbyterorum ordinis*, 2; implicit references, *L.G.*, 11, 33, and *Apostolicam actuositatem*, 3.

42 See Scheeben, Matthias, *The Mysteries of Christianity, op. cit.*, pp. 573-574, 582-592; Leeming, Bernard, *Principles of Sacramental Theology, op. cit.*, Section II, caps. 4-8, pp. 129-279.

43 Cf. Leeming, Bernard, *ibid.*, pp. 143-167.

44 Cf. Saint Thomas Aquinas, *S.T., op. cit.*, 3a, 63, 3 ad 3 and 3a, 63, 6, ad 1, pp. 357 and 359.

45 Vatican II, *L.G.*, 11, citing *S.T.*, 3a, 63, 2; English translation, *V.II.*, p. 361.

46 Cf. Scheeben, Matthias, *The Mysteries of Christianity, op. cit.*, p. 598.

47 This is a development beyond Kasper's reiteration of the "domestic church" in *Lumen Gentium*, 11; cf. Kasper, Walter, *Theology of Christian Marriage, op. cit.*, p. 38. As "sacrament of the Church," Marriage is the sacrament of the family in an ecclesial way; see below, Chapter Eight, pp. 227-229.

48 Cf. Scheeben, Matthias, *The Mysteries of Christianity, op. cit.*, pp. 604-606.

49 Vatican II, *G.S.*, 48; Pius XI, *C.C.*, 41; *C.I.C.*, Canon 1134.

50 See below, Chapter Five, pp. 224-227.

51 Cf. Kasper, Walter, *Theology of Christian Marriage, op. cit.*, p. 37.

52 Vatican II, *L.G.*, 39; English translation, *V.II., op. cit.* p. 396.

53 Cf. *C.I.C.*, Canon 1605, #1.

54 Clérissac, Humbert, OP., *Le Mystère de l'Église*, (préface de Jacques Maritain), Dismas, Dion-Valmont (Belgique), 1985, p. 52.

55 John Paul II, *F.C.*, 13; English translation, p. 25.

56 Kasper, Walter, *Theology of Christian Marriage, op. cit.*, p. 36.

57 Cf. Paul VI, *H.V.*, 9, citing Vatican II, *G.S.*, 50, to qualify love which is fruitful.

58 In the context of repeating the universal call to holiness, the Bishops declared: "*Imprimis est promovenda spiritualitas coniugum quae in sacramentum matrimonii innititur et maximi momenti est in opere traditionis fidei ad futuras generationes.*" *Relatio Finalis*, II. A. 5.

Chapter Three: THE QUEST FOR THE SIGN

1 For example, Joyce, G.H., *Christian Marriage, op. cit.*, and Schillebeeckx, Edward, *Marriage: Human Reality and Saving Mystery, op. cit.*, and to some degree Mackin, Theodore, *What Is Marriage?, op. cit.* Schillebeeckx and Mackin tend to "slant" their history towards their respective ends: a human "secular" emphasis and a non-biblical "covenant" view of Marriage.

2 Cf. Saint Pius X, *Lamentabili, Errores modernistarum*, 51, DS., 3451.

3 For a description of these rites, see Schillebeeckx, Edward, *Marriage: Human Reality and Saving Mystery, op. cit.*, pp. 233-244.

4 Saint Ignatius of Antioch, *Ad Polycarpum*, 3 (*P.G.*, 5, 724).

5 Cf. Joyce, G.H., *Christian Marriage, op. cit.*, p. 165.

6 Tertullian, *Ad uxorem*, 2.9. (*P.L.*, 1, 1302): "*quod ecclesia conciliat, et confirmat oblatio, et obsignat benedictio, angeli renuntiant Pater rato habet.*" Cited by John Paul II, *F.C.*, 13.

7 Cf. Schillebeeckx, Edward, *Marriage: Human Reality and Saving Mystery, op. cit.*, p. 246.

8 Tertullian, *Ad uxorem*, 2.7. (*P.L.*, 1, 1299): ". . . *ex parte divinae gratiae patrocinium.*"

9 Cf. Schillebeeckx, Edward, *Marriage: Human Reality and Saving Mystery, op. cit.*, p. 246.

10 Cf. Clement of Alexandria, *Stromata*, 3.10. (*P.G.*, 8, 1169, 1170).

11 Cf. *Ibid.*, 3.12. (*P.G.*, 8, 1187, 1188).

12 Cf. Mackin, Theodore, *What Is Marriage?, op. cit.*, pp. 83-90.

13 Origen, *In Matthaeum commentarii*, 14.16. (*P.G.*, 13, 1229).

14 Saint Ambrose, *Ep. 19 ad Vigilium*, 7, (*P.L.*, 16, 958).

15 Saint Ambrose, *Ep 42 ad Siricium P.*, 3. (*P.L.*, 16, 1124): "*sanctificatum a Christo.*"

16 Ambrosiaster, *In Eph.*, 5:31, 32. (*P.L.*, 17, 399).

17 Cf. Saint Epiphanius, *Adversus haereses Panarium*, 51.30. (*P.G.*, 41, 941).

18 Saint Cyril of Alexandria, *In Ioan.*, 2.1. (*P.G.*, 73, 224).

19 Theodoret, *Haereticarum fabularum compendium*, 5.25. (*P.G.*, 83, 537).

20 Saint Leo the Great, *Ep. 167 ad Rusticum*, 4 (*P.L.*, 54, 1204, 1205).

21 Cf. Didymus, *Contra Manichaeos*, 8.9. (*P.G.*, 39, 1096).

22 Saint Ambrose, *De institutione virginis*, 6.41. (*P.L.*, 16, 316): ". . .*non enim defloratio virginitatis facit coniugium sed pactio coniugalis.*"

23 Saint Augustine, *De Genesi ad litteram*, 9.7.12. (*P.L.*, 34, 397): ". . . *in sacramento autem (attenditur), ut coniugium non separetur, et dimissus aut dimissa nec causa prolis alteri coniugatur.*" Cited by Pius XI, *C.C.*, 101. Also *In Peccato Originali* 2.39. (*P.L.*, 44 404).

24 See Schillebeeckx, Edward, *Marriage: Human Reality and Saving Mystery, op. cit.*, pp. 285-287. Failing to take account of Augustine's philosophical background, Schillebeeckx wishes to reduce the objectivity and mystery of "*sacramentum*" in line with his own non-ontological sacramentalism, evident even before his Eucharistic phenomenology and denial of indelible character.

25 Cf. Saint Augustine, *De nuptiis et concupiscentia*, 1.11.12. (*P.L.*, 44, 420, 421) where he speaks of "binding indissolubility" as a "*quiddam coniugale.*"

26 Saint Augustine, *De bono coniugali*, 24.32. (*P.L.*, 40, 394): ". . . *sacramento Domini semel imposito non carebit, quamvis ad iudicium permanente.*"

27 Saint Augustine, *De nuptiis et concupiscentia*, 1.10.11. (*P.L.*, 44, 420): ". . . *velut de coniugio Christi recedens.*"

28 Cf. Saint Augustine, *De bono coniugali*, 44.32. (*P.L.*, 40. 394).

29 Saint Augustine, *In Ioannis evangelium tractatus*, 9.2. (*P.L.*, 35 1459).

30 *Ibid.*, 9.10. (*P.L.*, 35, 1463): "*Dormit Adam ut fiat Eva; moritur Christus ut fiat ecclesia.*"

31 Saint Augustine, *In epistulam Ioannis ad Parthos*, 2.2. (*P.L.*, 35, 1990).

32 Saint Augustine, *De nuptiis et concupiscentia*, 1.10.11. (*P.L.*, 44, 420): "... *ut vivens cum vivente in aeternum nullo divortio separetur.*"

33 Saint Augustine, *ibid.*, 1.11.12. (*P.L.* 44, 420).

34 Saint Augustine, *De consensu evangelistarum*, 2.1.2. (*P.L.*, 34, 1071).

35 Cf. Joyce, G.H., *Christian Marriage, op. cit.*, p. 168.

36 An example of the judgmental tendency, cf. Mackin, Theodore, *What is Marriage?, op. cit.*, pp. 130-138, a book also "nuanced" against procreation.

37 Schillebeeckx thought Saint Augustine knew the translation as "*sacramentum.*" See his *Marriage: Human Reality and Saving Mystery, op. cit.*, p. 286. Saint Pacian, writing late in the Fourth Century, in Spain, referred to the "*magnum sacramentum,*" implicitly citing Ephesians 5:32; see Chapter Two.

38 Cf. Saint Bede, *The Commentary on the Seven Catholic Epistles*, tr. David Hurst, OSB., Cistercian Publications, Kalamazoo, Michigan, 1985, p. 96.

39 Cf. Joyce, G.H., *Christian Marriage, op. cit.*, pp. 195-198.

40 Cf. Schillebeeckx, Edward, *Marriage: Human Reality and Saving Mystery, op. cit.*, pp. 256-260.

41 Cf. *Ibid.*, pp. 260-266, for an account of liturgical development.

42 Nicholas I, "*Ad Bulgaros,*" DS., 643: "*Matrimonium non facit coitus sed voluntas.*"

43 Cf. Joyce, G.H., *Christian Marriage, op. cit.*, pp. 362-379.

44 Cf. *Ibid.*, pp. 351-354, for an account of Pope Nicholas' struggle with Lothaire.

45 For the case, see Joyce, G.H., *Christian Marriage, op. cit.*, pp. 54-58.

46 Hincmar of Rheims, *De nuptiis Stephani* (*P.L.*, 126, 145).

47 Cf. Leeming, Bernard, *Principles of Sacramental Theology, op. cit.*, p. 258.

48 Alexander III, "*Ex publico instrumento,*" letter to the Bishop of Brescia, DS., 754, and "*Verum post,*" letter to the Archbishop of Salerno, DS., 755, 756.

49 Cf. Schillebeeckx, Edward, *Marriage: Human Reality and Saving Mystery, op. cit.*, pp. 292-294.

50 Cf. *C.I.C.*, Canon 1061, #1.

51 Cf. Leeming, Bernard, *Principles of Sacramental Theology, op. cit.*, pp. 567-569.

52 Cf. *Ibid.*, pp. 565-566.

53 Cf. Schillebeeckx, Edward, *Marriage: Human Reality and Saving Mystery, op. cit.*, p. 322.

54 Cf. *Ibid.*, pp. 320-324, for a fuller summary of Hugh's theology of Marriage.

55 Cf. Joyce, G.H., *Christian Marriage, op. cit.*, p. 171.

56 Cf. *Ibid.*, p. 169.

57 Cf. Schillebeeckx, Edward, *Marriage: Human Reality and Saving Mystery, op. cit.*, p. 319.
58 Peter Lombard, *Sententiae in IV libris distinctae, Lib. IV.*, Tom. II, Editiones Collegii S. Bonaventurae Ad Claras Aquas, Grottaferrata (Romae), 1981, d.1, cap. 4,2, p. 233: "...*signum gratiae Dei, et invisibilis gratiae forma, ut ipsius imaginem gerat et causa existat.*"
59 Cf. *Ibid.*, d.2, cap. 1,1, p. 240.
60 Cf. Peter Lombard, *Sententiae in IV libris distinctae, Lib. IV., op. cit.*, d.22, cap. 2,3, p. 289 and d.26, cap. 1,1, and 2, p. 416.
61 Cf. *Ibid.*, d.27, cap. 3,1 and 2, pp. 422, 423.
62 Cf. Joyce, G.H., *Christian Marriage, op. cit.*, p. 172.
63 Cf. Schillebeeckx, Edward, *Marriage: Human Reality and Saving Mystery, op. cit.*, pp. 334-336.
64 See Leeming, Bernard, *Principles of Sacramental Theology, op. cit.*, pp. 291-293, and the Scotist view, sacramental Grace as an aspect of Sanctifying Grace, p. 99.
65 Cf. Schillebeeckx, Edward, *Marriage: Human Reality and Saving Mystery, op. cit.*, pp. 336, 337, citing Saint Albert, *In IV Sent.*, d.26, a 14.
66 Cf. Lucius III, *Damnatio errorum sectarum laicalium*, DS., 761.
67 Cf. Innocent III, *Professio Valdesii, "Eius exemplo,"* DS., 794.
68 Cf. Innocent III, *"Quantum te magis,"* letter to Bishop Hugo of Ferrara, May 1, 1199, DS., 769. It is doubtful whether the Twelfth Century magisterial references can begin with Canon 23, Second Lateran Council (DS., 718) which is really only a condemnation of unspecified anti-marriage heretics.
69 Cf. Biffi, Inos, *La Teologia e un Teologo: San Tommaso d'Aquino*, Edizioni Piemme, Casale Monferrato, 1984, pp. 88, 89.
70 Cf. Saint Thomas Aquinas, *In IV., op. cit.*, 26.1.1, pp. 581, 582 (*S.* 41.1.).
71 Cf. *Ibid.*, 26.1.1. ra.2, p. 582 (*S.* 41.1. ad.2.).
72 Cf. Saint Thomas Aquinas, *S.C.G., op. cit.*, Lib. III, cap. 123, 2959-2966, pp. 183, 184.
73 Saint Thomas Aquinas, *In IV., op. cit.*, 26.1.1. ra.4, p. 582 (*S.* 41.3. ad.4). *"similitudinem actus inordinati."*
74 *Ibid.*, 26.2.1. ra.1,2, p. (*S.* 42.1. ad.1,2).
75 See Joyce, G.H., *Christian Marriage, op. cit.*, pp. 184-186.
76 Saint Thomas Aquinas, *In IV., op. cit.*, 26.2.1. ra.3, p. 583 (*S.* 42.1. ad.3), and see his *S.T., op. cit.*, 3a. 64. 7., p. 366.
77 See Introduction under "Memorial, Actuation, Prophecy," pp. xviii-xxii.
78 Cf. Saint Thomas Aquinas, *In IV., op. cit.*, 26.2.1. ra.4, p. 583 (*S.* 42.1. ad.4).
79 *Ibid.*, 26.2.1. ra.5, p. 583 (*S.* 42.1. ad.5).

80 Cf. Saint Thomas Aquinas, *Ad Ephesios*, *op. cit.*, cap. v, lect. x, 333, 334, pp. 76-77.

81 Cf. Saint Thomas Aquinas, *In IV.*, *op. cit.*, 26.2.4. (*S*. 42.4.).

82 *Ibid.*, 27.1.3b. ra.1, p. 586 (*S*. 61.3. ad.1): "*illam coniunctionem quae est Christi ad animam per gratiam,*" and "*. . . quantum ad assumptionem humanae naturae in unitatem personae, quae omnino est indivisibilis.*"

83 Cf. *Ibid.*, 27.1.3b co and ra.2.

84 Saint Thomas Aquinas, *In IV.*, *op. cit.*, 27.1.2a. ra.2, p. 585 (*S*. 45.1. ad.2): "*. . . nec consensus, proprie loquendo, coniunctionem Christi ad ecclesiam significat, sed voluntas eius, qua factum est ut ecclesiae coniungaretur.*"

85 See Chapter Four under "Consent as Efficient Cause," pp. 130-131.

86 Cf. Saint Thomas Aquinas, *S.T.*, *op. cit.*, 3a.29.2c, p. 167.

87 Cf. Saint Thomas Aquinas, *S.C.G.*, *op. cit.*, Lib. III, cap. 126, 2987-2992, p. 187.

88 Saint Thomas Aquinas, *Super Epistolas S. Pauli Lectura, Ad Corinthios*, ed. Raphaelis Cai, OP., lib. I, Marietti, Torino e Roma, 1953, on 1 Cor 7:2-3, p. 329.

89 Cf. Saint Thomas Aquinas, *In IV.*, *op. cit.*, 31.1.3. ra. 5, p. 594 (*S*. 49.3. ad.5).

90 Cf. *Ibid.*, 27.1.1a. ra.1 and ra.2, p. 584 (*S*. 44.1. ad.1 and ad.2).

91 *Ibid.*, 26.2.3. ra.2, p. 583 (*S*. 42.3 ad.2), "*. . . dispositive operetur ad gratiam.*"

92 Saint Thomas Aquinas, *S.C.G.*, *op. cit.*, Lib. III, cap. 78, 4122: "*Et quia sacramenta efficiunt quod figurant, credendum est quod nubentibus per hoc sacramentum gratia conferatur . . . per quam ad unionem Christi et Ecclesiae pertineant . . . quod eis maxime necessarium est, ut sic carnalibus et terrenis intendant quod a Christo et Ecclesia non disiunguntur.*"

93 Saint Thomas Aquinas, *In IV.*, *op. cit.*, 31.1.3. co., p. 594 (*S*. 49.3. co.): "*. . . sicut etiam homini est essentialis esse naturae quam esse gratiae, quamvis esse gratiae sit dignius.*"

94 Cf. *Ibid.*, *op. cit.*, 31.2.1. sc.2, p. 594 (*S*. 49.4. co.): "*. . . non solum bonus sed etiam sanctus.*"

95 *Ibid.*, 31.1.2. ra.4, p. 594 (*S*. 49.2. ad.4): "*. . . in sacramento non solum intelligenda est indivisio, sed omnia illa quae consequuntur matrimonium ex hoc quod est signum coniunctionis Christi et ecclesiae.*"

96 *Ibid.*, *op. cit.*, 31.1.2. ra.7, p. 594 (*S*. 49.2. ad.7): "*. . . sed etiam omnia quae ad significationem ipsius pertinent.*"

97 Saint Thomas Aquinas, *Ad Ephesios*, *op. cit.*, cap. v, lect. x, 335, p. 77: "*. . . et implendum est in aliis in figura Christi.*"

98 Cf. Leeming, Bernard, *Principles of Sacramental Theology*, *op. cit.*, pp. 99-100 and pp. 108-118.

99 Cf. Saint Thomas Aquinas, *S.T., op. cit.*, 3a.72.7. ad.3, p. 428, stating, without reasons, that the Grace of Baptism differs from that of Confirmation.

100 *Ibid.*, 3a.65.3. co., p. 373.

101 See Schroeder, H.J., *Disciplinary Decrees of the General Councils*, Herder, St. Louis, 1937, pp. 324-327, a concise account of the Second Council of Lyons.

102 Cf. *Professio fidei Michaelis Palaeologi imperatoris*, DS., 860.

103 Saint Thomas Aquinas, *In IV., op. cit.*, 26.2.1. ad.1, p. 583 (*S.* 42.1. ad.1).

104 Cf. *Ibid.*, 27.1.2b, sc.2; 27.1.2c. ra.2, p. 585 (*S.* 42.1. ad.1): "*de futuro*" versus "*de praesenti.*"

105 Cf. Fourth Lateran Council, Canon 51, DS., 817, and in Schroeder, H.J., *Disciplinary Decrees of the General Councils, op. cit.*, pp. 280-281.

106 Cf. Perrone, Johannes, *Praelectiones Theologicae*, Vanlinthout et Vandenzande, Louvain, 1842, *Tractatus de matrimonio*, Vol. VII, cap. 1, 20, p. 212.

107 John XXII, *Gloriosam Ecclesiam*, January 23, 1318, DS., 916: ". . . *coniugii venerabile sacramentum.*"

108 Cf. Council of Florence, *Exultate Deo, Decretum pro Armeniis*, DS., 1327: "*Causa efficiens matrimonii regulariter est mutuus consensus per verba de praesenti expressus.*" Indissolubility was affirmed in the "*matrimonii vinculum legitime contracti.*"

109 Cf. Luther, Martin, *Omnium Operum Reverendi Patris Viri Dei D. Mart. Luth.*, Tom. II, *De captivitate babylonica ecclesiae: Praeludium*, Tobias Steinman, Jena, 1600, pp. 279-280.

110 On the early Protestants' view of Marriage, see Adnès, Pierre, *Le mariage*, Desclée, Tournai, 1963, pp. 95-99, and on "reflexive faith" and sacraments, Hacker, Paul, *The Ego in Faith: Martin Luther and the Origin of Anthropocentric Religion (Das Ich in Glauben bei Martin Luther)*, Franciscan Herald Press, Chicago, 1970, pp. 8-19, and cap. V, pp. 91-121.

111 Cf. Calvin, John, *Institutes of the Christian Religion*, lib. iv., cap. 19, nos. 34-37, in *Joannis Calvini Opera Selecta*, ed. P. Barth, G. Niesel, ed. 3, Kaiser, Munich, 1974, pp. 467-471.

112 Cf. Hughes, Philip, *The Reformation in England*, 3 volumes in one, revised, Burns & Oates, London, 1963, vol. III, pp. 87 and 153.

113 Cf. Council of Trent, *Canones de sacramentis in genere*, 1., DS., 1601, Seventh Session, March 3, 1547.

114 Cf. Cano, Melchior, *De Locis Theologicis, De Auctoritate Doctorum Schol.*, lib. viii, cap. v, in his *Opera*, Auroy, Paris, 1706, pp. 328-330.

115 Cf. McDermott, Charles, *The Tridentine Canon on the Sacramentality of Marriage*, Faculty of Theology, Gregorian University, Rome, 1978, p. 355.

116 Cf. Caffarra, Carlo, "Marriage as a Reality in the Order of Creation and Marriage as a Sacrament," I.T.C., op. cit., pp. 133-134.

117 See Jedin, Hubert, and Reinhardt, Klaus, *Il Matrimonio, una ricerca storica e teologica (Ehe Sakrament in der Kirche des Herrn)*, tr. F. Meneghini, Morcelliana, Brescia, 1981; especially Jedin's historical work, pp. 9-87 and Reinhardt's theology, pp. 114-124.

118 Council of Trent, *Canones de sacramento matrimonii*, 1, DS., 1801: "*Si quis dixerit, matrimonium non esse vere et proprie unum ex septem Legis evangelicae sacramentis, a Christo Domino institutum, sed ab hominibus in Ecclesia inventum, neque gratiam conferre: anathema sit.*"

119 Cf. McDermott, Charles, *The Tridentine Canon on the Sacramentality of Marriage, op. cit.*, p. 364.

120 Cf. Council of Trent, *Doctrina de sacramento matrimonii*, DS., 1799.

121 See, Colli, Pietro, *La pericope paolina ad Ephesios 5:32 nella interpretazione dei SS. Padri e del Concilio di Trento*, Parma, 1951 (doctoral dissertation, Gregorian University, Rome), and Lawrence, Ralph J., *The Sacramental Interpretation of Ephesians 5:32 from Peter Lombard to the Council of Trent*, Catholic University of America Studies in Theology, 2nd Series, 145, Catholic University of America Press, Washington, DC, 1963.

122 Cf. Council of Trent, "*Tametsi*," November 11, 1563, DS., 1813-1816.

123 For an account see Gomes, W.Z., *De matrimoniis clandestinis in Concilio Tridentino*, Pontificium Athenaeum Urbanianum de "Propaganda Fide," Rome, 1950.

124 Cf. Leeming, Bernard, *Principles of Sacramental Theology, op. cit.*, pp. 422-423.

125 Cf. De Cock, Joseph, *L'Église et le Sacrament de Mariage d'après les Actes du Concile de Trente*, Pontificia Universitas Gregoriana Facultas Theologica, Rome, 1966, pp. 70-73.

126 Cf. Saint Pius V, *Professio fidei Tridentina*, November 13, 1564, DS., 1864.

127 Cf. *Catechism of the Council of Trent, op. cit.*, pp. 342, 350, 351.

128 *Ibid.*, p. 354.

129 But not the only theologian to maintain permanent sacramentality in Marriage; see Gerke, Leonard, *Christian Marriage, a Permanent Sacrament*, Catholic University of America Studies in Theology, 2nd Series, 161, Catholic University of America Press, Washington, DC, 1965.

130 Saint Robert Bellarmine, *De controversiis christianae fidei adversus huius temporis haereticos*, Tom. III, *De sacramento matrimonii*, liber I Apud Joannem Malachinum, Venice, 1721, cap. v, p. 626.

131 *Ibid.*, cap. vi, p. 628: "*Nam coniugii Sacramentum duobus modis considerari potest. Uno modo dum fit. Altero modo, dum permanet postquam factum est. Est enim Matrimonium simile Eucharistiae, quae non solum dum fit, sed etiam dum permanet, Sacramentum est: dum enim coniuges vivunt, semper eorum societas Sacramentum est Christi, et Ecclesiae.*"

132 Pius XI's encyclical, *Casti Connubii*, is covered further on in this chapter under the heading, "The Twentieth Century."

133 Saint Robert Bellarmine, *De controversiis*, Tom. III, *op. cit.*, cap. vi, p. 626: "*Si vero consideratur Matrimonium iam factum, et celebratum, negari non potest ipsos coniuges simul cohabitantes, sive externam coniugum societatem et coniunctionem, esse materiale symbolum exterum, repraesentans Christi et Ecclesiae indissolubilem coniunctionem: quemadmodum in Sacramento Eucharistiae, consecratione peracta remanent species consecratae, quae sunt symbolum sensibile atque externum, interni alimenti spiritualis.*"

134 See above, pp. 88, 94, 100, 104-105.

135 Cf. Saint Robert Bellarmine, *De controversiis*, Tom. III, *op. cit.*, cap. vii, pp. 630-631: "*Ex quo intelligimus Cani opinionem etsi omnino singularem, et novam. . . .*"

136 Cf. *Ibid.*, cap. viii, p. 632: ". . . *sed a Christo evectum ad ordinem rerum sacrarum.*"

137 See Caffarra, Carlo, "Marriage as a Reality in the Order of Creation and Marriage as a Sacrament," *I.T.C., op. cit.*, pp. 126-127.

138 Cf. *Ibid.*, pp. 139-141.

139 On Emperor Joseph II of Austria, see Joyce, G.H., *Christian Marriage, op. cit.*, pp. 255-262.

140 Cf. Tanquerey, Adolphe, *Synopsis Theologiae Moralis et Pastoralis*, Tom. I, Editio decima, Desclée, Paris, 1925, n. 828, p. 488.

141 Cf. Saint Alphonsus Liguori, *Theologia Moralis*, Tom. IV, Lib. VI, Tract. VI, *De Matrimonio*, ed. Leonardi Gaudé, Typis Polyglottis Vaticanis, Rome, 1912, 1953, n. 897, n. 898, pp. 75-79.

142 For a recent excellent synopsis, see Mullady, Brian T., "The Mystery of Marriage in Matthias Joseph Scheeben," *M.J. Scheeben teologo cattolico d'ispirazione tomista* (various authors), Studi Tomistici 33, Pontificia Accademia di S. Tommaso, Libreria Editrice Vaticana, 1988, pp. 435-441.

143 Scheeben, Matthias, *The Mysteries of Christianity, op. cit.*, p. 592.

144 *Ibid.*, pp. 578-579 and 604-605.

145 *Ibid.*, p. 606.

146 Cf. *Ibid.*, p. 606, n. 10.

147 Cf. Pius IX, *Errores de matrimonio christiano*, 65, 66, DS., 2965-2974.

148 Cf. Leo XIII, *Arcanum Divinae Sapientiae*, 9, DS., 3142; English translation, Carlen, Claudia, *The Papal Encyclicals, 1878-1903*, McGrath, Wilmington, North Carolina, 1981, p. 31.

149 Cf. *Ibid.*, 23, 24, DS., 3145, 3146; English translation, p. 34.

150 Cf. Tanquerey, Adolphe, *Synopsis Theologiae Moralis et Pastoralis*, Tom. I, *op. cit.*, pp. 470-471.

151 Cf. Prümmer, Dominic, *Manuale Theologiae Moralis secundum principia S. Thomae Aquinatis*, Tom. III, ed. decima, Herder, Barcelona, 1946, pp. 457-458.

152 Cf. Leeming, Bernard, *Principles of Sacramental Theology, op. cit.*, p. 368.

153 Pius XI, *Casti Connubii*, 40, DS., 3714; English translation, Carlen, Claudia, *The Papal Encyclicals, 1903-1939, op. cit.*, p. 397.

154 Cf. Leeming, Bernard, *Principles of Sacramental Theology, op. cit.*, p. 106.

155 Pius XI, *C.C.*, English translation, p. 398, cited, Vatican II, *G.S.*, 48, n.7.

156 *Ibid.*, 42; English translation, p. 398.

157 See Chapter Five under "Consecration" and "The Bond of Love," pp. 150-154.

158 Pius XI, *C.C.*, 110; English translation, p. 409, citing Saint Robert Bellarmine, *De controversiis*, Tom. III, *op. cit.*, cap. vi, p. 628.

159 *Ibid.*, 111; English translation, pp. 409-410.

160 Pius XII, *Mystici Corporis Christi*, 20, June 29, 1943; English translation, Carlen, Claudia, *The Papal Encyclicals 1939-1958, op. cit.*, p. 41.

161 Pius XII, *Sacra Virginitas*, 37, March 25, 1954, DS., 3911; English translation, Carlen, Claudia, *op. cit.*, p. 254.

162 Cf. Von Hildebrand, Dietrich, *Marriage, the Mystery of Faithful Love, op. cit.*, "Introduction" by Alice Von Hildebrand, pp. x-xiv.

163 Cf. *De finibus Matrimonii*, Decretum S. Officii, 1 April 1944, DS., 3838.

164 Vatican II, *G.S.*, 47; English translation, *V.II., op. cit.*, p. 949.

165 *Ibid.*, 48; English translation, pp. 950-951.

166 Cf. Paul VI, *H.V.*, 8.

167 See Chapter Seven under "The Sacrament and Contraception," pp. 212-219.

168 See Congregation for the Doctrine of the Faith, *Documenta inde a Concilio Vaticano Secundo Expleto Edita (1966-1985)*, Libreria Editrice Vaticana, 1985, Letter of Cardinal Seper on indissolubility, April 11, 1973, p. 48.

169 Cf. *Rituale Romanum ex decreto sacrosancto oecumenici Concilii Vaticani II instauratum auctoritate Pauli PP. VI promulgatum, Ordo Celebrandi Matrimonium*, Editio typica, Typis Polyglottis Vaticanis, 1972, Praenotanda n. 7, p. 8.

170 Cf. Newman, John Henry, *An Essay on the Development of Christian Doctrine*, Longmans Green, London, 1894, the seven notes, cap. v., pp. 109-206.

Chapter Four: THE SACRAMENTAL CONSENT

 1 *C.I.C.*, Canon 1057, #2; English translation, *The Code of Canon Law in English Translation*, Canon Law Society, Great Britain, Ireland, Australia, New Zealand and Canada, Collins, London, 1983, p. 189.
 2 Cf. *Ibid.*, Canon 1096, #1.
 3 Cf. *Ibid.*, Canon 1098.
 4 Cf. *Ibid.*, Canon 1103.
 5 Cf. *Ibid.*, Canon 1102, #1.
 6 Cf. *Ibid.*, Canon 1101, #1.
 7 Cf. Evdokimov, Paul, *Sacrement de l'amour: le mystère conjugal à la lumière de la tradition orthodoxe*. Éditions de l'epi, Paris, 1977, p. 190, nn. 47, 48.
 8 Cf. *Ibid.*, p. 185.
 9 John Paul II, *F.C.*, 12; English translation, p. 24.
10 Cf. John Paul II, "Nelle parole del consenso coniugale il segno del'profetismo del corpo," General Audience, January 18, 1983, *Insegnamenti di Giovanni Paolo II, op. cit.*, VI.1, 1983, p. 157.
11 See Chapter Seven under "Faith and Sacrament," pp. 192-199.
12 Cf. Vatican II, *L.G.*, 16.
13 John Paul II, *F.C.*, 68; English translation, pp. 101, 102.
14 Cf. Laroche, Michel, *Une seule chair, op. cit.*, pp. 84, 85.
15 Cf. John Paul II, "Nelle parole . . .," *op. cit.*, VI.1, 1983, p. 155.
16 Cf. Volta, Giovanni, "Indagine filosofica sull'amore," in *Enciclopedia del matrimonio*, ed. Tullo Goffi, Editrice Queriniana, Brescia, 1968, pp. 182, 183.
17 Cf. Von Hildebrand, Dietrich, *Marriage, the Mystery of Faithful Love, op. cit.*, pp. 11, 12.
18 Cf. Evdokimov, Paul, *La femme et le salut du monde*, Théophanie, Desclée de Brouwer, Paris, 1978, pp. 194, 195.
19 Cf. *Ibid.*, pp. 258, 259.
20 Cf. Pius XI, *C.C.*, 115; John Paul II, *F.C.*, 66.
21 Cf. Volta, Giovanni, *op. cit.*, pp. 187, 188.
22 See Belmans, Theo G., *Le sens objectif de l'agir humain, Pour relire la moral conjugale de Saint Thomas*, Libreria Editrice Vaticana, 1980, pp. 292-295.
23 Cf. Volta, Giovanni, *op. cit.*, pp. 191, 192.

24 Paul VI, *H.V.*, 8; English translation, Vatican Polyglot Press, Catholic Truth Society, London, 1968, p. 10.

25 Cf. Saint Thomas Aquinas, *In IV, op. cit.*, 27.1.2c ra.2, p. 585 (*S.*, 45.3.ad.2).

26 *Ibid.*, 27.1.2b co., p. 585 (*S.*, 45.2. co.).

27 Cf. Lyons, James P., *The Essential Structure of Marriage, A Study of the Thomistic Teaching on the Natural Institution*, Catholic University of America Press, Washington, DC, 1950, pp. 16, 17.

28 Saint Thomas Aquinas, *In IV, op. cit.*, 27.1.2a ra.2, p. 585 (*S.*, 45.1. ad.2).

29 Scheeben, Matthias, *The Mysteries of Christianity, op. cit.*, p. 610. Also see Caffarra, Carlo, "Marriage as a Reality in the Order of Creation and Marriage as a Sacrament," *I.T.C., op. cit.*, pp. 150-154.

30 Cf. Hervada, Javier, "la inseparabilidad entre contrato y sacramento en el matrimonio," in *C.F.M.F., op. cit.*, pp. 260-264.

31 *C.I.C.*, (1983), Canon 1055, #2; *C.I.C.*, (1917), Canon 1012, #2.

32 See Lawler, Michael G., *Secular Marriage, Christian Sacrament*, Twenty-Third Publications, Mystic, Connecticut, 1985, p. 68.

33 Irish Theological Commission, *What God Has Joined . . .*, Irish Messenger Publications, Dublin, 1982, p. 5.

34 Cf. Paul VI, *H.V.*, 9.

35 Irish Theological Commission, *op. cit.*, p. 5.

36 Lawler, Michael G., *op. cit.*, p. 74.

37 Pius XII, *Haurietis Aquas*, 49; English translation, Carlen, Claudia, *The Papal Encyclicals 1939-1958, op. cit.*, p. 297.

38 *Ibid.*, 63, p. 299.

39 *Ibid.*, 64, p. 299.

40 *Ibid.*, 65, p. 299.

41 *Ibid.*, 89, pp. 301-302, citing Saint Thomas Aquinas, *S*, 42.1. ad.3.

42 *Ibid.*, 90, p. 302.

43 *Ibid.*, 93, p. 302.

44 Cf. Evdokimov, Paul, *op. cit.*, pp. 44-46.

45 Nash, Andrew and Dora, *Christian Marriage, Covenant in Christ*, Faith Pamphlets, Wallingford, Surrey, 1983, pp. 11, 12.

46 Cf. Volta, Giovanni, *op. cit.*, p. 189.

47 See Chapter Five under "The Sacramentality of the Body," pp. 155-162.

48 See, Gil Hellín, Francisco, "El matrimonio: amor e institución," in *C.F.M.F. op. cit.*, pp. 236-237, a non-romantic, pragmatic understanding of fundamental conjugal love.

49 Von Balthasar, Hans Urs, *The Christian State of Life (Christlicher Stand)*, tr. Sr. Mary Frances McCarthy, Ignatius Press, San Francisco, 1983, p. 238.

50 *C.I.C.*, Canon 1099; English translation, p. 196.

51 Cf. Kasper, Walter, *Theology of Christian Marriage, op. cit.*, pp. 82, 83.

Chapter Five: THE SACRAMENTAL BOND

1 See Chapter Three under "Saint Augustine."

2 See Chapter Three under "Signification in Saint Thomas Aquinas" and "The Grace of Marriage in Saint Thomas." Also Saint Thomas Aquinas, *In IV, op. cit.*, 12.1.3b co. and ra.2. ra.3, p. 586 (*S.* 61.2. co and ad.2 ad.3.).

3 John Paul II, *F.C.*, 13, citing his "Address to the Delegates of the Centre de Liaison des Équipes de Recherche," November 3, 1979, *Insegnamenti di Giovanni Paolo II, op. cit.*, II.2, 1979, p. 1032.

4 Cf. John Paul II, "Il linguaggio del corpo nella comunion degli sposi," 6, General Audience, January 5, 1983, *Insegnamenti di Giovanni Paolo II, op. cit.*, VI.1, 1983, p. 44.

5 Pius XI, *C.C.*, 35, DS., 3712; English translation, Carlen, Claudia, *The Papal Encyclicals, 1903-1939, op. cit.*, p. 396, noting the use of "*foedus*," but translated as "contract" in the English text chosen by Sr. Carlen.

6 See Chapter One under "Marriage in Creation," "In Eden, the Creation Accounts," pp. 6-9.

7 Saint Thomas Aquinas, *In IV, op. cit.*, 27.1.3b ra.1, p. 586 (*S.* 61.3. ad.1.): ". . . *quantum ad assumptionem humanae naturae in unitatem personae, quae omnino est indivisibilis.*"

8 Cf. Scheeben, Matthias, *The Mysteries of Christianity, op. cit.*, pp. 184-186.

9 Saint Augustine, *De nuptiis et concupiscentia*, 1.10.11. (*P.L.*, 44, 420): ". . . *vivens cum vivente in aeternum nullo divortio separetur.*"

10 Pius XII, *Mystici Corporis*, 58; English translation, Carlen, Claudia, *The Papal Encyclicals, 1939-1958, op. cit.*, p. 48.

11 Cf. Hagerty, Cornelius J., *The Holy Trinity*, Christopher, North Quincy, Massachusetts, 1976, pp. 143-145.

12 Scheeben, Matthias, *The Mysteries of Christianity, op. cit.*, p. 599.

13 *Ibid.*, p. 600. Also see pp. 602-603.

14 *Ibid.*, p. 171 where he cites Saint Bernard, *Serm. VIII in Cantica*, 9 (*P.L.*, 183, 814).

15 *Ibid.*, pp. 109-110.

16 *Ibid.*, p. 566.

17 See Chapter Two under "Spouses Consecrated by the Holy Spirit," pp. 67-69.

18 Cf. Saint Thomas Aquinas, *S.T., op. cit.*, 3a.63.3. ad.3. and 63.6. ad.1., Tom. III, pp. 357 and 359.

19 See Chapter Two under "Christians, Sealed by the Holy Spirit," pp. 64-67.

20 Cf. Scheeben, Matthias, *The Mysteries of Christianity, op. cit.*, pp. 604-606; Pius XI, *C.C.*, 41, 110; Vatican II, *G.S.*, 48.

21 Robinson, Geoffrey, *Marriage, Divorce and Nullity*, Dove Communications, Melbourne, 1984, p. 7.

22 See Chapter Three, pp. 105-107, 111-113.

23 John Paul II, *F.C.*, 13.

24 Saint Thomas Aquinas, *S.T., op. cit.*, 1a.37.1. ra.3, Tom. I, p. 189: "... *dicendum quod Spiritus Sanctus dicitur esse nexus Patris et Filii inquantum est Amor.*" and "... *medius nexus duorum ab utroque procedens.*" "... *in unitate Spiritus Sancti.*"

25 Scheeben, Matthias, *The Mysteries of Christianity, op. cit.*, p. 107.

26 Cf. John Paul II, "Realizzazione del valore del corpo secondo il disegno del Creatore," 2, General Audience, October 22, 1980, *Insegnamenti di Giovanni Paolo II*, III.2, 1980, p. 949.

27 Cf. Grisez, Germain, *The Way of the Lord Jesus, op. cit.*, p. 138.

28 Cf. John Paul II, "L'uomo-persona divenuta dono nella libertà dell'amore," 1-3, *Insegnamenti di Giovanni Paolo II, op. cit.*, III.1, 1980, pp. 148-150.

29 Cf. John Paul II, "Il significato biblico della conoscenza nella convivenza matrimoniale," General Audience, March 5, 1980, *Insegnamenti di Giovanni Paolo II, op. cit.*, III.1, 1980, pp. 517-521, especially, 4, pp. 519-520.

30 Gosling, Justin C., *Marriage and the Love of God*, Chapman, London, 1965, p. 65.

31 See Chapter Three under "After Saint Augustine."

32 Cf. Saint John Chrysostom, *Hom. xxi in epist. ad Corinth.* (*P.G.*, 61, 257-259).

33 Cf. Saint John Chrysostom, *Hom. xii in epist. ad Coloss. cap. iv.* (*P.G.*, 62, 385-392, especially 388). See also Messenger, E.G., *Two in One Flesh*, 3 vols. Newman Press, Westminster, Maryland, 1948, vol. 2, pp. 143-145.

34 Cf. Pampaloni, Pio, "Il matrimonio nella scholastica," *Enciclopedia del Matrimonio, op. cit.*, pp. 332-337.

35 See Chapter Three under "Signification in St. Thomas."

36 Cf. Saint Thomas Aquinas, *In IV, op. cit.*, 26.1.3. co., p. 582 (*S.* 41-3. co.).

37 For example, Messenger, E.G., *Two in One Flesh, op. cit.*, vol. 1, pp. 1-12.

38 Cf. Council of Trent, *Canones de sacramento matrimonii*, Can. 10, DS., 1810; Pius XII, *Sacra Virginitas*, March 25, 1954, DS., 3911, 3912; and Moioli, Giovanni, "Matrimonio e verginità," *Enciclopedia del Matrimonio, op. cit.*, pp. 401-403.

39 Cf. Gosling, Justin C., *Marriage and the Love of God, op. cit.*, p. 64.

40 Sattler, Henry V., "Adultery within Marriage," *Homiletic and Pastoral Review*, New York, December 1981, pp. 30-31.

41 Cf. John Paul II, "La concupiscenza come distacco dal significato sposale del corpo," General Audience, September 10, 1980, *Insegnamenti di Giovanni Paolo II*, III.2, 1980, pp. 589-593.

42 Cf. John Paul II, "Realizzazione del valore del corpo secondo il disegno del Creatore," 5, General Audience, October 22, 1980, *Insegnamenti di Giovanni Paolo II*, *op. cit.*, III.2, 1980, p. 961.

43 Vatican II, *G.S.*, 49; English translation, *V.II.*, pp. 952-953.

44 Cf. Council of Trent, *Canones de sacramento matrimonii*, Can. 7, DS., 1807, reinforced by Pius XI, *C.C.*, 88 (*A.A.S.*, 22, 1930, p. 574).

45 Cf. Descamps, A.L., "The New Testament Doctrine on Marriage," *I.T.C.*, *op. cit.*, pp. 241-249.

46 See Joyce, G.H., *Christian Marriage*, *op. cit.*, pp. 584-600.

47 See above, pp. 79-82.

48 Saint Thomas Aquinas, *In IV*, *op. cit.*, 33.2.1. ra.2, p. 600 (*S.* 67.1. ad.2.):
"*. . . inseparabilitas competit matrimonio secundum quod est signum perpetuae coniunctionis Christi et ecclesiae, et secundum quod est in officium naturae ad bonum prolis ordinatum.*"

49 Martelet, G., "Sixteen Christological Theses on the Sacrament of Marriage," *I.T.C.*, *op. cit.*, n. 13, p. 282.

50 See Hamel, E., "The Indissolubility of Completed Marriage: Theological, Historical and Pastoral Reflections," *I.T.C.*, *op. cit.*, pp. 189-198.

51 As in Lawler, Michael G., *Secular Marriage, Christian Sacrament*, *op. cit.*, pp. 50-55.

52 *Ibid.*, p. 118.

53 Cf. Council of Trent, *Canones de sacramento matrimonii*, Can. 8, DS., 1808, "*separatio tori et mensae.*"

54 Descamps, A.L., "The New Testament Doctrine on Marriage," *I.T.C.*, *op. cit.*, p. 260, and see note 130, p. 359.

55 See Joyce, G.H., *Christian Marriage*, *op. cit.*, pp. 275, 276, 295, 296, as against Lawler, Michael G., *Secular Marriage, Christian Sacrament*, *op. cit.*, pp. 86-87, and as modifying the problems in Descamps, A.L., "The New Testament Doctrine on Marriage," *I.T.C.*, *op. cit.*, pp. 226-228 and 235-236.

56 See Chapter Seven, pp. 203-208. For a detailed objective account of the history of Eastern views, see Bressan, Luigi, *Il divorzio nelle chiese orientali: ricerca storica sull'attegiamento cattolico*, Edizione Dehoniane, Bologna, 1976.

57 Cf. Saint Thomas Aquinas, *In IV*, *op. cit.*, 27.1.1a ra.1., p. 584 (*S.* 44.1. ad.1).

58 Paul VI, "The Family, School of Holiness," Address to the "Équipes de Notre-Dame," 6, *Insegnamenti di Paolo VI*, Libreria Editrice Vaticana, VIII, 1970, p. 427: "*Le don n'est pas une fusion, en effet. Chaque personnalité demeure distincte, et loin de se dissoudre dans le don mutuel, s'affirme et s'affine, grandit à longeur de vie conjugale, selon cette grande loi de l'amour; se donner l'un à l'autre pour se donner ensemble.*"

59 Cf. Vatican II, *Apostolicam Actuositatem*, 11.

60 Mersch, Émile, *The Theology of the Mystical Body*, (*La Théologie du corps mystique*), tr. Cyril Vollert, SJ., Herder, St. Louis, Missouri, 1951, p. 446.

61 Saint Augustine, *De bono coniugali*, 18.21. (*P.L.*, 40, 388): *"Sicut ergo sacramentum pluralium nuptiarum illius temporis significat futuram multitudinem Deo subjectam in terrenis omnibus gentibus; sic sacramentum nuptiarum singularum nostri temporis significat unitatem omnium nostrum subjectam Deo futuram in una coelesti civitate."*

Chapter Six: THE SACRAMENTAL COVENANT

1 The covenants: with Noah, cf. Genesis 8:20; 9:8-17 and see Hebrews 11:7; with Abraham, cf. Genesis 15:1-20; 17:13 and see Hebrews 6:13; with Moses, cf. Exodus 6:7; 34:1-10, 27-28; with David, cf. 2 Samuel 7:5-16; 23:5.

2 Cf. McCarthy, Dennis J., *Treaty and Covenant, a study in form in the Ancient Oriental Documents and in the Old Testament*, Analecta Biblica 21a (revised text), Pontifical Biblical Institute, Rome, 1978, pp. 253, 256, 295, 296.

3 Cf. *Ibid.*, pp. 297, 298 and 263 on the "familial" dimension of covenant.

4 See Chapter One under "Israel: Towards the 'Great Mystery'."

5 Cf. Tosato, Angelo, *Il matrimonio israelitico, una teoria generale, op. cit.*, pp. 105-106.

6 Cf. Most, William, *Covenant and Redemption*, St. Paul Publications, Athlone, Ireland 1975, pp. 31-32.

7 Cf. McCarthy, Dennis J., *op. cit.*, p. 204.

8 Cf. Most, William, *op. cit.*, p. 39.

9 Cf. John Paul II, "Gli aspetti morali della vocazione dei cristiani," 7, General Audience, September 15, 1982, *Insegnamenti di Giovanni Paolo II*, V.3, 1982, p. 462.

10 Cf. Ernst, Wilhelm, "Marriage as Institution and the Contemporary Challenge to It," *I.T.C., op. cit.*, p. 47.

11 Cf. De La Potterie, Ignace, "La donna e il mistero della Chiesa," *La donna nella Chiesa oggi, op. cit.*, p. 115.

12 Sorci, Pietro, "Il tema della Chiesa-sposa nelle liturgie nuziali," *Ho Theologos, op. cit.*, p. 95.

13 Cf. Most, William, *op. cit.*, pp. 64-65.

14 See Chapter Two under "Saint Paul": "new" in the "new creation," pp. 46-47.

15 Cf. Hogan, Richard, and Le Voir, John M., *Covenant of Love*, Doubleday, New York, 1985, p. 163.

16 Cf. De La Potterie, Ignace, *op. cit.*, pp. 120-121.

17 Cf. John Paul II, "La perdità del sacramento originale reintegrata con la redenzione nel matrimonio-sacramento," 2-5, General Audience, October 13, 1982, *Insegnamenti di Giovanni Paolo II*, V.3, 1982, pp. 811-814.

18 Cf. Council of Trent, *Canones de sacramentis in genere*, Canons 1, 2, 4, 6, 8, DS., 1601, 1602, 1604, 1606, 1608; *Canones de sacramento matrimonii*, Canon 1, DS., 1801.

19 John Paul II, *F.C.*, 13; English translation, pp. 25-26.

20 Cf. John Paul II, "Il matrimonio è parte integrante della nuova economia sacramentale," 5, General Audience, October 20, 1982, *Insegnamenti di Giovanni Paolo II*, V.3, 1982, p. 859.

21 Cf. Pius XI, *C.C.*, 32 and 34, DS., 3710 and 3712; see Chapter Five, Footnote 5.

22 Cf. *V.II., op. cit.*, pp. 950-951, 954. This is one instance where Abbot, Walter M., *The Documents of Vatican II*, Guild Press, New York, 1966, pp. 250-252, 255, is to be preferred, where *"foedus"* is consistently "covenant."

23 Vatican II, *G.S.*, footnote 1; English translation, *V.II.*, p. 903.

24 For the text, see Vatican II, *Acta Synodalia Sacrosancta Concilii Oecumenici Vaticani II*, Typis Polyglottis Vaticanis, Rome, 1970-1978, Vol. I, Pars IV, pp. 718-771.

25 Cf. Mackin, Theodore, *What is Marriage?*, *op. cit.*, pp. 248-265, noting his bias.

26 Cf. Vatican II, *G.S.*, 47.

27 Vatican II, *G.S.*, 48; English translation, *V.II.*, p. 950.

28 Cf. Vatican II, *Acta Synodalia*, *op. cit.*, Vol. IV, Pars I, p. 536.

29 Cf. *Ibid.*, Vol. IV, Pars VII, pp. 476-477.

30 Claimed by Häring, Bernard, "Fostering the Nobility of Marriage and the Family," *Commentary on the Documents of Vatican II*, Herder and Herder, Burns and Oates, New York, London, 1969, Vol. V, pp. 232-233.

31 *C.I.C.*, Canon 1055, #1.

32 Cf. *Ibid.*, Canon 1055, #2.

33 *Ibid.*, Canon 1057, #2; English translation, *The Code of Canon Law*, *op. cit.*, p. 189.

34 Heavily influenced by the American crisis in Marriage, these are the nuances found in Lawler, Michael G., *Secular Marriage, Christian Sacrament*, *op. cit.*, pp. 50-55.

35 See Chapter Three under "After Trent," pp. 105-107.

36 Cf. John Paul II, *F.C.*, 13.

37 Cf. *Ibid.*, 56, citing Vatican II, *G.S.*, 48, on the abiding presence of Jesus Christ filling the lives of spouses with Faith, Hope and Charity.

38 *Catechism of the Council of Trent*, *op. cit.*, p. 354.

39 Pius XI, *C.C.*, 110; English translation, Carlen, Claudia, *The Papal Encyclicals 1903-1939, op. cit.*, p. 409.
40 Von Balthasar, Hans Urs, *The Christian State of Life, op. cit.*, pp. 244-245.
41 Cf. *C.I.C.*, Canons 1151-1155, separation permitted while the bond remains.
42 Cf. John Paul II, *F.C.*, 58.
43 Cf. John Paul II, *Reconciliatio et Paenitentia*, Post-Synodal Apostolic Exhortation, 27, *Insegnamenti di Giovanni Paolo II, op. cit.*, VII.2, 1984, p. 1480.
44 John Paul II, *F.C.*, 57; English translation, p. 86.
45 Grisez, Germain, *The Way of the Lord Jesus, op. cit.*, p. 801.
46 Cf. Pieper, Josef, *Sull'amore* (Über die Liebe) trad. di Gianni Poletti, Morcelliana, Brescia, 1974, pp. 98-99.
47 Cf. *Ibid.*, pp. 130-132.
48 Cf. *Ibid.*, pp. 41-46.
49 Cf. *Ibid.*, 47-48 and 128-129, "... *la gratitudine per il fatto che noi realmente otteniamo ciò che per natura desideriamo ed amiamo.*"

Chapter Seven: SACRAMENTAL PROBLEMS

1 Vatican II, *Sacrosanctum Concilium*, 59; English translation, *V.II., op. cit.*, p. 20.
2 The two texts of *Sacrosanctum Concilium*, 59, see Vatican II, *Acta Synodalia, op. cit.*, Vol. II, Pars II, p. 550, noting the strengthening in the "*textus definitivus.*"
3 *Rituale Romanum, Ordo Celebrandi Matrimonium, op. cit.*, Praenotanda n. 7, p. 8: "*Imprimis pastores foveant nuptriantque fidem nupturientium: Sacramentum enim Matrimonii fidem supponit atque expostulat.*"
4 For example, in English: Kilmartin, Edward, "When is Marriage a Sacrament?", *Theological Studies*, 34, 1973, pp. 275-286; Cuenin, Walter, *The Marriage of Baptized Non-Believers*, Gregorian University Press, Rome, 1977; Cuenin, Walter, "Questions: Faith, Sacrament and Law," *Origins*, November 9, 1978, pp. 321-328.
5 International Theological Commission, *Propositions on the Doctrine of Christian Marriage*, 2.3, *I.T.C., op. cit.*, pp. 14-15, and see pp. 18-19.
6 Cf. Lehmann, Karl, "The Sacramentality of Christian Marriage," *I.T.C., op. cit.*, pp. 100-111.
7 Caffarra, Carlo, "Marriage as a Reality in the Order of Creation and Marriage as a Sacrament," *I.T.C., op. cit.*, p. 180, and see pp. 175-180.
8 Cf. Synod of Bishops, 1980, *De muneribus familiae christianae in mundo hodierno, Elenchus Propositionum*, E Civitate Vaticana, 1980, pp. 26-27.

9 Cf. *Il Sinodo dei Vescovi, Quinta Assemblea Generale*, a cura di Giovanni Caprile, S.I., Edizioni "La Civiltà Cattolica," 1981, *Relatio post dicepationem, De sacramento matrimonii, Fides et sacramentum*, 2, pp. 762-763.

10 John Paul II, *F.C.*, 68; English translation, pp. 101-103.

11 See Chapter Four under "Words of Faith and Obedience."

12 Cf. Vatican I, *Dei Filius*, cap. 3, *De fide*, DS., 3014, 3036 and see DS., 2738.

13 Cf. Vacant, Jean-Michel-Alfred, *Études théologiques sur les Constitutions du Concile du Vatican*, Delhomme et Briguet, Paris, Lyon, 1895, Tome II.

14 Cf. *C.I.C.*, Canon 1071, #1(4°), 1071, #2. See also Canon 1125.

15 Cf. Vacant, Jean-Michel-Alfred, *op. cit.*, pp. 168-170, 173-179.

16 Cf. Vatican I, *Dei Filius*, cap. 2, *De revelatione*, DS., 3004, 3026.

17 *Ibid.*, DS., 3010.

18 Cf. Vacant, Jean-Michel-Alfred, *op. cit.*, Tome I, pp. 288-291.

19 See S. Congregatio de Propaganda Fide, *Collectanea*, I, An. C. 1860, n. 1188, pp. 649-650.

20 Vatican II, *L.G.*, 16; English translation, *V.II., op. cit.*, p. 368.

21 Cf. Council of Trent, *Decretum de iustificatione*, Cap. 7, DS., 1528, 1529.

22 See Leeming, Bernard, *Principles of Sacramental Theology, op. cit.*, pp. 495-496 on the intention of the recipient, and pp. 266-267, 278-279 on the reviviscence of Grace, including Marriage.

23 Cf. Jadraque, Fernando, "Necesidad de la fe en quienes contraen el sacramento del matrimonio," *C.F.M.F., op. cit.*, p. 173.

24 See Caffarra, Carlo, *op. cit.*, pp. 175-178.

25 Cf. Council of Florence, *Decretum pro Armeniis*, DS., 1312.

26 Cf. *C.I.C.*, Canons 1057, 1096, 1099, 1101.

27 Cf. Perez, Tomaz Rincon, "Fe y sacramentalidad del matrimonio," *C.F.M.F.*, pp. 196-198.

28 *C.I.C.*, Canon 1096, #1; English translation, *The Code of Canon Law, op. cit.*, p. 195.

29 Cf. *Ibid.*, Canon 1099.

30 See *Errores Iansenistarum*, Decretum S. Officii, December 7, 1690, 12-15, DS., 2312-2315, errors condemned, which do not allow for attrition.

31 John Paul II, *F.C.*, 78; English translation, pp. 119-120. For theologians' differing views on the problem, see Adnès, Pierre, *Le mariage, op. cit.*, pp. 153-155 and Schleck, Charles A., *The Sacrament of Matrimony, a Dogmatic Study*, Bruce, Milwaukee, 1964, pp. 104-108.

32 Paul VI, *Matrimonia Mixta*, Apostolic Letter, January 7, 1970, *A.A.S.*, 62, (1970), p. 258; English translation, *V.II., op. cit.*, p. 509.

33 Cf. Lehmann, Karl, *op. cit.*, p. 111.

34 Cf. Ernst, Wilhelm, "Marriage as Institution and the Contemporary Challenge to It," *I.T.C., op. cit.*, pp. 68-69.

35 See Chapter Three under "The Schoolmen," p. 89.

36 Saint Thomas Aquinas, *In IV, op. cit.*, 39.1.2. ra.1, p. 618 (*S.* 59.2. ad.1).

37 See especially John Paul II, "La perdità del sacramento originale reintegrata con la redenzione nel matrimonio-sacramento," 1, General Audience, October 13, 1982, *Insegnamenti di Giovanni Paolo II, op. cit.*, V. 3, 1982, p. 810.

38 See Maritain, Jacques, *Ragione e ragioni, Saggi sparsi (Raison et raisons. Essais détachés)*, Vita e Pensiero, Milano, 1982, cap. VI, "La dialettica immanente del primo atto di libertà," pp. 102-131, especially pp. 115-119.

39 Vatican II, *G.S.*, 22; English translation, *V.II., op. cit.*, p. 923.

40 This would suggest great caution and prudence in applying Canon 1146, 2°, allowing for the Pauline Privilege at a later stage in these Marriages.

41 Cf. Paul VI, *Matrimonia Mixta, A.A.S.*, 62 (1970), p. 258, referring only to such Marriages as have been authorized by the appropriate Catholic authority.

42 See Chapter Three, pp. 101-102, noting high-Lutheran exceptions.

43 Cf. Congregation for Oriental Churches, *Crescens Matrimoniorum*, February 22, 1967, *A.A.S.*, 59 (1967), pp. 165-166; English translation, *V.II., op. cit.*, pp. 481-482.

44 Cf. Asnaghi, Adolfo, "Teologia di matrimonio presso gli Orientali," *Enciclopedia del Matrimonio, op. cit.*, pp. 450-451.

45 For example, Laroche, Michel (Orthodox archpriest), *Une Seule Chair, op. cit.*, and Evdokimov, Paul, *Sacrement de l'amour, op. cit.*

46 Cf. Saint John Chrysostom, *In Matt. opus imperfectum*, hom. 32, (*P.G.*, 56, 802A).

47 Cf. Meyendorff, John, *Marriage: An Orthodox Perspective*, St. Vladimir's Seminary Press, Crestwood, New York, revised edition, 1975, p. 19.

48 See Chapter Four under "The Sacramental Word," p. 121.

49 Cf. Meyendorff, John, *op. cit.*, pp. 24-25.

50 Cf. Alavistos, Hamilcar S., *Marriage and Divorce in Accordance with the Canon Law of the Greek Orthodox Church*, Faith Press, London, 1948, pp. 14-15, and Asnaghi, Adolfo, *op. cit.*, pp. 449-450. Note that impotence is seen as a ground for divorce when a divorce system replaces a nullity system.

51 Cf. Joyce, G.H., *Christian Marriage, op. cit.*, p. 378.

52 Cf. Meyendorff, John, *op. cit.*, pp. 15-16.

53 *Ibid.*, p. 16. In practice, the Orthodox permit a heavily "penitential" rite of Marriage after the death of a spouse.

54 See Joyce, G.H., *op. cit.*, pp.362-379.

55 Cf. Saint Basil the Great, *Ad Amphilochium*, Ep. 188. 9 (*P.G.*, 32, 677).

56 See Joyce, G.H., *op. cit.*, pp. 324-326.

57 Cf. Saint Basil the Great, Ep. 207. 78 (*P.G.*, 32, 804, 805).

58 Cf. Joyce, G.H., *op. cit.*, pp. 327-328.

59 *Ibid.*, pp. 392-394.

60 Cf. *Ibid.*, pp. 396-397, and Hamel, E., "The Indissolubility of Completed Marriage: Theological, Historical and Pastoral Reflections," *I.T.C., op. cit.*, pp. 202-203.

61 Council of Trent, *Canones de sacramento matrimonii*, Canon 7, DS., 1807. For an account of the evolution of this Canon, see Bressan, Luigi, *Il divorzio nelle chiese orientali, op. cit.*, pp. 95-115.

62 Anglican-Roman Catholic International Commission, *Anglican-Roman Catholic Marriage*, Church Information Office, Catholic Information Office, U.K., 1975, no. 21, pp. 10-11.

63 See Joyce, G.H., *op. cit.*, p. 181.

64 Cf. Lacey, T.A., *Marriage in Church and State*, revised by R.C. Mortimer, S.P.C.K., London, 1912, 1957, pp. 38-40.

65 As in Sherwin, Bailley Derrick, *The Mystery of Love and Marriage*, S.C.M. Press, London, 1952, but the author approved of contraception, see pp. ix, x.

66 Cf. Hughes, Philip, *The Reformation in England, op. cit.*, vol. II, p. 133.

67 Cf. Joyce, G.H., *op. cit.*, pp. 424-425.

68 Cf. *Ibid.*, pp. 428 and 629.

69 See Lacey, T.A., *op. cit.*, pp. 208-213, but also Joyce, G.H., *op. cit.*, pp. 583-584.

70 Cf. Joyce, G.H., *op. cit.*, pp. 428-429 and 629 for the text of the Resolutions of the 1930 Lambeth Conference.

71 See *Putting Asunder, a Divorce Law for Contemporary Society*, S.P.C.K., London, 1966.

72 For example, Winnett, A.R., *The Church and Divorce*, A.R. Mowbray, London, 1968, pp. 101-108, noting his disfavor for the "medieval" *vinculum*, p. 105.

73 See *Marriage, Divorce and the Church*, S.P.C.K., London, 1971, pp. 66-67.

74 See McManus, Patrick A., *Divorce and Remarriage: A Comparative Study of the Teaching and Practice of the Church of England and the Roman Catholic Church*, Pont. Studiorum Universitas a Sancto Thoma in Urbe, Rome, 1972.

75 Cf. Oppenheimer, Helen, *The Marriage Bond*, Faith Press, Leighton Buzzard, 1976; pp. 96-98.

76 *Ibid.*, p. 57.

77 See The Church Union, *The Theology of Marriage*, Church Literature Association, London, 1978.

78 Cf. Anglican-Roman Catholic International Commission, *op. cit.*, nos. 41-49, pp. 18-22.

79 Vatican II, *Unitatis Redintegratio*, 13; English translation, *V.II.*, *op. cit.*, p. 463.

80 Cf. John Paul II, *F.C.*, 32.

81 Cf. Saint Thomas Aquinas, *In IV*, *op. cit.*, 31.1.3., p. 594 (*S.* 49.3.) and see Grisez, Germain, *The Way of the Lord Jesus*, *op. cit.*, p. 802.

82 John Paul II, *F.C.*, 32; English translation, p. 52.

83 Cf. Quay, Paul M., *Contraception and Marital Love*, revised from *Theological Studies*, vol. 22, 1, March 1961, Family Life Bureau, Washington, D.C., 1962, p. 25.

84 John Paul II, *F.C.*, 32; English translation, p. 52.

85 Cf. Paul VI, *H.V.*, 12.

86 Cf. Quay, Paul M., *op. cit.*, p. 22.

87 See Grelot, Pierre, *Le couple humain dans l'Écriture*, *op. cit.*, pp. 104-106 on the couple as sinners, and pp. 106-110 on the Grace of the Cross offered to them.

88 Cf. Von Balthasar, Hans Urs, *The Christian State of Life*, *op. cit.*, p. 246.

89 Cf. Paul VI, *H.V.*, 25.

Chapter Eight: THE SACRAMENT OF THE FAMILY

1 Cf. Miralles, Antonio, "Naturaleza y sacramento en la doctrina del Concilio Vaticano II sobre el matrimonio," *C.F.M.F.*, *op. cit.*, pp. 165-167.

2 Vatican II, *G.S.*, 50; English translation, *V.II.*, *op. cit.*, p. 954.

3 *Ibid.*,

4 See Introduction under "Among the Great Sacraments," pp. xxv-xxvi.

5 Cf. Saint Thomas Aquinas, *S.C.G.*, *op. cit.*, Lib. IV, cap lviii, 3974, p. 361: "... *ad cultum divinum.*"

6 Joint Commission for Theological Dialogue between the Roman Catholic Church and the Orthodox Church, *Church, Eucharist, Trinity, The Mystery of the Church and of the Eucharist in the Light of the Mystery of the Holy Trinity*. First Statement of the Joint Commission, Archdiocese of Thyateira and Great Britain, Catholic Truth Society, London, 1984, no. 4, p. 12.

7 Von Balthasar, Hans Urs, *The Christian State of Life*, *op. cit.*, p. 242.

8 Vatican II, *Presbyterorum Ordinis*, 16; English translation, *V.II.*, *op. cit.*, p. 893.

9 Cf. McNamara, Kevin (Archbishop of Dublin), *The Family Today*, Irish Messenger Publications, Dublin, 1984, p. 21.

10 *Ibid.*, p. 27.

11 A favorite phrase which my own father often used to describe the Church.

12 John Paul II, *F.C.*, 63; English translation, pp. 92-93.

13 *Ibid.*, English translation, p. 78.

14 *Ibid.*, English translation, p. 79.

15 Cf. John Paul II, *F.C.*, 55, 56.

16 *Love is for Life*, A Pastoral Letter issued on behalf of the Irish Hierarchy, Veritas Publications, Dublin, 1985, no. 47, p. 13.

17 Escrivá de Balaguer, Josemaría, *Conversations with Monsignor Escrivá de Balaguer*, Sinag Tala, Manila, 1977, p. 146.

18 See Aranda Gonzalo, "Relación entre los conyuges y valor del matrimonio a luz de Ef 5, 22-33," *C.F.M.F., op. cit.*, p. 121. A strong doctrinal basis for family spirituality is found in Tettamanzi, Dionigi, *I due saranno una carne sola, Saggi teologici su matrimonio e famiglia*, Leumann, Turin, 1986.

19 John Paul II, *F.C.*, 86; English translation, p. 129.

20 See Chapter One under "The Love of the Trinity."

21 See Schmitt, John, "Families and the Trinity," *Fidelity*, (U.S.A.), September, 1983, pp. 15 and 24, an excellent approach to this mystery.

22 For an historical survey of the Trinity-family theology, see Gendron, Lionel, *Mystère de la Trinité et symbolique familiale*, Pontificia Universitas Gregoriana, Facultas Theologiae, Rome, 1975.

Bibliography

Scripture quotations in Greek and Latin are taken from *Novum Testamentum Graece et Latine*, ed. Augustinus Merk, SJ., editio x, Sumptibus Pontificii Instituti Biblici, Romae, 1984. Scripture quotations in English are taken from *Holy Bible, Revised Standard Version (Catholic Edition)*, Nelson, London, 1966.

Patristic references are taken from Migne, J.P., *Patrologia Graeca*, 161 volumes, Paris, 1857-1865 and Migne, J.P., *Patrologia Latina*, 217 volumes, Paris, 1878-1890.

A. SOURCES

Saint Alphonsus Liguori, *Theologia Moralis*, editio nova, Tom. IV, ed. Leonardi Gaudé, Typis Polyglottis Vaticanis, Romae, 1912, 1963.

Saint Ambrose, *De institutione virginis*, *P.L.*, 16; *Epistula 19 ad Vigilium*, *P.L.*, 16; *Epistula 42 ad Siricium*, *P.L.*, 16.

Ambrosiaster, *In Ephesios*, *P.L.*, 17.

Saint Augustine, *De Genesi ad litteram*, *P.L.*, 34; *De consensu evangelistarum*, *P.L.*, 34; *In Ioannis evangelium tractatus*, *P.L.*, 35; *In epistulam Ioannis ad Parthos*, *P.L.*, 35; *De bono coniugali*, *P.L.*, 40; *In peccato originali*, *P.L.*, 44; *De nuptiis et concupiscentia*, *P.L.*, 44.

Saint Basil the Great, *Ad Amphilochium*, Ep. 188, *P.G.*, 32; Ep. 207, *P.G.*, 32.

Saint Bede, *The Commentary on the Seven Catholic Epistles*, tr. David Hurst, OSB., Cistercian Publications, Kalamazoo, Michigan, 1985.

Carlen, Claudia, *The Papal Encyclicals*, McGrath, Wilmington, North Carolina, 1981. *The Papal Encyclicals, 1878-1903*, English translation of Leo XIII, *Arcanum Divinae Sapientiae*. *The Papal Encyclicals, 1903-1939*, English translation of Pius XI, *Casti Connubii*. *The Papal Encyclicals, 1939-1958*, English translation of Pius XII, *Mystici Corporis Christi, Sacra Virginitas, Haurietis Aquas.*

Catechism of the Council of Trent, tr. John A. McHugh, OP., Charles C. Callan, OP., Wagner, New York, 16th Edition, 1962.

Clement of Alexandria, *Stromata*, 2, *P.G.*, 8.

Codex Iuris Canonici, Auctoritate Ioannis Pauli P.P. Promulgatus, Libreria Editrice Vaticana, 1983.

Congregation for the Doctrine of the Faith, *Documenta inde a Concilio Vaticano Secundo Expleto Edita (1966-1985)*, Libreria Editrice Vaticana, 1985.

Congregation for Oriental Churches, *Crescens Matrimoniorum*, February 22, 1967, *A.A.S.*, 59 (1967).

Congregation for the Propagation of the Faith, *Collecteana*, I., An. C., 1860.

Saint Cyril of Alexandria, *In Ioannem*, *P.G.*, 73.

Denzinger H., Schönmetzer A., *Enchiridion Symbolorum Definitionum et Declarationum de Rebus Fidei et Morum*, editio xxxvi, emendata, Herder, Freiburg, 1976.

Didymus, *Contra Manichaeos*, *P.G.*, 39.

Saint Epiphanius, *Adversus haereses Panarium*, *P.G.*, 41.

Saint Gregory the Great, *In Evangelica*, lib. II, hom. 38, *P.L.*, 76.

Hincmar of Rheims, *De nuptiis Stephani*, *P.L.*, 126.

Saint Ignatius of Antioch, *Ad Polycarpum*, *P.G.*, 5.

Saint Irenaeus, *Adversus haereses*, *P.L.*, 7.

Blessed Isaac of Stella, *Discursus* 51, *P.L.*, 194.

Saint John Chrysostom, *De coemeterio et de cruce*, *P.G.*, 49. *In Matthaeum opus imperfectum*, Hom. 32, *P.G.*, 56. *Hom. xxi in epist. ad Corinthios*, *P.G.*, 61. *Hom. xii in epist. ad Coloss.*, *P.G.*, 62.

John Paul II, General Audiences, Catechesis on Sexuality and Marriage, *Insegnamenti di Giovanni Paolo II*, Libreria Editrice Vaticana, II-VII, 1979-1984. Apostolic Exhortation, *Familiaris Consortio*, English translation, Vatican Polyglot Press, St. Paul Editions, Boston, 1981. Apostolic Exhortation, *Reconciliatio et Paenitentia*, *Insegnamenti di Giovanni Paolo II*, VII. 2., 1984.

Saint Leo the Great, *Ep. 167 ad Rusticum*, *P.L.*, 54.

Leo XIII, *Arcanum Divinae Sapientiae*, English translation, Carlen, Claudia, *The Papal Encyclicals (1878-1903)*, *op. cit.*, pp. 29-40.

Missale Romanum, ex Decreto Sacrosancti Oecumenici Concilii Vaticani II Instauratum, Auctoritate Pauli PP. VI Promulgatum, Typis Polyglottis Vaticanis, 1971.

Origen, *In Matthaeum commentarii*, *P.G.*, 13.

Saint Pacian, *Sermo de baptismo*, *P.L.*, 13.

Paul VI, *Humanae Vitae*, *A.A.S.*, 60 (1968), pp. 481-503; English translation, Vatican Polyglot Press, Catholic Truth Society, London, 1968. Apostolic Letter on Mixed Marriages, *Matrimonia Mixta*, *A.A.S.*, 62 (1970), pp. 257-273; English translation, *V.II.*, *op. cit.*, pp. 508-514. Speech to the Representatives of the "Équipes de Notre Dame" (May 4, 1970), *Insegnamenti di Paolo VI*, Libreria Editrice Vaticana, VIII, 1970.

Peter Lombard, *Sententiae in IV libris distinctae, Lib. IV.*, Tom. II, Editiones Collegii S. Bonaventurae Ad Claras Aquas, Grottaferrata (Romae), 1981.

Pius XI, *Casti Connubii*, *A.A.S.*, 22 (1930), pp. 539-592; English translation, Carlen, Claudia, *The Papal Encyclicals (1903-1939)*, *op. cit.*, pp. 391-414.

Pius XII, *Mystici Corporis Christi*, *A.A.S.*, 35 (1943), pp. 193-248; English translation, Carlen, Claudia, *The Papal Encyclicals (1939-1958)*, *op. cit.*, pp. 37-63. *Sacra Virginitas*, *A.A.S.*, 46 (1954), pp. 161-191; English translation, Carlen, Claudia, *The Papal Encyclicals (1903-1939)*, *op. cit.*, pp. 239-253. *Haurietis Aquas*, *A.A.S.*, 48 (1956), pp. 309-353; English translation, Carlen, Claudia, *The Papal Encyclicals (1939-1958)*, *op. cit.*, 291-313.

Rituale Romanum ex Decreto Sacrosancti Oecumenici Concilii Vaticani II Instauratum, Auctoritate Pauli PP. VI Promulgatum, Ordo Celebrandi Matrimonium, editio typica, Typis Polyglottis Vaticanis, 1972.

Saint Robert Bellarmine, *De controversiis christianae fidei adversus huius temporis haereticos*, Tom. III, *De sacramento matrimonii*, Apud Joannem Malachinum, Venice, 1721.

Synod of Bishops (1980), *De muneribus familiae christianae in mundo hodierno, Elenchus Propositionum*, E Civitate Vaticana, 1980. *Il*

Sinodo dei Vescovi, quinta assemblea generale, a cura di Giovanni Caprile S.I., Edizioni "La Civiltà Cattolica", 1981.

Tertullian, *Ad uxorem, P.L.*, 1.

Theodoret, *Haereticarum fabularum compendium, P.G.*, 83.

Saint Thomas Aquinas, *S. Thomae Aquinatis Opera Omnia*, 1., *In IV Sententiarum*, (004-4SN), curante Roberto Busa, S.I., Frommann-Holzboog, Stuttgart-Bad Connstatt, 1980. *Super epistulas S. Pauli lectura, Ad Corinthios*, Lib. I, *Ad Ephesios*, Lib. II, cura Raphaelis Cai, OP., ed. viii, revisa, Marietti, Torino e Roma, 1953. *Summa Contra Gentiles*, cura Ceslai Pera, OP., Marietti, Torino e Roma, 1961. *Summa theologiae* (with *Supplementum*), cum textu ex recensione Leonina, cura P. Caramello, Marietti, Roma, 1956.

Vatican II, *Acta Synodalia Sacrosancta Concilii Oecumenici Vaticani II*, (Four Volumes in Parts), Typis Polyglottis Vaticanis, Rome, 1970-1978. Latin text of the Documents, Sacrosanctum Oecumenicum Concilium Vaticanum II, *Constitutiones Decreta Declarationes*, cura et studio Secretariae Generalis Concilii Oecumenici Vaticani II, Typis Polyglottis Vaticanis, 1974. English translation of the Documents, Flannery, Austin, *Vatican Council II, The Conciliar and Post Conciliar Documents*, Costello, New York, 1975. English translation of the Documents also used, Abbott, Walter M. *The Documents of Vatican II*, Guild Press, New York, 1966.

B. SECONDARY AUTHORITIES

Adnès, Pierre, *Le mariage*, Desclée, Tournai, 1963.

Alavistos, Hamilcar S., *Marriage and Divorce in Accordance with the Canon Law of the Greek Orthodox Church*, Faith Press, London, 1948.

Anglican-Roman Catholic International Commission (A.R.C.I.C.), *Anglican-Roman Catholic Marriage*, Church Information Office, Catholic Information Office, U.K., 1975.

Belmans, Theo G., *Le sens objectif de l'agir humain, Pour relire la morale conjugale de Saint Thomas*, Libreria Editrice Vaticana, 1980.

Biffi, Inos, *La teologia e un teologo: San Tommaso d'Aquino*, Edizioni Piemme, Casale Monferrato, 1984.

Bover, José M., *Teología de San Pablo*, cuarta edición, Biblioteca de Autores Cristianos, Madrid, 1967.

Bressan, Luigi, *Il divorzio nelle chiese orientali: ricerca storica sull'attegiamento cattolico*, Edizione Dehoniane, Bologna, 1976.

Caffarra, Carlo, "Verità ed ethos dell'amore coniugale", Giovanni Paolo II, *Uomo e donna lo creò, catechesi sull'amore umano*, Città Nuova Editrice Libreria Editrice Vaticana, Roma, 1985, Introdduzione generale, pp. 12-24.

Calvin, John, *Institutes of the Christian Religion, Joannis Calvini Opera Selecta*, ed. P. Barth, G. Niesel, ed. 3, Kaiser, Munich, 1974.

Cano, Melchior, *De Locis Theologicis, De Auctoritate Doctorum Schol., Opera*, Auroy, Paris, 1706.

Capello, Felix, *De Sacramentis Tractatus Canonico-Moralis*, Tom. III, Marietti, Roma, 1933.

Cerfaux, Lucien, *Christ in the Theology of Saint Paul*, Herder, Freiburg, 1962.

Clérissac, Humbert, *Le Mystère de l'Église*, Dismas, Dion-Valmont (Belgique), 1985.

De Cock, Joseph, *L'Église e le Sacrement de Mariage d'après les Actes du Concile de Trent*, Pontificia Universitas Gregoriana Facultas Theologica, Roma, 1966.

De La Potterie, Ignace, "La donna e il mistero della Chiesa, principi ermeneutici per l'interpretazione della visione biblica sulla donna", *La donna nella Chiesa oggi*: a cura di Adriano Capriolo e Luciano Vecarro, Edizioni Elle Di Ci, Torino, 1981, pp. 106-129.

De Vaux, Roland, *Ancient Israel*, Vol. I, McGraw Hill, New York, 1965.

Durrwell, F.X., *The Resurrection, A Biblical Study*, tr. Rosemary Sheed, Sheed and Ward, New York, 1960. *In the Redeeming Christ, Towards a Theology of Spirituality*, tr. Rosemary Sheed, Sheed and Ward, New York, 1963.

Elliott, Peter, "The 'Propositional' View of Revelation", *Compass*, Chevalier Press, Sydney, vol. 4, no. 2, September-October, 1970, pp. 131-134. "Talking of Sacraments: a Case for Plain English", *Bulletin of Christian Affairs*, no. 21, April, 1972, Holy Name Press, Melbourne.

Enciclopedia del Matrimonio, a cura di Tullo Goffi, Editrice Queriniana, Brescia, 1968. Articles cited as follow: Asnaghi, Adolfo, "Teologia del matrimonio presso gli Orientali", pp. 448-456. Moioli, Giovanni, "Matrimonio e verginità", pp. 387-413. Pampaloni, Pio, "Il matrimonio nella scholastica", pp. 297-341. Volta, Giovanni, "Indagine filosofica sull'amore", pp. 139-197.

Escrivá De Balaguer, Josemaría, *Conversations with Monsignor Escrivá de Balaguer*, Sinag Tala, Manila, 1977.

Evdokimov, Paul, *Sacrement de l'amour: le mystère conjugal à la lumière de la tradition orthodoxe*, Éditions de l'epi, Paris, 1977. *La femme et le salut du monde*, Théophanie, Desclée de Brouwer, Paris, 1978.

Feuillet, André, *Johannine Studies*, Alba House, New York, 1964.

Gosling, Justin C., *Marriage and the Love of God*, Chapman, London, 1965.

Grelot, Pierre, *Le couple humain dans l'Écriture*, Les Éditions du Cerf, Paris, 1969.

Grisez, Germain, *The Way of the Lord Jesus*, Vol. I, *Christian Moral Principles*, Franciscan Herald Press, Chicago, 1983.

Hacker, Paul, *The Ego in Faith, Martin Luther and the Origin of Anthropocentric Religion (Das Ich in Glauben bei Martin Luther)*, Franciscan Herald Press, Chicago, 1970.

Hagerty, Cornelius J., *The Holy Trinity*, Christopher, North Quincy, Massachusetts, 1976.

Häring, Bernard, "Fostering the Nobility of Marriage and the Family", *Commentary on the Documents of Vatican II*, Vol. 5, Herder and Herder, Burns & Oates, New York, London, 1969, pp. 225-245.

Hogan, Richard, Le Voir, John M., *Covenant of Love*, Doubleday, New York, 1985.

Hughes, Philip, *The Reformation in England*, 3 volumes in one, revised, Burns & Oates, London, 1963.

International Theological Commission (1978), *Contemporary Perspectives on Christian Marriage*, ed. Richard Malone, John R. Connery, SJ., Loyola University Press, Chicago, 1984. *I.T.C., Propositions on the Doctrine of Christian Marriage* pp. 7-36. Position Papers cited as follows: Caffarra, Carlo, "Marriage as a Reality in the

Order of Creation and Marriage as a Sacrament", pp. 119-180. Descamps, A.L., "The New Testament Doctrine on Marriage", pp. 217-273. Ernst, Wilhelm, "Marriage as Institution and the Contemporary Challenge to It", pp. 39-90. Hamel, E., "The Indissolubility of Completed Marriage: Theological, Historical and Pastoral Reflections", pp. 181-203. Lehmann, Karl, "The Sacramentality of Christian Marriage, the Bond between Baptism, Faith and Marriage", pp. 91-115. Martelet, G., "Sixteen Christological Theses on the Sacrament of Marriage", pp. 275-283.

Irish Theological Commission, *What God Has Joined* . . ., Irish Messenger Publications, Dublin, 1982.

Jedin, Hubert, Reinhardt, Klaus, *Il Matrimonio, una ricerca storica e teologica (Ehe Sakrament in der Kirche des Herrn)*, tr. F. Meneghini, Morcelliana, Brescia, 1981.

Saint John of the Cross, *Poems of St. John of the Cross*, tr. Roy Campbell, Collins, London, 1951.

John Paul II, Karol Wojtyla, *Sign of Contradiction*, tr. Mary Smith, Hodder and Stoughton, London, 1979.

Joint Commission for Theological Dialogue between the Roman Catholic Church and the Orthodox Church, *Church, Eucharist, Trinity, The Mystery of the Church and of the Eucharist in the Light of the Mystery of the Holy Trinity*, First Statement of the Joint Commission, Archdiocese of Thyateira and Great Britain, Catholic Truth Society, London, 1984.

Joyce, G.H., *Christian Marriage: An Historical and Doctrinal Study*, Sheed and Ward, London, 1948.

Kasper, Walter, *Theology of Christian Marriage*, Burns & Oates, London, 1980.

Kevane, Eugene, "Apostolicity, Indefectibility and Catechesis", *Divinitas, Pontificiae Academiae Theologicae Romanae Commentarii*, Rome, September, 1985, pp. 207-233.

Lacey, T.A., *Marriage in Church and State*, revised by R.C. Mortimer, S.P.C.K., London, 1912, 1957.

A Lapide, Cornelius, *Commentaria in Scripturam Sacram*, Tom. XVI, *Commentaria in Ioannem*, ed. Augustine Crampon, editio nova, Vivès, Paris, 1877. Tom. XVIII, *In Epistolas Divi Pauli*,

Commentaria in Epistolam ad Ephesios, ed. Augustine Crampon, editio nova, Vivès, Paris, 1880.

Laroche, Michel, *Une Seule Chair, l'aventure mystique du couple*, Nouvelle cité, Paris, 1984.

Lawler, Michael G., *Secular Marriage: Christian Sacrament*, Twenty Third Publications, Mystic, CT, 1985.

Leeming, Bernard, *Principles of Sacramental Theology*, Newman Press, Westminster, Maryland, 1956.

Love is for Life, A Pastoral Letter issued on behalf of the Irish Hierarchy, Veritas Publications, Dublin, 1985.

Luther, Martin, *De captivitate babylonica ecclesiae: Praeludium, Omnium Operum Reverendi Patris Viri Dei D. Mart. Luth.*, Tom. II, Tobias Steinman, Jena, 1600.

Lyons, James P., *The Essential Structure of Marriage, A Study of the Thomistic Teaching on the Natural Institution*, Catholic University of America Press, Washington, D.C., 1950.

Mackin, Theodore, *What is Marriage?*, *Marriage in the Catholic Church*, Paulist Press, New York, 1982.

Maritain, Jacques, *Ragione e ragioni, Saggi sparsi (Raison et raisons, Essais détachés)*, Vita e Pensiero, Milano, 1982.

Marriage, Divorce and the Church, S.P.C.K., London, 1971.

McCarthy, Dennis J., *Treaty and Covenant, a study in form in the Ancient Oriental Documents and in the Old Testament*, Analecta Biblica 21a, (revised text), Pontifical Biblical Institute, Rome, 1978.

McDermott, Charles, *The Tridentine Canon on the Sacramentality of Marriage*, Faculty of Theology, Gregorian University, Rome, 1978.

McNamara, Kevin, *The Family Today*, Irish Messenger Publications, Dublin, 1984.

Mersch, Émile, *The Theology of the Mystical Body (La théologie du corps mystique)*, tr. Cyril Vollert, SJ., Herder, St. Louis, 1951.

Messenger, E.G., *Two In One Flesh*, 3 volumes, Newman Press, Westminster, Maryland, 1948.

Meyendorff, John, *Marriage: An Orthodox Perspective*, St. Vladimir's Seminary Press, Crestwood, New York, revised edition, 1975.

Most, William, *Covenant and Redemption*, St. Paul Publications, Athlone, Ireland, 1975.

Mühlen, Heribert, *Una Mistica Persona, La Chiesa come il mistero dello Spirito Santo in Cristo e nei cristiani: una persona in molte persone*, Città Nuova, Roma, 1968.

Nash, Andrew and Dora, *Christian Marriage, Covenant in Christ*, Faith Pamphlets, Wallingford, Surrey, 1983.

Newman, John Henry, *Selected Treatises of St. Athanasius*, Vol. II, Longmans Green, London, 1895. *Lectures on the Doctrine of Justification*, Longmans Green, London, 1838, new impression, 1924. *Parochial and Plain Sermons*, Vol. V, Longmans Green, London, 1891. *An Essay on the Development of Christian Doctrine*, Longmans Green, London, 1894. *Callista, a Tale of the Third Century*, Longmans Green, London, 1855, new impression, 1928.

Norris, Thomas, "Why the Marriage of Christians is one of the Seven Sacraments", *Irish Theological Quarterly*, Vol. 5, No. 1, 1985, pp. 37-51.

O'Callaghan, Denis, "Marriage as Sacrament", *Concilium*, English, May, 1970, pp. 101-110.

Oppenheimer, Helen, *The Marriage Bond*, Faith Press, Leighton-Buzzard, 1976.

Perrone, Johannes, *Praelectiones Theologicae, Tractatus de matrimonio*, Vol. VII, Vanlinthout et Vandenzande, Louvain, 1842.

Pieper, Josef, *Sull'amore (Über die Liebe)*, trad. di Gianni Poletti, Morcelliana, Brescia, 1974.

Prat, Fernand, *The Theology of Saint Paul (La théologie de Saint Paul)*, tr. John L. Stoddard, Newman Press, Westminster, Maryland, 2 Volumes, 1927.

Prümmer, Dominic, *Manuale Theologiae Moralis secundum principia S. Thomae Aquinatis*, Tom. III, ed. decima, Herder, Barcelona, 1946.

Quay, Paul M., *Contraception and Marital Love*, revised from *Theological Studies*, Vol. 22, 1, March, 1961, Family Life Bureau, Washington, D.C., 1962.

Rahner, Karl, "Marriage as a Sacrament" ("Die Ehe als Sakrament", *Geist und Leben*, 40, 1967), *Theology Digest*, 17, 1969, pp. 4-8.

Ratzinger, Joseph, *Introduction to Christianity*, tr. J.R. Foster, Herder and Herder, New York, 1969. *Rapporto sulla Fede* (con Messori, Vittorio), Edizioni Paoline, Milan, 1985.

Robilliard, J.A., "Le symbolisme du mariage selon Saint Paul", *Revue des Sciences Philosophiques et Théologiques*, no. 21, 1932, pp. 242-247.

Robinson, Geoffrey, *Marriage, Divorce and Nullity*, Dove Communications, Melbourne, 1984.

Sattler, Henry V., "Adultery within Marriage", *Homiletic and Pastoral Review*, New York, December, 1981, pp. 26-33.

Scheeben, Matthias J., *The Mysteries of Christianity (Die Mysterien des Christentums)*, tr. Cyril Vollert, SJ., Herder, St. Louis, 1951. *Nature and Grace (Natur und Gnade)*, tr. Cyril Vollert, SJ., Herder, St. Louis, 1954. *The Glories of Divine Grace*, Benzinger, New York, 1885.

Schillebeeckx, Edward, *Christ the Sacrament of the Encounter with God*, Sheed and Ward, New York, 1963. *Marriage: Human Reality and Saving Mystery*, Sheed and Ward, London, 1965, 1976.

Schleck, Charles A., *The Sacrament of Matrimony, a Dogmatic Study*, Bruce, Milwaukee, 1964.

Schmitt, John, "Families and the Trinity", *Fidelity*, (U.S.A.), September, 1983, pp. 14-26.

Schroeder, H.J., *Disciplinary Decrees of the General Councils*, Herder, St. Louis, 1937.

Il Simposio Internacional de Teología de la Universidad de Navarra, *Cuéstiones Fundamentales sobre Matrimonio y Familia*, ed. Augustino Sarmiento, Eloy Tejero, Teodoro López, José Manuel Zumaquero, Ediciónes Universidad de Navarra, S-A, Pamplona, 1980. Symposium Papers cited as follows: Aranda, Gonzalo, "Relación entre los conyuges y valor del matrimonio a luz de Ef 5, 22-33", pp. 119-131. Ausin, Santiago, "Matrimonio y designo di Dios, anotaciones exegéticas a Gen 2, 4-25", pp. 133-148. Delicado Baeza, José, "El matrimonio en el mistero de Cristo", pp. 81-102. Gil Hellín, Francisco, "El matrimonio: amor e institución", pp. 231-244. Hervada, Javier, "La inseparabilidad entre contrato y sacramento en el matrimonio", pp. 259-272. Jadraque, Fernando, "Necesidad de la fe en quienes contraen el sacramento del matrimonio", pp. 169-182. Miralles, Antonio, "Naturaleza y sacramento en la doctrina del Concilio Vaticano II sobre el matrimonio", pp. 149-168. Perez Tomaz, Rincon, "Fe y sacramentalidad del matrimonio", pp. 183-200.

Sorci, Pietro, "Il tema della Chiesa-sposa nelle liturgie nuziali", *Ho Theologos*, Facoltà Teologica di Sicilia, Nuova Serie, Anno 1, num. 1, 1983, pp. 67-110.

Tanquerey, Adolphe, *Synopsis Theologiae Moralis et Pastoralis*, Tom. I, Editio decima, Desclée, Paris, 1925.

Tosato, Angelo, *Il matrimonio israelitico, una teoria generale, Analecta Biblica*, 100, Biblical Institute Press, Rome, 1982.

Vacant, Jean-Michel-Alfred, *Etudes théologiques sur les Constitutions du Concile du Vatican*, Tome I, Tome II, Delhomme er Briguet, Paris, Lyon, 1895.

Vawter, Bruce, *On Genesis: A New Reading*, Doubleday, New York, 1977.

Von Balthasar, Hans Urs, *The Christian State of Life (Christlicher Stand)*, tr. Sr. Mary Frances McCarthy, Ignatius Press, San Francisco, 1983.

Von Hildebrand, Dietrich, *Marriage, the Mystery of Faithful Love*, Sophia Institute Press, Manchester, New Hampshire, 1984.

Von Speyr, Adrienne, *The Cross, Word and Sacrament (Kreuzeswort und Sakrament)*, tr. Graham Harrison, Ignatius Press, San Francisco, 1983.

Winnett, A.R., *The Church and Divorce*, A.R. Mowbray, London, 1968.

C. WORKS CITED GENERALLY

Brown, Raymond, *The Semitic Background of the Term "Mystery" in the New Testament*, Fortress Press, Philadelphia, 1968.

The Church Union, *The Theology of Marriage*, Church Literature Association, London, 1978.

Colli, Pietro, *La pericope paolina ad Ephesios V.32 nella interpretazione dei SS. Padri e del Concilio di Trento*, Parma, 1951 (doctoral dissertation, Gregorian University, Rome).

Cuenin, Walter, *The Marriage of Baptized Non-Believers*, Gregorian University Press, Rome, 1977. "Questions: Faith, Sacrament and Law", *Origins*, November 9, 1978, pp. 321-328.

Gendron, Lionel, *Mystére de la Trinité e symbolique familiale* (Vol. I) Pontificia Universitas Gregoriana, Facultas Theologiae, Rome, 1975.

Gerke, Leonard, *Christian Marriage, a Permanent Sacrament*, Catholic University of America Studies in Theology, 2nd Series, 161, Catholic University of America Press, Washington, D.C., 1965.

Gomes, W.Z., *De Matrimoniis Clandestinis in Concilio Tridentino*, Pontificium Athenaeum Urbanianum de "Propaganda Fide", Catholic Book Agency, Rome, 1950.

Kilmartin, Edward, "When is Marriage a Sacrament?", *Theological Studies*, 34, 1973, pp. 275-286.

Lawrence, Ralph J., *The Sacramental Interpretation of Ephesians 5:32 from Peter Lombard to the Council of Trent*, Catholic University of America Studies in Theology, 2nd Series, 145, Catholic University of America Press, Washington, D.C., 1963.

McManus, Patrick A., *Divorce and Remarriage: A Comparative Study of the Teaching and Practice of the Church of England and the Roman Catholic Church*, Pont. Studiorum Universitas a Sancto Thoma in Urbe, Rome, 1972.

Mullady, Brian T., "The Mystery of Marriage in Matthias Joseph Scheeben", *M.J. Scheeben teologo cattolico d'ispirazione tomista*, (various authors) Studi Tomistici 33, Pontificia Accademia di S. Tommaso, Libreria Editrice Vaticana, 1988.

Putting Asunder, a Divorce Law for Contemporary Society, S.P.C.K., London, 1966.

Ratzinger, Joseph, *Daughter Sion (Die Tochter Zion)*, tr. Charles McDermott, Ignatius Press, San Francisco, 1983.

Sherwin, Bailey Derrick, *The Mystery of Love and Marriage*, S.C.M. Press, London, 1952.

Tettamanzi, Dionigi, *I due saranno una carne sola, Saggi teologici su matrimonio e famiglia*, Leumann, Turin, 1986.

Index